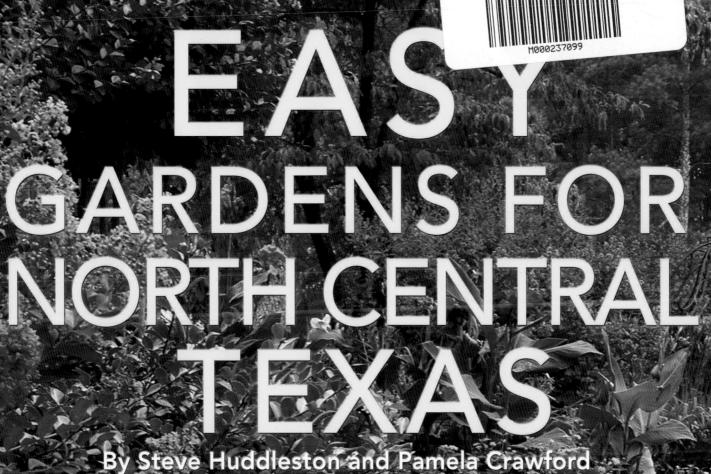

EASY
GARDENS FOR
NORTH CENTRAL
TEXAS

By Steve Huddleston and Pamela Crawford

For any Texan who has ever killed a plant!

Where to Buy "Easy Gardens for the South"

The book is available through many garden centers and book sellers. It is also available through www.amazon.com. To locate your nearest source or place an order with the publisher, contact us at:

Pamela Crawford & Associates, Lake Worth, Florida
Phone: 561-371-2719
Web site: www.pamela-crawford.com
Email: info@pamela-crawford.com

Credits:

Authors: Steve Huddleston and Pamela Crawford, with additional writing help from Barbara Pleasand and Harvey Cotten
Managing Editor: Barbara Hadsell
Cover Design and Graphic Design: Elaine Weber Designs, Inc. (www.ewdlogos.com)
Proofreader: Barbara Iderosa, Best Editing Service, Wellington, Florida
Researcher: Tammy Brogan and Sheila Allen
Bargain Gardening Consultant: Joan Ahrens

Printing: Asianprinting.com, Korea

Published by Pamela Crawford & Associates, Inc., Lake Worth, FL. First printing: 2009
Library of Congress Catalog Card Number pending

ISBN 10: 0-9712220-8-8
ISBN 13: 978-0-9712220-8-3

This book is not designed as a source to the possible toxicity of each plant. Do not eat any plant in this book and teach your children to never eat any plant unless you can find it in the produce department of your grocery store.

Title page photo and the photo on this page from the home of Mrs. Bill Taylor, Jr. in

Contents

Easy Plants and Symbols

What are Easy Plants?

This book includes many plant profiles, which are descriptions of the plants. Large profiles take up two pages. Here are the criteria for double-page profiles:

❀ Ability to withstand climate conditions in Texas, including warming trends and moisture extremes.

❀ Attractive appearance with trimming three times a year or less.

❀ Consistent behavior for at least two years in multiple locations.

❀ Ability to adapt to a variety of urban and suburban situations.

❀ Plants of various heights and environmental tolerances to provide a complete plant palette for many residences and commercial establishments.

To evaluate the plants further, we put them on a spreadsheet and classified them by how many times a year they had to be touched. The easiest plants are designated by a blue ribbon and the next easiest by a red ribbon (defined on pages 12 to 13). It is amazing to see how many Texas plants only need care once or twice a year!

At the end of each chapter (chapters two to five), we include smaller profiles of other plants that deserve mention.

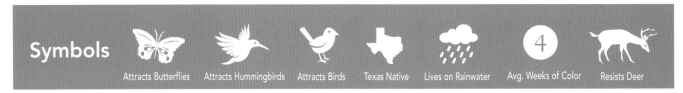

Symbols — Attracts Butterflies · Attracts Hummingbirds · Attracts Birds · Texas Native · Lives on Rainwater · Avg. Weeks of Color · Resists Deer

Each double-page plant profile includes symbols at the top of the page to make it easier to determine key characteristics of the plant without having to read a lot of text.

❀ The butterfly and hummingbird symbols denote the plants whose flowers produce nectar for butterflies or hummingbirds.

❀ The bird symbol denotes the plants that provide either shelter or food for birds.

❀ The "Texas Native" symbol indicates plants that are native to Texas, defined as growing in Texas before Columbus discovered America.

❀ The "Lives on Rainwater" symbol refers to those plants that live on natural rainwater without any supplemental irrigation.

❀ "Average Weeks of Color" refers to the number of weeks that the plant has either flowers or colorful leaves.

❀ The deer symbol refers to those plants that are almost never eaten by deer. Deer will eat anything when they are starving, but they like some plants more than others. In addition to plants that are almost never damaged, we have further classified the plants as 'Frequently damaged,' 'Often damaged,' or 'Seldom damaged.' Those classifications appear in the left sidebar under 'Cautions.'

North Central Texas Environment

Many newcomers to north central Texas are disappointed to find they can't grow the rhododendrons they grew up north. The climate in this region is humid subtropical with hot summers; but, it also includes some low winter temperatures. Summer daytime temperatures frequently exceed 100°. Rainfall occurs mostly in spring and fall and averages 30 to 44 inches a year. There are many beautiful plants that thrive in this tough environment. This book includes the best plants the region has to offer.

Fort Worth Botanic Garden

Steve Huddleston has been the senoir horticulurist at the Fort Worth Botanic Garden since 1994. All of the plants in this book have been at the garden for years, so he knows them well. Stop by the garden to see the plants, and don't miss their spring and fall plant sales there.

The oldest botanic garden in the state of Texas, the Fort Worth Botanic Garden (FWBG) consists of 109 acres and touts itself as an outdoor museum of plants. It is the perfect place to see and learn about the plants mentioned in this book. Much of the garden is in a natural state that features a variety of trees native to the region. In other locations of the garden, trees from elsewhere in the country and around the world are featured.

The FWBG consists of 23 theme gardens, including a world-famous Japanese garden, a historical rose garden full of old garden and Earth-Kind™ roses, the largest public trial garden in north central Texas that features over 250 perennials, a conservatory filled with tropical plants from around the world, and a water conservation garden that features low water-use native and adapted plants. Learn more about the FWBG and what it has to offer by visiting its website at www.fwbg.org.

Photo Credits

All photos by Pamela Crawford except for the following:

Aceshot1: Burning Bush, p. 266. Albert Mednelewski: Grape hyacinth, p. 175. Antique Rose Emporium: 'Caldwell Pink' roses, p. 240; 'Belinda's Dream', p. 242, 243. Armitage Images: Turk's cap, p. 21, 40, 169, 305, Summer snowflake, p. 166, Verbena 'Blue Princess', p. 170; Amaryllis, p. 106; Mexican mint marigold, p. 111, 149. Ball Seed: Dragon wing begonia, p. 45; Pansies, p. 49, 72, 73, 87, 167; Portulaca, p. 80, 81; Dahlberg daisy, p. 58; 'Cora' vinca, p. 63, 79, 81, 83, 91, 94, 95; Salvia 'Black and Blue', Hibiscus, p. 40, 95, 147, 157; Viola, p. 72; Petunias, p. 78, 79; Portulaca, p. 80, 81; Zinnia, p. 18, 97; Alternanthera, p. 99; 'Luna Park Swirl' hibiscus, p. 23; Coneflower 'Primadonna Deep Rose', p. 117; Hibiscus, p. 134, 135; 'Sequins' ice plant, p. 136, 137; 'Harlequin Blue' scabiosa, p. 158; Guara, p. 174. Bailey Nursery: Smoke tree, p. 17; Bridalwreath spiraea, p. 17, 41, 249; Siberian Iris, p. 139; Spiraea, p. 248; Wintercreeper, p. 267; Trumpet Creeper, p. 267; 'Endless Summer' hydrangea, p. 143, 220; 'Stella deOro', p. 207; 'John Clayton' honeysuckle, p. 218; Ginkgo, p. 284; Fringe tree, p. 306; Weeping willow, p. 307; Poplar, p. 307. Bill Adams: 'Texas Gold' columbine, p. 104, 105, 107, 167, 231.

Candace Garber: Redbud, p. 16; 'Chinese Snowball' viburnum, p. 17, 41, 252, 253; Japanese maple, p. 40, 290; 'Doublefile' viburnum, p. 41, 254, 255; Southern magnolia, p. 14; 'Butterfly Blue' scabiosa, p. 158, 173, 207, 229; 'Kern's Pink' viburnum, p. 252. Carlos Gi: Camellia, p. 197. Casa Flora: Fern, holly, p. 21, 127; Japanese painted fern, p. 40, 126. Cathleen Clapper: Agave, p. 182. Chamblee Roses: 'Caldwell Pink' rose, p. 241; 'Perle d'Or' rose, p. 241; 'Georgetown Tea' rose, p. 241. Chris Starbuck, Missouri Botanical Garden: Yew shrub, p. 261. Conrad Pyle, Rob Cardillo: 'Knock Out' rose, p. 40, 103, 109, 151, 159, 165, 185, 229, 246, 247; 'Blushing Knock Out' rose, p. 247; 'Sunny Knock Out' rose, p. 219, 247; 'Pink Knock Out' rose, p. 247, 'Double Knock Out' rose, p. 247. Syl Arena: 'Pink Double Knock Out' rose, p. 247, 'Rainbow Knock Out' rose, p. 247. Cynthia McKenney: Amaryllis, p. 106; Aster, p. 110, 111. Agarita shrub, p. 180, Oaks, p. 292. Derek Fell: Lenten Rose, p. 140, 141, 227; Naked ladies, Black-eyed susan, p. 142; Stokesia, p. 164.

Encore: Azaleas, p. 23, 41, 105, 163, 188, 189, 201. Flowerwood: Cleyera, p. 21, 205; Azalea, p. 141; 'Bronze Beauty' cleyera, p. 261; White azalea, p. 197; Japanese boxwood, p. 193. Gail Johnson: Sycamore, p. 307. Gene Joyner: Pindo palm; p. 307. G. Kling: Mahonia, p. 230. Gardener's Confidence Collection (© Michael Dirr): 'Cherry Dazzle' crapemyrtle, p. 113, 123, 153, 179, 185, 206, 207; also from Gardener's Confidence Collection, McCorkle Nursery (courtesy of): Hydrangea, p. 255; Loropetalum, p. 228, 273. Glenn Kopp, Missouri Botanical Garden: Yew, p. 205, 259, 260, 261.

Harvey Cotten: Crapemyrtle, p. 12, 42, 273; 'Rose Creek' abelia, p. 14, 17, 40, 178, 273; Glossy abelia, p.179; Bald cypress, Elm lacebark, 'Parsons' juniper, 'Grey Owl' juniper, p. 16, 274; Wax myrtle, naked ladies lily, holly, dwarf yaupon, p. 17, 41, 142, 143, 258, 259, 274, 275; Lenten rose, p. 21; Joe Pye weed, p. 23; Butterflies, p. 34, 39; Black-eyed susan, p. 112; Pink muhly grass, p. 131; Maiden grass, p.133; Mexican bush sage, p. 149, 157; 'Autumn Joy' sedum, p. 160; Fall aster, p. 161; Loropetalum, p. 176, 248; Abelia, p. 179; Juniper, p. 224, 225; 'Leatherleaf' viburnum, p. 267; Boxwoods, p. 192; Hydrangeas, p. 222, 223; Lacebark elm, p. 280; Yaupon holly, p. 286. Hillstar: Daffodils, p. 167. Horticopia: Clematis, p. 201; Redbud, p. 302. Jackson & Perkins: 'Seafoam' rose; p. 239; 'The Fairy' rose, p. 241; Crapemyrtle, p. 273. Jesse Eldora Roberton: Mexican feather grass, p. 181, 183, 277. Jill Lang: Coreopsis, p. 171 and 195. Jim Manhart: Texas sage, p. 250; Desert willow, p. 277. Joy Brown: Bench, p. 212. KBR Photos: Black-eyed-susan, p. 112; Kathleen Cook: 'Color Guard' yucca, p. 264. Keith Johansson: Ginkgo, p. 268; Shantung maple, p. 269, 291. Lady Bird Johnson Wildflower Center: Andy and Sally Wasowski: Soapberry, p. 305; Joseph Marcus: Agarita, p. 181; Desert willow, p. 276; Harry Cliffe: Eve's necklace, p. 283.

©McCorkle Nursery (courtesy of): Loropetalum, p. 14, 15, 199, 203, 211, 228, 229; All hedge pictures, p. 15; Kerria, p. 17, 21, 189, 226, 227; Hydrangea, p. 177; Carolina jessamine, p. 41, 198, 199; Crapemyrtle, p. 179; 'Lady Banks' rose, p. 238, 239; Boxwood hedges, p. 192; Ginkgo, p. 284, 285. Megan R. Hoover: Pecan, p. 307. Martin Heaney: Viburnum, Burkwood, p. 267. Martin Anderson: Wisteria, Japanese & Chinese, p. 267. Michael Shake: Dawn redwood; p. 307. Mountain States Nursery: Texas sage, p. 250, 251. Nancy Tripp: Live oak, p. 294. Neale Cousland: Agave, p. 183. Novalis: Amaryllis, p. 107; Lily, oxblood, p. 175.

Park Seed: Dahlberg daisy, p. 59, 65; Salvia, p. 40; Zinnia, p. 96; Japanese Iris, p. 137; Louisiana Iris, p. 137; 'Sarah Taylor' bearded iris, p. 139; Lenten rose 'Royal Heritage Strain', p. 140; 'Purple Pixie' stokesia, 'Peachy' stokesia, p. 164; Hosta, p. 175; Pomegranate, p. 234; Rosemary, p. 236; Autumn sage, p. 251, 277; 'Ivory Tower' yucca, p. 262; Joe Pye weed, p. 175; 'Davidii' mix, p. 194; 'Margarita' Carolina jessamine, p. 198; Clematis, white, p. 200; 'Harlequin' honeysuckle, p. 218. Paul Marcus: Loquat, p. 306. Pam Penick: Mexican plum, p. 199, 209, 283, 301. Patricia Davis: Coreopsis, p. 118; Patti Steib: Live oak with house, p. 294. Plant Delights Nursery: Turk's Cap, p. 168. PDSI: Honeysuckle, p. 17; Japanese painted fern, p. 21, 40, 126, 127; 'Color Wheel' stokesia, p. 164, Summer Snowflake, P. 166, 167; Autumn fern, p. 233, Dwarf wax myrtle, p. 258, Acuba, p. 187; Little Leaf Boxwood, p. 193; Cleyera, p. 204; 'Mardi Gras' honeysuckles, p. 218.

Proven Winners: Cuphea, bat-face 'Flamenco Samba', 'Flamenco Cha cha', 'Flamenco Rumba', p. 56, 57, 63, 97, 135; Lantana 'Patriot Fire Wagon', p. 65, 69, 71; Gomphrena 'Globe Purple', p. 65; Coneflower 'Twilight', p. 71, 116, 117, 195; Coneflower 'Big Sky After Midnight', p. 69, 116, 117; Coneflower 'Big Sky Sunrise', p. 116, 117, 159; 'Purple Emperor' butterfly bush, p. 69, 117, 135, 173; 'Totally Tempted' cuphea, p. 56; Melampodium 'Sunflake Gold', p. 71; Petunias, p. 19, Heuchera, p. 21, 40; Althea, 'Rose of Sharon', p. 25, 184; Butterfly bush, p. 40, 98, 195; Persian shield, p. 77, 89; Sweet potato vine, p. 88; Torenia, trailing, p. 85, 92, 93, 221; Euphorbia, 'Diamond Frost' p. 98; Dicondra, 'Silver Falls', p. 98; Lantana, p. 117; Elephant ear, p. 124; Purple fountain grass, p. 131; Cleome, p. 145; Foxglove, p. 174; Scaevola, p. 82; Coleus, p. 83; 'White Chiffon' althea, p. 184; Althea, p. 185; Hosta, p. 187; 'Peacock' butterfly bush, p. 194.

RA Howard: Desert willow, p. 277. Robert Mohlenbrock: Wisteria, American, p. 267. Rose Smith: Black-eyed-susan, p. 113. Scheeper's Bulbs: Daffodils, p. 17, 120, 121, 167, 209; Iris, p. 137, Lilies, p. 73; Yucca, p. 301. Sharon Day: Dianthus, p. 174. Shutterstock: Redbud, p. 41, 301, 303; Coreopsis, p. 118, 119; Ice plant, p. 136; Spider lily, p. 146, 147; Red-hot poker, p. 154; Kerria, p. 227; Fraser, Red-Tip Photinia, p. 266; Black walnut, p. 307; Sweet gum, p. 307. Southern Bulb: Lilies, p. 144, 145. Stokes Seed: Dahlberg daisy, p. 58.

Steve Huddleston: 'Gold Star' Esperanza, p. 62, 63, 79, 145; Lantana horrida, p. 68; Elm, Cedar, Shumard oak, p. 16; Maiden grass, Mexican feather grass, Lindheimer's muhly grass, Inland sea oats, Southern wood fern, p. 21, 131, 132, 133, 143, 169, 189, 191, 203, 205, 231, 261, 283; Salvia, p. 40, 111; Crossvine, Clematis, Aster, p. 41, 110, 251, 200, 202, 203, 208, 209; Tapioca, p. 81, 90, 91; 'Powis Castle' artemisia, p.108; Hibiscus, p. 134; Mexican mint marigold, p. 148; Autumn Sage, p. 149, 157, 181, 219; Phlox, 'John Fanick', p. 150, 15, 179; Zexmenia, Lily of the Field, p. 175; Agarita, p. 180; Mahonia, p. 231; Nandina, 232, 233; Dwarf pomegranate portrait, p. 234; Pomegranate flower, p. 235; Rosemary, p. 237; Climbing Pinkie, p. 239; Texas sage, p. 250; Virginia creeper, p. 256, 257; 'Rusty Blackhaw' Viburnum, p. 257; Yucca, p. 265; 'Ducher' rose, p. 243, Agarita, p. 180; Zexmenia, p. 183; Hollies, p. 216, 217; Yaupon holly, p. 275, 286, 287; Desert willow, p. 276; Cedar elm, p. 281; Eve's necklace, p. 282; Oaks, p. 293, 295; Soapberry, p. 304, 305. Steven Van Horn: Hummingbird, p. 11

Texas A & M University: 'Marie Daly' rose, p. 241.'Duchesse de Brabant' rose, p. 243; 'Carefree Beauty' rose, p. 243. Tesslar: 'Tropicanna' canna leaf, p. 114. Tom Wichman: Wisteria, p. 267. William Travis: Dutch Iris, p. 139. W. Woyke: Crocus, p. 174.

Climate and Acknowledgments

Zone Map of North Central Texas

This book covers zones USDA cold hardiness zones 7a, 7b, and 8a in north central Texas, as shown on this map. The map is divided into zones based on minimum temperatures established by the USDA. Plants are classified by zone numbers to determine where they can grow based on the lowest temperature they can take.

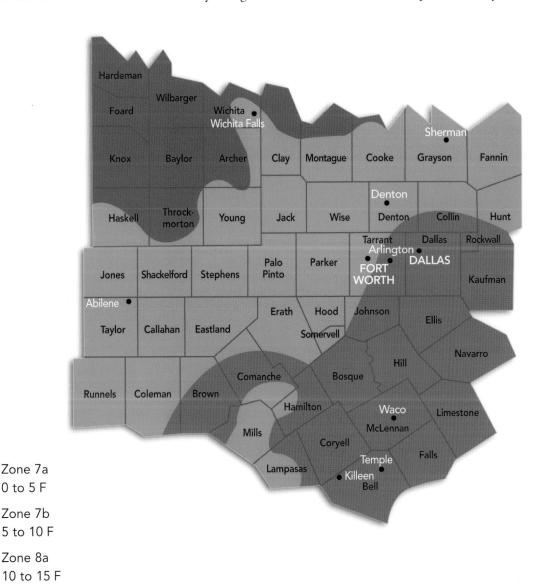

Zone 7a
0 to 5 F

Zone 7b
5 to 10 F

Zone 8a
10 to 15 F

Annual minimum temperatures

Thank You

Barbara Hadsell   *Elaine Golob Weber*

We want to thank Barbara Hadsell, Pamela Crawford's assistant. She worked tirelessly on making this book a reality.

Elaine Weber, the graphic designer, worked enthusiastically with Pamela on some very tight deadlines. She showed great patience with her last-minute requests.

Chapter 1

Easy Basics for Sustainable Gardening

After

Before

It's time to learn a new way of gardening in north central Texas. Our temperatures are rising while our rainfall amounts are either too much or too little. We are all concerned that the activities of man might actually be harming our environment.

At the same time, people are busier than ever, and few have time to devote to maintenance-intensive landscapes. Budgets are stretched to the limit.

The purpose of this book is to show plants and gardening techniques that help our environment and fit into our busy, budget-driven lifestyles.

These photos show gardens that use the principles in this chapter, both in planting and maintenance. Each principle considers the environment first and then details easy shortcuts that will save you time, money and trouble. Skim this chapter before putting your first plant in the ground. Look for easy instructions on the following key sustainable principles:

✿ Choose plants that can take our changing climate. The plants in this book adapt to warmer temperatures as well as the rainy years and droughts that are forecast for our future.
✿ Learn how to grow healthy plants naturally by placing them in the right spot, preparing the soil, planting, and watering in a way that keeps the plant healthy. Healthy plants resist pests and use less water.
✿ Determine which plants bloom the longest, so your butterflies will have enough food.
✿ Discover how to keep your plants healthy with natural compost, mulch, and the best fertilizers for the environment.
✿ Find out how to save water and how to use water from your roof to water your plants. This information will free you from high water bills and watering restrictions.
✿ Gather information about the latest plants. Breeders are working to produce plants that bloom longer and require less care than before. Some are worth the money, and others aren't. Make it a habit to take this book with you to your garden center so you can check out the plants BEFORE you buy them!

(Above and left): These gardens include many side-planted container gardens, as shown here. These baskets and column kits are available from www.kinsmangarden.com. That website also shows quick videos of the planting and installation of these containers and columns.

Seven Worst Gardening Mistakes

1. Buying the Wrong Plants

Most beginners buy plants that don't meet their expectations simply because they don't understand the plant's flowering habits - or the plant is an erratic performer. Take this book with you to your garden center. If you stick to the blue ribbon plants described on page 12, you will have a great chance of success with tough plants that are well adapted to the Texas environment. Most plants you see in your garden center will be described in this book, with both good and bad qualities. It is much better to know how they grow before you buy them. See pages 18 and 19 for more plant shopping tips.

2. Planting in Areas with Poor Drainage

Most plants that are grown in soil that is constantly wet die pretty quickly. Drainage problems are the major cause of wet spots in the garden. See pages 22 and 23 to learn how to check your soil and how to fix it. If you can't fix your drainage problems, these pages tell you which plants are the best and worst for wet spots.

3. Purchasing the Wrong Fertilizer

Several times, we have killed plants by using fertilizers. One of our first lawns died from over fertilization. An entire garden done by a local landscaping company died because the popular, slow-release fertilizer they used released all three month's worth of nutrients at once. Water activates the fertilizer, and we had a lot of rain. No one wants to kill plants because of such a routine occurrence! See pages 36 to 39 for information regarding good, easy fertilizers.

4. Watering Incorrectly

Plants need quite a bit of water right after they are planted, particularly if planted in spring or summer. If they don't get enough in the beginning, they can die. If you give them too much later, they can also die. Read pages 28 to 31 to learn how to water easily and efficiently.

5. Piling Soil Around the Stem of the Plant

If soil or organic mulch comes into contact with the stem of many plants, the stem rots, and the plant dies. It is quite easy to avoid this plight by simply planting the plants a little higher. To help retain water, most people put organic mulch on top of the soil after they have planted. Learn to pull the mulch away from the trunk or stem when you are mulching. Learn how to plant properly on pages 26 and 27.

6. Spacing Plants Incorrectly

Each plant requires a certain amount of space to grow properly. If you plant them too close together, they won't grow properly, nor will they flower profusely. If you plant them too close to your house, they will eventually have to be removed. See the individual plant profiles in chapters two through five to find the proper spacing for each plant.

7. Placing Plants in the Wrong Amount of Light

Different plants need different amounts of light. A petunia likes sun, while a hosta likes shade. But how much sun is enough for sun plants? The rule of thumb is at least four to six hours of direct sun a day. In other words, if your petunia gets just two hours of sun with shade the rest of the day, it will not do well. For your shade-only plants, if they are left in the sun, the leaves and flowers will burn. Of the two, shade plants are more complicated to place than sun plants. See pages 20 and 21 for more information on shade gardening.

Six Tips That Benefit the Environment

1. Learn the Latest Water Saving Methods

You will learn about many plants that breezed through our recent droughts with nothing but rainwater. You'll find them in chapters two through five, with the symbol indicating "Lives on Rainwater" in the green band on the top of the right-hand pages. Plant them in fall when you won't need much water to establish them. Use these for your main planting areas. If you want more diversity, plant thirstier plants in separate areas that can easily be watered with the water you collect from your roof, air conditioner, or shower. Use the most drought-tolerant grass for your climate zone. Buffalo grass lived fine through the worst droughts Texas has ever seen, although it did turn brown when it went without water for periods of three weeks or more. Read pages 32 to 33 to learn lots more ways to save water.

2. Appreciate Our Wonderful Native Plants

North central Texas is replete with fabulous native plants, many of which flower beautifully, like rusty blackhaw viburnum and Mexican plum. You'll find them in chapters two through five, with the symbol of the state of Texas in the green bar that runs along the top of each page. Appreciate natives both for their natural fit in the environment and for their cultural significance. Understand, however, that all natives are not necessarily low water plants. Our surveys showed that native azaleas and dogwoods were among the plants that suffered most in the recent droughts. Many native plants, like azaleas, are native to areas near streams where they have frequent moisture. Other natives, like eastern red cedar, are quite adaptive to different moisture levels, taking rainy periods or droughts equally as well.

3. Look for Plants That Can Adapt to Our Changing Environment

The temperatures in Texas have risen substantially since 1990. We have also had historic droughts. The climate scientists tell us to prepare for more heat as well as water extremes (drought years alternated with years of high rainfall). Look for plants that can adapt to these changes. Crapemytle, for example, does fine if the temperature goes up a few degrees. It can also take high rainfall years as well as droughts. This book is loaded with plants that are ready for our new environment.

4. Use Environmentally-Friendly Fertilizers and Pesticides

We have all read about links between toxic chemicals and disease. Many fertilizers pose health risks by contaminating our ground water. Learn how to use environmentally-friendly fertilizers and pesticides on pages 34 to 39.

5. Attract Butterflies and Hummingbirds to Your Garden

Because of human encroachment and loss of natural habitat, butterflies have fewer sources of nectar. It it easy to attract both butterflies and hummingbirds by simply planting the flowers that offer the nectars they drink. Look for the butterfly and/or hummingbird symbols on the top of the right page of the plant profile to find the best plants for butterflies and hummingbirds.

6. Draw Birds to Your Garden

Recent reports have shown that our songbird population is diminishing. Plant trees and shrubs that provide both nesting spots and food for birds. Look for the bird symbol on the top of the right page of the plant profiles in chapters two to five to find plants that are friendly to birds.

1ST Blue Ribbon Means Easy!

The blue ribbon plants require no more than one chore from you per year, in addition to proper planting, watering, and fertilization. Although we discuss many other plants in this book, we recommend that beginners or serial plant killers stick to the blue ribbon plants until they have some successful growing experiences.

Characteristics of the Blue Ribbon Perennials, Shrubs, Vines, & Trees

✿ Requires touching (trimming, deadheading, etc.) no more than once a year.

✿ Is very well adjusted to the Texas climate (drought years as well as years with normal or above normal rainfall).

✿ Fares well with little susceptibility to pests.

✿ Has an established record (it has been around for enough years to understand its requirements).

✿ Needs water once or twice a week at the most after the establishment period (see pages 28 to 29). Many blue ribbon plants need no supplemental irrigation at all.

Left to right: Lantana, crapemyrtle, and 'Homestead Purple' verbena are all blue ribbon plants.

Characteristics of the Blue Ribbon Annuals

✿ Performs the same way every year (dependable).

✿ Requires little to no trimming.

✿ Is very well adjusted to the Texas environment, including high heat and humidity.

✿ Lives a long life (at least the four to six months of your growing season).

✿ Fares well with little susceptibility to pests.

✿ Has an established record (it has been around for enough years to understand its requirements).

✿ Blooms continuously for a minimum of five to six months (except for cacti, bromeliads, and plants used primarily for leaf color).

✿ Needs water, at the most, once or twice a week after it is established.

2ND Red Ribbon, Almost as Easy

Red ribbon plants are not far behind the blue ribbon plants in overall performance. The only difference is that red ribbon plants require more care - up to three chores per year, if they are planted, watered, and fertilized correctly. Some may have susceptibility to pests and require occasional deadheading. Red ribbon plants may be watered up to twice a week.

Characteristics of the Red Ribbon Perennials, Shrubs, Vines & Trees

✿ Requires touching (trimming, deadheading, etc.) no more than three times per year.

✿ Is very well adjusted to Texas climate (years with droughts as well as normal or above normal rainfall).

✿ Has an established record (it has been around for enough years to fully understand its requirements).

✿ Needs water, at the most, once or twice a week.

Above: Hydrangeas are red ribbon plants because they require more water than blue ribbon plants.

Left: Hydrangeas in a home garden

Characteristics of the Red Ribbon Annuals

✿ Performs the same way every year (dependable).

✿ Adjusts well to most climates.

✿ Requires trimming every month or so

✿ Has a long lifespan, at least the four to six months of our growing season.

✿ May have some susceptibility to pests.

✿ Has an established record (it takes many years on the market for a plant to be a reliable success).

✿ Blooms continuously for a minimum of five to six months (except for cacti and bromeliads or plants used primarily for leaf color).

Easy Hedges and Screens

For easy hedges, use evergreen plants with dense forms that don't require much trimming. The following plant lists are excellent choices. And don't forget color! Many of these plants either have colored leaves or flowers. See page 24 for tips on saving money when you buy plants.

Small Hedges, 1 to 4 Feet

'Rose Creek' Abelia

1' to 4'

Abelia, 'Rose Creek' (light shade - sun)
Azalea, dwarf (light shade)
Boxwood (light shade - sun)
Holly (light shade - sun)
Loropetalum, smaller cultivars (light shade - sun)

Loropetalum

Medium Hedges, 4 to 12 Feet

'Knock Out' Rose

4' to 8'

Abelia, larger varieties (light shade - sun)
Aucuba (dense - medium shade)
Azalea (light shade)
Boxwood (light shade - sun)
Camellia (light shade)
Cleyera (medium shade, light shade, sun)
Holly (light shade - sun)
Loropetalum (light shade - sun)
'Knock Out' rose (sun)
Wax Myrtle, dwarf (light shade - sun)

8' to 12'

Camellia (light shade)
Cleyera (medium shade, light shade, sun)
Holly (light shade - sun)
Loropetalum (light shade - sun)
Wax myrtle (light shade - sun)
Yaupon holly (light shade - sun)

Tall Hedges, 12 Feet Plus

Southern Magnolia

12' to 25'

Eastern red cedar (light shade - sun)
Holly (light shade - sun)
Magnolia, 'Little Gem' (light shade - sun)
Wax myrtle (light shade - sun)

25' Plus

Eastern red cedar (light shade - sun)
Magnolia, southern (light shade - sun)

Eastern Red Cedar

Low hedges are often used for geometric gardens. Boxwood (left and above) is a good choice for these hedges because it grows densely and slowly. Holly is less expensive than boxwood, but grows faster, so it requires more frequent trimming.

Loropetalum (right and below) comes in many different sizes, so be sure the variety you choose fits your space. They flower for part of the season, but the leaves retain their color all year, making this one of the few plants that offers color 365 days per year.

Loropetalum hedges require very little care.

Easiest Plants in this Book

All of the blue ribbon plants in this book are easy, but which are the easiest of the bunch? And which can live on rainwater? The plants on these two pages combine both very low water and very low care requirements. Granted, things can change. North central Texas could turn into a desert. New plant diseases could wipe out whole species. Who knows what the future will bring? But, for now, these are the best bets for serial plant killers, people who don't want to do much work, and people who live in homes with no automatic irrigation systems.

Maintenance Time: Almost Nothing

About the only way you can kill these trees is to plant them incorrectly (see pages 26 to 27) or give them poor drainage (see pages 22 to 23). They grow well in almost any soil, live on rainwater (after two-year establishment period, page 28), and seldom need trimming. These twelve are not currently susceptible to any serious pests or diseases. And look at all those flowers!

Most of theses trees lose their leaves once a year, which requires raking, if you have grass underneath them. Why not forgo the grass? Plant easy, low water shrubs underneath and just mulch for groundcover. This way, you don't even have to rake the leaves, unless they fall on your drive or walk.

Cypress, Bald
Profile: Page 274
60' - 80' tall
Full sun

Desert Willow
Profile: Page 282
15' - 25' tall
Full sun

Elms, Cedar and Lacebark
Profile: Page 280
60' - 80' tall
Light shade - sun

Eve's Necklace
Profile: Page 280
15' - 25' tall
Light shade - sun

Holly, Yaupon
Profile: Page 286
15' - 20' tall
Light shade - sun

Mexican Plum
Profile: Page 300
15' - 25' tall
Light shade - sun

Oaks, Bur and Lacey
Profile: Page 294
35' - 80' tall
Light shade - sun

Oaks, Live and Shumard
Profile: Page 294
80' - 100' tall
Light shade - sun

Redbud
Profile: Page 302
10' - 20' tall
Light shade - sun

Soapberry
Profile: Page 304
20' - 30' tall
Full sun

Maintenance Time: About One Minute Per Year

We have had junipers in our trial gardens for about three years. We have never touched them - no water, no fertilizer, no trimming, no spraying. The only reason you might need a minute a year for your junipers is to fertilize them if your soil needs it. The only way you can kill junipers (other than running them over with your car) is to plant them in a location with poor drainage. See pages 22 to 23 for information about how to avoid that.

Juniper 'Blue Rug'
Profile: Page 224
6" - 8" tall
Sun

Juniper 'Grey Owl'
Profile: Page 224
3' tall
Sun

Juniper 'Nick's Compact'
Profile: Page 224
2.5' tall
Sun

Juniper 'Parsons'
Profile: Page 224
2' tall
Sun

Eastern Red Cedar
Profile: Page 278
40' tall
Sun

No Irrigation*, Little Care

Maintenance Time: About Two Minutes Per Year

These plants are also incredibly easy, requiring only about five minutes of care a year - either fertilizing or trimming. And, like the other plants on these two pages, they live on rainwater after establishment (page 28), except in the most extreme conditions. Many of the plants have substantial bloom periods. Abelia blooms for about six months and both crapemyrtle and red yucca for about two to three months. (See the individual plant profiles for more information).

Abelia
Profile: Page 178
3' to 10' tall
Light shade - sun

Agarita
Profile: Page 180
3' - 6' tall
Light shade - sun

Agave
Profile: Page 182
2' - 5' tall
Full Sun

Coral Honeysuckle
Profile: Page 218
2' - 5' tall
Light shade - sun

Crapemyrtle
Profiles:
Page 206 & 272
3' - 25' tall
Sun

Holly, Dwarf Yaupon
Profile: Page 286
2' - 5' tall
Light shade - sun

Red Yucca
Profile: Page 264
3' tall
Sun

Yucca
Profile: Page 262
2' - 3' tall
Light shade - sun

Maintenance Time: About Five Minutes Per Year

These plants are also incredibly easy, only requiring about five minutes of care a year, either for fertilization or trimming. And, like the other plants on these two pages, they live on rainwater after establishment (page 28) except in the most extreme conditions. Texas sage gives year-round color from its leaves and Turk's cap blooms for most of the warm season with almost no time from you! Daffodils and amaryllis create traffic-stopping color. See the individual plant profiles for more information.

Amaryllis
Profile: Page 106
2' tall
Light shade - sun)

Beautyberry
Profile: Page 190
2' - 2.5' tall
Light shade - sun

Daffodils
Profile: Page 120
6" -16" tall
Sun (in winter)

Summer Snowflake
Profile: Page 166
12" - 15" tall
Shade or sun

Texas Sage
Profile: Page 250
3' - 5' tall
Light shade - sun

Turk's Cap
Profile: Page 168
2' - 4' tall
Light shade - sun

*Lives on rainwater after establishment in all but the most extreme conditions

Take This Book with You...

BUDGET GARDENING TIP:
SAVE MONEY ON PLANTS

✿ Buy the smallest size you can. A shrub in a 1 gallon pot costs about 1/3 as much as the same shrub in a 3 gallon pot.

✿ Buy annuals in multi-packs. We like the 18 packs the best. The roots of the plants are about 3 inches across. The same plant in a 4 inch pot is at least twice as much money! And, it only takes about a week for the smaller plants to grow as large as the more expensive ones!

✿ Seeds are the cheapest way to buy new plants. Buy an old book from a used book supplier called *Park's Success with Seeds* by Ann Reilly. It will only cost a few dollars and is the best book we know for fast and easy success with seeds.

✿ In each individual plant profile (chapters 2 to 5), we explain how to propagate the plant. In most instances, it's easy! Learn how to use root cuttings, and you will have a gorgeous garden for nothing!

✿ Trade with your neighbors. Have everyone divide their perennials, trade with each other at a block party, and color your neighborhood!

✿ Look for local gardening events. Often, home growers sell plants really cheap.

✿ Abandoned properties that are scheduled to be cleared can be great places to find plants. Be sure to get permission from the owner. Check with your local city hall to find out how to find the owner's name.

✿ Space plants correctly. Each plant profile (chapters 2 to 5) tells you the proper spacing. If you plant them too close, you waste a lot of money. For example, it takes 4 times as many plants for 1 foot of spacing than for a 2 foot spacing.

Take this book with you when you go to garden centers. When you see a plant you need information on, check the index to find the appropriate pages. The information can save you a lot of time, frustration, and money. This book not only covers the great plants but also describes many of the not-so-great ones as well. We don't want you to make the same mistakes we did!

Some Plants Won't Meet Your Expectations

Pamela Crawford (one of the authors of this book) purchased gerber daisies, thinking they would bloom throughout her growing season, or at least six months or so. Not so. They bloomed for a month and never even set another bud. She thought she had done something wrong until she found out that gerber daisies are supposed to only bloom for a month. Had she known that, she would have bought one plant instead of the six she planted in a container that cost her $4 each!

But the label didn't say how long the plant bloomed, and the garden center lady told her she thought they bloomed for months. She was wrong.

Pamela had the same experience with kalanchoe. It looked great the day she planted it, but it only stayed in bloom for about a month.

Many garden center personnel are encyclopedias of plant knowledge. Others are novices in gardening.

The hardest information to find is how long the plant blooms. So, take this book with you. The plant you are looking for may not be here, but chances are it will.

If you see a plant you like that is not in this book, by all means ask the garden center personnel. Be sure to ask if they have any personal experience with the plant.

Name Confusion

Zinnias are widely planted in north central Texas. Some (right, top) look great in the pot at the garden center but are very susceptible to disease and won't look very good in your garden for long.

On the other hand, 'Profusion' zinnias (right, bottom) are blue ribbon plants and are labeled with their name at the garden centers. They have consistently bloomed for six month periods in our trial gardens with no care other than watering! Take this book with you so you can check out all the plants you buy before you plant them!

When You Shop for Plants.

Great Plants That are Hit or Miss

Petunias are one of the most popular annuals in Texas. We've had great luck with some of the Wave petunias from Pan American Seed as well as the Supertunias from Proven Winners (shown left, at one of their growing facilities in Vancouver).

So, why aren't they blue ribbon plants? Several reasons:

❀ Many petunias sold today are unnamed. The label just says "Petunia." Quite a few of these died on us. We're afraid if we classify them as the best of the best, you might end up with one of these bad ones and be quite disappointed.

Many other blue ribbon plants are also sold as unnamed plants, but the species are so strong that all of them do well. Wax begonias and impatiens are both examples of this. They are almost foolproof - named or unnamed.

❀ One of the most important criteria for blue ribbon annuals is at least a four to six month lifespan. Most petunias won't last that long, particularly if the weather is quite hot.

Erratic Performers

Calibrachoa, or million bells, is one of the hottest and prettiest plants in container gardening. However, when they are good, they are very, very good; but when they are bad, they are awful!

We're not sure why. Probably, some of the new ones haven't been tried in certain climates and might not like it there. Eventually, they will sort themselves out.

Once again, take this book with you to your garden center so you will have a better shot at assessing your risk with certain plants. In many instances, they are so inexpensive that cost is not an issue. However, it is important that both new gardeners and serial plant killers have successful gardening experiences. So, stick with the blue ribbon plants if you fall into either of these categories.

New Plants

New plants as well as new cultivars and varieties of old plants are showing up by the thousands. We have tested many of these new plants at Fort Worth Botanic Garden. Many are really superior to older varieties - more flowers, longer bloom period, etc. Others are not so great. We have written about lots of them in chapters two to five. Take this book with you to make plant shopping much easier.

Understand Light

Different plants need different amounts of light. A petunia likes sun, while a hosta likes shade. But how much sun is enough for sun plants? The rule of thumb is at least four to six hours of direct sun per day for sun plants. In other words, if your petunia just gets two hours of sun with shade the rest of the day, it will not do well.

If you put a plant (that just likes shade) in the sun, the leaves and flowers will burn. And, shade is more complicated than sun. It's pretty easy to tell whether your area is in sun; but, shade is trickier. Many plants are quite sensitive to varying degrees of shade - light, medium, and dense. Sit in the same location you are considering for a plant and look around.

Light Shade

Light shade is often characterized by morning sun and afternoon shade. Many plants do well in light shade. If you are under trees, try this exersize to determine if you are in light shade. Look up, and you will see about 20-30% leaves and the rest sky. The trees are planted farther apart in light shade than in medium shade. Look down, and notice many types of plants growing. Look around, and see many patches of sky from any direction.

Plants that grow well in light shade also thrive in part-sun, part-shade situations - provided the sun is in the morning hours. If your area gets sun all afternoon, choose plants that tolerate full sun.

Medium Shade

Look up, and you will see medium shade from trees. Look for about 50% or more of sky. Look down, and see ferns or other shade plants growing. Look around, and see more trees but not much open sky on the south or west sides. Sun from the south or west is strong and too much for most medium shade plants.

Fewer plants grow in medium shade than light shade, but your choices are still wide enough to make a great, colorful garden.

Dense Shade

Look up, and you will see the dense shade of very thick trees or the roof of a building. Less than 30% of the sky is visible. Look down, and see almost nothing growing, except possibly a few weeds. Look all around, and you will still see very little sky but rather more thickly-leafed trees or buildings.

Many plants thrive in light to medium shade. Dense shade, however, is a difficult situation. Most flowering plants require more light than dense shade provides.

Easy Shade Plants

Plants for light shade are easy to find - over half the plants in this book thrive in light shade. Azaleas and hydrangeas love that light condition. Finding plants for medium to dense shade is more difficult than for light shade. Here are some good shrub, groundcover, and perennial choices.

Dense Shade Perennials, Groundcovers, and Shrubs

Aucuba
Profile: Page 198

Fern, Holly
Profile: Page 126

Fern, Painted
Profile: Page 126

Grass, Liriope
Profile: Page 128

Grass, Mondo
Profile: Page 128

Ivy
Profile: Page 212

Pachysandra
Profile: Page 212

Medium Shade Perennials, Groundcovers, and Shrubs

Aucuba
Profile: Page 198

Cleyera
Profile: Page 204

Elephant Ears
Profile: Page 124

Fern, Autumn
Profile: Page 126

Fern, Southern Wood
Profile: Page 126

Fern, Holly
Profile: Page 126

Fern, Painted
Profile: Page 126

Grass, Liriope
Profile: Page 128

Grass, Mondo
Profile: Page 128

Heuchera
Profile: Page 194

Inland Sea Oats
Profile: Page 130

Ivy
Profile: Page 212

Kerria
Profile: Page 226

Lenten Rose
Profile: Page 140

Mahonia
Profile: Page 230

Pachysandra
Profile: Page 212

Phlox, Woodland
Profile: Page 150

Turk's Cap
Profile: Page 168

Vinca Vine
Profile: Page 94

Yew
Profile: Page 260

Check Drainage Before Planting

Bad Drainage Usually Kills Plants

Planting in a bed that drains poorly is one of the easiest ways to kill a plant. Compacted soil can keep a plant's root system from growing. Without a good root system, the plant will never be able to live without a ton of water. Many die without it.

Areas Most Likely to Have Drainage Problems

'Bathtub,' a potential drainage problem

✿ 'Bathtub' is an area in between the house and the walk. Since the walk often interrupts the drainage pattern, this area is among the first you need to check. It often drains poorly.

✿ Drainage issues can be found in any area that could have had heavy equipment running over the soil. Heavy equipment can compact the soil, making it hard. Roots cannot grow well into hard, concrete-like soil.

✿ Any area of clay soil. Since clay is such a dense soil, it drains poorly.

An Easy Way to Check Your Drainage

Check your drainage by digging a hole about two feet square by one foot deep. Does the soil you removed look really hard? Fill the hole with water. If it hasn't drained in 12 hours, you have a drainage problem.

Fixing Drainage Problems

✿ Till your soil to a depth of 8 to 12 inches. Try the drainage test again.

✿ If it still doesn't drain, you may have a hardpan or concrete-like shelf under your soil. A deep auger can loosen it up. Or, you can punch holes through it with a shovel to give the water a way out, like the drainage holes in flower pots.

✿ Coarse-textured soil amendments, like expanded shale and pine bark, added to the top of the soil and tilled down to a 12-inch depth, also helps drainage. Don't use sand. Clay plus sand makes concrete.

✿ Ask for advice if you don't know what to do. Many garden centers and nurseries know how to solve drainage problems. Look for the nurseries that have heavy equipment. It might cost less than you think to hire a machine and an operator for an hour or so to fix your problem.

✿ French drains can be dug and filled with gravel. Once again, get a professional opinion before going to the trouble and expense of installing a French drain.

Plants for Wet Spots

If you cannot fix your drainage problem and the water stays in your test hole for 24 hours, you need to call in professionals for help. However, if it drains in between 12 and 24 hours, there are some plants that might work in that situation. Here are your best bets.

Best Plants for Wet Spots (or Areas of Poor Drainage)

Joe Pye weed

Bald cypress
Canna
Carolina jessamine
Elephant ears
Fern, autumn
Fern, holly
Fern, painted
Grass, acorus
Hibiscus
Holly, yaupon
Honeysuckle
Joe Pye weed
Magnolia 'Little Gem'
Magnolia, Southern
Maple, red
Palm, sable
Salvia 'Black and Blue' and
        'Argentine Skies'
Wax myrtle

'Luna Pink Swirl' Hibiscus

Worst Plants for Wet Spots

'Autumn Twist' Encore azalea

Aucuba
Azalea, evergreen
Boxwoods
Camellia
Daffodils
Eastern red cedar
Grass, purple muhly
Grass, switch
Heuchera
Holly, Chinese
Holly, dwarf yaupon
Holly, Japanese
Holly 'Nellie R. Stevens'
Hosta
Ice plant
Iris (except Louisiana iris)
Juniper
Pachysandra
Phlox
Red hot poker plant

Sedum
Smoke tree
Spanish bluebell
Yew

Preparation

Identifying Your Soil

There are many different types of soil in north central Texas, from clay, to sand, to loam - as well as many combinations of the three. If you don't know what type of soil you have, call your county extension service and ask them. Also ask them for instructions on soil amendments to add to your soil before planting. Since clay is the most common soil in north central Texas, here are instructions for dealing with clay.

Beautiful gardens are easily grown in clay soil if it is properly prepared.

Preparing Clay for Planting Beds

Most annuals and perennials don't do well at all when planted in straight clay or sand. It is better to prepare an entire planting bed instead of preparing one hole at a time. Beds on clay are better raised somewhat to encourage drainage. If possible, plan to raise the level of the bed about six inches by adding soil amendments. If that's not possible, remove the top six inches of the clay, so the level of the finished bed will remain at the same level it was before the preparation. Add six inches of soil amendments.

Organic amendments - like compost, peat moss, pine bark, and manure - come from living things. They improve both water and nutrient retention of the soil. They also allow for more aeration, which helps roots grow healthy and strong. Organics help to provide a healthy environment for beneficial organisms like earthworms. Inorganic amendments come from things that were never alive, like expanded shale, perlite, or vermiculite. Inorganic amendments are used strictly to improve drainage. They have little nutritional value.

The Texas AgriLife Extension Service recommends its EarthKind™ approach to soil improvement. For clay soil, add three inches of expanded shale to the bed, and incorporate by rototilling. (Expanded shale is shale that has been heated to a high temperature. As it heats, it expands, thus creating more air space within each particle of shale. These shale particles in a clay soil loosen it up and add air to the soil.) Next, apply three inches of aged compost on top of the clay and expanded shale mixture, and rototill into the underlying soil. The compost helps loosen up the clay soil. For sandy soils, add only three to six inches of aged compost, and rototill into the soil. The incorporated compost will supply nutrients and help the soil retain moisture.

It's very important to blend soil amendments into the existing clay soil. If you don't, water will pass through the amendments and stop on top of the clay. You will have created a bathtub instead of a planting bed, and many plants will drown.

We recommend planting shrubs in beds instead of in single holes in the middle of grass. However, trees are often planted alone. Do not add amendments to tree holes. See page 27, "Planting Single Trees or Shrubs from Containers," for preparation instructions.

Plants That Do Well in Unimproved Clay

Many university studies have found that shrubs and trees don't need organics incorporated into the top layer of soil because their roots quickly outgrow them. Here is a list of shrubs, vines, and trees that we think have a good chance of doing well in unimproved clay, provided it is loosened up quite a bit and not compacted.

Althea, or rose of Sharon, is one of the shrubs that can be planted in unimproved clay.

Shrubs

Althea, rose of Sharon
Butterfly bush
Crapemyrtle
Forsythia
Holly
Spiraea, bridalwreath
Viburnum, Chinese snowball
Viburnum, doublefile
Wax myrtle

Trees

Bald cypress
Chaste tree, Vitex
Chinese elm
Chinese pistache
Crapemyrtle
Eastern red cedar
Ginkgo

Holly
Magnolia
Maple
Palms, European fan, needle, sabal,
             and windmill
Redbud
Oak
Smoke tree

Vines

Carolina jessamine
Honeysuckle

Preparing Soil for Grass

Grass requires drainage, so find out if your soil is compacted, and how much. If it feels hard, it is best to till the top six inches. This can be quite hard work, but it will ensure the health of your grass. Add an inch of top soil or organics, and blend it into the top three inches of soil. Rake the bed to remove clods, rocks, etc., so you can have a smooth bed. This raking is time-consuming but necessary. Avoid creating 'birdbaths' (small, low spots that collect water).

If you are planting grass at a new house, the soil could be really compacted and almost impossible to till by hand. Check with a local garden center or landscaper to find out what they would charge to do the work with a machine. It could be worth it in the long run.

Planting

When to Plant

It is best to plant shrubs, trees, and perennials in fall or winter because they require less water during these cooler periods. Also, cooler temperatures are less stressful for the plants than summer heat. The roots of plants installed in fall continue to develop most of the winter, even when the tops of the plants aren't growing. However, most garden centers sell perennials and blooming shrubs when they are flowering, which could be June. You can plant most plants from containers anytime, but it will take more water to establish them. Summer annuals, some bulbs, and some other plants can't be planted in fall or winter. Check each individual plant profile for specifics.

Spacing the Plants Appropriately

Spacing plants appropriately is very important. We have the proper spacing listed on each plant profile. Plants need room for their roots to expand as well as room for their branches to grow long enough to bloom or fruit. They also need to be far enough away from a building to allow for cleaning and painting. Understand the mature plant size (also detailed in the plant profiles), and place the plant so it will be two to three feet away from a building when it is mature.

Space plants according to their mature size to reduce competition for water. Overcrowding increases the need for water in that area. It may also increase bugs and diseases.

If you follow proper spacing guidelines, your garden may appear bare on planting day. Fill in with annuals for the first season if this open space bothers you.

This garden exemplifies proper plant spacing. Each plant has enough room to grow without overtaking its neighbors.

Planting Trees or Large, Single Shrubs from Containers

Since tree and shrub roots quickly grow beyond your soil amendments, most soils (including clay) are not amended prior to planting individual trees or shrubs. Dig a hole three to four times the width of the root ball, to a depth of one inch less than the height of the pot. We use a tape measure to make this faster. Loosen up the soil that has been removed. It could be quite solid, especially if you are in a new home. Heavy equipment driving over clay will turn it quite hard. Since roots have a hard time growing through that, loosen up the removed soil, so it has a good, soft consistency. If it is not loosened up, the tree will have a hard time growing into the existing soil. (See pages 22 and 23 for information on checking and fixing drainage problems.)

Do not add organic matter to the holes of large shrubs or trees. It acts as a sponge, absorbing all the water. The roots of the plants will have more trouble growing away from the sponge. Roots can also suffocate in wet, waterlogged soil, which is a leading cause of plant death in north central Texas.

Remove the plant from its container. If the roots are growing in a circular shape around the root ball, use your hand to loosen them up. Set the plant in the middle of the hole, and check to see that it is at the right depth. The top of the root ball should be one inch above the level of the surrounding soil. Fill in around the root ball, half way up to the top. Water thoroughly until you see no more bubbles coming up from the bottom. Fill in to the top of the hole, and water again. Fill in where the soil settles. The goal is to remove any air bubbles from the soil.

Be sure the root ball is slightly out of the ground and that no soil is piled up around the trunk (a really fast way to kill your tree!). Fertilize if it is spring or summer with the slow-release product described on page 37. Do not fertilize in fall or winter. Mulch according to the instructions on page 32.

Planting Balled and Burlapped Trees

Planting balled and burlapped trees is exactly like planting trees from containers (as described above) except for handling the burlap. Do not remove it because it keeps the roots together and naturally rots in the soil after planting. Set the tree in the hole with the burlap intact. Cut the twine or string so that you can fold back the burlap from the top of the root ball. Tuck this burlap down around the lower sides of the root ball and into the planting hole. Proceed with filling around the roots the same way you would with a containerized tree (see above).

Planting Annuals, Perennials, and Shrubs in Prepared Beds

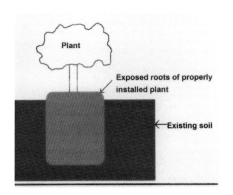

Plant

Exposed roots of properly installed plant

Existing soil

After your soil is prepared, planting is fairly easy, if your soil is soft. If it is rocky, digging can be difficult, so sharpen the edge of your shovel (with an electric grinder sold at home improvement stores) or rent a mechanical digging tool. Dig a hole slightly wider and one inch shallower than the root ball. Take the plant out of the pot. If any roots are circling, loosen them slightly, so they can grow straight into the soil and not in a circle. This step is very important, especially for annuals. Their roots are often so tight, the root ball looks white! If they are not loosened, the plant won't grow much. Place the plant in the hole. Fill in the sides with the same soil. Do not put any additional soil on top of the root ball. It should be slightly out of the ground, as shown in the diagram. The major cause of plant death is planting the plant too deep. Soil piled up on top of the root ball and covering the stem can kill the plant. Water the plant, so the soil is settled in the hole, and there are no air pockets. If you see bubbles coming from the soil you used to fill in around the roots, there are still air pockets.

Establishment Watering

Plants need lots of water right after they are planted. That water is called establishment watering. Most plants store water in their roots. Since their roots are small when they are in nursery containers, they need more water until the roots can grow large enough to store more.

Observe Your Garden Carefully for Its First Growing Season

Recently installed plants need frequent, deep watering to establish their roots in the ground. The watering schedule depends upon the plants' environment. Shade gardens require half the water of sun gardens. Windy gardens require more water than calm gardens. Plants require much more water if planted in summer than if planted in fall.

Your plants will tell you when they need water. Observe them carefully for their first season. If a plant is wilting, it needs water. If the soil feels dry when you insert your finger, it needs water. Plants that are grown in containers are usually grown in a different soil than your garden soil. They can quickly dehydrate if you plant them in clay. The clay can absorb the water in the potting soil quickly. The clay is damp, but your plant is wilted. Push your finger into the potting mix, and give it water if it is dry. After about two weeks, the roots will begin growing into the clay, and the water needs will be somewhat reduced. But the plant will still need extra water for the remainder of that growing season.

Field-grown trees present another problem. These are trees that were grown in the ground on a tree farm. Their roots were cut so that they could be transplanted into your landscape. They require more water than containerized plants because their root balls are larger (often two to three feet in depth), and they have been through the trauma of having their roots cut. They will need more water than smaller plants because the water needs to be absorbed deeper into the soil. They won't need water as frequently as a small, container plant because their soil will be similar to the one you are planting in, and the water will not be sucked out of the rootball into the surrounding soil.

How Much Water to Apply

On the average, you'll need to apply enough water to soak into the soil to a depth of six to eight inches. That will take different amounts of time, depending on your watering method. Slow watering directly on the soil is better than a fast hit with the hose because the roots have more time to absorb water if it is applied slowly. It takes about 45 minutes for our drip irrigation system to apply that much water. Since watering systems vary greatly in their application time, you need to see how long yours takes to apply that much water.

Deep watering is very important. It encourages deep, healthy, root growth. A common mistake is to give too little water with each watering. The plants will never be their best unless their roots are encouraged to grow deeply.

Watch the Plants for Two Years

Most plants are well-established after their first growing season. However, the larger the plant, the longer it takes to establish. So, watch trees and shrubs carefully the second season as well. If a plant is wilting, it needs water. If the soil feels dry when you insert your finger, it needs water.

New Fall Plantings: How Often to Water

Water the plants right after planting them. Mulch them well. Most of the time, that's all you have to do if you plant in November because the temperatures are cool, and it often rains in the fall. The plants aren't using that much water. But be sure to check them closely. If the temperatures rise to the 70's and it doesn't rain for a while, the plants will dry out and could die. Put your finger in the soil around the roots. If the soil feels dry, water.

Fall Planting Saves a Lot of Water

New Summer Plantings: How Often to Water

Plants installed in fall need the least amount of water to establish, and those planted in summer need the most. The first two weeks is the most critical period. The roots have not left their root ball, and they might need water twice a day until they do, which takes about two weeks. That is unusual, however. The most we have ever watered in clay soil was every two days and once a day in sand. However, remember to observe your plants closely during this critical period. The need for water will diminish during the second two week period and will continue to diminish for the remainder of the season. Expect to water about twice a week from the second week until the end of the season.

This bed mixes plants with low or very low water requirements. They need frequent watering immediately after planting if they are planted in summer, less if planted in fall. Once they are established, they need only occasional water to supplement the rainfall. Plants include crapemyrtle, daylilies, purple heart, lantana, and coneflower.

Watering the Established Garden

Overwatering is the gravest error gardeners commit. This common practice shortens a plant's life, causes disease, and increases the maintenance requirements of each plant. Root rot is the biggest problem for plants in clay soil. Also, the plant grows faster with more water and, therefore, needs more trimming. The growth is often leggy because the plant is frantically trying to figure out where to store all this water; thus, long stems result. Overwatered plants also require more fertilizer than properly watered plants because the water washes the fertilizer through the soil.

Different Plants Need Different Amounts of Water

Different kinds of plants have different watering needs. Each plant profile tells you how often the plant needs water during the growing season. Most people don't water much in winter unless they have planted annuals, such as pansies.

Native plants have differing water needs, just like plants from other places. It is a common misconception that native plants tolerate drought better than non-natives. Some native trees, like lacey oaks, are very drought tolerant. Others, like dogwoods, show quite a bit of damage in a drought. Bald cypress is a native tree that adapts to both wet and dry conditions. We have included water needs of each plant and classified them as high, medium, low, or very low water users (in the individual plant profiles, chapters two to five).

It is easiest to water a garden that has beds with plants that have the same water needs. Many gardeners use low-irrigation plants in most of their garden and put higher water-use plants together in a small, highly visible location.

These flowers are impatiens, which are some of the thirstiest flowers used in Texas. They are easy to water if they are kept in a small area, such as in this gazebo.

How Often to Water

It is best to water plants when they need it rather than putting them on a set schedule. Here are some tips:

✿ Wait until the plant shows it needs water. Most plants show they need water by wilting or turning a pale, grayish-green color.

✿ Watering too frequently causes the plant's root to develop only close to the surface. Your goal should be working to grow large, deep roots on the plants, so they have large areas to store water in times of drought.

✿ Water at night or early morning to avoid water loss to evaporation.

✿ Grass turns a dull, grayish-green color when it needs water. If you can see your footprints after walking on it, then you should water.

✿ Watering frequency depends on many environmental factors:
- Plants in shade require about one third as much water as those in sun.
- Plants in clay soil require much less water than those planted in sand.
- Plants need more water when temperatures are higher.
- Plants need more water if it is windy.

✿ Shrubs, vines, and trees generally have larger root systems than perennials, so they may not need water as often.

Annuals, like these petunias require more frequent watering than more permanent plantings.

How Much to Water

✿ Water deeply to encourage deep root growth. Check your soil to see how long it takes to penetrate to a depth of six to eight inches.

✿ For hand watering, apply about five gallons per ten square feet, which takes about one minute with an average gardening hose. Larger shrubs need more.

✿ For grass, apply one inch of water per week during summer. During spring and fall, apply one to two inches of water every two weeks. If you water more, your grass will never grow a healthy enough root system to look its best. Put a coffee can in the grass and see how long your sprinklers take to fill it up to one inch.

Water containers until a steady stream flows from the bottom. Since they require frequent watering, we have them hooked up to a drip irrigation system that waters automatically from our rainwater collection system. Containers and posts from www.kinsmangarden.com.

12 Easy Tips for Saving Water

1. Set Up Different Areas for Plants with Different Water Needs

✿ Plant high water-use plants, like annuals, in one area so it's easier to water them. Since annuals are short-lived, they never have a chance to develop root systems large enough to store much water, so they need frequent watering. Moisture-retaining polymers can be mixed in with the soil when planting annuals. They reduce the water needs of these small plants. Be sure to follow the instructions, or they can harm your plants. These polymers don't work for larger plants because their roots quickly outgrow the area with the polymers.

✿ Place plants according to their water needs - very low water (no irrigation after establishment), low water, medium, or high water use. Temporary irrigation can be used for all the very low water use areas because you should only need it during the eight to ten week establishment period. Or, if you plant in late fall, plants won't even need that much water for establishment.

✿ Use plants that don't need irrigation for the majority of your plants. Use drip irrigation lines for smaller areas with higher water use plants.

2. Mulch

Mulch does a great job of holding moisture in the soil as well as preventing weeds and adding organic matter to keep your plants healthier. Here are some tips (see page 39 for sources of free mulch):

✿ Apply three inches of mulch on top of the soil after planting. Take care not to pile it up around the stem (or trunk) of the plant because wet mulch can rot a trunk. Keep it completely away from trunks and stems. Use your hands to pull it two to three inches away from trunks as you are applying it.

✿ Pine straw is very attractive but doesn't insulate the soil as well as finer mulches, like ground up pine bark or hardwood mulch. Pine bark is the most popular mulch in most of Texas, but it can easily wash away during a heavy rain. Shredded hardwood and cypress mulch stay in place better.

3. Reduce Areas of Grass

Grass uses more water than any other plant in your garden (unless you plant impatiens in full sun!). It also needs a lot of care - cutting, aerating, etc. Areas of grass are shrinking in newer landscapes. Landscape designers and architects are installing a much higher percentage of beds and a lower percentage of grass. Some areas of the country, like Las Vegas, are actually paying people one dollar per square foot to take grass out!

4. Water Your Plants Only When They are Thirsty!

Don't set your sprinkler timer to water whether the plants are thirsty or not! Most plants show they need water by wilting or turning a pale, grayish-green color. Or, push your finger a few inches into your soil and see if it feels dry.

✿ Buy a rain gauge, so you can easily see how much rain actually falls in your garden. If you get half an inch of rain or more, it gives your plants a good watering. If it is only a sprinkle, it doesn't do much good.

✿ Install a rain sensor on your sprinkler system. These sensors keep the system from operating when it is raining. Soil moisture sensors are quite a bit more sophisticated. They measure the moisture content of the soil and turn on your sprinklers only when the soil is dry. University studies are giving these moisture sensors rave reviews for saving water.

5. Create Shade

Shady areas can be 20 degrees cooler than sunny spots. Plants need MUCH less water in shade than in sun. We have been amazed at how little water shade containers need compared to their sun counterparts. This window box needed water about once a week. It is large (36-inch side-planted, from www.kinsmangarden.com), and we used potting mix that included moisture-retaining granules.

The sun baskets that were near this window box needed water every day! That means this shade container required SEVEN TIMES less water than those in direct sun!

6. Plant Low Water-Use Plants

Many of the plants in this book need minimal to no water after they are established. They are well-adapted to Texas and can take Texas' rainfall as well. Many desert plants grow on almost no water but will die in the 30 inches of annual rainfall that occurs in north central Texas.

7. Use Drip Irrigation

Drip irrigation waters the roots of the plants instead of spraying water up in the air, as traditional irrigation systems. They are suitable for beds and containers but not for grass. Drip systems use 20 to 70 percent less water than traditional irrigation systems do.

8. Plant in Fall Rather Than Spring or Summer

Gardens planted in November need very little water to establish. The same garden planted in July could require water every other day (or sometimes every day) for many weeks.

9. Space Plants Appropriately

Space plants according to their mature size to reduce competition for water. Overcrowding increases the need for water in that area. It also increases the number of bugs and diseases.

10. Collect the Rainwater that Falls on Your Roof

About 32,000 gallons of water come off the average Texas roof each year. That's a lot of water! See our website at www.easygardencolor.com for more information on rainwater collection systems.

11. Take Care When Planting Under Trees

The root systems of trees are quite large, generally extending three times the diameter of the drip line (the outer limit of the leaves). If you plant shrubs or groundcovers under these trees, there may not be enough room for all the roots. Since roots store water, the smaller plants may suffer.

12. Fertilize Correctly

Healthy plants use less water than unhealthy ones. Learn to use slow release fertilizers that send nutrients slowly to the plant roots rather than liquids or granular products that can overdose your plant on chemicals. Overfertilization causes plants either to get sick or go into hypergrowth, which causes plants to use more water than they need.

Maintaining Your Garden

Healthy Pest Control

Many of the plants in this book don't attract any bugs that will harm the plant, so don't make the mistake of using toxic chemicals just to keep bugs from arriving. Many common garden pesticides are quite toxic to people and pets, so take great care before using them. Here are some tips for minimizing pesticide use:

❀ Healthy plants don't get as many pests as weak plants, just like people. Weak people are more likely to get sick than strong, healthy people. Keep your plants healthy with the proper amount of water, fertilizer, and mulch.

❀ If you see holes in the leaves, let them alone for a while. Many bugs will take a few nibbles out of a plant and then abandon it for another, especially if the plant is healthy.

❀ Plants are particularly vulnerable to pests immediately after planting. They are in a weakened state and actually send out signals that attract pests. If you see bugs on the plants, they are normally very easy to remove. Aphids, for example, are clustered on the ends of the branches where they eat the new growth. They look like little dots. Simply remove them by cutting the tip of the plant off and throwing it away. If they return, spray the plant with something that will make it taste bad to bugs but won't hurt the plant, like insecticidal soap, garlic, or pepper. None of these will kill birds, butterflies, pets, or people! Garden centers sell sprays containing these natural products.

❀ If you see holes in the leaves but cannot see the bug, the culprits are probably snails, slugs, or caterpillars. Most stay hidden in the daytime, feeding only at night. If you can see the caterpillar, take a photo and have your county extension office identify it. If it is a butterfly caterpillar, you might want to leave it alone. It won't kill the plant; it will just eat some leaves (sometimes, quite a few leaves)!

If the damage becomes severe, take the leaves to a garden center or your county extension office, so they can tell you what kind of bug or disease is causing the damage. Once you know the cause, ask them for the least-toxic remedy. If you buy a pesticide, look it up on the Internet prior to using it to find out the risks. Also, the internet is a great source for natural remedies for pests and diseases. Check out www.gardeninsects.com for beneficial insects.

❀ The only really bad pest we have in our trial gardens is the Japanese beetle, which comes in May and stays until late June or early July. We made a big mistake when we first saw them: we bought Japanese beetle traps. They attracted the entire Japanese beetle population of north central Texas to our gardens! After three years, we no longer spray our beetles. They leave in June or July anyway, so we put up with some holes in the leaves of some plants. The only plants we had that were almost completely ruined by the beetles were hollyhocks, which we removed. They took quite a bit of our sweet potato vines as well. Our 'Knock Out' roses were quite chewed up in June but recovered quickly in July after the beetles left.

Weeding: Some Time-Saving Tips

Weeds are always a problem but particularly right after planting: soil has been disturbed (which uncovers every weed seed in the area); water is being applied heavily; and the new plantings have lots of space in between (which gives weeds room to grow). Here are some tips for saving time with your weeding chores:

✿ There are two classes of herbicides - pre-emergent herbicides and post-emergent. Look for products you trust, as many herbicides are toxic. More safe, natural products are coming on the market all the time. Many home-brew recipes for healthy weed killers are showing up. Check out http://www.garden-counselor-lawn-care.com/vinegar-weed-killer.html for some great ideas.

✿ Pre-emergent herbicides inhibit weed seeds from germinating. You spray (or broadcast) them on top of the mulch after planting. They do not hurt the existing plants. They simpy inhibit weed seeds from germinating. There are many different types on the market. Follow the instructions closely. This type of herbicide can cut your weeding chores down by 70 percent. You need to re-apply them, however, so be sure to follow the instructions. Proper timing of the application is critical.

✿ Post-emergent herbicides are made up of two types: selective and non-selective. Selective herbicides kill the targeted species like dandelions in a Bermuda lawn (Weed-B-Gon). Non-selective herbicides kill everything they touch - Glyphosate (Round-up) being the most common product. Spray in the early morning, when the wind is down. Herbicide drift (herbicide that hits plants you don't want to kill) is a common problem. Be sure to check out the dangers of any herbicide before using it.

✿ Weeds that sprout close to plants must be removed by hand.

✿ Mulch can greatly decrease weeding.

✿ Spacing your plants so they will eventually grow together without leaving much light on the ground is another way to combat weeds.

✿ Many weed cloths are on the market. Do not use plastic that will not let water through because it will not allow water to get through to the roots of the plants. Do not use weed cloth under mulch if you want the mulch to break down to add organic matter to the soil. If weed cloth is placed under paths or other areas that are not planted, the mulch or gravel must be thick enough to cover it.

✿ Boiling water will kill most weeds in your garden. Just fill up your tea kettle, boil some water, and pour away! Be careful to avoid the good plants with the hot water!

Fertilizer

Plants need 16 elements to grow. In ideal conditions, all of these elements come from nature. Picture a natural forest. Leaves fall from the trees and break down into organic matter that is constantly feeding the roots of the plants. Contrast that with a residential garden. Since plant roots grow out three times the diameter of the plant itself, much of their roots are covered with grass, houses, walkways, and driveways. So, we fertilize to give the plants the nutrients they need. There are many different kinds of fertilizers on the market.

✿ Grass fertilizers are different from the fertilizer you will use on the rest of your plants. Buy a brand name you trust. Follow the instructions very carefully. It is easy to apply too much and kill the grass. Also, check to see if the fertilizer stains so that you will be careful around pavement.

✿ Liquid fertilizers (which usually come in powder form that is used with a hose-end sprayer) are good for plants. They need to be applied with great frequency, like every two weeks. This frequent application is hard on you as well as your groundwater. The liquid goes into the groundwater and has been banned in some areas.

✿ Granular fertilizers also have drawbacks. They need to be applied less often than liquids but more often than slow-release fertilizers. Many of them stain hardscapes. Some are also quite harsh and capable of burning plants.

✿ Slow-release fertilizers are best. They are milder, and most don't burn plants. The nutrients are released slowly, so they don't contaminate your groundwater. And, they don't have to be applied as frequently as the rest, making it easier for you as well.

✿ Organic fertilizers are made from things that were once living. This does not mean they are perfect, however. Some, like Milorganite, can easily burn plants. We used it generously around the edge of our planting beds one year to repel deer, and all the plants along the edge died! However, you can build up the nutrients in your soil over time by using organics. See pages 38 and 39 for information.

Fertilizer Tips

✿ Avoid placing harsh, granular fertilizers in planting holes. They can damage plant roots.

✿ Testing your soil is the best gauge of the need for fertilizer. It is important that you keep your soil healthy because healthy plants store water more efficiently and therefore need less water.

✿ Use slow release fertilizers to get a more uniform, water-efficient growth rate. They also decrease plant burn.

✿ Avoid overfertilization, which can cause plants to grow too quickly. Excessive growth can cause lanky, misshapen plants that require more water. Excess nitrogen present in many granular and liquid fertilizers is the primary culprit.

✿ Fertilization frequency depends on the type of plant and the type of fertilizer used. For easy gardening, use a slow-release product that has to be applied only once a year (like the one recommended on the next page).

✿ Early spring is the best time to fertilize.

Best Slow-Release Fertilizer: For Containers, Annuals, & Perennials

We have killed many plants with fertilizer and also have been through other fertilizers that simply didn't make the grade. They included some but not all of the elements a plant needs. Weird, hard-to-diagnose nutritional deficiencies developed that were time consuming, annoying, and definitely not easy.

Plants are like people - they need lots of different nutrients to keep them alive. If you have a vitamin deficiency, you might get quite sick. Same thing for a plant. Learn to read the fertilizer label to make sure it includes *all* the nutrients your plants need.

Most fertilizers include nitrogen, phosphorus (phosphate), and potassium (potash). Most, including some of the best-selling brands, don't include the micronutrients that plants need. *So look for boron, copper, iron, manganese, and magnesium as well. Do not buy a slow-release product that doesn't include these micronutrients, or your plants could suffer later.*

We have found only one fertilizer that works perfectly every time, and it is forgiving. If you use too much, it doesn't burn the plants. It is also excellent for the environment, having won the 2005 Gulf Guardian Award from the EPA Gulf of Mexico Program Partnership.

This fertilizer is slow-release, meaning its little pellets release the nutrients over a period of time. It is a great improvement over the liquids you apply weekly with a hose sprayer! However, there are many slow-release products on the market. We have tested every one we could get our hands on, and none came close to this one. Some either don't last as long or don't have all the nutrients plants need. Others release all their nutrients at once and burn plants.

This fertilizer lasts nine months under 'average' conditions. If you see the plants yellowing a bit, just add some more. Sprinkle it on top of the potting mix, following the instructions on the label.

We recommend this fertilizer for all your container, annual, and perennial plantings. We use it on all our shrubs as well. This fertilizer is available from www.kinsmangarden.com.

Signs That Plants Need Fertilizer

❧ The best method is to get a soil nutrient test through your county extension office.

❧ Abnormal leaf color is usually a sign of nutrient deficiency, although it is also symptomatic of some plant diseases.

❧ If all the leaves are lighter green than normal, the plant probably has a nitrogen deficiency.

Organic Fertilizer and Mulch

Differences between Chemical and Organic Fertilizers

✿ Chemical fertilizers can include any and all nutrients a plant needs to grow. Organic fertilizers either have only one element or several in very low levels.

✿ Organic fertilizers are usually slow-release, which is good. However, they take quite a while to work. The idea behind organics is to improve slowly the structure of the soil and not to provide quick nutrients. So, if your plants need nutrients quickly, like annuals or plants in container gardens, we recommend the chemical fertilizer shown on page 39. It has both slow and fast-acting elements, and it includes all 16 elements your plants need to grow. Plus, it is not an environmental threat.

✿ Organic fertilizers are free from many sources. All chemical fertilizers cost money.

✿ The long term effects of organics are excellent because they can greatly diminish the amount of chemicals needed in your yard.

✿ Learn about any organic fertilizer prior to using it so that you understand specific risks and benefits. Go to www.cdcg.org/goOrganic.html for more information.

Composting: Free Soil & Fertilizer from Kitchen and Garden Waste

✿ Composting is using garden and kitchen waste to create healthy soil. See www.guvswd.org/compost for complete instructions.

✿ You'll need a place to store your compost. We just have a waste pile in our backyard. Some people construct two chicken wire boxes next to their house. One box is for new waste (which requires time to break down and turn into soil), and the other is for the compost that is ready to use. Many fancy, compost bins are for sale at garden centers and through online suppliers.

✿ It takes certain microorganisms to turn your leaves into soil. These microorganisms are present in green waste, like grass clippings or fruit and vegetable waste. Layer green waste with dry waste like leaves. Add water and mix it together occasionally. If it is not breaking down and turning into soil, buy a compost starter at your garden center.

✿ Some composters keep turning the waste to be sure it is well mixed. It will get quite hot (150 degrees), and turning helps that process work evenly. Other composters just leave the pile alone for a year or two and let nature do the work.

✿ Use compost as an amendment for new planting beds (see pages 24 to 25 for instructions) or to spread around existing plants in your beds. Organic gardeners use compost instead of chemical fertilizers.

✿ Wear gloves and long-sleeved shirts when handling compost to keep from getting bacterial infections.

✿ The University of Minnesota reports that there have been rare cases of compost piles catching on fire without anyone lighting a match. No documented cases have been reported on compost piles under seven feet tall.

✿ Avoid putting weeds in your compost pile. Weed seeds could end up in your finished compost!

✿ Avoid putting in meat or dairy products, pet manure, fats, or oils.

Building Up Your Soil Naturally

BUDGET GARDENING TIPS:

FREE MULCH

✿ Rake the leaves in your yard, and sweep them from your street. Check with your neighbors to see if you can rake up their leaves as well.

✿ Some tree companies give away chipped wood. Look them up in the yellow pages, and ask. If you see a tree company chipping up trees in your neighborhood, ask them if they will dump it at your house.

✿ Some counties will deliver free mulch. Call, and ask. Be sure to ask how much they deliver so you'll know if you have room for it.

✿ Free mulch is not sterilized like many sold mulches, so you might get weed seeds. Also, fresh tree mulch needs to age for six months to a year before you can use it on your garden.

FREE FERTILIZER

✿ Look in the yellow pages for stables. Call, and ask them if they have any manure they want hauled away, or if they know anyone who does.

✿ Manure must be aged six to twelve months because it burns plants when it is fresh.

✿ Only use manure from herbivores, like horses, chickens and cows. Manure from meat eaters, like dogs and cats, can contain unwanted bacteria.

The Role of Organic Mulch

✿ Mulch is discussed on page 38. Organic mulch acts much like leaves in a forest. It breaks down into the nutrients your plants need to grow. Apply it at least once a year.

Manure

✿ Livestock manure (sheep, cattle, horses, pigs, chickens) provides nutrients to the soil that plants need to grow. It also helps the water holding capacity of the soil.

✿ Use only what you need, as manure contains nitrates that can leach into the groundwater. Take your soil to your local county extension office for testing before applying manure.

✿ Weed seeds are common in free manure (other than chicken droppings). Purchased manure has probably been sterilized, meaning no weed seeds.

✿ Chicken manure has the most nutrients, but it is also the 'hottest,' burning plants (more than the rest) unless it has been composted.

Homemade Fertilizer

✿ Coffee grounds are wonderful for acid-loving plants like azaleas and roses. Just sprinkle the grounds on the soil around the plants. In addition to being acidic, coffee grounds include nitrogen, magnesium, and potassium–all essential elements for plant growth.

Color Your Garden!

Easiest, Colorful Plants

✿ The easiest, colorful plants are shown on pages 22 and 23.

✿ Shrubs, trees, and vines are the easiest sources of color on the whole. Most don't require either deadheading (removing dead flowers) or dividing, which is the norm with perennials. Some don't require any care at all for years!

✿ Annuals offer the most color for a long time (five to seven months for blue ribbon annuals), but they have to be replaced each year.

✿ Perennials offer color from two weeks to five months. Many require deadheading (removing of dead flowers) to look good. Most require dividing every three to five years. Some exceptions to both of those rules are 'Homestead Purple' verbena, purple heart, agastache, hibiscus, and lenten roses. These five perennials are the easiest of all, but all of them require at least one cutback per year. Although that quick chore might seem easy to most gardeners, some shrubs, vines, and trees don't even require that.

✿ Bulbs are perennials with short but very intense bloom periods, adding more color impact than other perennials. They are worth planting to give that traffic-stopping impact that many of us are looking for. Most are easy to grow. Use different bulbs in clumps throughout your garden, where they show extremely well when blooming but hide when they are not in flower.

Perennials, Shrubs, Vines, and Trees with the Longest Color Period

These plants offer color from leaves or flowers for more than four months each year. If you really like color, use them as the main plants in your garden, accenting with plants that have shorter color seasons.

Abelia Profile: Page 178

Artemisia Profile: Page 108

Autumn Sage Profile: Page 156

Aucuba Profile: Page 198

Butterfly Bush Profile: Page 194

Canna Profile: Page 114

Fern, Painted Profile: Page 126

Heuchera Profile: Page 194

Hibiscus Profile: Page 134

Loropetalum Profile: Page 228

Maple, Japanese Profile: Page 290

Purple Heart Profile: Page 152

Rose 'Knock Out' Profile: Page 246

Rose of Sharon Profile: Page 184

Salvia 'Black & Blue' Profile: Page 156

Salvia 'Henry Duelberg' Profile: Page 168

Turk's Cap Profile: Page 168

Verbena 'Homestead Purple' Profile: Page 170

Yucca Profile: Page 262

Perennials, Shrubs, Vines, and Trees with the Strongest Color Impact

These plants are the traffic-stoppers–those with more color impact than any other reasonably easy plant for Texas. Most plants with a lot of color impact don't bloom for long. These average two to four weeks of flowers, except for the crapemytle (two to four months) and the chaste tree (three to four months). Use these plants to accent a garden loaded with longer bloomers.

Aster, Fall
Profile: Page 110

Azaleas
Profile: Page 188

Carolina Jessamine
Profile: Page 198

Chaste Tree
Profile: Page 270

Clematis,
Sweet Autumn
Profile: Page 200

Crapemyrtle
Profiles:
Pages 206 & 272

Crossvine
Profile: Page 208

Daffodils
Profile: Page 120

Forsythia
Profile: Page 210

Hydrangea
Profiles:
Pages 220 - 222

Iris
Profile: Page 138

Kerria
Profile: Page 226

Lilies
Profiles: Pages
144 - 146

Phlox, Woodland
Profile: Page 150

Redbud
Profile: Page 302

Mexican Bush Sage
Profile: Page 156

Sedum
Profile: Page 160

Spiraea
'Bridalwreath'
Profile: Page 248

Viburnum
'Chinese Snowball'
Profile: Page 252

Viburnum
'Doublefile'
Profile: Page 254

Rebloomers

Encore Azalea
Profile: Page 188

Plant breeders have been quite busy recently producing new plants that bloom more than the originals. New daylilies, azaleas, irises, hydrangeas, and many more flowering plants now bloom longer than their ancestors. Look for plants labeled 'rebloomers,' and you will be pleasantly surprised!

'Mini Penny'
Reblooming Hydrangea
Profile: Page 220

Seasonal Gardens

Most of our Texas plants are seasonal bloomers. Luckily, the temperate climate of Texas proves mild enough to produce blooms for twelve months each year. Have fun planting seasonal gardens, one for each of our four seasons. Since each garden will have lots of plants blooming at the same time, the effect is quite spectacular!

Chapter 2

Annuals

Annuals are plants that just last one season. Why buy annuals when you could have perennials or shrubs that live much longer?

✿ Annuals have a much higher percentage of color than most flowering perennials or shrubs.

✿ Annuals bloom quite a bit longer than most perennials or shrubs. Azaleas, for example, are gorgeous in bloom but only flower for about two weeks. Even the re-blooming azaleas bloom for only about four weeks. Expect 28 to 31 weeks of blooms from most of the annuals in this chapter.

✿ Annuals are quite a bit less expensive than perennials or shrubs.

✿ Annuals are fun! And who can resist stopping at a garden center in spring and loading up the trunk with beautiful flowers? Many cost less than a dollar!

Annuals bloom all year in most of Texas, with summer annuals lasting for about five or six months and winter annuals the same.

Be sure to take this book with you when you shop for annuals. Many annuals are for sale that don't last an entire season. Look them up in this book, so you know what to expect before you buy them!

Above: Butterfly on a lantana blossom

Left: This garden showcases many of our highest performing annuals. Lantana is planted on the ground. The yellow lantana on the left conceals a large container planted with red dragon wing begonias and golden shrimp plants. The basket on the column (www.kinsmangarden.com) is planted with a croton as the centerpiece and is surrounded by coleus, sweet potato vines, and some blanket petunias at the end of their bloom cycle. Go to www.easygardencolor.com to see a series of three-minute videos about column installation, as well as planting one of these side-planted containers.

Begonia, Dragon Wing

CHARACTERISTICS

Plant Type: Annual

Average Size: About 12 to 24 inches tall by 12 to 18 inches wide.

Growth Rate: Medium

Leaf: Dark, glossy green. About 3 inches long by 1 1/2 inches wide. Shaped like a wing.

Flower: Hanging clusters that measure about 4 inches across.

Lifespan: 7 months, but won't take freezes. Easily lasts for an entire growing season.

Origin: Begonias are native to the new world tropics. This one is a hybrid.

Spacing: About 12 inches on center (measure from the center of each plant). Closer in containers.

Cautions: Irritant, if eaten, which can result in breathing difficulties. Seldom damaged by deer.

Colors: Red or pink flowers

Pink dragon wing begonias form the centerpiece of this side-planted Imperial planter from www.kinsmangarden.com. Wax begonias are alternated with coleus and creeping Jenny both through the side holes and along the top edge.

Dragon wing begonias are one of the best annuals for Texas gardens - in medium to light shade. They rate a blue ribbon* because they bloom all season long with no attention other than watering.

Dragon wings grow beautifully planted in the ground or in containers.

Dragon wing begonias are quickly becoming one of the most valuable sources of garden color in Texas. Plant them when danger of frost is over, and don't touch them for the entire growing season - other than periodic watering. They are beautiful in shade gardens, with a high percentage of color, low water requirements, and a distinctive appearance. Dragon wings are larger and showier than wax begonias but share the begonia habit of a long bloom period with very little care.

Color Period: Spring, summer, and fall - continuously. They keep blooming until the first freeze.

Buying Tips: Good dragon wing begonias are easy to find at your local garden center. We have bought many that are simply labeled 'Dragon Wing Begonias,' and all have done extremely well. They look gorgeous in the larger, gallon nursery pots. However, they don't look spectacular in smaller, four inch nursery pots. Don't hesitate to buy them in small containers, however, because they will fill out before you know it. Also, be sure to look for dark green leaves and red or pink flowers, like the ones shown on these pages. Lots of angel wing begonias (with spotted leaves and lighter flowers) are for sale with similar characteristics, but they don't bloom anywhere near as long.

*Blue ribbon plants are defined on page 12. For blue ribbon performance, follow the planting and maintenance guidelines on pages 22 to 39.

Companions: Pink dragon wings work well with pastel colors. Either pink or red dragon wings look wonderful with white. Both also do quite well paired with bright colors - particularly yellow, blue, and purple. Try either color with the bright plants shown below - planted either in the ground or in containers.

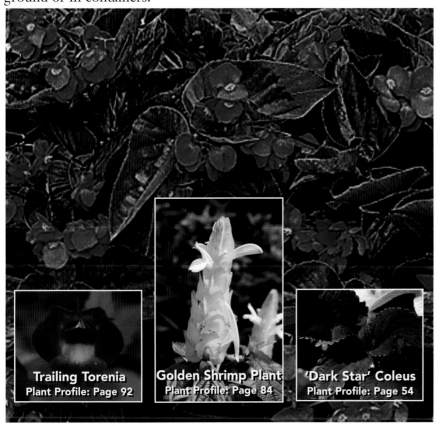

Trailing Torenia
Plant Profile: Page 92

Golden Shrimp Plant
Plant Profile: Page 84

'Dark Star' Coleus
Plant Profile: Page 54

Dragon wing begonias with some companion plants

Trailing Torenia (above, left) makes a great border for dragon wings. It is frequently sold in hanging baskets but also thrives when planted in the ground. The purple color is a perfect contrast to the red begonia. Plant this combination in medium to light shade (in a location where they get some break from afternoon sun in the heat of summer).

Golden Shrimp Plant (above, center) is one of the best companions for dragon wings because both the flower color and shape are different. Plant the shrimp plants behind the shorter dragon wings because the dragon wings are easier to trim if they grow taller than the shrimps. Shrimp plants last all season, like the dragon wings, and require no care other than watering. Plant this combination in medium to light shade (in a location where they get some break from afternoon sun in the heat of summer).

'Dark Star' Coleus (above, right) is one of many different coleus plants that looks good bordering dragon wing begonias. These coleus last for the entire growing season, like the begonias and shrimp plants. Plant this combination in medium to light shade (in a location where they get some break from afternoon sun in the heat of summer).

GROWING CONDITIONS

Light: Medium to light shade. Takes morning sun but definitely needs shade in the afternoon.

Water: Medium. Ideal is once or twice a week in shade or twice a week in sun (after the establishment period, pages 28 to 29). Takes water up to three times a week. Do not overwater because the plant is susceptible to fungus. Requires more water when grown in containers.

Soil: For the garden, plant in any fertile, well-drained soil that has been enriched with organic matter. Use only good-quality potting mix for containers. See pages 22 to 25 for specific instructions on soil preparation.

Hardiness: Use as an annual. Takes temperatures down to 32 degrees.

Propagation: Cuttings

Pest Problems: Rare. We have never had a problem in over 10 years of trials. However, if the leaves or stems develop brown spots or slimy areas, the plant has fungus. Cut down on water. Spray with a fungicide only if it becomes severe. If holes appear in the leaves, they are from caterpillars or snails.

PLANTING & MAINTENANCE

When to Plant: Spring is ideal, so that you can enjoy the plants for the entire growing season. However, the plants can be planted any time the temperatures are over 32 degrees.

Trimming: None needed unless they grow taller than you like. Pinch them back anytime this occurs.

Fertilization: Fertilize at planting time with a timed-release product. See pages 36 to 39 for more instructions.

Begonia, Wax

CHARACTERISTICS

Plant Type: Annual

Average Size: About 8 inches tall by 8 inches wide.

Growth Rate: Medium

Leaf: Rounded, glossy green or bronze leaves, 1 to 2 inches long and wide.

Flower: Hundreds of small, open-centered blossoms.

Lifespan: 7 months

Origin: Brazil

Spacing: About 8 inches on center (measure from the center of each plant). Closer in containers.

Cautions: Irritant, if eaten, which can result in breathing difficulties. Seldom damaged by deer.

Colors: White, red, or pink flowers on green or bronze leaves.

1. *White wax begonia*
2. *Pink wax begonia*
3. *Red wax begonia*
4. *'Cherry Blossom' double wax begonia.*

Wax begonias are one of the best annuals for Texas gardens - in sun or shade. They rate a blue ribbon* because they bloom all season long with no attention other than watering.

Red and pink wax begonias with silver dusty miller planted in front

Wax begonias bloom constantly, from early spring until the first freeze takes them down. Their constancy of color is truly remarkable, as is their ability to adapt to sun or partial shade. Wax begonias also transition beautifully from cool to hot weather and back to cool weather again in the fall. Plants grow into rounded mounds that always look neat with very little care. Wax begonias are small enough to use as edging plants along walkways, and they are unsurpassed for unifying flower beds planted with a number of different flowers.

Color Period: Late spring to late fall, blooming constantly

Buying Tips: Good wax begonias are one of the easiest annuals to find at your local garden center. We have bought many that are simply labeled 'Wax Begonias,' and all have done extremely well. If you need more than 18, look for them in the money-saving multi-packs.

*Blue ribbon plants are defined on page 12. For blue ribbon performance, follow the planting and maintenance guidelines on pages 22 to 39.

Companions: Wax begonias are truly go-with-everything flowers. Their neat, mounded form brings discipline to the scene when sprawling, informal plants – like cleomes – are used as background plants. They work well in formal gardens as well. Try the pink begonias with the plants shown below - planted either in the ground or in containers.

White Begonia
Plant Profile: Page 44

Persian Shield
Plant Profile: Page 76

Caladium
Plant Profile: Page 50

Wax begonias with some companion plants

White Begonias (above, left) are one of the best annuals to use for borders of pink begonias or any other flowers in your garden. They work with all colors and last the entire season with no care other than watering, if they are planted correctly.

Persian Shield (above, center) can be added for a dramatic color accent with pink and white begonias. Alternate the two colors of begonias as a border around the Persian shield, either in a container or in the ground. This combination lasts all season, from spring to the first frost of fall. Plant them in medium to light shade.

Caladiums (above, right) are a natural companion for begonias. Use begonias that coordinate with the colors in the caladium leaves. Plant the begonias as the border because they are smaller than the caladiums. Most caladium cultivars require shade, but others take sun. Generally, the thick-leafed varieties take more sun than the thinner-leafed types. Either works well with the light requirements of wax begonias.

GROWING CONDITIONS

Light: Light shade to full sun. Most varieties of begonias with green leaves do better in light shade, but some of the newer ones take sun as well. All of the bronze-leafed begonias take light shade to full sun.

Water: Medium. Deep watering two to three times a week is ideal for wax begonias in sun, once or twice a week in shade after the establishment period (pages 28 to 29).

Soil: For the garden, plant in any fertile, well-drained soil that has been enriched with organic matter. Use only good-quality potting mix for containers. See pages 22 to 25 for specific instructions on soil preparation.

Hardiness: If you cover plants to protect them through light frosts in fall, they will continue to bloom until the first hard freeze kills the plants.

Propagation: Seeds or cuttings

Pest Problems: Rare. Root rot can develop if plants are kept too wet.

PLANTING & MAINTENANCE

When to Plant: Set out bedding plants when they become available in spring. The fibrous roots usually fill the containers, so it's helpful to split the bottom of the root mass to encourage new roots to spread into surrounding soil.

Trimming: None required unless they are in too much shade. If this happens, they might get leggy. Cut them back a bit to restore a tighter form.

Fertilization: Fertilize at planting time with a timed-release product.

BUDGET GARDENING TIP

Wax begonias are fairly easy to grow from seeds, and one package results in hundreds of plants!

Cabbages or Kale, Ornamental

CHARACTERISTICS

Plant Type: Annual

Average Size: About 8 to 12 inches tall by equally as wide.

Growth Rate: Medium

Leaf: Large, cabbage-type leaves with curled or frilled edges.

Flower: Yellow flowers in spring; grown primarily for foliage.

Lifespan: 5 months

Origin: North Africa and Europe

Spacing: About 10 inches on center (measure from the center of each plant). Closer in containers.

Cautions: Leaves are edible and often used for garnishes, but they are not as flavorful as those of culinary kale. Occasionally eaten by deer.

Colors: White, red, pink, or purple leaves.

1. *Cabbages get their color during cool weather.*
2. *As the temperatures cool, their leaf color intensifies, turn beautiful colors, like this white one...*
3. *or this purple one.*

Ornamental cabbages and kale are two of the best sources for color when the temperatures cool. Plant them in fall, and enjoy all winter long. When the temperatures approach the twenties, be sure to cover them. They miss a ribbon because of their temperature limitations.

Cabbages are planted in the side holes of a side-planted basket from www.kinsmangarden.com. Juncus grass and pansies are planted in the top.

Ornamental cabbages and kale join pansies and violas as the stars of winter gardens in Texas. They make wonderful companions for these flowers but do require covering when temperatures approach the twenties. Plant them in a warm spot (south side of your home or on a sheltered patio), and you can enjoy them for most of the winter with little to no care other than occasional watering. Cabbages do quite well in containers but feel the cold more; therefore, they should be covered as well when temperatures approach the twenties.

Color Period: Begins in late October as cabbage leaves need cool weather to show leaf color. As cool weather persists, leaf color will intensify and last through most of the winter. Cabbages flower in spring with tall, spikes of yellow flowers. Some people like the flowers, and some don't. Cut them off if they bother you.

Buying Tips: We use these every winter at the Fort Worth Botanic Garden in containers and beds. Buy them in four inch or one gallon pots in late October.

Botanical Name: *Brassica oleraceae acephala*
Family: Brassicaceae/Cruciferae

ANNUALS

Companions: Mix cabbages with other winter flowers, like snapdragons, dusty miller, violas, and pansies. Since violas and pansies bloom longer than the others, they are the highest performing flower companions for cabbages. Both violas and pansies show some damage when temperatures drop into the low 20's, but they recover quickly and keep blooming until late spring.

Choose companions you like for the different-colored ornamental cabbages. Here are some ideas for the purple ones.

Yellow Violas
Plant Profile: Page 72

Red Pansies
Plant Profile: Page 72

Light Purple Pansies
Plant Profile: Page 72

Ornamental cabbages with some companion plants

Yellow Violas (above, left) are great companions for cabbages because they will bloom the entire time the cabbages thrive - and yellow is a great companion for purple. Use violas if you plant the cabbages in a partial shade situation because they take shade better than pansies. The violas grow shorter than the pansies, so use them as a border.

Red Pansies (above, center) contrast well with purple cabbages. Use them in sun. For maximum color impact, plant the cabbages with both red and yellow flowers. Pansies grow shorter than cabbages, so use them as a border.

Light Purple Pansies (above, right) provide a quieter combination than the bright red and yellow. Add some pink for a gentle contrast. The pansies will bloom the entire time the cabbages thrive. Pansies grow shorter than cabbages, so use them as a border in sunny situations.

GROWING CONDITIONS

Light: Light shade to full sun. Plants need 6 hours of sun daily to develop the best leaf color.

Water: Medium in warm weather, low in cool weather. We seldom water our cabbages in winter. However, take care to check the dryness of the soil if a hard cold spell is forecast. Severe cold spells frequently dry out the soil, so water before one arrives.

Soil: For the garden, plant in any fertile, well-drained soil that has been enriched with organic matter. Use only good-quality potting mix for containers. See pages 22 to 25 for specific instructions on soil preparation.

Hardiness: Do best in temperatures ranging from 20 to 60 degrees in the ground; 25 degrees minimum in containers.

Propagation: Seeds

Pest Problems: Caterpillars occasionally.

PLANTING & MAINTENANCE

When to Plant: Fall. For winter hardiness, plant early enough in fall (late October) for the plants to establish themselves before the cold arrives.

Trimming: None generally needed. Trim the flowers off in spring if you don't like them.

Fertilization: Fertilize at planting time with a timed-release product. See pages 36 to 39 for more instructions.

Caladium

1ST

CHARACTERISTICS

Plant Type: Tropical perennial tuber, grown as an annual.

Average Size: From 8 to 20 inches tall, 4 to 14 inches wide. Be sure to know the mature size of the variety you buy so you can use it appropriately.

Growth Rate: Medium

Leaf: Large heart- or lance- shaped leaves, splashed with red, pink, white and green; often with contrasting veins.

Flower: Insignificant, finger-shaped spikes.

Lifespan: 6 to 7 months

Origin: South America

Spacing: About 8 to 12 inches on center (measure from the center of each plant).

Cautions: Poisonous, if eaten; sap may irritate skin. Occasionally damaged by deer.

Colors: Red, pink, white, or green leaves.

1. *Caladium 'Candidum'*
2. *Caladium 'Carolyn Whorton'*
3. *Caladium 'Frieda Hemple'*
4. *Caladium 'White Queen'*

Caladiums are one of the best choices for annual leaf color in Texas gardens - in sun or shade. They rate a blue ribbon* because they provide color all season long, with no attention other than watering.

White caladiums surrounding Miscanthus grass

Caladiums have been popular throughout Texas for decades. Plant them when the temperatures have warmed into the 70's (late April), and don't touch them for the entire growing season - other than periodic watering and removing a brown leaf or two. Even in the very hot weather that is typical of Texas summers, caladiums appear cool and elegant. Traditionally used only in shade gardens, some new cultivars do equally as well in sun.

Regional Differences: Caladiums need temperatures above 70 degrees to grow. In zone eight, the knobby tubers can be planted directly in the ground in spring. In zone seven, begin with purchased plants, or start the tubers inside to give them a head start on summer.

Color Period: The flowers are insignificant, but the plants will produce a nice show of colorful leaves by early summer. With good care, they will keep their handsome good looks until nights cool down in the fall.

Buying Tips: All caladiums we have planted, regardless of the name on the tag, have done well for us. However, they come in a wide variety of sizes, from eight to 20 inches tall. Be sure you know the height of the ones you are buying. While garden centers are ideal choices for purchasing caladium plants, a huge variety of tubers can be purchased online or from catalogs. Tubers are generally fresher when purchased directly from a grower.

*Blue ribbon plants are defined on page 12. For blue ribbon performance, follow the planting and maintenance guidelines on pages 22 to 39.

ANNUALS

Companions: Since wide- and narrow- leafed plants show well next to each other, combine caladiums with the narrowest leaves you can find, as shown with the grasses, left. The narrow leaves of the grass really accentuate the large leaves of the caladiums.

Caladiums make excellent centerpieces for container gardens. Whether you use them in the ground or in containers, mix them with leaves or flowers that coordinate with the leaf patterns shown in the examples below.

Caladiums with some companion plants

Wax Begonias (above, left) form nice borders for caladiums because they bloom the entire time the caladiums thrive. Although these begonias are shorter than most caladiums, check the caladium label to be sure the variety you are buying grows over 12 inches tall, so it will remain taller than the begonias. Choose the color of the begonia flower to coordinate with the leaf of the caladium. Since wax begonias take sun or shade, they will do well with either sun or shade caladiums.

Coleus (above, center) works well as a mid layer, in between the caladiums and the begonias. Once again, coordinate the coleus color with the caladium leaf. Be sure the caladiums are on the tall side, at least 18 inches tall.

Torenia (above, right) coordinates well bordering this caladium in sun (if the caladium take sun) to light shade. Although torenia doesn't last quite as long as the begonias, the combination looks terrific!

GROWING CONDITIONS

Light: Most cultivars require shade, but some varieties take sun. Check the tag at the garden center.

Water: Medium in shade and high in sun. Ideal water is twice a week in shade and three to four times a week in sun (after establishment, pages 28 to 29). Requires more water when grown in containers.

Soil: For the garden, plant in any fertile, well-drained soil that has been enriched with organic matter. Use only good-quality potting mix for containers.

Hardiness: Grows wherever temperatures stay about 70 degrees for a few months.

Propagation: Tubers

Pest Problems: Slugs and snails may cause light damage.

PLANTING & MAINTENANCE

When to Plant: After soil temperatures have risen above 60 degrees, usually in late April.

Trimming: Occasional, if at all. Clip off any old leaves that bend over and lose their color if you like. Some people don't like the look of the flowers and clip them off as well.

Fertilization: Fertilize at planting time with a timed-release product.

PLANTING & STORING TUBERS

Planting: Place the knobby side up, and cover with one inch of soil. After the summer season, dig them up when temperatures dip into the 50's. Leave the leaves on the tubers as well as a small amount of soil around them.

Storage: Let them dry out in a warm, dry location. Place them on dry wood shavings or sphagnum moss. and don't let the tubers touch each other. Clean off the leaves and soil in about 3 to 4 weeks. Cut the leaves gently, leaving some of the base attached to the tuber. Store in a cool, dry location for the winter.

Cleome

Plant Type: Annual that often reseeds itself.

Average Size: Old fashioned cleomes grow to about 4 feet tall by 2 feet wide. The 'Sparkler' series tops out at about 2 feet tall by 18 inches wide. 'Linde Armstrong' is the smallest, about 16 inches tall.

Growth Rate: Fast

Leaf: Green leaves consisting of 5 to 7 pointed leaflets. Short spines are often present where leaves attach to main stems.

Flower: Rounded clusters of delicate, open blossoms borne at stem tips.

Lifespan: 4 to 7 months

Origin: Brazil and Argentina

Spacing: About 10 inches on center for the smaller ones and 20 to 24 inches on center for the larger ones, including 'Senorita Rosalita' (measure from the center of each plant). Closer in containers.

Cautions: The large, old fashioned varieties have an unpleasant scent. Seldom damaged by deer.

Colors: Pink, mauve, white, rose, or lavender flowers.

'Serena' angelonias are planted on either side of these cleomes in this side-planted window box from www.kinsmangarden.com. Scaevola and wax begonias are planted in the side holes and along the edge.

Cleomes are easy to grow but don't bloom as long as the four to six month minimum we require for annuals to get a ribbon. However, the smaller varieties are worth growing for the distinctive appearance of the flowers.

Cleomes bordered by impatiens

Use of cleomes in the garden has greatly increased recently due to the introduction of new, smaller, and more compact varieties. Old cleomes are large and lanky, seeding freely in the garden. While some might welcome the new plants produced by these seeds, others consider them a weed. Old cleomes also have the annoying habit of falling apart halfway through the summer. The new cleomes are smaller and much better mannered, seldom popping up the next year. Most cleomes sold in garden centers are the new, smaller varieties. 'Senorita Rosalita' is a new variety highly recommended by the Dallas Arboretum. This variety blooms constantly from late spring to fall, does not produce seed pods, and has foliage with no odor. It grows two to four feet tall and tolerates heat and drought.

Color Period: Continuous bloom from early summer to fall, if deadheaded regularly. We never have had time to deadhead the cleomes in our trial gardens, where they have bloomed on and off for about half of the growing season.

Buying Tips: Be sure to check the size that is printed on the tag.

Attracts Butterflies

Attracts Hummingbirds

14
Avg. Weeks of Color

Botanical Name: *Cleome hassleriana*
Family: Capparaceae

ANNUALS

Companions: Finding companions for cleomes is great fun, and easiest to do at the garden center. Put a cleome in your cart and wheel it around to find other flowers that look good with it. Use your eyes to see which combinations make you smile! Be sure to take this book with you, so you can check out the characteristics of the flowers you like.

Cleomes are such complex flowers that they look best with simple companions, like the petunias, gomphrena, and pentas shown below.

Pink Petunia
Plant Profile: Page 78

Gomphrena
Plant Profile: Page 64

Pentas
Plant Profile: Page 74

Cleomes with some companion plants

Petunias (above, left) are great companions for cleomes, working well as a front border. Both 'Tidal Wave Cherry' and 'Tidal Wave Silver' combine very well with cleomes.

Gomphrena (above, center) works well as another front border plant. The globe-shaped flowers contrast with the pink and lavender hues of the cleome flower.

Pentas (above, right) are a good choice for a mid layer cleome companion. They are one of the best flowers for attracting butterflies. Check the tag on the pentas to be sure the variety stays smaller than your cleomes.

GROWING CONDITIONS

Light: Light shade to full sun

Water: Medium. Healthy cleomes can tolerate drought, but flower production is best when plants receive enough water to soak the roots at least once a week after the establishment period (pages 28 to 29). Requires more water when grown in containers.

Soil: For the garden, plant in any fertile, well-drained soil that has been enriched with organic matter. Use only good-quality potting mix for containers. See pages 22 to 25 for specific instructions on soil preparation.

Hardiness: Annual that grows in the summer throughout the country.

Propagation: Seeds for the older varieties. Some new ones grow from cuttings.

Pest Problems: Very rare

PLANTING & MAINTENANCE

When to Plant: Spring or summer

Trimming: New, smaller varieties do not require trimming but benefit from removing the old blooms, if you have time. The old, large varieties need a mid summer trimming. Use sharp pruning shears to cut back stem tips after the flowers fade, which keeps the plants from using their energy to produce long, stringy seed pods and encourages them to develop bud-bearing branches. Some gardeners let their cleomes go until late summer and then prune back the plants by one-half their size. This is a good practice if you want your plants to reseed.

Fertilization: Fertilize at planting time with a timed-release product. See pages 36 to 39 for more instructions.

Coleus

CHARACTERISTICS

Plant Type: Annual

Average Size: 6 to 36 inches tall, depending on variety. Leaf pattern also varies with variety; most coleus are as wide as they are tall.

Growth Rate: Medium

Leaf: Intricately variegated leaves vary in shape, with some quite thin and thread-like, others broad and oval, and many with curled or frilled edges.

Flower: Spikes of pale blue flowers are usually clipped off to encourage production of leaves.

Lifespan: 7 months

Origin: Mediterranean region

Spacing: About 8 to 18 inches on center (measure from the center of each plant), depending on cultivar. Closer in containers.

Cautions: Seldom damaged by deer.

Colors: Burgundy, lime green, chartreuse, pink, purple, and white leaves, in endless combinations.

1. 'Defiance' coleus
2. 'Gay's Delight' coleus
3. 'Dark Star' coleus
4. 'Crime Scene' coleus

Coleus is consistently one of the top-rated summer annuals for long-season color in Texas. Requires more water than some other annuals, however. Just misses a blue ribbon* because it needs monthly pinching.

These three layers of coleus demonstrate the height differences of different varieties. The back layer is 'Mississippi Summer Sun;' middle layer, 'Giant Webfoot;' border, 'Wizard Golden' coleus. Layering like this is difficult unless you know the mature height of each coleus used.

Coleus are one of the most popular annuals for shade and sun in Texas. Their tolerance for heat, coupled with long lifespan, have ranked them as a top annual for Texas gardens. However, most seed-grown coleus (like the 'Wizard' series) don't last as long as coleus grown from cuttings. And coleus like more water than drought and water restrictions can sometimes handle. Traditionally thought of as shade plants, their tolerance for sun has greatly increased with new varieties.

Color Period: Continuous from spring until the temperatures drop to 40 degrees in the fall. Coleus are grown for their colorful leaves, which are more abundant when flower spikes are clipped off as soon as they appear. Most varieties grown from cuttings flower much less than those grown from seed.

Buying Tips: Coleus are fast growers, so buying smaller plants pays off. Since coleus vary from six to 36 inches tall, it helps if the plant tags in the garden centers include the height, so you know how to design with them.

Red ribbon plants are defined on page 13. For red ribbon performance, follow the planting and maintenance guidelines on pages 22 to 39.

Companions: Coleus come in so many different colors and sizes that you will never run out of neat ways to use them. A popular approach is to combine two varieties - one chartreuse and one dark red or purple - to form a tapestry of high contrast color. For neon color, try the combination shown below.

Coleus with some companion plants

Dragon Wing Begonia (above, left) not only blooms nonstop all season but also looks great with this red and yellow coleus. Plant the coleus as a border for the dragon wings, or use it as a side planting, with the dragon wing as the centerpiece in a container.

Golden Shrimp Plant (above, center) blooms constantly all season in medium to light shade. The yellow flowers coordinate perfectly with the yellow in the coleus leaf. Since the shrimp plant gets taller than the coleus, use the coleus as the border. Be sure to buy shrimp plants whose flowers are identical to the one shown above. There are many others in the garden centers, but this one is the best.

Persian Shield (above, right) can be added to this bright mix, and you could stop traffic in your neighborhood! Use all of them in a container, or plant them in the ground. For a dynamite garden accent planting, alternate three each of the begonias, shrimp plants, and Persian shield and border all of them with coleus. Be sure to use dragon wing begonias and not wax begonias because the wax begonias don't grow tall enough for a coleus border.

GROWING CONDITIONS

Light: Full sun to medium shade, depending on variety. Check plant tags for light preferences.

Water: High in sun, medium in shade. To save time, install a soaker hose in beds planted with coleus. In summer, plants need water three times a week in sun and once or twice a week in shade, after the establishment period (pages 28 to 29). Requires more water when grown in containers.

Soil: For the garden, plant in any fertile, well-drained soil that has been enriched with organic matter. Use only good-quality potting mix for containers.

Hardiness: Shows cold damage at about 40 degrees.

Propagation: Seeds or cuttings

Pest Problems: Most coleus are pest free, but very wet soil can cause root rot problems. They have been pest free in the Fort Worth Botanic Garden.

PLANTING & MAINTENANCE

When to Plant: Spring, summer, or fall. It makes the most sense to plant in spring, so you can enjoy them longer!

Trimming: We pinch the tips of our coleus about once a month. Clip off flower spikes when they appear, if you have time. Should plants become leggy, shear them back by one-third their size.

Fertilization: Fertilize at planting time with a timed-release product. See pages 36 to 39 for more instructions.

BUDGET GARDENING TIP

Coleus are very easy to root from cuttings. Just cut a piece about 4 inches long, strip the bottom leaves off, and put it in a glass of water. You'll see roots shortly.

Cuphea, Bat-Face

CHARACTERISTICS

Plant Type: Tropical perennial grown as an annual in Texas.

Average Size: Bat-face cuphea is about 2 feet tall by 18 inches wide. 'Totally Tempted' is about 12 inches tall by 15 inches wide.

Growth Rate: Medium

Leaf: Small, green, pointed leaves

Flower: Small, bi-colored flowers

Lifespan: 6 to 7 months

Origin: Mexico

Spacing: About 12 to 18 inches on center (measure from the center of each plant), depending on the variety. Closer in containers.

Cautions: None known

Colors: Bi-colored flowers are either red or pink with purple centers.

These photos are all of the 'Flamenco' series, which is larger and a little less compact than 'Totally Tempted.'
1. *'Flamenco Rumba'*
2. *'Flamenco Cha Cha'*
3. *'Flamenco Tango'*
4. *'Flamenco Samba'*

Bat-face cuphea is a great plant for Texas, flowering all season - right through both heat and drought. Be sure to give it good drainage, and it will repay the favor with lots of blooms that attract both butterflies and hummingbirds. It rates a red ribbon* because it sometimes requires trimming.

'Totally Tempted' cuphea in container

Sporting unique red and purple flowers, the bat-face cuphea was the beginning of plant hybridization that has produced some fabulous plants for Texas. *Cuphea llavea* 'Bat-face' has the ability to bloom all season, but its growth habit is large and loose, so it needs trimming mid season. 'Totally Tempted' is a new hybrid from Proven Winners that offers the advantages of a long bloom period but also is much more compact, requiring no trimming at all. Its flowers are about twice as large as those on the 'Bat-face' variety. The 'Flamenco' series comes in more colors but is larger than the 'Totally Tempted.' 'Flamenco,' 'Cha Cha,' and 'Samba' have performed very well in beds and containers at the Fort Worth Botanic Garden. These cultivars tolerate heat and flower all summer long.

Color Period: From spring until the first frost of fall, non-stop

Buying Tips: 'Totally Tempted' as well as the 'Flamenco' series are available at many nurseries and garden centers in four inch pots.

*Red ribbon plants are defined on page 13. For red ribbon performance, follow the planting and maintenance guidelines on pages 22 to 39.

Companions: At the Fort Worth Botanic Garden, esperanza 'Gold Star' has combined very well with 'Flamenco Samba.' The lavender 'Cora' vinca has combined very well with 'Flamenco Cha Cha.' 'Totally Tempted' cuphea looks good with plants with leaf color, like coleus, variegated grasses, or yuccas. Yellow lantana also works well with this cuphea, along with plants with spiky flowers, like salvia or angelonia. Here are some specific suggestions for great companion plantings.

'Dark Star' Coleus
Plant Profile: Page 54

Variegated Yucca
Plant Profile: Page 262

Trailing Torenia
Plant Profile: Page 92

'Totally Tempted' bat-face cuphea with some companion plants

'Dark Star' Coleus (above, top) is a fabulous companion for this cuphea. Its purple color brings out the purple in the center of the cuphea flower. Since the coleus gets taller than the cuphea, use the cuphea as a border, either in the ground or in a container.

Variegated Yucca (above, center) makes a great centerpiece surrounded by this cuphea in a container. Add some dark coleus for a dramatic accent. And, since the yucca is an evergreen perennial, you can leave it in the same container all year, changing the flowers that are planted along the edge with the seasons.

Trailing Torenia (above, bottom) also picks up the purple color in the center of the cuphea flower. Both trail over the edges of containers. For a simple and long-lasting container garden, plant yucca as a centerpiece and surround it by torenia and cuphea.

ANNUALS

GROWING CONDITIONS

Light: Full sun, at least 6 hours per day.

Water: Low, after establishment (pages 28 to 29). Once a week works well. Requires more water when grown in containers. Our container-grown cupheas did better with routine watering rather than waiting for them to wilt as a signal to water. In other words, water them before they wilt.

Soil: For the garden, plant in any fertile, well-drained soil that has been enriched with organic matter. Use only good-quality potting mix for containers. See pages 22 to 25 for specific instructions on soil preparation.

Hardiness: Use as an annual in Texas. Not tolerant of temperatures below 25 degrees.

Propagation: Cuttings

Pest Problems: Rare. Root rot can develop if plants are kept too wet.

PLANTING & MAINTENANCE

When to Plant: Spring or summer

Trimming: The smaller varieties, like 'Totally Tempted,' don't require trimming at all. Other, taller varieties could become leggy in late summer. Shearing them back by one-third will restore their form and encourage a late flush of fresh blossoms.

Fertilization: Fertilize at planting time with a timed-release product. See pages 36 to 39 for more instructions.

Dahlberg Daisy

CHARACTERISTICS

Plant Type: Annual

Average Size: About 6 to 12 inches tall by 6 to 12 inches wide.

Growth Rate: Medium

Leaf: Lime green, deeply-divided, thread-like leaves that have a pungent, lemony odor when crushed or bruised.

Flower: 1/2 inch wide, daisy-like flowers consisting of golden yellow petals and yellow centers.

Lifespan: 6 to 7 months

Origin: South central Texas and northern Mexico.

Spacing: About 8 to 12 inches on center (measure from the center of each plant). Closer in containers.

Cautions: None known. Deer almost never damage this plant.

Colors: Yellow flowers

This sunny yellow flower makes a bold statement in the landscape. Its six to seven month bloom period, combined with easy care, rates a blue ribbon.*

Dahlberg daisies do equally as well planted in containers or in the ground.

The Dahlberg daisy's long bloom season, along with its excellent performance in heat and drought, has made it a long time favorite at the Fort Worth Botanic Garden. This colorful annual makes an excellent, low edging, border, or rock garden plant. Dahlberg daisy also looks good in containers and between stepping stones, attracting butterflies wherever you plant it. It is easy to grow - just plant it in a sunny location with well drained soil and water twice a week.

Foliage has a pungent, lemony odor when crushed or bruised.

Color Period: From spring (April 1) to mid November, blooming constantly.

Buying Tips: Most often sold in four inch pots, which are the best starting size for this plant. Commonly available in local garden centers in spring and summer.

Blue ribbon plants are defined on page 12. For blue ribbon performance, follow the planting and maintenance guidelines on pages 22 to 39.

Attracts Butterflies

31
Avg. Weeks of Color

Resists Deer

Texas Native

Botanical Name: *Thymophylla tenuiloba*
Family: Asteraceae

Companions: Dahlberg daisy combines well with red, orange, blue and purple flowers. In particular, it looks good with purple heart, purple gomphrena, scaevola, 'Profusion' zinnias and 'Cora' vincas.

Dahlberg daisy and some companions

Pentas
Plant Profile: Page 74

Purple Heart
Plant Profile: Page 152

GROWING CONDITIONS

Light: Full sun, at least 6 hours a day.

Water: Medium. Twice weekly after the establishment period (pages 28 to 29). Requires more water when grown in containers.

Soil: For the garden, plant in any fertile, well-drained soil that has been enriched with organic matter. Use only good-quality potting mix for containers. See pages 22 to 25 for specific instructions on soil preparation.

Hardiness: Grows in all U. S. zones during the hot summer. In Texas, grows in zones 6 to 8 as an annual and in zones 9 to 11 as a short-term perennial. In north central Texas, dies after a hard freeze (usually around November 15).

Propagation: Seeds

Pest Problems: Rare

PLANTING & MAINTENANCE

When to Plant: Plant when they become available in spring, after after all danger of frost has passed, or in summer.

Trimming: None required, although deadheading (removing spent flowers) encourages additional bloom.

Fertilization: Fertilize at planting time with a timed-release product. See pages 36 to 39 for more instructions.

Pentas (above, left) are a good companion with the daisy because the flowers are so much larger. Combining large and small flowers makes each flower show up better. And pentas, like the daisies, attract butterflies. The taller pentas, growing about two feet tall, work well as the tallest layer of this grouping.

Purple Heart (above, right) combines well with this daisy and the pentas. It is a perennial that keeps its purple color all summer long. Since purple heart grows to about 12 inches tall, plant it as a mid layer, in between the taller pentas and the shorter daisies. All three do well in well-drained soil and full sun.

Dusty Miller

CHARACTERISTICS

Plant Type: Perennial grown as hardy annual.

Average Size: 8 to 12 inches tall, equally as wide.

Growth Rate: Medium

Leaf: Deeply-cut, grey leaves covered with fine, felt-like hairs.

Flower: Small clusters of yellow flowers develop on year-old plants, but they usually are removed.

Lifespan: 7 months. Occasionally lives up to one year.

Origin: Mediterranean region

Spacing: About 8 inches on center (measure from the center of each plant). Closer in containers.

Cautions: All parts of the plant are poisonous if eaten. Seldom damaged by deer.

Colors: Grown for its frosty, grey leaves.

1. Close up of flower
2. Dusty miller works well as a border for these blue salvia and pink wax begonias.

An easy annual that makes most flowers look better. Sometimes lives longer than just one season. Tolerant of frost. Dusty miller rates a blue ribbon.*

Dusty miller planted around Miscanthus grass

All flowers are pretty, but many look even prettier when grown in the company of plants that provide strong contrast in color and texture, which is exactly what you get with dusty miller. The gentle, grey leaves flatter bright reds and deep pinks, making them appear sharper, and they also amplify blues beautifully. True go-with-everything plants, dusty miller does an amazing job of separating masses of different-colored flowers. When used as an edging, dusty miller makes a bed look as if it is trimmed with lace.

Dusty miller needs contrasting companions to look good. It doesn't work well when planted alone.

Regional Differences: Dusty miller is easy to grow in the summer in zones six through eight; in winter, it does well in zone eight. In very warm, rainy years, it may be troubled by root rot diseases.

Color Period: Dusty miller's silver-grey leaves provide contrast to flowering plants for the entire growing season. Not known for its flowers.

Buying Tips: All the dusty millers we have purchased have done well, regardless of the other names on the tags.

*Blue ribbon plants are defined on page 12. For blue ribbon performance, follow the planting and maintenance guidelines on pages 22 to 39.

ANNUALS

Companions: It is hard to name a flower that does not partner well with dusty miller, but some make such fantastic bedfellows that they should be high on your list of choices. Use plants that are quite different from dusty miller. The grass (shown on the opposite page) looks good with dusty miller because its leaves are such different sizes and shapes. Also, the grey color really sets off hot pinks and purples. Try dusty miller as an annual accent for a perennial garden featuring those colors, as shown below.

'Homestead Purple'
Verbena
Plant Profile: Page 170

Dragon Wing
Begonia
Plant Profile: Page 44

Purple Heart
Plant Profile: Page 152

Dusty miller with some companion plants

'Homestead Purple' Verbena (above, left) works well as a border for dusty miller. It blooms on and off all summer and returns year after year.

Dragon Wing Begonias (above, center) are added as the tallest plant in this perennial/annual grouping. The begonias grow about two feet tall and bloom from spring until the first frost of fall.

Purple Heart (above, right) is possibly the best perennial companion for dusty miller because its color contrasts so beautifully and it keeps its color from spring until the first frost of fall. Border dusty miller with the shorter-growing purple heart.

To combine them all, plant the begonias as the tallest plants, bordered by dusty miller. Alternate groups of three verbena with groups of three purple heart as the border. Since two of these four plants are perennials, they will last for many years to come.

GROWING CONDITIONS

Light: Light shade to full sun

Water: Medium. Dusty miller grows best when soil never becomes completely dry after the establishment period (pages 28 to 29). Requires more water when grown in containers.

Soil: For the garden, plant in any fertile, well-drained soil that has been enriched with organic matter. Use only good-quality potting mix for containers. See pages 22 to 25 for specific instructions on soil preparation.

Hardiness: Dependably hardy in zones 8 to 10 and often hardy in zone 7 when grown in a protected place. Although some lucky people have dusty miller that has lasted them for years, that's the exception rather than the rule.

Propagation: Seeds, though they are very tiny and slow to grow. Stem cuttings root with the help of rooting powder.

Pest Problems: Root knot nematodes can stunt the growth of dusty miller.

PLANTING & MAINTENANCE

When to Plant: Set out plants in early spring, after hard freezes have passed.

Trimming: When buds rise up on overwintered plants, you may want to clip them off. The flowers are not showy, and plants that have bloomed usually deteriorate quickly.

Fertilization: Fertilize at planting time with a timed-release product. See pages 36 to 39 for more instructions.

Esperanza 'Gold Star'

CHARACTERISTICS

Plant Type: Annual

Average Size: 4 feet tall by 3 feet wide.

Growth Rate: Medium

Leaf: Green leaves; 2 to 4 inches long and about 1 inch wide.

Flower: Trumpet-shaped, yellow flowers that are 2 inches long by about 1 inch wide. Flowers are slightly fragrant. Flowers are followed by narrow, bean-like capsules up to 8 inches long that appear later in the summer.

Lifespan: 6 to 7 months

Origin: South Texas, New Mexico, Arizona to Central America, South America, and parts of the Caribbean. 'Gold Star' is a cultivar that Greg Grant, Texas horticulturist, discovered growing in a garden in San Antonio, Texas.

Spacing: About 3 feet on center (measure from the center of each plant). Closer in containers.

Cautions: Seeds from pods reportedly are toxic. Do not ingest. Deer almost never damage this plant.

Colors: Yellow flowers

This heat-tolerant plant is a great source of yellow color. It blooms all season with very little care. It rates a red ribbon* because it requires one maintenance chore: removing the seed pods, if you don't like them.

Designated as a Texas Superstar™ plant (by Texas A&M AgriLife Extension Service), esperanza is a summer staple in north central Texas. Fort Worth Botanic Garden uses it each summer in both mass plantings and containers. Esperanza 'Gold Star' rates these high marks because it provides continuous, yellow-colored flowers from early summer until frost. It is also very easy to grow because it thrives in the Texas heat.

Esperanza has additional benefits: it adds a tropical look to the landscape and attracts butterflies. There are no bad characteristics, unless it's the seed pods that follow the flowers, but even they are attractive and add interest to the plant.

Color Period: June 1st until the first hard frost in mid November, blooming continuously.

Buying Tips: Readily available in one gallon pots, which is the best size to start with. Another cultivar you may wish to plant is *Tecoma x* 'Sunrise,' which has a burnished copper color on the flower buds and the back of the flower; the flowers are golden yellow streaked with orange. This plant is relatively new, so if you see it at your garden center buy it immediately as you may not see it again for awhile!

Esperanza is planted as the centerpiece of this basket.

Red ribbon plants are defined on page 13. For red ribbon performance, follow the planting and maintenance guidelines on pages 22 to 39.

Companions: Esperanza 'Gold Star' combines well with yellow-variegated foliage, and with flowers that are orange, red, blue, or purple. Such companions as the 'Flamenco' cupheas, Chinese hibiscus, lantana, and 'Cora' vincas combine very well with esperanza 'Gold Star.'

'Flamenco' Cuphea
Plant Profile: Page 56

'Cora' Vinca
Plant Profile: Page 94

Esperanza with some companion plants

'Flamenco' Cuphea (above, top) contrasts well with the bright yellow flowers of esperanza 'Gold Star.' These cupheas are annuals and reach a mature height of 15 to 18 inches and a width of 12 to 15 inches. The cupheas work well as a front layer for the taller, four foot esperanza. Or, for three layers of color, plant the cupheas as a mid layer in between the esperanza and the vinca.

'Cora' Vinca (above, bottom) works well as a companion for both the esperanza and the cuphea. The deep lavender flowers in the vinca provide a striking contrast with the bright yellow flowers of esperanza and the red cuphea flowers. Vinca are summer annuals that grow 14 to 16 inches tall and spread up to two feet wide. Plant the 'Cora' vinca as a front border for the cupheas and the esperanza. All three of these plants bloom throughout spring, summer, and fall.

GROWING CONDITIONS

Light: Full sun. At least six hours a day.

Water: Medium. Requires twice a week watering after the establishment period (pages 28 to 29). More often in containers.

Soil: For the garden, plant in any fertile, well-drained soil that has been enriched with organic matter. Use only good-quality potting mix for containers. See pages 22 to 25 for specific instructions on soil preparation.

Hardiness: Summer annual in north central Texas; winter hardy further south in zone 9.

Propagation: Seeds or cuttings

Pest Problems: Rare

PLANTING & MAINTENANCE

When to Plant: Plant in spring or summer after all danger of frost has passed, which is usually April 1st.

Trimming: You may opt to remove dead flowers to increase amount of blooms. You may also remove seed pods to encourage rebloom.

Fertilization: Fertilize at planting time with a timed-release product. See pages 36 to 39 for more instructions.

ANNUALS

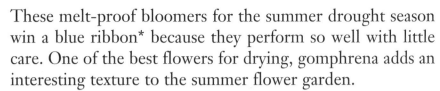

1ST

CHARACTERISTICS

Plant Type: Annual

Average Size: 9 to 24 inches tall, 10 to 14 inches wide, depending on variety.

Growth Rate: Moderate at first; faster after hot weather arrives.

Leaf: Rounded, glossy, green or bronze leaves, 1 to 2 inches long and wide.

Flower: 1 inch, ball-shaped, papery-textured, clover-like flower.

Lifespan: 7 months

Origin: Central America

Spacing: Plant the smaller varieties about 8 inches on center and the larger ones about 12 inches on center (measure from the center of each plant). Closer in containers.

Cautions: None known. Slightly deer resistant.

Colors: White, pink, purple, orange, red, and magenta.

These melt-proof bloomers for the summer drought season win a blue ribbon* because they perform so well with little care. One of the best flowers for drying, gomphrena adds an interesting texture to the summer flower garden.

Gomphrena 'Globe Purple'

Gomphrena, also known as globe amaranth, deserves much wider use in Texas gardens. Plants take off fast once hot weather arrives, and soon each stem tip is topped by one or more round flowers. Gomphrena needs less water than most other summer flowers, and the stiff stem has no trouble staying upright. Tall varieties that grow upwards of two feet include beautiful 'Bicolor Rose' and pinkish-orange 'Strawberry Fields.' Both are well worth the trouble of starting from seed. In addition to looking lovely in beds or containers, they make great cut flowers and can even be dried and enjoyed in the winter. These tall varieties are used as companion plants in the Republic of Texas rose garden at the Fort Worth Botanic Garden.

Dwarf gomphrenas (including deep purple 'Buddy') are widely sold as bedding plants, but they are not as pretty or productive as taller selections.

Color Period: Blooms continuously from summer to fall

Buying Tips: Since different kinds of gomphrenas vary from nine to 24 inches tall, be sure the plant tag at the garden center tells you how tall yours will get so you can use it appropriately.

Blue ribbon plants are defined on page 12. For blue ribbon performance, follow the planting and maintenance guidelines on pages 22 to 39.

Companions: Whenever you notice that a flower bed has become borderline boring because it includes too many plants with flat flowers, gomphrena can solve the problem with its pom-poms of color. For a drought-tolerant flower bed, pair gomphrena with other warm-season bloomers, including lantana and Dahlberg daisies, as shown below.

Right: Perilla forms the centerpiece of this container, accented by Acorus grass and gomphrena. The container is www.globalpottery.com's 'Handled Planter' in kiwi (12"H x 11"W).

GROWING CONDITIONS

Light: Full sun, at least 6 hours a day.

Water: Medium when plants are young. Once they are well rooted, gomphrenas tolerate dry conditions and need water only once a week, in most situations, after the establishment period (pages 28 to 29). Requires more water when grown in containers.

Soil: For the garden, plant in any fertile, well-drained soil that has been enriched with organic matter. Use only good-quality potting mix for containers. See pages 22 to 25 for specific instructions on soil preparation.

Hardiness: Cannot tolerate frost

Propagation: Seeds

Pest Problems: Rare. In very wet years, plants can have trouble with root rot.

PLANTING & MAINTENANCE

When to Plant: Plant bedding plants or seeds in late spring, after the soil is warm.

Trimming: We haven't deadheaded (removed the dead flowers) from the gomphenas at the Fort Worth Botanic Garden, and they have looked pretty good. However, a true, cut-and-come-again flower, gomphrena blooms more often when you gather blossoms, which can be used for indoor arrangements.

Fertilization: Fertilize at planting time with a timed-release product. See pages 36 to 39 for more instructions.

Lantana 'Patriot Firewagon'
Plant Profile: Page 68

Dahlberg Daisy
Plant Profile: Page 58

Gomphrena with some companion plants

Lantana 'Patriot Firewagon' (above, left) is a terrific companion for purple gomphrena. It is the brightest lantana we tried, doing incredibly well in a long, hot summer and reaching about two feet in height. Plant it alongside of larger gomphrenas or behind shorter ones.

Dahlberg Daisy (above, right) is a good companion for gomphrena because the flowers are a different shape and color. Border the taller gomphrenas and lantana with the shorter Dahlberg daisy.

Impatiens

CHARACTERISTICS

Plant Type: Annual

Average Size: About 12 to 18 inches tall by equally as wide.

Growth Rate: Fast

Leaf: Rounded, with a point on the end. Medium green or variegated. About 1 inch long by equally as wide in regular impatiens. New Guineas' leaves can be twice as large.

Flower: Regular impatiens measure about 1 1/2 inches wide. New Guineas are about twice as large.

Lifespan: 7 months

Origin: Africa

Spacing: About 12 inches on center (measure from the center of each plant). Closer in containers.

Cautions: Frequently damaged by deer.

Colors: Many shades of red, purple, pink, peach, orange, and white. Most impatiens have green leaves, but many New Guineas feature darker-colored or variegated leaves.

1. *Double pink impatiens*
2. *'Little Lizzy' orange impatiens*
3. *New Guinea lipstick impatiens*
4. *Regular 'Blue Pearl' impatiens*

Impatiens are the most popular bedding plant in the world but are too thirsty for most Texas gardeners to plant extensively. However, they are great for containers, especially the New Guinea and 'Little Lizzy' series.

New Guinea impatiens surrounding a bromeliad. Container from www.campaniainternational.com's Fiberglass Collection, 'Round Leaf Planter,' on 'Square Frame Pedestal.'

Impatiens perform best in spring and fall in Texas. The plants seem to "melt" during the summer, and high, nighttime temperatures keep them from recovering. But many Texans have good luck with impatiens in spring and fall. The New Guinea impatiens, which feature larger leaves and flowers than the regular impatiens, are one of the most colorful plants in the world and use the least water of any impatiens. We only had to water them only twice a week in large, shade containers. The 'Little Lizzy' series is smaller than regular impatiens and is also more colorful in containers. The 'Accent' series of regular impatiens does especially well in the Dallas-Fort Worth area. And don't forget the double impatiens, which are one of the most beautiful flowers for containers that are viewed from up close.

Color Period: Late spring and in fall, blooming constantly. Throughout the growing season, if planted in containers in shade.

Buying Tips: Regular impatiens are one of the easiest plants to find in the garden centers in spring. New Guineas and double impatiens are also showing up everywhere. 'Little Lizzies' are harder to find. All the impatiens we have purchased have done well for us, regardless of the name on the tag.

*Red ribbon plants are defined on page 13. For red ribbon performance, follow the planting and maintenance guidelines on pages 22 to 39.

ANNUALS

Companions: One of our favorite designs with any of the impatiens is to alternate jewel-toned flowers - orange, red, purple, or hot pink. Both of the container designs on these two pages feature orange, purple, and red New Guinea impatiens, alternated. The container shown below also features white begonias and pink caladiums, which quiet down the wild colors of the impatiens.

Wax Begonia
Plant Profile: Page 44

Caladium
Plant Profile: Page 50

Impatiens
Plant Profile: Page 66

Impatiens with some companion plants

Wax Begonias (above, left) are one of the best annuals to use for shady areas. They tone down the intensity of the bright impatiens' flowers.

Caladiums (above, center) are an excellent choice for centerpieces of shady container gardens. They contrast well with the other plants in this group because their leaves are so much bigger.

Put them all together in a 16 inch, side-planted basket (#ZGBS16) on a 36 inch border column (#ZGBC36) from www.kinsmangarden.com. First, the impatiens are planted through the side holes in the basket. Second, the caladium is planted in the center. Third, the begonias are tucked in along the edge. The basket is mounted on a wooden post that is sunk into the garden itself. See the Kinsman web site for short videos showing this technique. You won't believe how easy it is!

GROWING CONDITIONS

Light: Medium to light shade. Some New Guineas, called 'Sunpatiens,' take more sun. Regular impatiens are often planted in full sun in the spring and fall.

Water: High. Regular impatiens need daily water in light shade in the ground during the hottest time of summer. New Guineas need less. We have watered them as little as twice a week in large containers in shade.

Soil: For the garden, plant in any fertile, well-drained soil that has been enriched with organic matter. Use only good-quality potting mix for containers. See pages 22 to 25 for specific instructions on soil preparation.

Hardiness: Very sensitive to the slightest frost.

Propagation: Seeds or cuttings

Pest Problems: Fungus, slugs, Japanese beetles.

PLANTING & MAINTENANCE

When to Plant: Spring or fall

Trimming: Should plants become leggy in late summer, shearing them back by 1/3 will restore their form and encourage a late flush of fresh blossoms.

Fertilization: Fertilize at planting time with a timed-release product.

New Guinea impatiens lining a path.

Lantana

1ST

CHARACTERISTICS

Plant Type: Tropical perennial used primarily as an annual in Texas, other than *Lantana horrida*, which is a perennial.

Average Size: Varies by variety, from 1 to 5 feet high by 1 1/2 to 4 feet wide. *Lantana montevidensis*, (purple) is 12 inches high by 3 to 4 feet wide. 'New Gold' is 2 feet tall by 3 to 4 feet wide.

Growth Rate: Fast

Leaf: Medium green and pointed. About 1 inch long by 1/2 inch wide.

Flower: Clusters of tiny flowers forming larger flowers of about 1 inch across.

Lifespan: 7 months for annual lantana

Origin: Tropical America

Spacing: About 18 to 24 inches on center (measure from the center of each plant). Closer in containers.

Cautions: Poisonous to humans, dogs, and livestock. Can cause serious illness or death. Almost never damaged by deer.

Colors: White, red, pink, yellow, purple, or orange.

1. 'Landmark Rose Glow' lantana
2. 'Landmark White' lantana
3. *Lantana horrida*, a perennial in Texas
4. *Lantana montevidensis*

If you could choose just one annual, make it lantana. Unstoppable garden color from early summer to fall. This heat-loving, blue ribbon plant* blooms like crazy and requires very little maintenance.

'New Gold' is a low growing lantana that is covered with blooms all season long.

Lantanas are extremely useful plants in Texas gardens. They tolerate heat and drought and bloom prolifically all summer. Out of 21 varieties of lantana trialed at the Dallas Arboretum in 2007, 'Luscious Tropical Fruit' emerged as a winner of the 2007 North Texas Winner's Circle Awards. Lantana 'New Gold' has been designated as a Texas Superstar™ plant by the Texas A & M AgriLife Extension Service. It tolerates heat and drought and produces an abundance of golden-yellow flowers all summer long. Since 'New Gold' doesn't produce seed, all of its energy goes into profuse flower production, as shown in the photo above. Also a Texas Superstar™ plant, purple trailing lantana (*Lantana montevidensis*) produces purple flowers and demonstrates excellent heat, wind, and drought tolerance. A native Texas lantana, *Lantana horrida*, is a perennial that produces orange and yellow flowers on plants that reach four to five feet tall and bloom from May through November.

Color Period: From April until the first frost, non stop

Buying Tips: Remember that, while most lantanas bloom from spring until the first frost, purple lantanas peak in spring and fall, blooming a bit less in the heat of summer. Also, since the height of lantana varies from one to five feet, check the plant tag at your garden center to be sure the selection fits your space.

*Blue ribbon plants are defined on page 12. For blue ribbon performance, follow the planting and maintenance guidelines on pages 22 to 39.

Attracts Butterflies

Attracts Hummingbirds

Resists Deer

31
Avg. Weeks of Color

Botanical Name: *Lantana camara*
Family: Verbenaceae

ANNUALS

Companions: Lantanas are excellent color accents for perennial gardens. Most perennials don't bloom anywhere near as long as lantana does, so adding lantana ensures constant color in your bed. And, if you use perennials that also attract butterflies, like the ones shown below, you will attract clouds of them!

Yarrow
Plant Profile: Page 172

'Purple Emperor'
Butterfly Bush
Plant Profile: Page 194

'Big Sky After
Midnight'
Coneflower
Plant Profile: Page 116

Lantana 'Patriot Firewagon' with some companion plants

Yarrow (above, left) is an easy perennial companion for lantana. Yellow yarrow lights up a garden for about two to three months in summer and contrasts wonderfully with this 'Patriot Firewagon' lantana. Since yarrow grows to about 18 inches tall, place it so it shows up with the size of lantana you choose.

'Purple Emperor' Butterfly Bush (above, center) may be added for a dramatic color accent with the yarrow and lantana. Most of the newer, compact butterfly bushes, like this 'Purple Emperor,' grow to about four feet tall, so put it in the center or back of the bed surrounded by the yarrow and lantana. It, too, blooms for about two months in summer.

'Big Sky After Midnight' Coneflower (above, right) is a great, pinkish-purple color that contrasts well with the other flowers in this grouping. Since it grows to about 18 inches tall, place it so that it shows well with the lantana. This coneflower blooms at about the same time as the yarrow and butterfly bush.

GROWING CONDITIONS

Light: Full sun

Water: Low. Ideal watering is once or twice a week after the initial establishment period (pages 28 to 29). Tolerates water up to three times per week at the most. Requires more water when grown in containers.

Soil: For the garden, plant in any fertile, well-drained soil that has been enriched with organic matter. Use only good-quality potting mix for containers.

Hardiness: Lantana is used primarily as an annual in Texas (zones 6 to 8). Grows as a short-term perennial in zones 9 to 10, occasionally in zone 8. 'New Gold' lantana has often overwintered at the Fort Worth Botanic Garden.

Propagation: Cuttings

Pest Problems: If brown spots appear on the leaves, it is a fungus. These spots are routine, especially in the summer. If possible, cut back on water. Spray only if they become quite severe.

PLANTING & MAINTENANCE

When to Plant: Spring and summer.

Trimming: Accept lantana as an informal plant, if you are looking for low maintenance. We never trimmed ours in the Fort Worth Botanic Garden.

Fertilization: Fertilize at planting time with a timed-release product. See pages 36 to 39 for more instructions.

BUDGET GARDENING TIP

Lantana is sometimes twice as expensive as other annuals. However, it usually cover 4 to 6 times as much space, so it is much cheaper because you will need fewer to fill your garden.

Melampodium

CHARACTERISTICS

Plant Type: Annual

Average Size: We have purchased many unnamed melampodium (tag just says 'Melampodium'), and they all grew to about 12 to 18 inches tall by 12 inches wide. 'Derby,' 'Golden Globe,' 'Sunflake Gold,' 'Lemon Delight,' and 'Million Gold' are dwarfs of about 12 inches tall and equally as wide. 'Showstar' is about 24 inches tall and equally as wide. 'Medallion' can grow to 36 inches tall.

Growth Rate: Fast

Leaf: Medium green leaves, 2 to 3 inches long.

Flower: Inch-wide yellow daisies with yellow centers.

Lifespan: 7 months

Origin: Tropical America

Spacing: About 10 inches on center for the dwarfs; up to 2 feet on center for the largest varieties (measure from the center of one plant to the center of another). Closer in containers.

Cautions: Reseeds readily, even to the point of becoming a nuisance. Seldom damaged by deer.

Colors: Light yellow or gold, depending on variety.

BUDGET GARDENING TIP

Melampodium are really easy to grow from seeds. You can sow them directly in your garden, and they sprout in 7 to 10 days. The plants also show up again next year in your garden (although not necessarily where you want them!) because they reseed naturally. Some consider these new plants nuisances, but budget gardeners love free plants, and move them wherever they like!

One of the top annuals for sun and heat. Thrives from spring until frost with almost no care. Rates a blue ribbon* because of its long bloom period and ease of care.

Melampodiums are informal plants but look quite neat with a formal, clipped border.

If your plans for any sunny spot call for bright yellow, melampodium should be a top contender. Although the flowers are small, they appear so abundantly and continuously that the plants are always gloriously clad with deer-resistant color. You can start with bedding plants, but melampodium is also easy to sow from seed. As long as the soil is warm, melampodium seeds sprout quickly and begin blooming in a few short weeks. They reseed themselves, too, and volunteer seedlings are easy to dig and move to wherever you want them to grow and bloom. The taller varieties tend to fall over in mid summer, which isn't visible if they are planted in a mass but shows quite a bit in containers or in formal borders. Stick to the smaller varieties if compact form is needed.

Color Period: Early summer to fall, continuously

Buying Tips: Since melampodiums vary from 10 to 36 inches tall, be sure to check the plant tag at your garden center (or the description in the seed catalog) to be sure the selection fits your space.

*Blue ribbon plants are defined on page 12. For blue ribbon performance, follow the planting and maintenance guidelines on pages 22 to 39.

Companions: Melampodium is great to use wherever yellow color is needed. The list of garden allies is long indeed and includes sun lovers from agastache to zinnia. A packet of seeds can quickly and inexpensively fill a large space for a mass planting.

Melampodium mixes equally well with annuals and perennials. Try the combination below for a mix of each.

Lantana 'Patriot Firewagon'
Plant Profile: Page 68

Agastache 'Blue Fortune'
Plant Profile: Page 102

Coneflower 'Twilight'
Plant Profile: Page 116

'Sunflake Gold' melampodium with some companion plants

Lantana 'Patriot Firewagon' (above, left) is a terrific companion for melampodium. It is the brightest lantana we tried, doing incredibly well in a long, hot summer and growing to about two feet tall. Plant it alongside of tall melampodium or behind shorter ones.

Agastache 'Blue Fortune' (above, center) is one of the longest-blooming of the easy southern perennials and looks great with melampodium. Since it reaches three feet tall, plant the melampodium in front of the taller agastache.

Coneflower 'Twilight' (above, right) is a perennial with a fairly long bloom period that likes sun and reaches about two feet tall. Use the most common melampodiums as a border for this flower.

To combine them all, alternate the agastache with lantana. Plant the coneflowers along the sides, and border all of them with melampodium.

GROWING CONDITIONS

Light: Full sun

Water: Medium. Established plants tolerate short periods of drought but grow and bloom best with water twice weekly in summer after establishment (pages 28 to 29). Requires more water when grown in containers.

Soil: For the garden, plant in any fertile, well-drained soil that has been enriched with organic matter. Use only good-quality potting mix for containers. See pages 22 to 25 for specific instructions on soil preparation.

Hardiness: Cannot tolerate frost

Propagation: Seeds

Pest Problems: Large insects, including blister beetles and grasshoppers, occasionally chew the foliage, but they seldom weaken these vigorous plants.

PLANTING & MAINTENANCE

When to Plant: Spring or summer

Trimming: None needed

Fertilization: Fertilize at planting time with a timed-release product.

Melamodium planted around a tropical chenille plant.

Pansies and Violas

1ST

CHARACTERISTICS

Plant Type: Hardy annual

Average Size: 6 inches tall and equally wide.

Growth Rate: Medium

Leaf: Dark green, scalloped leaves on short stems that stay close to the ground.

Flower: Pansy flowers range from 1 inch wide mini-pansies to 2 inch wide 'Panolas'; large-flowered varieties have 4 inch wide, flat blossoms.

Lifespan: 6 to 7 months

Origin: Europe

Spacing: About 6 to 8 inches on center (measure from the center of each plant). Closer in containers.

Cautions: Frequently damaged by deer.

Colors: Flowers are white, yellow, blue, pink, purple, orange, red, or a variety of bicolors.

1. 'Sorbet Blue Heaven' viola
2. 'Matrix Blue Blotch' pansy
3. 'Matrix Rose' pansy
4. 'Sorbet Yellow Delight' viola

Cold tolerant and easy to please, pansies and violas are one of the best flowers to plant for the fall-to-spring season. They rate a blue ribbon* because of their high performance and ease of care.

Pansies do well planted in containers or in the ground. However, they feel the cold more in containers.

Pansies and violas love winter in Texas and are the most popular annuals for our cool months. They are grown primarily as winter annuals in Texas and spring annuals in the north. Pansies and violas come in either solid colors or with blotches in the center. The solid ones show up better from a distance. Pansies with smaller flowers generally bloom more than those with larger blooms.

Violas are closely related, but their performance is different. They generally recover from extreme cold faster than pansies and bloom in light shade to full sun. Violas have smaller flowers that are not as impressive as pansies when viewed from a distance; however, they cover themselves with flowers all winter long. The 'Sorbet' and 'Penny' series perform well in Dallas-Fort Worth.

Color Period: Most of the fall, winter, and spring. Although they stop blooming and don't look too happy when temperatures drop to the mid-twenties, they bounce back quickly when temperatures rise.

Buying Tips: The Dallas Arboretum relies on pansies in the following series: 'Bingo,' 'Delta,' 'Crown,' 'Panola,' 'Clear Sky,' 'Skyline,' and 'Baby Bingo.' However, most of the pansies and violas you see at your garden center grow pretty well in this area.

Blue ribbon plants are defined on page 12. For blue ribbon performance, follow the planting and maintenance guidelines on pages 22 to 39.

Companion: Pansies combine very well with the attractive and colorful foliage of ornamental cabbage and kale. Or, to keep it simple, pansies and violas often come in mixes of colors that are professionally chosen for good design. You can't go wrong choosing one of these mixes.

Pansies and violas long bloom period includes late winter and early spring, when few other annuals flower. Try them with other shrubs and bulbs that bloom at the same time, as shown below.

'Matrix Blue Blotch' pansies and some companion plants

Iris (above, left) blooms for about two weeks from early to late spring, depending on the cultivar you choose. Since both its flowers and leaves are quite different from pansies, it makes a great companion.

Forsythia (above, center) is a great shrub companion for pansies because it blooms for an extended period of time in late winter or early spring. Its yellow flowers contrast well with blue or purple pansies. Since it gets quite tall, plant the pansies as the front border.

Asiatic Lilies (above, right) bloom for a few weeks from late spring to early summer, so they would take over for tall bloomers after the iris and forsythia have stopped blooming.

To put it all together, plant forsythia as the tallest layer; alternate clumps of Asiatic lilies and iris in front, as the middle layer; border with the pansies. Blooms from February to May. Two or three out of four of the plants should flower at the same time.

GROWING CONDITIONS

Light: Full sun for pansies. Violas grow in light shade to full sun.

Water: Medium. Supplemental water is often needed after planting in fall, when dry weather often prevails. After Thanksgiving, winter rains are usually sufficient for pansies. However, cold spells often dry out plants, so water before really cold weather threatens if the soil is dry. Requires more water when grown in containers.

Soil: For the garden, plant in any fertile, well-drained soil that has been enriched with organic matter. Use only good-quality potting mix for containers.

Hardiness: Violas and pansies are winter hardy to zone 6. Although pansies and violas will tolerate temperatures down to 19 degrees, their foliage suffers damage and turns brown under such low temperatures. At the Fort Worth Botanic Garden, we cover pansies and violas with row covers when temperatures fall into the 20's and then remove when the temperatures come back into the low 30's.

Propagation: Seeds

Pest Problems: Rare. Root rot can develop if plants are kept too wet.

PLANTING & MAINTENANCE

When to Plant: Pansies grow best when they develop good roots before soil temperatures drop into the 40's. Plant in mid to late October.

Trimming: You don't have to remove the dead blooms from pansies but doing so will help the plants bloom longer and stronger. Pull up plants in mid April because they cannot tolerate hot weather.

Fertilization: Fertilize at planting time with a timed-release product. See pages 36 to 39 for more instructions.

Pentas

CHARACTERISTICS

Plant Type: Tropical perennial grown as an annual.

Average Size: 1 to 4 feet tall; 12 to 24 inches wide, depending on variety.

Growth Rate: Medium

Leaf: Dark green leaves with pointed tips; prominent leaf veins give the leaves a quilted texture.

Flower: Rounded clusters of star-shaped, 5-petaled flowers.

Lifespan: 7 months. Larger varieties usually outlive dwarfs.

Origin: Tropical Africa

Spacing: Set dwarf plants 12 inches on center (measure from the center of each plant); mid-sized varieties do well with 18 inch spacing. Grow tall varieties as specimen plants because they grow to the size of bushy 3 to 4 foot tall shrubs. Place closer in containers.

Cautions: Seldom damaged by deer.

Colors: Red, pink, lilac, lavender, purple, or white.

1. *Pentas 'Butterfly Deep Pink'*
2. *Pentas 'Butterfly White'*
3. *Pentas 'Butterfly Rose Deep'*

Pentas take all the Texas heat and are one of the favorite foods of both butterflies and hummingbirds. Although they don't rate a ribbon because they don't bloom constantly for the whole summer, they are definitely worth planting for the butterflies.

Pentas 'Butterfly Deep Pink'

The original pentas were shrubs that grew to four feet tall in tropical areas. Since they bloomed continuously and took heat well, hybridizers began working to get a more compact plant. The new varieties, particularly the dwarfs, have lost some of the strength of their taller ancestors, however. They are a little more susceptible to fungus and don't bloom continuously. However, even the dwarfs bloom about 75 percent of the time and attract butterflies and hummingbirds like crazy. Pentas are well worth planting in areas with long, hot summers. Pentas 'Butterfly Deep Pink' was a 2006 winner of the North Texas Winner's Circle Awards.

Color Period: Spring, summer, and fall; about 75 percent of the time for the smaller ones. The larger ones bloom continuously.

Buying Tips: If you are lucky, you might see some of the old-fashioned, red pentas in your garden centers. They bloom dependably all summer but get up to four feet tall. More likely, you will see the 'Butterfly' series, which gets about 16 inches tall and blooms on and off from spring until fall.

ANNUALS

Companions: Phenomenal plants for attracting butterflies and hummingbirds, pentas partner perfectly with other butterfly magnets, such as butterfly bush, lantana, salvia, and zinnias. For clouds of butterflies, plant the combinations shown below.

Scabiosa
Plant Profile: Page 158

Butterfly Bush
Plant Profile: Page 194

Lantana
Plant Profile: Page 68

Pentas 'Butterfly Deep Pink' and some companion plants

Scabiosa (above, left) is a small (12 to 18 inches tall) perennial that is one of the best for butterflies, particularly right after it goes into bloom. It blooms for two to four months, starting in May. Plant it as a border for mid-sized pentas.

Add a purple butterfly bush (above, center) for another butterfly favorite. Most of the newer, compact butterfly bushes, like this 'Peacock,' grow to about four feet tall, so put it in the center or back of the bed, surrounded by the pentas, scabiosa, and lantana. It blooms for about two months in summer.

Lantana (above, right) has attracted more butterflies than any other plant. The annual variety will flower from spring until fall. The pink and yellow one (shown) usually grows to about two feet tall, but check the plant tag to be sure.

To put it all together, plant the butterfly bush as the tallest layer, the pentas and lantana (side by side) as the mid-layer, and border with the scabiosa.

GROWING CONDITIONS

Light: Full sun to light shade

Water: Medium. Once or twice a week after plants are established (pages 28 to 29). Requires more water when grown in containers.

Soil: For the garden, plant in any fertile, well-drained soil that has been enriched with organic matter. Use only good-quality potting mix for containers. See pages 22 to 25 for specific instructions on soil preparation.

Hardiness: Easily killed by hard freezes.

Propagation: Seeds or cuttings

Pest Problems: Powdery mildew sometimes causes white patches to form on the leaves. It weakens but does not kill the plants.

PLANTING & MAINTENANCE

When to Plant: Set out plants in late spring, when the soil is warm. Pentas thrive in humid heat, so they can be planted well into early summer.

Trimming: Most pentas currently sold in garden centers don't need trimming because they have a dense form and only grow to about 18 to 24 inches tall. Removing the dead flowers increases the blooming, however. Taller pentas might become leggy in late summer. If this happens, shearing them back by 1/3 will restore their form and encourage a late flush of fresh blossoms.

Fertilization: Fertilize at planting time with a timed-release product. See pages 36 to 39 for more instructions.

Persian Shield

CHARACTERISTICS

Plant Type: Tropical perennial grown as an annual.

Average Size: About 2 to 3 feet tall by 2 feet wide. Smaller in containers.

Growth Rate: Medium

Leaf: 6 inch long, pointed leaves with serrated edges; reddish purple beneath and purple above, with dark green leaf veins.

Flower: Small, blue flowers occur primarily on year old plants that survive winter; not showy. Grow this one for the leaf color.

Lifespan: 6 to 7 months. Does not look good after that, regardless of how warm it is.

Origin: Burma

Spacing: About 18 inches on center (measure from the center of each plant). Closer in containers.

Cautions: None known. Seldom damaged by deer.

Colors: Leaves are purple

Persian shield makes a great centerpiece for container gardens. Red wax begonias, 'Dark Star' coleus, and Lysimachia 'Outback Sunset' are planted along the edge and through the side holes of this side-planted hanging basket. 16" double Imperial planter (#ZGIPD16) from www.kinsmangarden.com

Persian shield is possibly the most beautiful foliage plant in the world. Its purple leaves are almost iridescent. Tolerant of heat, it rates a blue ribbon* because of its long lifespan and ease of care. It is hard to believe a plant this beautiful is actually easy to grow! And it even produces lots of color in shade.

Persian shield with lime coleus and 'Blue Pearl' impatiens planted in front

Easy to grow, Persian shield thrives in our hot, humid Texas summers in shade. Since it is too large to use for borders, plant it as an accent in the garden, as shown above, or as the centerpiece of a container, as shown left.

Persian shield is supposed to be a perennial in the tropics. However, we tried it in areas that don't freeze, and it still lived for only about six to seven months.

Color Period: Grow Persian shield for its leaf color instead of its insignificant and seldom-seen flowers. Its leaves offer color anytime temperatures stay above 32 degrees.

Buying Tips: Persian shield is getting more popular in garden centers. We have used hundreds of them over a number of years, and they all have done well, so this is an easy one to find. Any Persian shield you see should do quite well in your garden!

Blue ribbon plants are defined on page 12. For blue ribbon performance, follow the planting and maintenance guidelines on pages 22 to 39.

ANNUALS

Companions: Persian shield is quite versatile, looking great with a variety of different colors. Red dragon wing begonias and golden shrimp plants combine with the purple for a traffic-stopping combination. Pale pink flowers, like wax begonias, also look good with Persian shield, particularly if silver dusty miller is added to the mix. Or, pair it with lime green and different shades of purple, as shown below.

Persian shield forms the centerpiece of this side-planted basket from w w w . k i n s m a n g a r d e n . c o m . Impatiens and white begonias complete the design.

Gomphrena
Plant Profile: Page 64

'Gay's Delight' Coleus
Plant Profile: Page 54

Persian shield and some companion plants

Gomphrena (above, left) is an annual that comes in different shades of purple that coordinate well with Persian shield. Most stay shorter than the Persian shield and bloom for much of the summer in sun to light shade. They make an excellent border for Persian shield.

'Gay's Delight' Coleus (above, right) has lime green leaves with dark purple veins. It looks like it was custom made for Persian shield! It grows to about two feet tall when planted in the ground- the same size as the Persian shield - so it works very well planted on either side of it. This coleus grows well in sun to light shade.

GROWING CONDITIONS

Light: Light to medium shade to full sun.

Water: Average to high. Persian shield wilts when its roots become dry, so watering about twice weekly in hot weather is often necessary after the establishment period (pages 28 to 29). More water in containers.

Soil: For the garden, plant in any fertile, well-drained soil that has been enriched with organic matter. Use only good-quality potting mix for containers. See pages 22 to 25 for specific instructions on soil preparation.

Hardiness: Survives a slight freeze, but only lives about 6 or 7 months - even in warm weather. Treat this plant like a summer annual.

Propagation: Cuttings. You can increase your supply of plants by pinching off 4 inch long stem tips, stripping off the leaves from all but the tip and rooting them in damp potting mix.

Pest Problems: Rare

PLANTING & MAINTENANCE

When to Plant: Spring or summer

Trimming: Should plants become leggy, trim them back by half their size. They generally don't need trimming when planted in containers but need it occasionally when planted in the ground. The warmer the season, the more trimming they require.

Fertilization: Fertilize at planting time with a timed-release product. See pages 36 to 39 for more instructions.

Petunia, 'Tidal Wave' Series

CHARACTERISTICS

Plant Type: Summer annual

Average Size: 18 to 24 inches tall by 2 1/2 to 4 feet wide.

Growth Rate: Medium

Leaf: Medium green, 1 to 2 inches long; oval in shape and slightly fuzzy.

Flower: 2 to 3 inches wide, funnel-shaped.

Lifespan: 7 months

Origin: South America

Spacing: 18 to 24 inches on center

Cautions: To avoid build-up of harmful disease pathogens, do not plant petunias in the same beds every year. Petunias don't like water on their flowers, although 'Tidal Wave' flowers recover more rapidly after rains and overhead irrigation than other types of petunias. Deer will frequently eat petunias.

Colors: 'Tidal Wave Cherry' is a bright cherry red. 'Tidal Wave Silver' is a light lavender or silvery white.

Trailing petunias that hold up to the heat and humidity of north central Texas and bloom all summer long in bright cherry red or pale lavender/silvery white. Designated by the Texas A & M AgriLife Extension Service as Texas SuperStar™ plants. Definitely a blue ribbon* plant.

'Tidal Wave Silver' petunias

Petunias used to be difficult to grow in Texas until new cultivars became available. At Fort Worth Botanic Garden, we have had the best luck with the 'Tidal Wave' petunias. They are heat-tolerant, easy to grow, and provide summer long color. The 'Tidal Wave Cherry' provides show stopping color and combines well with other bright colors, or it can be toned down with more subtle flower and foliage colors. 'Tidal Wave Silver' combines well with purple foliage and flowers in cool color schemes. You do not have to deadhead (remove dead flowers) for blooms to be continuous. These two colors have been our favorites for the last few years.

Although this plant is primarily used as a summer annual, it also tolerates cold temperatures well, including winters in north central Texas, as long as the soil is well drained. Flowering stops during the winter but will resume with the first warm days of late winter and early spring.

Color Period: Seven months (April 1 to November 1)

Buying Tips: Commonly available in better nurseries and garden centers. Other 'generic' petunias will die out with the advent of summer's heat. Avoid petunias that only say 'Petunia' on the label.

*Blue ribbon plants are defined on page 12. For blue ribbon performance, follow the planting and maintenance guidelines on pages 22 to 39.

Companions: 'Tidal Wave Silver' (shown, left and right) combines well with plants having silver leaves, like artemisia and dusty miller. It also looks good with other purple flowers of different sizes, like vinca and lantana.

'Tidal Wave Cherry' combines well with ornamental grasses, as shown in the photo to the far left. The dark grass is 'Purple Majesty Millet.' Or, try it with bright colors that bloom during the heat of summer. Esperanza 'Gold Star' and purple vinca make great companions, as shown below.

GROWING CONDITIONS

Light: Full sun, at least 6 hours a day.

Water: Medium. Two times a week after the establishment period (pages 28 to 29). Requires more water when grown in containers.

Soil: For the garden, plant in any fertile, well-drained soil that has been enriched with organic matter. Use only good-quality potting mix for containers. See pages 22 to 25 for specific instructions on soil preparation.

Hardiness: Summer annual in all U.S. zones; marginally winter hardy in Zone 8. Winter hardy in zones 9 and south.

Propagation: Seeds or cuttings

Pest Problems: Slugs can be a problem on petunias where the leaves meet the soil. One solution is to place small tubs of beer in the bed among the petunias. The slugs will crawl into the beer and meet their fate. Other solutions are mulching with pecan shell hulls or sprinkling snail and slug bait granules available at your local garden center. Be sure to check out the dangers of any snail bait you purchase. It is easiest to find that information online.

PLANTING & MAINTENANCE

When to Plant: Spring or summer

Trimming: Can be lightly trimmed in mid to late summer if desired to stimulate more bloom in the fall. Removing the dead flowers is not necessary.

Fertilization: Fertilize at planting time with a timed-release product. See pages 36 to 39 for more instructions.

Esperanza 'Gold Star'
Plant Profile: Page 62

'Cora Deep Lavender' Vinca
Plant Profile: Page 94

'Tidal Wave Cherry' petunias and some companions

Esperanza 'Gold Star' (above left) provides striking contrast in form and color with 'Tidal Wave Cherry.' This yellow flowered plant is an annual in north central Texas and grows three to four feet tall. Because of its height, use it behind petunias. Esperanza 'Gold Star' blooms all summer and fall.

'Cora Deep Lavender' Vinca (above right) combines well with both the petunia and the 'Gold Star.' This vinca is a summer annual that grows 14 to 16 inches tall, so plant it as a border for the taller 'Gold Star' and petunias. All three plants do well in full sun.

Portulaca and Purslane

Purslane flowers

Portulaca and purslane are heat-tolerant, low-growing annuals that produce a profusion of bright, cheerful flowers in many colors. They bloom for five to seven months. Flowers close on cloudy days or in the afternoon on sunny days, which limits their use and keeps them from qualifying for a blue ribbon.* Their heat tolerance and low water needs make them useful annuals for the hot Texas summer.

Double portulaca flowers (left) look like little roses. Purslane flowers (right) are usually single, which are simpler.

Purslane and portulaca provide a profusion of colorful flowers all summer long. Both stay lower than most other annuals, making them useful as ground-hugging borders. However, their flowers close in the afternoon on sunny days and do not open on cloudy days. The flowers of the 'Yubi' purslane stay open later in the afternoon, however. This annual has been featured in the Fort Worth Botanic Garden's flower clock. The low, spreading quality allows the hands of the clock to pass over the plant with no maintenance. One disadvantage of the 'Yubi' purslane is its tendency to reseed, which can become a nuisance.

Color Period: April 1 to November 15

Buying Tips: 'Samba Bicolor Pink' and 'Samba White' portulaca were designated as 2007 Flame Proof Winners at the Dallas Arboretum, which is a testament to their heat tolerance. The 'Yubi Series' is the best kind of purslane and has flowers twice as large as older varieties. Designated a Texas SuperStar™ plant by the Texas A & M AgriLifeExtension Service, it will grow with almost no extra water.

Blue ribbon plants are defined on page 12. For blue ribbon performance, follow the planting and maintenance guidelines on pages 22 to 39.

Companions: Purslane and portulaca combine well with bright-colored flowers. 'Flamenco' cuphea, Dahlberg daisy, gomphrena, lantana, and vinca are good companions. For traffic-stopping color, try the neon combination shown below.

Purslane flowers do well in containers.

GROWING CONDITIONS

Light: Full sun, at least 6 hours a day.

Water: Medium. Once or twice a week in beds after the establishment period (pages 28 to 29); more often in containers.

Soil: For the garden, plant in any fertile, well-drained soil that has been enriched with organic matter. Use only good-quality potting mix for containers. See pages 22 to 25 for specific instructions on soil preparation.

Hardiness: Hardy as a summer annual in all U. S. and Texas hardiness zones.

Propagation: Seeds or cuttings

Pest Problems: Rare. No serious pests. Portulaca is susceptible to root rot in poorly-drained soil, thus it is important to plant in well-drained soil in full sun.

PLANTING & MAINTENANCE

When to Plant: After all danger of frost is passed (April 1).

Trimming: None needed

Fertilization: Fertilize at planting time with a timed-release product. See pages 36 to 39 for more instructions.

Variegated Tapioca
Plant Profile: Page 90

'Cora Deep Lavender' Vinca
Plant Profile: Page 94

Portulaca flowers and some companions

Variegated Tapioca (above left) is a summer annual that thrives in the same summer sun and heat the portulaca and purslane love. Since it grows three to four feet tall, use the smaller purslane or portulaca as a border.

'Cora Deep Lavender' Vinca (above right) combines well with both the portulaca and the variegated tapioca. This vinca is a summer annual that grows 14 to 16 inches tall, so plant it in between the other two plants. All three plants do well in full sun.

Portulaca flowers

Scaevola, Fan Flower

CHARACTERISTICS

Plant Type: Tropical perennial used as an annual in Texas.

Average Size: About 6 inches tall by 12 to 18 inches wide.

Growth Rate: Medium

Leaf: Medium green, oblong and pointed.

Flower: Small flowers shaped like a fan.

Lifespan: 7 months

Origin: Australia

Spacing: About 12 inches on center (measure from the center of each plant). Closer in containers.

Cautions: Rabbits love them! Sometimes damaged by deer.

Colors: Blue or white

1. Scaevola 'Whirlwind Blue'
2. Scaevola 'Whirlwind White'

Excellent annual for Texas gardens. Blooms all season with very little care. Butterflies love it! Plant it properly in spring, and don't touch it (other than water) all summer long. Rates a blue ribbon* for its high performance and ease of care.

Scaevola thrives in hot, humid climates, where it produces fan-shaped flowers that bloom all season long. It blooms all spring, summer, and fall, never taking a break. Scaevola is a bit pickier about performing well when planted in the ground, however. If it is a year of average or below average rainfall (20 to 33 inches), scaevola does incredibly well. It cannot take either too much rain (60 inches plus) or poor drainage when planted in the ground, though. Scaevola also takes heat beautifully. It performs especially well in containers. Scaevola 'New Wonder' has been designated a Texas SuperStar™ plant by the Texas A & M AgriLife Extension Service.

However, it takes longer to get going than most other annuals. Don't expect it to grow and thrive until it has been planted for about three weeks. We have noticed it going into a wilt shortly after planting, even if the soil is moist. Don't give it extra water (unless it stays in a wilt for more than a day or two), and it will perk up shortly.

Color Period: Spring through fall, continuously

Buying Tips: We have never had any trouble with scaevola. All cultivars have excelled in our gardens.

*Blue ribbon plants are defined on page 12. For blue ribbon performance, follow the planting and maintenance guidelines on pages 22 to 39.

ANNUALS

Companions: Blue scaevola needs bright companions if it is to be viewed from a distance. Yellow (like melampodium and lantana) and red flowers (like 'Tidal Wave Cherry' petunias) are ideal companions for distance viewing.

If you are planting scaevola in a location for up-close viewing, try using other shapes of blue or lavender flowers accented with colorful foliage, as shown below.

'Cora Deep Lavender' Vinca
Plant Profile: Page 94

'Dark Star' Coleus
Plant Profile: Page 54

Blue scaevola and some companion plants

'Cora Deep Lavender' Vinca (above, left) makes an excellent companion for scaevola and creates a cool, soothing color scheme. These nonstop, all-summer-long blooming annuals get 14 to16 inches tall and should be placed behind the shorter scaevola.

'Dark Star' Coleus (above, center) can be added as well. It matures at 15 inches tall and can be placed on either side of the vinca or alone behind the scaevola.

GROWING CONDITIONS

Light: Sun to light shade

Water: Medium. Once or twice a week after establishment. Requires more water in containers.

Soil: For the garden, plant in any fertile, well-drained soil that has been enriched with organic matter. Use only good-quality potting mix for containers. See pages 22 to 25 for specific instructions on soil preparation.

Hardiness: Winter hardy in zones 10 through 11.

Propagation: Seeds or cuttings

Pest Problems: No serious insect or disease problems.

PLANTING & MAINTENANCE

When to Plant: Spring or summer

Trimming: None required

Fertilization: Fertilize at planting time with a timed-release product. See pages 36 to 39 for more instructions.

Our favorite scaevola container combines it with salvia and creeping jenny. Easy-to-plant container and column are from www.kinsmangarden.com.

1ST

CHARACTERISTICS

Plant Type: Tropical shrub used as an annual in Texas.

Average Size: About 12 to 18 inches tall and wide.

Growth Rate: Medium

Leaf: Green and pointed, 2 to 4 inches long.

Flower: Dramatic, yellow spike with white accent; about 3 inches long.

Lifespan: Lives for about 5 years in areas that don't freeze. Count on it for one growing season in Texas.

Origin: Peru

Spacing: About 12 inches on center (measure from the center of each plant). Closer in containers.

Cautions: Sometimes damaged by deer.

Colors: Be sure to buy the shrimp plant with the yellow flower shown here. There are many more available, but none do as well as this one.

Shrimp plant with coleus and creeping Jenny in a container.

Shrimp plants bloom all season - at least seven months - with no care whatsoever other than watering! This newcomer to Texas has been doing well for generations in the tropics. It loves heat and blooms in part sun or shade. The golden shrimp plant easily merits a blue ribbon.*

Shrimp plant with blue torenia and pink dragon wing begonias. Shrimps do equally well when planted in containers or in the ground.

Shrimp plants are one of the best sources for color in medium to light shade during Texas summers. They bloom in sun as well but prefer some break from the afternoon blast, especially in the heat of August. Shrimp plants are relatively new to Texas, but should be used much more.

Color Period: Late spring to late fall, blooming constantly

Buying Tips: Golden shrimp plants are relatively new to Texas, and many garden centers have not yet discovered them. If you can find them, be sure to buy only the yellow one shown on these two pages. The other colors do not perform as well as the yellow. Try online suppliers if your local sources don't have the golden shrimps.

Blue ribbon plants are defined on page 12. For blue ribbon performance, follow the planting and maintenance guidelines on pages 22 to 39.

Attracts Butterflies   Attracts Hummingbirds

ANNUALS

Companions: Golden shrimp plants are primarily used as an accent planted in beds or as a centerpiece of a container garden. Since there are so few yellow shade plants that bloom all season, they are extremely useful with many companions. Use them with blues and pink, as shown below, for a soft combination.

Torenia
Plant Profile: Page 92

Dragon Wing Begonia
Plant Profile: Page 44

'Painted Lady' Coleus
Plant Profile: Page 54

Golden shrimps and some companion plants

Torenia (above, left) does well in the light shade planted either in a container (as shown, opposite) or planted as a border to the shrimp plants in the ground. Either trailing or upright torenia works with the shrimps.

Dragon Wing Begonias (above, center) are one of the best companions for golden shrimp plants because the two together have more color impact than either one alone. Plant them in a container (as shown, opposite) or in the ground. Both plants are annuals.

'Painted Lady' Coleus (above, right) looks great with shrimps, torenia, and dragon wings.

Put them all together by planting either the shrimp or the dragon wings as the tallest plant, whichever is larger on planting day. Border with the torenia and the coleus. All four of these plants are annuals.

GROWING CONDITIONS

Light: Medium to light shade. We have used them in full sun, and they do okay; but, they do better in some shade.

Water: Medium. Once or twice a week after establishment (pages 28 to 29), depending on light conditions. Requires more water in containers.

Soil: For the garden, plant in any fertile, well-drained soil that has been enriched with organic matter. Use only good-quality potting mix for containers. See page 22 to 25 for specific instructions on soil preparation.

Hardiness: Not tolerant of freezes. Lasts for about 5 years in zones 9B to 11.

Propagation: Cuttings

Pest Problems: Rare

PLANTING & MAINTENANCE

When to Plant: Spring or summer

Trimming: None required when shrimp plants are used as an annual.

Fertilization: Fertilize at planting time with a timed-release product. See pages 36 to 39 for more instructions.

Shrimp plant with coleus and dragon wing begonias in a side-planted wall pot from www.kinsmangarden.com.

Snapdragon

Plant Type: Annual

Average Size: 6 to 36 inches tall, depending on variety, and 10 to 14 inches wide.

Growth Rate: Slow in fall, fast in spring.

Leaf: Green, narrow leaves with pointed tips clothe the base of the plants.

Flower: Vertical spikes of delicate flowers that open from the bottom upward.

Lifespan: 2 to 6 months

Origin: Mediterranean region

Spacing: About 8 to 12 inches on center (measure from the center of each plant). Closer in containers.

Cautions: Seldom damaged by deer.

Colors: White, yellow, red, pink, peach, or bicolors.

Charming, old-fashioned flowers for the fall-to-spring garden. Plant this one in fall. Removal of dead flowers required on tall varieties, which takes some time.

Tall snapdragons bordered by impatiens

Of all the flowers you can plant in fall for bloom in spring, snapdragons are the only ones that have an upright growth habit. They typically stay low and green through the winter and then explode with new growth and blooms as the weather warms in spring. The tall spikes make excellent cut flowers, and secondary spikes emerge after the first flower spike is removed. Snapdragons make excellent bedding and container plants.

Snapdragons come in a wide variety of sizes, from six inch dwarfs to three foot background plants. We have been very happy with the ease of growth of the small ones. They offer a carpet of high-impact color and are very useful in areas where low stature is required. The tall ones are spectacular, with tall, spire-like flowers that look like the kind of flower that would never grow in Texas. However, the tall ones require deadheading (removing of dead flowers), which takes quite a bit of time.

Color Period: Blooms most in early spring, for about three months.

Buying Tips: We have never had problems with snapdragons. Every one we have bought (several different cultivars) has excelled in our gardens.

Companions: Snapdragons look great with spring bulbs, particularly irises. They also work with other cool weather flowers like pansies. Mix tall snaps (over 16 inches tall) with different colored pansies and add some evergreen grasses, like 'Dwarf White Striped Sweet Flag,' for a textural change, as shown below.

White snapdragons and some companion plants

Pansy 'Panola Rose' (above, top) will stay in bloom for most of the late fall, winter, and spring. Plant it as a border for snapdragons.

Dwarf White-Striped Sweet Flag Grass (above, center) grows to about 15 inches tall and is evergreen. Plant it as a mid layer between the pansies and the taller snapdragons.

Pansy 'Matrix Deep Blue Blotch' (above, bottom) gives the final touch to this red, white, and blue color scheme. Alternate it with the rose pansies along the border.

Put them all together by planting the tall snapdragons in the center of the bed. Border it with the two colors of pansies, alternated. Plant the grass as a mid-sized layer, in between the snapdragons and the pansies. Plant all of them in fall. The pansies and grasses will stay for most of the fall, winter, and spring, with the snapdragons blooming in fall, going dormant for the winter, and re-appearing in spring.

GROWING CONDITIONS

Light: Full sun or at least 6 hours of direct sun each day. When grown in reduced light, flower spikes will curve toward the sun.

Water: Medium. Water twice weekly after planting in fall, when dry weather usually prevails. Winter and spring rains are usually sufficient for snapdragons, but check the soil before cold spells to be sure the flowers don't go into the cold, dry weather with dry soil.

Soil: For the garden, plant in any fertile, well-drained soil that has been enriched with organic matter. Use only good-quality potting mix for containers. See pages 22 to 25 for specific instructions on soil preparation.

Hardiness: Always hardy in zone 8, provided the plants are well-rooted when cold weather arrives. In zones 6 and 7, plants rest through the winter and re-appear in spring. They bloom now and again in winter during warm spells.

Propagation: Seeds or cuttings

Pest Problems: Rare

PLANTING & MAINTENANCE

When to Plant: Plant in fall with enough time for the plants to become well rooted before the really cold weather comes. Late October is ideal.

Trimming: Should plants become leggy in late summer, shearing them back by 1/3 will restore their form and encourage a late flush of fresh blossoms.

Fertilization: Fertilize at planting time with a timed-release product. See pages 36 to 39 for more instructions.

Sweet Potato Vine

CHARACTERISTICS

Plant Type: Tuberous, tropical perennial grown as an annual.

Average Size: Vines grow 6 to 12 inches tall by 3 to 8 feet long, depending on variety.

Growth Rate: Very fast

Leaf: Leaf shapes include heart shapes, pointed palmate leaves or as in the variety, 'Sweet Caroline,' deeply cut leaves.

Flower: Insignificant; usually does not bloom on most varieties. A few have attractive flowers.

Lifespan: Lasts for one, full growing season in Texas because it won't tolerate freezes.

Origin: Tropical America

Spacing: About 12 to 18 inches on center (measure from the center of each plant). Closer in containers.

Cautions: Frequently damaged by deer.

Colors: Leaf colors include chartreuse, lime green, bronze, burgundy, or green with pink variegation.

1. 'Tricolor' sweet potato
2. 'Sweet Caroline Blackie'
3. 'Sweet Caroline Bronze'
4. 'Marguerite' sweet potato

Calling sweet potato vines easy might be a stretch because they grow too fast and attract insects. However, some new ones are much easier than their predecessors. Vibrant foliage stays lush from early summer to fall. Excellent, heat-proof foliage to mix with vigorous, spreading, summer flowers.

Sweet potato vines are most often used in containers. This window box (#ZWBS30 from kinsmangarden.com) features a Juncus grass as the centerpiece, surrounded by 'Dark Star' coleus, red wax begonias, and 'Black Heart' sweet potato vine.

Sweet potato vines tolerate heat extremely well and are not as thirsty as many other annuals. They are extremely easy to grow if you know what kind to buy and can put up with some holes in the leaves. We found the plants with heart-shaped leaves (like the leaves shown above) grew like a Jack-and-the-beanstalk and required frequent trimming. The ones shaped more like a maple leaf (see photo 2, left) grew much slower and were much easier to control, particularly the 'Sweet Caroline' variety. The lime and purple grew at about the same rate. The pink ones grew quite a bit slower but were not as dependable as the lime and purple ones.

Color Period: Occasionally, vines may produce small, morning glory-type flowers in late summer. Breeders are working on sweet potato vines that bloom more freely.

Buying Tips: Easy to find in the spring. Look for the ones with the maple-shaped leaves (see photos two and three , left) for the easiest care.

ANNUALS

Companions: Combine sweet potatoes with other plants that coordinate with the individual leaf colors. For a traffic-stopping color accent, plant lime green sweet potato with bright reds and purples, as shown below.

'Marguerite' sweet potato and some companion plants

Dragon Wing Begonias (above, left) are one of the brightest red flowers and contrast well with the lime green sweet potato. They grow taller than the sweet potato, so plant them as the tallest layer, surrounded by sweet potato.

Persian Shield (above, center) can be added for a dramatic color accent with the red begonias. Alternate the two taller plants, and border with the sweet potato.

'Defiance' Coleus (above, right) contrasts really well with lime sweet potato.

Put them all together in a container by using the Persian shield in the center, with a dragon wing begonia planted on either side. Alternate the 'Defiance' coleus and the lime sweet potato vines around the edge. Plant this mix in spring in a container 16 inches wide or larger, with top-quality potting mix and the fertilizer shown on page 37, and it will last you all season until the first frost of fall. Expect to trim the sweet potato a few times as well as pinch the tips off the coleus monthly. Place your container in light shade (or morning sun with afternoon shade) for best results.

GROWING CONDITIONS

Light: Light shade to full sun

Water: Medium. Keep soil lightly moist for 3 weeks after planting. Once established (pages 28 to 29), these vines can get by with weekly watering, if they are mulched. More water in containers.

Soil: For the garden, plant in any fertile, well-drained soil that has been enriched with organic matter. Use only good-quality potting mix for containers. See pages 22 to 25 for specific instructions on soil preparation.

Hardiness: Vines die when exposed to frost. Tubers must be stored above 55 degrees through the winter. Winter hardy in zones 9 through 11.

Propagation: Rooted cuttings; slips that grow from tubers.

Pest Problems: Flea beetles sometimes make pinholes in leaves; various June bugs may casually eat the leaves, too, particularly Japanese beetles. Deer love sweet potato vine foliage.

PLANTING & MAINTENANCE

When to Plant: Set out plants in late spring, after the soil has warmed. Tubers can be saved through winter in a warm, dry place and then planted in a warm bed in spring. "Slips" that grow from the tubers are easily transplanted to new beds or containers when they are 6 inches long.

Trimming: Stems can be trimmed back any time to control their spread. You can increase your supply of plants by rooting 4 inch long stem tips in damp potting soil.

Fertilization: Fertilize at planting time with a timed-release product. See pages 36 to 39 for more instructions.

Tapioca, Variegated

CHARACTERISTICS

Plant Type: Tropical plant that performs as an annual in north central Texas.

Average Size: About 3 to 4 feet tall by 5 feet wide.

Growth Rate: Medium

Leaf: Medium-green leaf margins with creamy-yellow centers and red leafstalks.

Flower: Inconspicuous; planted for foliage.

Lifespan: 7 months

Origin: Brazil

Spacing: About 3 to 4 feet on center (measure from the center of each plant).

Cautions: All parts of the plant (roots, leaves, etc.) contain cyanide compounds and SHOULD NOT BE EATEN. Pets won't eat enough to hurt themselves because all parts of the plant contain distasteful cyanide compounds and have a rough texture. Deer will eat tapioca, but it does not spoil the venison.

Colors: Flowers are inconspicuous. Leaves are green and yellow.

This plant provides bold, colorful foliage all summer long and takes all the heat that Texas has to offer! Adds a tropical look to the summer landscape. The Texas A & M AgriLife Extension Service has designated this plant a Texas Superstar™ plant. Rates a blue ribbon* for its ease of care.

This bold-leafed plant offers show-stopping color during the hottest part of the summer and adds a tropical look to the summer landscape. Variegated tapioca is easy to grow if it is planted in well-drained soil watered correctly (see 'Water' on opposite page). The plant's best characteristic is its variegated foliage, which rivals the color of any flower in the garden. It has been a staple at the Fort Worth Botanic Garden for several years in both beds and containers because it loves the intense heat of summer. Its worst characteristic is that all parts of the plant are poisonous if ingested by humans.

Color Period: From spring until the first, hard, frost of fall, continuously. Foliage is predominant. Flowers are inconspicuous.

Buying Tips: Readily available at better nurseries and garden centers

*Blue ribbon plants are defined on page 12. For blue ribbon performance, follow the planting and maintenance guidelines on pages 22 to 39.

Companions: Variegated tapioca combines well with any vibrant colored flower or foliage for a hot, tropical look. Red, orange, and purple look great with variegated tapioca. Ideal companion plants include red-leafed sun coleus, violet vinca, purple coneflower, hibiscus, and lantana.

Variegated tapioca works well as a background plant for vinca and purple heart, as shown below.

Variegated tapioca and some companion plants

'Cora Punch' Vinca (above, left) makes an excellent companion for tapioca. These non-stop, all-summer-long blooming annuals get 14 to 16 inches tall and should be placed in front of the taller tapioca.

Purple Heart (above, right) is a perennial ground cover that grows to about one foot tall, fitting nicely as a border in front of the vinca. purple heart gives you constant color from May until the first frost of fall. All three plants grow well in full sun.

GROWING CONDITIONS

Light: Full sun to partial sun; more intense color in full sun.

Water: Medium. Twice a week for plants in beds after the establishment period (pages 28 to 29); more water in containers.

Soil: For the garden, plant in any fertile, well-drained soil that has been enriched with organic matter. Use only good-quality potting mix for containers. See pages 22 to 25 for specific instructions on soil preparation.

Hardiness: Strictly a summer annual in north central Texas.

Propagation: Cuttings

Pest Problems: Rare

PLANTING & MAINTENANCE

When to Plant: After May 1. Does not grow vigorously until night temperatures are above 60 degrees.

Trimming: If any solid green leaves should appear, cut them out or they will become dominant over the variegated foliage.

Fertilization: Fertilize at planting time with a timed-release product. See pages 36 to 39 for more instructions.

ANNUALS

Torenia, Trailing

CHARACTERISTICS

Plant Type: Annual

Average Size: Trailing torenia grows only 2 to 6 inches tall by about 12 inches wide.

Growth Rate: Medium

Leaf: Medium green. About 3/4 inch long.

Flower: Small, tubular, trumpet-shaped flower.

Lifespan: The trailing form lasts the entire spring, summer, and fall growing season.

Origin: Vietnam

Spacing: About 12 inches on center for the trailing forms (measure from the center of each plant). Closer in containers.

Cautions: Sometimes damaged by deer.

Colors: Blue, purple, pink, white

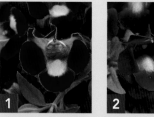

1. 'Catalina Midnight Blue'
2. 'Summer Wave Large Violet'
3. 'Summer Wave Amethyst'
4. 'Summer Wave Blue'

Trailing torenia is one of the best performing annuals in our trials, blooming from spring until the first frost of fall with very little care. This high performance earns it a blue ribbon.*

Torenia 'Summer Wave Large Violet' is the best performer of our torenia trials. It does equally well planted in containers or in the ground.

Torenia is a relatively new plant that deserves more use in Texas gardens. There are two main types: upright (we tested the 'Clown' series) and trailing (we tested the 'Summer Wave' series). The 'Clown' series did acceptably well, taking the early summer heat with ease but giving out in August. We still use it because of its beauty and shade tolerance. The trailing type did very well, lasting from spring until the first frost of fall with no care other than water. The 'Summer Wave,' 'Moon' and 'Catalina' series made the "Arboretum Approved" list at the Dallas Arboretum.

Color Period: Late spring to late fall, continuously

Buying Tips: Upright torenia is often sold in four inch pots or multipacks. You may need to look up at the hanging baskets for the trailing torenia.

Blue ribbon plants are defined on page 12. For blue ribbon performance, follow the planting and maintenance guidelines on pages 22 to 39.

Companions: Torenias make great borders for most plants that bloom in spring, summer, or fall. For a long-blooming garden, pair it with the shrubs and perennials shown below. If you can't find any of them at your local garden center, there are lots of internet suppliers.

'Catalina Midnight Blue' torenia

GROWING CONDITIONS

Light: Medium shade to full sun

Water: Medium. Ideal water is twice a week after establishment (pages 28 to 29), if the plants are in shade. In sun, during the hottest days of summer, they may require water 2 to 3 times per week. Requires more water when grown in containers.

Soil: For the garden, plant in any fertile, well-drained soil that has been enriched with organic matter. Use only good-quality potting mix for containers. See pages 22 to 25 for specific instructions on soil preparation.

Hardiness: Not tolerant of even cool (45 degree) temperatures.

Propagation: Seeds or cuttings, depending on variety.

Pest Problems: Rare

PLANTING & MAINTENANCE

When to Plant: Spring or summer

Trimming: None required

Fertilization: Fertilize at planting time with a timed-release product. See pages 36 to 39 for more instructions.

'Let's Dance Starlight' Hydrangea
Plant Profile: Page 220

'Stella de Oro' Daylily
Plant Profile: Page 122

'Summer Wave Large Violet' torenia and some companion plants

'Let's Dance Starlight' Hydrangea (above, left) is one of the newer, reblooming hydrangeas that blooms for about three months in summer, June through August. Again, trailing torenia is a gorgeous border for this shrub.

'Stella de Oro' Daylily (above, right) is one of the longest blooming perennial daylilies, blooming for up to three months each summer. Torenia is an ideal border for daylilies and the hydrangea. Plant all three in light shade.

'Summer Wave Amethyst' torenia with New Guinea impatiens and vinca 'Illumination.'

Vinca, 'Cora' Series

1ST

CHARACTERISTICS

Plant Type: Annual

Average Size: 14 to 16 inches tall; 2 feet wide.

Growth Rate: Fast

Leaf: Glossy, dark green, oblong leaves with prominent central leaf veins.

Flower: Flat blossoms to 2 inches across, often with contrasting eyes.

Lifespan: 6 to 7 months

Origin: Madagascar

Spacing: About 10 inches on center (measure from the center of each plant). Closer in containers.

Cautions: Seldom damaged by deer. A leaf extract is used in the treatment of cancer.

Colors: Apricot, pink, burgundy, lavender, deep lavender, violet or white.

1. 'Cora Pink' vinca
2. 'Cora Punch' vinca
3. 'Cora White' vinca
4. 'Cora Lavender' vinca

Demonstrating heat, drought, and disease resistance, the 'Cora' series of vinca makes an outstanding bedding plant for hot summers in north central Texas. Easily rates a blue ribbon* if provided with excellent drainage.

'Cora Deep Lavendar' vinca

The 'Cora' series of vinca represents a major breakthrough for vinca. In the past, vinca succumbed to a disease that made many gardeners in Texas stop using vinca altogether. The 'Cora' series is resistant to this disease and one of the easiest annuals for north central Texas.

'Cora' vinca takes heat and drought very well, but insists on good drainage. Planting it in a raised bed is an easy way to ensure the drainage it needs.

The 'Cora' series earned both the "Arboretum Approved" and the "Flame Proof" awards for 2007 at the Dallas Arboretum; in addition, this series is a 2007 winner of the North Texas Winner's Circle Awards. Vincas often reseed in the garden, but the offspring of hybrid plants are seldom as vigorous or colorful as their parents. It is best to pull them out.

Color Period: Late spring to late fall, continuously

Buying Tips: Extremely easy to find at the garden centers in spring and summer. All we bought did quite well, provided it didn't rain too much.

*Blue ribbon plants are defined on page 12. For blue ribbon performance, follow the planting and maintenance guidelines on pages 22 to 39.

Companions: Vincas are great companions for any other annuals in this chapter that like sun. They also make great accents in perennial beds. Try 'Cora Burgundy' vinca with the perennials shown below, and you will have about five months of color in your bed.

'Cora Burgundy' vinca and some companion plants

'Luna' Hibiscus
Plant Profile: Page 134

'Stella de Oro' Daylily
Plant Profile: Page 122

Purple Heart
Plant Profile: Page 152

'Luna' Hibiscus (above, left) is an excellent perennial companion for vinca. It reaches about two to three feet tall and blooms from July until September. Its flowers are huge - up to seven inches across - and contrast well with the smaller vinca flowers. Use the vinca as a border for the hibiscus.

'Stella de Oro' Daylily (above, center) is one of the longest blooming perennial daylilies, blooming for up to three months each summer. It reaches about 18 to 24 inches tall. Vinca is an ideal border for daylilies.

Purple Heart (above, right) is another perennial companion for vinca. They have color for the entire spring, summer, and fall growing season and reach about a foot tall - the same as most vincas. Alternate clumps of vinca and purple heart for a low border for perennials.

Put them all together for a long blooming garden by planting the hibiscus as the tallest layer and the daylilies in the middle. Alternate clumps of vinca and purple heart as a border.

GROWING CONDITIONS

Light: Full sun, at least 6 hours per day.

Water: Medium to low. Water twice weekly for the first month after planting. Once established (pages 28 to 29), vincas can get by with weekly water, provided they are mulched. Requires more water in containers.

Soil: For the garden, plant in any fertile, well-drained soil that has been enriched with organic matter. Use only good-quality potting mix for containers. See pages 22 to 25 for specific instructions on soil preparation.

Hardiness: Not tolerant of frosts

Propagation: Seeds

Pest Problems: Root rot can develop if plants are kept too wet.

PLANTING & MAINTENANCE

When to Plant: In late spring or early summer, after most of the spring rains are over.

Trimming: None needed

Fertilization: Fertilize at planting time with a timed-release product. See pages 36 to 39 for more instructions.

'Cora Apricot' vinca

1ST

CHARACTERISTICS

Plant Type: Annual

Average Size: 12 to 18 inches tall and wide for the 'Profusion' series; 12 inches tall and 20 inches wide for 'Solcito.'

Growth Rate: Fast

Leaf: Oval, medium-green leaves with pointed tips.

Flower: 'Profusion' flowers are 1 1/2 to 2 inches wide; 'Solcito' flowers are 1 inch wide.

Lifespan: About 6 months

Origin: Mexico

Spacing: About 12 inches on center (measure from the center of each plant). Closer in containers.

Cautions: Seldom damaged by deer.

Colors: 'Profusion' series comes in apricot, cherry, fire, orange, or white; 'Solcito' flowers are dark, golden yellow with brown centers.

1. *'Profusion Apricot' zinnia*
2. *'Profusion Cherry' zinnia*
3. *'Profusion Deep Apricot' zinnia*
4. *'Profusion Fire' zinnia*

Zinnia 'Profusion' and 'Solcito' demonstrate compact growth habit, continuous flower production, and incredible resistance to powdery mildew and leaf spot. They definitely rate a blue ribbon* because of their summer-long, continuous bloom and ease of care.

'Profusion Coral Pink' zinnias

Many Texans have given up on zinnias because of frequent disease problems. However, there are two small zinnias that are disease-resistant and have proved very high performers in the tough Texas environment. The 'Profusion' and 'Solcito' zinnias bloom profusely and tolerate full sun, heat, and drought, which is typical of summers in north central Texas. The newest color of the 'Profusion' zinnias, 'Profusion Fire,' is a deep scarlet-orange that stands out from a distance. The drawback to 'Profusion Cherry' in our climate is that it fades during our sun-drenched summers. Both zinnias require very little care and bloom their heads off without deadheading (removing dead flowers). Butterflies love both zinnias as well.

Zinnia 'Solcito' hails from Hawaii and has tremendous disease resistance. The black and yellow flowers actually resemble little sunflowers.

Both the 'Profusion' and 'Solcito' zinnias won the 2007 'Flame Proof' designation at the Dallas Arboretum. 'Solcito' won the 2007 North Texas Winner's Circle Award.

Color Period: Late spring to late fall, blooming constantly

Buying Tips: Both these zinnias can be found in four inch pots or multipacks at many garden centers in spring.

Blue ribbon plants are defined on page 12. For blue ribbon performance, follow the planting and maintenance guidelines on pages 22 to 39.

Companions: 'Profusion' and 'Solcito' zinnias (right) combine well with annuals, such as purple gomphrena, portulaca, purslane, and vinca. They work well as borders for most shrubs and perennials.

For a country garden look, mix them with perennial salvias and lantana. Or, try the combination of annuals and shrubs shown below.

GROWING CONDITIONS

Light: Full sun

Water: Medium. Zinnias can tolerate drought but grow best when they receive water twice a week after the establishment period (pages 28 to 29). Require more water in containers.

Soil: For the garden, plant in any fertile, well-drained soil that has been enriched with organic matter. Use only good-quality potting mix for containers. See pages 22 to 25 for specific instructions on soil preparation.

Hardiness: Cannot tolerate frost

Propagation: Grows easily from seeds.

Pest Problems: None known

PLANTING & MAINTENANCE

When to Plant: Spring or summer

Trimming: None needed. Removing dead flowers will result in a few more blooms.

Fertilization: Fertilize at planting time with a timed-release product. See pages 36 to 39 for more instructions.

'Purple Emperor' Butterfly Bush
Plant Profile: Page 194

'Flamenco' Cuphea
Plant Profile: Page 56

'Solcito' zinnias and some companion plants

'Purple Emperor' Butterfly Bush (above, left) is a great companion for the 'Solcito' zinnia because the color, size, and shape of the flowers are so different. Most of the newer, compact butterfly bushes, like this 'Purple Emperor,' grow to about four feet tall, so put it in the back of the bed, surrounded by the zinnias and cuphea. It blooms for about five to six months in summer and fall.

'Flamenco' Cuphea (above, right) grows to about the same height as the zinnias. Alternate the cuphea with the zinnias, and plant both in front of the taller butterfly bush. All three plants like sun and bloom for the majority of the spring, summer, and fall season.

'Profusion White' zinnia

Other Annuals that Deserve Mention

Celosia
Celosia spp.

We've had mixed results with these plants. Some have lasted 6 months, while others have struggled to make it 2 months. Generally, taller varieties did better than dwarfs. 6 to 20 inches tall. Sun. Medium water.

Copper Leaf
Acalypha spp.

Excellent tropical shrub used as an annual in Texas. Used primarily for leaf color. Many varieties available. All the different ones we have tried did very well. Light shade to full sun. 2 to 8 feet tall in the tropics. Medium water.

Cosmos
Cosmos spp.

Summer annual that reseeds freely. Gorgeous flowers, but the plants don't stay in bloom continuously for the whole season. Lasts about 3 months. About 18 inches tall. Sun. Low water.

Croton
Codiaeum variegatum

An excellent tropical shrub used as an annual in Texas. Lasts from spring until fall. Overwinters well in a garage if you give it light and occasional water (weekly). Medium shade to full sun. 1 to 4 feet tall. Low water.

Dichondra 'Silver Falls'
Dichondra argenta 'Silver Falls'

A fabulous silver vine that is one of the best container plants for Texas summers. It requires almost no care and gives incredible performance. Lasts from spring to fall. Light shade to full sun. Trails down as far as 8 feet. Low water.

Dracaena
Dracaena spp.

One of the most common indoor plants. They work well outdoors, provided they are protected from frost. Really easy. Lasts all season and overwinters well indoors. Dense to light shade. 1 to 30 feet tall. Low water.

Duranta 'Gold Mound'
Duranta erecta 'Gold Mound'

An excellent, lime-green, foliage plant that breezes through the hottest summer Texas has to offer. Full sun. 8 inches tall. Low water.

Euphorbia 'Diamond Frost'
Euphorbia 'Diamond Frost'

We have had only one season's experience with this wildly popular plant. It performed quite well all summer in beds and containers at the Fort Worth Botanic garden. Light shade to sun. 12 to 18 inches tall. Low water.

Firebush
Hamelia patens

If butterflies are your thing, then your garden must have a firebush, even in the colder parts of zone 7 (treat as an annual). Orange flowers for 3 to 4 months on 3 to 4 foot mounded shrubs. Full sun. Medium water. Zones 8 to 11.

Gerber Daisy
Gerbera jamesonii

Lovely but very short-lived plant. Only lives and blooms for about a month. Some people have good luck with it as a perennial, but we never have. 12 inches tall. Sun. Medium water.

Heather, Mexican
Cuphea hyssopifolia

Extremely heat-tolerant annual that blooms for about 6 months in summer. Not showy. Mix with bright-colored, large-flowered companions. About 12 inches tall. Medium water. Light shade to full sun.

Hibiscus, Tropical
Hibiscus rosa-sinensis

Tropical shrub that is quite popular in Texas as a summer patio plant. Easy to overwinter in the garage. Grows 2 to 4 feet per season. Lots of colors. Medium water. Light shade to full sun.

Hyacinth Bean
Dolichos lablab

A fast grower, hyacinth bean vines will twine on any type of trellis, or you can let them ramble over a stump. Blooms from late summer to early fall. Easy to grow. 4 to 6 feet tall. Sun. Medium water.

Joseph's Coat
Alternanthera spp.

An up-and-coming plant that is getting rave reviews throughout Texas because of its heat tolerance. Use for leaf color. Full sun. Different varieties range from 4 to 20 inches tall. Low water.

Licorice Plant
Helichrysum petiolare

Did well in our containers but developed some mildew by the end of summer (didn't show much). Lasted 6 months. Great color for containers. Light shade to sun. 8 to 12 inches tall. Low water.

Lysimachia 'Outback Sunset'
Lysimachia 'Outback Sunset'

Semi-trailing plant that did very well in our container trials. Didn't bloom all summer, but the leaf color lasted. Takes some sun, but does better in medium to light shade. Grows about 8 inches down the sides of a pot. Medium water.

Mandevilla Vine
Mandevilla spp.

A tropical vine that does very well in hot, Texas summers as an annual. Bright, pink flowers on a fast-growing vine. Grows about 10 to 12 feet long. Full sun. Medium water.

Marigold
Tagetes spp.

Very popular Texas annual but only lasted a few months in our gardens. Melampodium is a much better yellow annual. Full sun. 6 to 30 inches tall. Medium water.

Mint, Variegated
Plectranthus coleoides 'Variegata'

Fabulous container plant. Lasts all season, from spring until the first frost of fall. Trails 36 inches down the sides of a container, but slowly. Medium to light shade. Medium water.

Perilla Magilla
Perilla frutescens 'Magilla'

Great plant that is very similar to coleus. Rates a red ribbon because it looks better with monthly pinching. Lasts all spring, summer, and fall in Texas. Medium to light shade. 2 to 4 feet tall. Medium water.

Phlox
Phlox spp.

The best annual phlox in our trials is 'Phlox Intensia' that blooms for most of the season. Perennial phlox are covered in chapter 3. Full sun. 12 to 14 inches tall. Medium water.

Phormium
Phormium spp

Phormium or flax is an excellent, blue ribbon plant. Extremely easy. Likes temperatures from 40 to over 100. Overwinter it inside with bright light. Light shade to full sun outdoors. 2 feet tall. Low water.

Plumbago
Plumbago auriculata

Plumbago is a great perennial in the ground in zones 9 to 11. It is taking off as an easy annual in north central Texas. Blooms for most of the spring, summer, and fall. Full sun. 2 to 3 feet tall. Low water.

Verbena, Annual
Verbena spp.

Trailing annual verbena lasts about 3 months each summer. The upright form died in about a month. See Chapter 3 for profile of perennial verbena. Sun. Medium water.

Chapter 3

Perennials

✿ Perennials are plants that come back to life year after year, usually following a winter rest. They do not need to be replanted each spring, which saves time and money.

✿ Most perennials are deciduous, meaning they die back in winter. However, some – like lenten rose, autumn ferns, some grasses, and heucheras – are evergreen.

✿ Perennials generally have soft stems that die back with the leaves in winter. Shrubs have hard, woody stems that do not die back, even if they lose their leaves.

✿ Perennials don't bloom as long as annuals. And, they usually do not have as much color impact. However, by combining perennials with other perennials or shrubs that bloom at the same time, major color impact can be achieved with plants that don't require yearly replacement.

✿ This chapter details color combinations that add wonderful color to your garden.

✿ Perennials in this chapter are basically easy to grow. All of them require at least one trimming a year. Many look better with deadheading (removal of dead flowers) but don't require it. Most have a longer flowering period if you have time to do this chore.

✿ Dividing is another maintenance chore common to most perennials, either to rejuvenate the clump or to get more plants. Some perennials require division every few years, and others don't.

Left: This garden features shrubs, annuals, and perennials. The dark-colored shrubs in the background are loropetalum. Perennials include daylilies, cannas, and purple heart. The pink vinca are annuals.

Agastache, Hummingbird Mint

1ST

CHARACTERISTICS

Plant Type: Deciduous perennial (dies back in winter).

Average Size: 36 inches tall and 18 inches wide.

Growth Rate: Medium

Leaf: Slightly-fuzzy, green leaves have a minty, licorice scent when crushed.

Flower: Tall, upright spikes studded with numerous tiny flowers that attract bees, hummingbirds, and butterflies.

Origin: Native species, such as *A. foeniculum*, crossed with others.

Spacing: About 18 inches on center (measure from the center of each plant). In 3 years, a single plant will form a 2 foot wide clump.

Cautions: Attracts bees, but almost never eaten by deer.

Flower Colors: Lavender-blue, pink, coral.

Agastache is a great butterfly and hummingbird plant, offering both ease of care and drought tolerance. Removal of dead flowers is not needed to keep it blooming for a full three months. Rates a blue ribbon* because it gives a lot for just a little bit of your time.

Agastache 'Tutti-Frutti' with caladiums and purple fountain grass

New varieties of agastache are definitely worthy of space in your perennial garden. 'Blue Fortune' is but one of several new hybrids making its way into nurseries. The Fort Worth Botanic Garden has been pleased with the performance of 'Blue Fortune' in its perennial trial garden.

Expect a modest bloom the first year, with a much more robust clump and heavier set of flowers in subsequent seasons.

Color Period: Late spring to late fall, blooming constantly

Buying Tips: Lots of new agastaches are constantly appearing. Some have the reputation for getting a bit rangy. We have only tried the three pictured (left) and have been happy with all of them.

1. *Agastache 'Blue Fortune'*
2. *Agastache 'Tutti-Frutti'*
3. *Agastache 'Acapulco'*

*Blue ribbon plants are defined on page 12. For blue ribbon performance, follow the planting and maintenance guidelines on pages 22 to 39.

Companions: Agastache likes plenty of sun and rather dry conditions, so it is best teamed up with other dry garden standouts, such as black-eyed Susans or ornamental grasses. 'Blue Fortune' looks great with mound-forming yellow flowers, such as coreopsis, or you can pair it with drought-tolerant annuals like cuphea, gomphrena, or 'Profusion' zinnia.

'Blue Fortune' grows three feet tall when it's in full bloom, so it has no trouble rising up behind a foreground planting of coreopsis. Because of its upright form and bottlebrush-shaped flower spikes, agastache is ideal for mixing with mounding plants that have daisy-shaped blossoms.

Since 'Blue Fortune' has such a long bloom period, pair it with some other Texas stars for a bed that blooms all season long, as shown below.

Agastache 'Blue Fortune' and some companions for easy color layers

Black-eyed Susans (above, left) are one of the best perennials to use with 'Blue Fortune' because they both bloom for most of the summer, like full sun, and have different shaped flowers. The blue and yellow colors contrast well, too. Since black-eyed Susans grow to about 18 inches tall, plant them in front of the 'Blue Fortune.'

'Knock Out' Roses (above, right) bloom spring, summer, and fall, so they will keep the bed in color for the entire growing season. These tough roses crave sun, like both the black-eyed Susans and agastaches. They grow taller than the 'Blue Fortune,' so plant them as the tallest plant in the bed.

GROWING CONDITIONS

Light: Full sun

Water: Medium after establishment. Likes water once or twice a week during the growing season.

Soil: For the garden, plant in any fertile, well-drained soil that has been enriched with organic matter. Use only good-quality potting mix for containers.

Hardiness: Zones 6 to 10

Propagation: Division in spring. Better yet, root 4-inch-long stem tip cuttings taken in early summer. Hybrid plants do not breed true from seed.

Pest Problems: Rare

PLANTING & MAINTENANCE

When to Plant: Agastache from containers can be planted anytime. Fall is best because they establish easier in cooler weather, but you are more likely to find them at your garden center in spring or summer when they are blooming. Expect a modest bloom the first year, with a much more robust clump and heavier set of flowers in subsequent seasons.

Trimming: Agastaches don't need much trimming when they are blooming. Removing dead flowers is not necessary, but the plants might need some neatening up at some point in the summer. Cut back the dead foliage (to the ground) in late fall or early winter after it freezes.

Fertilization: Medium. Fertilize at planting time and annually with a timed-release product. Less fertilizer is needed with the application of more organics.

Division: Divide in spring or fall, but fall is better. Division is not necessary to keep the plant healthy, so do it every 3 to 5 years, only if you want more plants.

PERENNIALS

Aquilegia, 'Texas Gold' Columbine

1ST

CHARACTERISTICS

Plant Type: Deciduous perennial (dies back in winter).

Average Size: 2 feet tall and 18 inches wide.

Growth Rate: Moderate

Leaf: Bluish-green with scalloped edges, about 1 inch across; delicate texture.

Flower: Cup with long spurs attached; about 3 inches long.

Origin: Moist, shady sites in the Big Bend area of west Texas.

Spacing: 18 inches on center (measure from the center of each plant).

Cautions: None; moderately deer-resistant.

Colors: Flowers are buttery-yellow

One of the best shade blooming perennials for north central Texas, 'Texas Gold' columbine produces attractive, buttery-yellow flowers in the spring, attracts hummingbirds, and holds up to the heat of Texas summers. This is definitely a blue-ribbon* plant, and it's rated a Texas Superstar™ plant by the Texas A & M AgriLife Extension Service.

'Texas Gold' columbine, when planted in drifts in dappled shade, makes a spectacular showing of graceful, buttery-yellow flowers during the month of April. 'Texas Gold' is a true perennial, persisting several years in the landscape without dying during the hot summers in north central Texas. The flowers attract hummingbirds during their spring migration, exude a pleasing fragrance, and make good cut flowers. 'Texas Gold' columbine foliage may suffer from spider mites or leaf miners mid to late summer, and plants will die if planted in dense shade.

Color Period: Late March through early May for about four weeks

Buying Tips: Many garden centers feature columbine hybrids from up north; these don't hold up to the heat during Texas summers and soon die. So be sure to look for 'Texas Gold,' which can be found in local garden centers, especially those that sell native plants.

*Blue ribbon plants are defined on page 12. For blue ribbon performance, follow the planting and maintenance guidelines on pages 22 to 39.

Companions: 'Texas Gold' columbine combines very well with spring-flowering bulbs, perennials, and ferns. Plant it in large drifts beneath deciduous trees for an excellent color accent. It's especially pretty when planted near southern wood ferns, daffodils, summer snowflakes, and Spanish bluebells.

Try the combination shown below for easy color layers.

Encore Azalea
Plant Profile: Page 188

Spanish Bluebells
Plant Profile: Page 162

Columbine with some companions

Encore Azaleas (above, left) bloom at the same time as columbine and create a colorful backdrop. Since the azaleas grow four to five feet tall, use the columbine in front. Both plants do well in light shade.

Spanish Bluebells (above, right) bloom at the same time as the columbine and like the same light shade. Since the bluebells reach a shorter height of 12 to 15 inches, plant them in a drift in front of the columbine.

GROWING CONDITIONS

Light: Light shade beneath deciduous trees is ideal. Avoid dense, continual shade.

Water: Medium after establishment. Likes water once or twice a week during the growing season, depending on its environment. See pages 28 to 33 for more information.

Soil: Well-drained, high in organic matter.

Hardiness: Zones 5 to 9

Propagation: Seed

Pest Problems: Spider mites and leaf miners may bother the foliage, leaving it unattractive by mid to late summer. If this happens, cut foliage down to a mound a few inches tall; new leaves will emerge when cooler, fall temperatures arrive.

PLANTING & MAINTENANCE

When to Plant: 'Texas Gold' from containers can be planted at any time. Fall is best because they establish more easily in cooler weather, but you are more likely to find them at your garden center in early spring when they are blooming.

Trimming: Summer, if the foliage looks tacky. Otherwise, cut back the dead foliage (to the ground) in late fall or early winter after it freezes.

Fertilization: Apply slow-release fertilizer high in nitrogen during October, December, and February to stimulate foliage production. See pages 36 to 39 for more instructions.

Division: Divide in fall if the original clump has died out in the center or you want more plants.

PERENNIALS

Amaryllis, Hardy Red

1ST

CHARACTERISTICS

Plant Type: Deciduous (dies back in winter) perennial bulb.

Average Size: 2 feet tall and equally as wide.

Growth Rate: Medium

Leaf: Medium green, smooth, strap-shaped, up to 2 feet long.

Flower: Trumpet-shaped, 4 to 5 inches wide, in clusters on 2 foot stems.

Origin: South America

Spacing: 1 foot on center (measure from the center of each plant).

Cautions: None known. Moderately deer resistant.

Colors: Flowers are bright red with a white stripe down the center of each petal.

Spectacular, spring-flowering bulb well-suited to the clay soils of north central Texas. This is a cold-hardy amaryllis that returns year after year to produce a myriad of flowers each spring. It is definitely a blue ribbon plant* because of its adaptability to our growing conditions, its low maintenance, and its show-stopping blooms.

Hardy red amaryllis is an easy-to-grow, heirloom bulb that makes a striking statement in the spring garden with its abundance of bright red, trumpet-shaped flowers. Plant this bulb in just about any kind of garden soil - even unamended clay - and leave it alone Within a few years, the original bulbs multiply and form a large clump. Leaves appear after the flowers bloom in the spring and persist through the summer. Partial shade is best for the foliage of the hardy red amaryllis, although the plant will grow in full sun if watered well during the summer.

Hardy red amaryllis is the earliest of all amaryllis hybrids. It was produced by an English watchmaker named Johnson somewhere between 1799 and 1812. The flowers of this hybrid may not be as large as the flowers of the modern Dutch hybrids, but it produces more flowers per stem. It also lives longer in the garden than the modern hybrids because most of them are bred for growing in pots.

Regional Differences: A zone eight plant

Color Period: Blooms continuously for about three weeks beginning in early April.

Buying Tips: This plant is occasionally available in some garden centers and through online bulb companies that specialize in heirloom plants. The Fort Worth Botanic Garden often offers this plant at its spring and fall plant sales.

*Blue ribbon plants are defined on page 12. For blue ribbon performance, follow the planting and maintenance guidelines on pages 22 to 39.

Companions: Hardy, red amaryllis combines very well with other spring-flowering plants, such as irises and columbines. Alternate clumps of those plants for a spectacular effect, as shown below.

'Texas Gold'
Columbine
Plant Profile: page 124

Iris
Plant Profile: Page 138

Amaryllis and some companions

'Texas Gold' Columbine (above, top) blooms at the same time as amaryllis and offers contrast in flower color, form of plant, and in leaf shape. Since the two plants grow about the same height (two feet), plant them in clumps beside each other.

Irises (above, bottom) bloom about the same time as the amaryllis and offer contrast in flower shape and color. Blue irises would contrast well with the yellow columbine and the red amaryllis. Irises grow in a wide range of sizes, so arrange the three plants based on the height of the iris. If your iris grows about two feet tall, it works well to alternate clumps in between the columbine and amaryllis. All three plants grow well in light shade.

*Lives on rainwater alone in all but the most extreme situations.

GROWING CONDITIONS

Light: Light shade to full sun

Water: Very low after establishment. Lives on rainwater alone, without supplemental water, in all but the most extreme conditions. See pages 28 to 33 for more information.

Soil: Any good, garden soil. Amaryllis does very well in the heavy clay soils of north central Texas.

Hardiness: Zones 7 through 10

Propagation: Division of clumps

Pest Problems: No serious insect or disease problems.

PLANTING & MAINTENANCE

When to Plant: Amaryllis from containers can be planted at any time. Fall is best because they establish more easily in cooler weather, but you are more likely to find them at your garden center in early spring when they are blooming.

Planting Depth: Cover with soil to the neck of the bulb.

Trimming: Remove old, dead leaves at the end of the summer.

Fertilization: Medium. Fertilize at planting time and annually with a timed-release product. Less fertilizer is needed with the application of more organics. See pages 36 to 39 for more instructions.

Division: Clumps may be divided in the fall after the leaves have died down; reset in the ground with the necks of the bulbs left slightly above ground level.

PERENNIALS

Artemisia

CHARACTERISTICS

Plant Type: Perennial that may hold its leaves well into the winter.

Average Size: 3 feet tall and equally as wide.

Growth Rate: Fast

Leaf: Silver, fine-textured, aromatic when crushed.

Flower: None

Origin: Mediterranean

Spacing: 3 feet on center (measure from the center of each plant).

Cautions: None. Moderately deer resistant.

Colors: No flowers on this cultivar; strictly a foliage plant. The leaves are silver.

Artemisia with petunias in a three-tiered planter from www.kinsman-garden.com.

Artemisia is an excellent, silver-leafed perennial that contrasts well with red, pink, or purple flowers. Its soft-textured, aromatic foliage is its most striking feature. These attributes, along with low water requirements, make this perennial a blue ribbon plant.*

'Powis Castle' artemisia is an easy-to-grow perennial that provides beautiful contrast to many colors in the garden. It makes a great "filler plant" – one that fills in the holes among other perennials and shrubs. However, if grown in wet, poorly-drained soils, it will die from root rot. Also, stems tend to lean outward during the summer, thus creating an open center.

Color Period: This artemisia does not bloom, but its leaves are colorful in spring, summer, and fall for about 27 weeks.

Buying Tips: Easily found at nurseries and garden centers

Blue ribbon plants are defined on page 12. For blue ribbon performance, follow the planting and maintenance guidelines on pages 22 to 39.

Companions: 'Powis Castle,' with its finely-textured and silvery foliage, makes a lovely foil for plants with red, pink, purple or blue flowers. It is combined with purple heliotrope in the container shown right.

'Knock Out' roses and purple heart make great companions for artemisia because they contrast well and offer months of color.

Artemisia with some companions

'Knock Out' Roses (above, left) bloom almost continuously spring to fall and really stand out against the silver foliage of 'Powis Castle.' Since 'Knock Out' roses easily grows four feet tall, plant the slightly lower 'Powis Castle' as a border in front of the roses. Plant this combination in full sun near your mailbox or in a prominent bed for traffic-stopping attention.

Purple Heart (above, right) is one of the best perennial companions for artemisia because its color contrasts so beautifully, and it keeps its color from spring until the first frost of fall. Border the artemisia with the shorter-growing purple heart. Both do well in sun.

GROWING CONDITIONS

Light: Full sun

Water: Low after establishment. Likes water every week or two during the growing season, depending on its environment. See pages 28 to 33 for more information.

Soil: Any fertile, well-drained soil that has been enriched with organic matter. Requires good drainage. See pages 22 to 25 for instructions.

Hardiness: Zones 6 to 9

Propagation: Underground rhizomes, division.

Pest Problems: No serious insect or disease problems.

PLANTING & MAINTENANCE

When to Plant: Artemisia from containers can be planted at any time. Fall is best because they establish more easily in cooler weather, but you are more likely to find them at your garden center in early spring.

Trimming: Cut back the dead foliage to six inches after it freezes in late fall or early winter.

Fertilization: Low. Fertilize at planting time with a timed-release product. Less fertilizer is needed with the application of more organics. In the years after planting, fertilization needs vary, based on the nutrients in your soil. See pages 36 to 39 for more instructions.

PERENNIALS

Aster, Fall

1ST

CHARACTERISTICS

Plant Type: Deciduous perennial (dies back in winter).

Average Size: About 2 feet tall by 3 feet wide.

Growth Rate: Medium

Leaf: Medium green, up to 1 inch long and 1/2 inch wide.

Flower: Daisy-like, 1 inch across

Origin: Great Plains of U.S.

Spacing: 2 to 3 feet on center (measure from the center of each plant).

Cautions: None known. Somewhat resistant to deer.

Colors: Flowers have lavender petals with yellow centers.

Native, fall-blooming perennial that produces showy lavender flowers that attract butterflies. The lavender flowers contrast nicely with the abundance of yellow and orange flowers that commonly bloom in the fall. Holds up to Texas' hot summers. Rates a blue ribbon* because of its low-maintenance requirements.

The showy, lavender flowers that absolutely cover this plant make a spectacular statement in the fall garden. Fall aster prefers full sun and grows easily in average, dry to medium, well-drained soil, even tolerating poor soils and drought. A compact, bushy plant, it draws little attention to itself during the summer as it waits its turn to put on a magnificent show in the fall. In addition to their beauty, asters serve as nectar plants for several species of butterflies, and monarchs often stop to sip aster nectar as they migrate southward in fall.

Color Period: Late September to October. Blooms last three to four weeks.

Buying Tips: Available at garden centers, especially those that specialize in native plants.

Blue ribbon plants are defined on page 12. For blue ribbon performance, follow the planting and maintenance guidelines on pages 22 to 39.

Companions: Fall aster is one of the few plants that produce lavender blooms in the fall. These daisy-like flowers contrast beautifully with yellow- and orange-blooming flowers commonly seen in the fall. The lavender color also looks good with the silver leaves of the artemisia.

For high color impact, combine the aster with yellow and pink flowers that bloom at the same time, as shown below.

Fall aster and some companions

Mexican Mint Marigold (above, left) is perhaps the very best companion for fall aster because it's the same height and blooms at the same time. The yellow flowers contrast beautifully with the lavender flowers of fall aster.

Autumn Sage (above, right) is a perennial that grows about the same height as both the aster and the marigold. It blooms from April through October, so its bloom period corresponds as well. Alternate clumps of the three plants, and keep them in full sun.

GROWING CONDITIONS

Light: Full sun

Water: Medium after establishment. Likes water once or twice a week during the growing season, depending on its environment. See pages 28 to 33 for more information.

Soil: Plant in any fertile, well-drained soil that has been enriched with organic matter. See pages 22 to 25 for specific instructions on soil preparation.

Hardiness: Zones 3 to 8

Propagation: In spring, use a hand trowel to dig up the small, rooted stems that emerge from the base of the old plant.

Pest Problems: No serious insect or disease problems.

PLANTING & MAINTENANCE

When to Plant: Asters from containers can be planted at any time. Fall is best because they establish more easily in cooler weather.

Trimming: In mid May, cut back stems by 1/3 to delay bloom until fall and to induce heavier blooming in the fall. Cut back the dead foliage (to the ground) after it freezes in late fall or early winter.

Fertilization: Low. Fertilize at planting time with a timed-release product. Less fertilizer is needed with the application of more organics. In the years after planting, fertilization needs vary, based on the nutrients in your soil. See pages 36 to 39 for more instructions.

Division: Divisions taken from established clumps can be dug and moved until the first of June. Every 2 to 3 years in spring, dig and divide established clumps. The outer growth usually has the most healthy plants. Discard the center if it looks bad.

PERENNIALS

Black-Eyed Susan

CHARACTERISTICS

Plant Type: Deciduous perennial (dies back in winter).

Average Size: About 2 feet tall by 1 to 2 feet wide for the 'Goldsturm' variety.

Growth Rate: Moderate for its first year; faster after that.

Leaf: Somewhat coarse green leaves, slightly hairy.

Flower: 3 to 6 inches across, daisy-like.

Origin: Native to central and eastern U.S.

Spacing: About 18 inches on center (measure from the center of each plant). They will grow together into clumps.

Cautions: None known. Occasional damage by deer.

Colors: Flowers have yellow-orange petals (sometimes with mahogany markings) surrounding a dark brown, black, or green center.

These are annual black-eyed Susans, which last only about 6 months. Be sure to check the plant tag on the black-eyed Susans you see at your garden center. They could be annuals rather than the 'Goldsturm' perennials described on these two pages.

One of the easiest and longest blooming perennials for Texas. Bold gold color all summer and into fall. Beyond providing vibrant summer color, black-eyed Susans attract butterflies and make superb cut flowers. Looks better when deadheaded (dead flowers removed), so it just misses a ribbon.

Black-eyed Susans are present in most perennial gardens in Texas for good reasons. Easy to grow and tolerant of heat and drought, vigorous varieties, such as 'Goldsturm,' often bloom for three months. 'Goldsturm' was named Perennial Plant of the Year in 1999 and is on the roster of Louisiana Select Plants, too. 'Goldsturm' grows about two feet tall by two and a half feet wide, a useful size for perennial gardens.

So many other new cultivars of black-eyed Susans come on the market each year that it is hard to keep up with all of them! We don't know if you can make a bad choice because all we have tried have done well, although the 'Goldsturm' is our favorite.

Color Period: June through July, if you don't deadhead (remove the dead flowers). June through September, if you do.

Buying Tips: Our favorite is 'Goldsturm,' which is usually well labeled at the garden center. Black-eyed Susans also come in an annual form (*Rudbeckia hirta)* that lives for only about six months.

Companions: Black-eyed Susans are one of the most valuable plants for summer gardens because of their color intensity and long bloom period. 'Knock Out' roses share the long bloom period and look good behind black-eyed Susans. Scabiosa also has a long bloom period and works well as a border for black-eyed Susans.

For both intense color and a long bloom period, combine black-eyed Susans with the plants shown below.

'Cherry Dazzle' Crapemyrtle
Plant Profile: Page 206

'Homestead Purple' Verbena
Plant Profile: Page 170

Black-eyed Susans with some companions for easy color layers

'Cherry Dazzle' Crapemyrtles (above, left) bloom for up to 90 days if you deadhead (remove the dead flowers). Their bloom period coincides with black-eyed Susans, and both plants thrive in full sun. Since dwarf crapemyrtles grow from three to five feet tall, use them behind the shorter (two to three foot) black-eyed Susans.

'Homestead Purple' Verbena (above, right) blooms for the entire warm season, from spring until fall. And, like the black-eyed Susan, it loves sun. Use this low-growing (about a foot tall) verbena as a front border for the crapemyrtle and the black-eyed Susans. This hot combo will stop traffic in your neighborhood!

GROWING CONDITIONS

Light: Full sun to partial afternoon shade.

Water: Medium after establishment. Likes water once or twice a week during the growing season, depending on its environment. See pages 28 to 33 for more information.

Soil: For the garden, plant in any fertile, well-drained soil that has been enriched with organic matter. Use only good-quality potting mix for containers.

Hardiness: Zones 3 to 9

Propagation: Division, rooted cuttings, seed.

Pest Problems: Powdery mildew sometimes causes white patches to form on leaves. It weakens plants but does not kill them.

PLANTING & MAINTENANCE

When to Plant: Black-eyed Susans from containers can be planted at any time. Fall is best because they establish more easily in cooler weather, but you are more likely to find them at your garden center in spring or summer, when they are blooming. Plant new divisions in spring.

Trimming: Deadhead (remove dead flowers) black-eyed Susans every two weeks to help prolong the blooming period. Cut back the dead foliage (to the ground) after it freezes in late fall or early winter.

Fertilization: Medium. Fertilize at planting time and annually with a timed-release product. Less fertilizer is needed with the application of more organics. See pages 36 to 39 for more instructions.

Division: Black-eyed Susans stay healthy without being divided. Divide them in spring only to get more plants or to control the size of the clump.

PERENNIALS

Canna

CHARACTERISTICS

Plant Type: Deciduous perennial (dies back in winter). It grows from a rhizome (large root).

Average Size: About 2 to 6 feet tall and 2 to 3 feet wide, depending on variety.

Growth Rate: Fast

Leaf: Large, banana-like leaves may be green, red or variegated. The foliage of some cannas is even more colorful than the flowers.

Flower: Clusters of large, open-faced, tubular blossoms atop upright stems.

Origin: Central and South America

Spacing: About 24 inches on center (measure from the center of each plant). Closer in containers.

Cautions: None known

Colors: Flowers come in yellow, orange, pink, peach, or red. Leaves are green, green and yellow, or multi-colored.

1. *Yellow canna flower*
2. *Red canna flower*
3. *Yellow-striped canna leaf*
4. *'Tropicanna' canna leaf*

Strong, textural plants that set a tropical mood for months. With big, bright flowers and flashy foliage, modern cannas set the summer garden on fire. They attract too many bugs to win a ribbon, however.

Red cannas with loropetalum planted behind them. Yellow daylilies peak out on the right side and purple heart is planted in front.

We shied away from cannas in our trial gardens for many years because of their reputation for requiring a lot of care. But their flowers are so spectacular that we gave into temptation one year and purchased some rhizomes from a catalog. We were pleasantly surprised by their performance. The biggest problem was holes in the leaves from caterpillars and Japanese beetles. At the Fort Worth Botanic Garden, we treat the plants with the least toxic alternative. Home gardeners who don't want to spray can groom the plants about once a month, cutting off the damaged leaves and flowers.

Color Period: Late spring to late fall, blooming constantly

Buying Tips: Large, blooming canna plants are common in garden centers in summer. Be sure to check out online suppliers to see the incredible variety of cannas that are easily available.

Companions: Consider both flower and foliage colors when partnering cannas with other plants. For cannas with dark leaves, consider lime green companions like marguerite sweet potato vines, as shown in this container (below, left).

To maximize the color punch of cannas that feature yellow-striped foliage, contrast them with bright flowers like the red dragon wing begonias shown in the green container (below, right).

Or, mix cannas with different colored leaves in the same garden, as shown in the bottom photo.

GROWING CONDITIONS

Light: Most cannas need full sun

Water: Medium after establishment. Likes water once or twice a week during the growing season, depending on its environment. See pages 28 to 33 for more information. Some cannas grow by the edges of ponds, but they adapt well to garden situations.

Soil: For the garden, plant in any fertile, well-drained soil that has been enriched with organic matter. Use only good-quality potting mix for containers.

Hardiness: Zones 7 to 10. Rhizomes may be left in the ground during winter.

Propagation: Most cannas grow from rhizomes, but a few grow from seeds. All can be divided.

Pest Problems: Canna leaf roller, Japanese beetles. Fungus, shown by brown spots on the leaves.

PLANTING & MAINTENANCE

When to Plant: Cannas from containers can be planted in spring or summer, when you see them for sale. Plant bare rhizomes from March 15 to April 15. Divide the rhizomes, so they contain only 2 or 3 "eyes" (little buds that look like bumps). Place the rhizome in the ground horizontally with the eyes up. Plant 24 inches apart, and cover with 2 inches of soil.

Trimming: Clip off old flowers to keep the plants looking neat. Cut back the dead foliage (leaving 6 inches) after it freezes in late fall or early winter.

Fertilization: Medium. Fertilize at planting time and annually with a timed-release product. Less fertilizer is needed with the application of more organics.

Division: If the center of the clump dies or if the clump simply looks too crowded, divide in spring.

PERENNIALS

Coneflower

CHARACTERISTICS

Plant Type: Deciduous perennial (dies back in winter).

Average Size: Most coneflowers average 2 to 3 feet tall by 18 inches wide. A few cultivars top out at over 3 feet tall.

Growth Rate: Medium

Leaf: Oval green leaves with pointed tips, 3 inches long and 2 inches wide.

Flower: Broad daisies, from 2 to 7 inches across, with centers comprised of a coppery-orange, bristly cone.

Origin: The prairies and eastern U.S.

Spacing: About 18 to 24 inches on center (measure from the center of each plant). Place smaller varieties closer together than larger ones.

Cautions: Attracts bees, but seldom damaged by deer. This flower has well known medicinal uses, but sometimes causes allergic reactions if ingested.

Colors: Flowers are mauve, white, orange, yellow, purple, bright pink.

1. *Traditional coneflower color*
2. *'Big Sky Sunrise' coneflower*
3. *'Big Sky Twilight' coneflower*
4. *'Big Sky After Midnight' coneflower.*

One of the most dependable bloomers in Texas. Long-blooming perennial attracts clouds of butterflies to the garden. Favorite of most perennial gardeners. Looks better when deadheaded (dead flowers removed), so it just misses a ribbon.

Visitors to Fort Worth Botanic Garden have seen as many as three to six butterflies on a single coneflower plant!

Coneflowers are one of the best perennials for Texas. While many perennials require frequent grooming to look good, coneflowers can make it with only one cutback in fall. They look neater with a few groomings (nipping off dried flower spikes) during the summer but look reasonably attractive without it. Since they bloom all summer with so little attention, most gardeners want them, but the number of new cultivars is daunting! You may see a dozen different kinds at one garden center! The good news is that we have never found a bad one - it looks like you can't make a bad choice! Most of the new hybrids are improvements over the originals - more compact, more intense colors, more colors, and more flowers on each plant. Among the many cultivars of coneflower featured in the Fort Worth Botanic Garden's perennial trial garden, 'Magnus' performs the best.

Color Period: Strongest bloom occurs in early summer. Very vigorous varieties continue to produce flowers through late summer and fall.

Buying Tips: Be sure to read the tag at the garden center to see how large your selection grows. They vary from two to over three feet tall, which can make a difference as to where you place it in your garden. If you don't see any you like, most of the new, exciting varieties are available online.

Companions: Use coneflowers in perennial beds filled with other easy perennials that bloom in summer. Salvia and agastache look good with coneflower because their spiky flowers contrast with the coneflower's round one. Or, combine different colored coneflowers together, as shown right.

For easy color layers, butterfly bush and 'New Gold' lantana make great partners for coneflower and attract droves of butterflies. Check out this combo below.

'Big Sky Twilight,' 'Sunrise,' and 'Sundown' coneflowers.

GROWING CONDITIONS

Light: Light shade to full sun

Water: Medium after establishment. Likes water once or twice a week during the growing season, depending on its environment.

Soil: For the garden, plant in any fertile, well-drained soil that has been enriched with organic matter. Use only good-quality potting mix for containers.

Hardiness: Zones 3 to 9

Propagation: Seeds or division

Pest Problems: Rarely serious, though Japanese beetles sometimes eat both flowers and leaves.

PLANTING & MAINTENANCE

When to Plant: Coneflowers from containers can be planted anytime. Fall is best because they establish more easily in cooler weather. Coneflowers grown from seeds are fine for wildflower meadows, but named varieties grown from cuttings provide much more color due to their vigor and extended season of bloom.

Trimming: Cut back the dead foliage (to the ground) after it freezes in late fall or early winter, unless you want to leave the flower heads intact during the winter for birds to eat.

Fertilization: Low. Fertilize at planting time with a timed-release product. Less fertilizer is needed with the application of more organics. In the years after planting, fertilization needs vary, based on the nutrients in your soil.

Division: When flower production declines in plantings more than 4 years old, dig, divide, and replant. Fall is the best time, but you can also divide them in spring.

'Purple Emperor'
Butterfly Bush
Plant Profile: Page 194

'New Gold' Lantana
Plant Profile: Page 68

Coneflower 'Primadonna Deep Rose' with some companion plants for easy layers.

'Purple Emperor' Butterfly Bush (above, top) is one of the newer, more compact butterfly bushes that grows to about four feet tall and, like coneflower, blooms for most of the summer. Plant it behind the shorter coneflowers.

'New Gold' Lantana (above, bottom) produces an abundance of golden yellow flowers all season long on plants two feet tall. Its yellow flowers contrast well with the rosy pink petals of most coneflowers. Since the lantana is shorter than many coneflowers, plant it as a border for both other plants. Plant all three in full sun.

PERENNIALS

Coreopsis, Threadleaf

CHARACTERISTICS

Plant Type: Deciduous perennial (dies back in winter).

Average Size: 18 to 24 inches tall by about 18 inches wide.

Growth Rate: Medium

Leaf: Narrow, thread-like, green leaves.

Flower: Flat, daisy-like blossoms with a tuft of yellow in the centers; 1 to 2 inches in diameter.

Origin: Southeastern U.S.

Spacing: About 18 inches on center (measure from the center of each plant). Closer in containers.

Cautions: Attracts bees but seldom damaged by deer.

Colors: Flowers are yellow

These easy, sun-loving flowers rebloom repeatedly all summer. The 'Moonbeam' variety won the Perennial Plant Association's 1992 Perennial Plant of the Year award. Soft texture for the perennial garden. Blooms for months with very little care. Rates a blue ribbon* because of its ease of care.

Coreopsis is one of the ten best-selling perennials. There are many different types, but most of our experience has been with threadleaf coreopsis, which differs from the rest because of its thin, needle-like leaves. Threadleaf coreopsis has the reputation for being one of the toughest of all of them and blooms for quite a while with no attention at all other than weekly watering. Many of the other kinds of coreopsis require frequent deadheading (removal of dead flowers) to keep blooming. Two of the best performers are 'Moonbeam,' (which is the best-known) and 'Zagreb' (which is sure to please). Both 'Moonbeam' and 'Zagreb' are featured in the Fort Worth Botanic Garden perennial trial garden.

Color Period: May or June through July, with a final flush of flowers in the fall. The best varieties bloom for three months or more.

Buying Tips: Threadleaf coreopsis doesn't look great in a nursery pot, as it is a bit thin and floppy when in a container. It does beautifully after it has been planted for just a short time.

Blue ribbon plants are defined on page 12. For blue ribbon performance, follow the planting and maintenance guidelines on pages 22 to 39.

Companions: Grow coreopsis with other perennials that take baking sun such as agastache and scabiosa. Since coreopsis is so fine-textured, the larger agastache and scabiosa flowers show up well with it.

The combination below shows coreopsis with 'Big Sky Twilight' coneflower and 'Homestead Purple' verbena. The three fit together well as three layers of different heights. And, with internet shopping, you can now find all these plants, even if you can't locate them at your local garden center.

'Big Sky Twilight' Coneflower
Plant Profile: Page 116

'Homestead Purple' Verbena
Plant Profile: Page 170

Coreopsis with some companions that form easy color layers

'Big Sky Twilight' Coneflower (above, top) is an excellent choice as a background for threadleaf coreopsis. The textures of the plants are quite different, they both like sun, and they share the same bloom period. This coneflower grows to about 30 inches tall. Place the 18 inch coreopsis in front of it.

'Homestead Purple' Verbena (above, bottom) blooms for the entire warm season, from spring until fall. And, like the coreopsis, it loves sun. Use this low-growing (about a foot tall) verbena as a front border for the coneflowers and the coreopsis. This hot combo will stop traffic in your neighborhood!

GROWING CONDITIONS

Light: Full sun, at least 6 hours per day.

Water: Low after establishment. Likes water every week or two during the growing season, depending on its environment. See pages 28 to 33 for more information.

Soil: Very well-drained soil that has been enriched with organic matter. Coreopsis does very well in heavy clay soil as long as it has been amended.

Hardiness: Zones 3 to 9

Propagation: Division

Pest Problems: Rare, but can develop fungus problems if overwatered.

PLANTING & MAINTENANCE

When to Plant: Coreopsis from containers can be planted anytime. Fall is best because they establish more easily in cooler weather, but you are more likely to find them at your garden center in early spring, when they are blooming.

Trimming: If the plants become unsightly in late summer, cut them back to 8 to 10 inches to encourage a rebound of healthy, new growth. Cut back the dead foliage (to the ground) after it freezes in late fall or early winter.

Fertilization: Low. Fertilize at planting time with a timed-release product. Less fertilizer is needed with the application of more organics. In the years after planting, fertilization needs vary, based on the nutrients in your soil. See pages 36 to 39 for more instructions.

Division: Divide every 2 to 5 years in fall or spring to maintain the vigor of the plants. The plants divided from the edges will be the healthiest. Discard the center if it appears weak.

PERENNIALS

Daffodils

CHARACTERISTICS

Plant Type: Deciduous perennial (dies back in winter). Grows from a bulb.

Average Size: 6 to 16 inches tall, depending on variety. Individual plants are 4 to 8 inches wide yet often grow into foot-wide clumps.

Growth Rate: Medium

Leaf: Green, narrow, strap-shaped leaves.

Flower: Flared petals around a central cup, with a great variety of types and sizes. Many are fragrant.

Origin: Mediterranean region

Spacing: See opposite page

Cautions: None known. Mice, deer, and other wildlife do not eat these bulbs.

Colors: Flowers are yellow, white, orange, or apricot-pink.

'Avalanche' daffodil, another excellent choice for north central Texas.

Daffodils are one of the easiest bulbs to grow in Texas. They live without irrigation, resist deer, grow in clay soil, and go for years requiring no care except occasional fertilization and division. Although each variety blooms for only two to three weeks, you can buy bulb mixes that will extend the blooming season for several months. Rates a blue ribbon* because of its ease of care.

'Falconet' daffodil, an excellent choice for north central Texas

Cheerful harbingers of spring and ideal for low-maintenance gardens, daffodils are one of the best bulbs for naturalizing (multiplying and persisting) in the garden. They are most effective when planted in drifts within beds, along creeks, or under deciduous trees. Plant them with other spring-flowering bulbs, shrubs, and annuals. After they're through blooming, it's best to let the foliage die down naturally because doing so helps the bulbs store up energy for blooming in the future.

Every spring, the Dallas Arboretum features "Dallas Blooms," a six-week-long, breathtaking display of every spring-blooming bulb imaginable.

Color Period: Late February to early April, depending on variety. Bulb nurseries offer many mixes with staggered blooming so the bed stays in bloom for months.

Buying Tips: Daffodils are available from local nurseries, catalogs, and online (try www.johnscheepers.com or www.brentandbeckysbulbs.com). The varieties are endless, but not all do well in north central Texas. Shop for the daffodils described on the opposite page to obtain plants that do well here. The divisions that have done best for us include the jonquillas and the tazettas (opposite page).

Blue ribbon plants are defined on page 12. For blue ribbon performance, follow the planting and maintenance guidelines on pages 22 to 39.

Daffodils are divided into different divisions according to common characteristics. Here are some that do well here. The jonquilla and tazetta divisions have done best for us.

'Fortune'

Cyclamineus Daffodils (Division 6, right): Look like cyclamen flowers with petals that fold back. Many bloom early, even in late February. Excellent varieties are 'February Gold' and 'Tête-á-Tête.' Cyclamineus daffodils grow 10 to 12 inches tall. Plant six inches deep and six inches apart.

'Waterperry'

Tazetta Daffodils (Division 8, right): One of the two best divisions for north central Texas. Produces four to eight fragrant flowers per stem. Plant six to eight inches deep and six inches apart. Varieties include 'Avalanche,' 'Cragford,' 'Falconet,' 'Geranium,' 'Grand Primo,' and 'Silver Chimes.'

Narcissus alba plenus odoratus

Large-cupped Daffodils (Division 2, left): Showy flower with a large cup in the center; grows 18 to 20 inches tall. Plant six to eight inches deep and six inches apart. The best varieties for north central Texas include 'Carlton,' 'Fortissimo,' 'Fortune,' 'Gigantic Star,' 'Ice Follies,' and 'St. Keverne.'

'Tête-á-Tête'

Jonquilla Daffodils (Division 7, left): One of the two best divisions for north central Texas. Slender foliage and stems that bear from two to six flowers. Plant six inches deep and six inches apart. Varieties include 'Bell Song,' 'Dickcissel,' 'Hillstar,' 'Quail,' 'Stratosphere,' 'Suzy,' and 'Waterperry.'

'Cragford'

Species and Wild Forms (Division 13, left): These dainty species include varieties of daffodils as they were originally found in the wild hundreds of years ago. Plant four to five inches deep and four to five inches apart. Good choices for north central Texas.

GROWING CONDITIONS

Light: Full winter sun, which may become filtered shade in late spring when trees leaf out. Morning sun is fine when the trees have leaves, but do give shade from hot afternoon sun.

Water: Very low. Because daffodils grow in the wet season, they seldom need supplemental water. These bulbs benefit from becoming dry in the summer.

Soil: Any well-drained soil that has been enriched with organic matter. Miniature daffodils can adapt to unimproved soil, provided they are fed properly, but large-flowered varieties need good, garden-quality soil.

Hardiness: Zones 3 to 8

Propagation: Division

Pest Problems: Rare

PLANTING & MAINTENANCE

When to Plant: Plant bulbs November through December in zones 7 and 8. Store bulbs in the refrigerator prior to planting. Take care to store them away from fruit, particularly apples or pears.

Planting Depth: Cover with soil to twice the height of the bulb.

Trimming: It is important to allow the foliage of daffodils to remain intact until it turns yellow in early summer, at which time it can be clipped off.

Fertilization: Fertilize once a year lightly with a low nitrogen fertilizer, just as the shoots emerge in early spring.

Division: Dig and divide to increase your supply or to relieve overcrowding. When adequately fed, daffodils should not need dividing more often than once a decade. If they stop blooming, they need either division or fertilization.

PERENNIALS

Daylily

CHARACTERISTICS

Plant Type: Deciduous perennial (dies back in winter) in colder areas. Some are evergreen in zone 8.

Average Size: 18 inches to 4 feet tall, depending on variety. The best, everblooming daylilies grow less than 2 feet tall and equally as wide.

Growth Rate: Fast

Leaf: Trumpet-shaped blossoms average 4 inches across, many with ruffled petals and contrasting throats.

Flower: Large, showy flowers; 4 to 6 inches across.

Origin: China

Spacing: About 12 inches on center (measure from the center of each plant) when planting nursery-grown plants. 6 to 8 inches apart for tubers.

Cautions: None known. Some types produce edible blossoms. Frequently eaten by deer, except for 'Stella deOro.'

Colors: Flowers are orange, yellow, red, pink, lilac, maroon, and in endless variations.

One of the easiest plants for Texas gardens. Reblooming selections provide colorful blossoms from early summer to fall. Rates a blue ribbon* because of its ease of care.

Daylilies have been one of the most popular plants in Texas gardens for generations. They hybridize easily, which explains why there are more than 20,000 cultivars from which to choose. The cultivars vary greatly in length of bloom time. Most bloom for about a month. But, for the gardener who wants longer-lasting color, the daylilies to plant are reblooming hybrids, which bloom heavily in early summer and then intermittently until fall. Three of the best rebloomers for Texas are 'Happy Returns,' 'Mack the Knife,' and 'Stella de Oro.' Many other daylilies have shorter bloom times, but they remain valuable for their exciting colors and forms.

Gardeners spend different amounts of time maintaining their daylilies. Some leave them alone most of the time; for these people, daylilies are an easy, blue ribbon plant. Others deadhead (remove dead flowers) daily, greatly increasing the maintenance as well as the floral display.

Color Period: Early summer to fall. The best reblooming types bloom from June to fall with deadheading (removal of dead flowers) but not as much without it. Daylilies that bloom only once do so in late spring or early summer.

Buying Tips: Widely available both in garden centers and online. Many local daylily societies have sales in September.

Blue ribbon plants are defined on page 12. For blue ribbon performance, follow the planting and maintenance guidelines on pages 22 to 39.

Botanical Name: *Hemerocallis* spp.

Family: Liliaceae

Companions: Daylilies are outstanding for mass plantings along driveways, or you can use them to soften fences. They do a great job of camouflaging the failing foliage of daffodils or other spring-flowering bulbs.

Daylily collectors often plant huge beds of just daylilies, putting lots of different kinds together.

Daylilies also work very well with other flowering shrubs and colorful groundcovers. The companions shown below offer months of color with very little care. The color time will be extended if you have time to remove the dead flowers from the daylilies and the crapemyrtle.

'Cherry Dazzle' Crapemyrtle
Plant Profile: Page 206

Purple Heart
Plant Profile: Page 152

Yellow reblooming daylily and some companions for easy color layers

'Cherry Dazzle' Crapemyrtle (above, left) blooms for up to 90 days if you remove the dead flowers. Its bloom period coincides with reblooming yellow daylilies (like 'Stella de Oro'), and both plants thrive in full sun. Since dwarf crapemyrtles grow from three to five feet tall, use them behind the shorter (two to three foot) daylilies.

Purple Heart (above, right) is a perennial ground cover that grows to about one foot tall, fitting nicely as a border in front of the daylilies and dwarf crapemyrtle. Purple heart gives you constant color from May until the first frost of fall.

*Reblooming daylilies bloom for up to 18 weeks.

GROWING CONDITIONS

Light: Full sun to partial shade

Water: Medium after establishment. Likes water once or twice a week during the growing season, depending on its environment. See pages 28 to 33 for more information.

Soil: Fertile, well-drained soil that has been amended with organic matter.

Hardiness: Zones 3 to 9

Propagation: Division is most common. Dig crowns from the outside of established clumps, and transplant them to other parts of your landscape.

Pest Problems: Few. Aphids sometimes overwinter in the old foliage and get on the new growth. Daylily rust, a fungal disease, occasionally causes problems.

PLANTING & MAINTENANCE

When to Plant: Daylilies from containers can be planted at any time. Fall is best because they establish more easily in cooler weather, but you are more likely to find them at your garden center in early spring.

Trimming: Clip off old flower stems. However, millions of daylilies bloom without being trimmed. Cut back the dead foliage (to the ground) after it freezes in late fall or early winter.

Fertilization: Medium. Fertilize at planting time and annually with a timed-release product. Less fertilizer is needed with the application of more organics. See pages 36 to 39 for more instructions.

Division: Daylilies produce fewer flowers after about 5 years. Divide them after they have bloomed. For instructions, go to http://www.daytonnursery.com/tips/Daylilies.html.

PERENNIALS

Elephant Ears

CHARACTERISTICS

Plant Type: Deciduous perennial (dies back in winter) or annual (lives for one season), depending on species and zone.

Average Size: Varies greatly by species. From about 18 inches tall and wide to 8 feet tall and 6 feet wide.

Growth Rate: Fast

Leaf: Large, reaching up to 3 feet long and 2 feet wide in the tropics.

Flower: Insignificant

Origin: Tropical and subtropical areas throughout the world.

Spacing: Depends on size. From 2 to 6 feet on center (measure from the center of each plant).

Cautions: None known. Seldom damaged by deer.

Colors: Flowers are insignificant. Plant this one for its leaves, which range from black to green.

Elephant ear planted as the centerpiece of a container. Dragon wing begonias and creeping Jenny are planted around the edge.

Great landscape or container plant for summer use. Commonly used as focal points of annual plantings in public places. In the warmer areas of Texas, it dies back in winter and reappears the next spring. Rates a blue ribbon* because it is so easy to grow.

Colocasia 'Illustris' elephant ear

Elephant ears are thought of as tropical plants but do quite well in much of Texas. Their large leaves add drama to the landscape. These plants are great for adding instant impact to otherwise mundane, boring beds. They are also one of the best centerpieces for container gardens - a sure-fire way of getting a good outcome. Just plant one in the middle and surround it with smaller plants, and it looks great every time.

Regional Differences: Elephant ears die back with the first frost of fall. In zone eight (along with protected areas of zone seven), they come back the next spring. In unprotected areas in zone seven, remove and store the tubers in fall for replanting the next spring (see instructions on opposite page).

Color Period: Flowers are insignificant. Use this one for the leaves.

Buying Tips: Good elephant ears are easy to find. We have never bought one that did poorly. However, it helps if the plant tag tells you how tall it gets. We purchased the one in the container, shown left, thinking it was a dwarf that would only get two feet tall. It grew to over five feet in height!

Blue ribbon plants are defined on page 12. For blue ribbon performance, follow the planting and maintenance guidelines on pages 22 to 39.

27

Avg. Weeks of Color

Botanical Name: *Alocasia* and *Colocasia* spp.
Family: Araceae

Companions: Use elephant ears with plants that contrast both with the size and color of the leaves. Lime green elephant ears look great in the middle of dark colored flowers and leaves. Conversely, dark elephant ears look good with light leaves, as shown in the container below. *Colocasia 'Illustris'* is planted as the centerpiece of this black and lime green container. Lime and black sweet potato vines are alternated with lime sedum 'Angelina.'

GROWING CONDITIONS

Light: Most prefer shade, but we have grown them in the Fort Worth Botanic Garden in full sun. Check the tag on any purchased plants for the light needs.

Water: Medium after establishment. Likes water once or twice a week during the growing season, depending on its environment.

Soil: For the garden, plant in any fertile, well-drained soil that has been enriched with organic matter. Use only good-quality potting mix for containers.

Hardiness: In zones 8 through 10, leave them in the ground. In protected areas of zone 7, they may or may not come back the next year.

Propagation: Tubers

Pest Problems: Rare

PLANTING & MAINTENANCE

When to Plant: Spring or summer. When planting tubers, the pointed end goes up and the blunt end goes down. Plant just deep enough to cover the tip.

Trimming: Cut back the dead foliage (to the ground) after it freezes in late fall or early winter.

Fertilization: Fertilize at planting time and annually with a top-quality, timed-release product that includes minor elements.

To Store Tubers: Dig up the tubers in fall, and let them dry outside for about a week. Store them in a cool (but not freezing), dry place over the winter. Be sure they neither rot nor dry out. Plant them in spring after the last frost.

Division: In spring, dig up the plant, and pull the tubers apart into 3 sections. Replant. They may wilt for a while. About 75% live.

PERENNIALS

Ferns

CHARACTERISTICS

Plant Type: Perennials, some evergreen, and some deciduous (dies back in winter). See individual descriptions on opposite pages for additional information.

Average Size: Japanese painted fern, 12 to 18 inches tall by equally as wide; holly fern, southern wood fern, and autumn fern, 2 feet tall by 2 feet wide.

Growth Rate: Medium for Japanese painted fern. Fast for holly fern, southern wood fern, and autumn fern.

Origin: Japanese painted fern, Japan; holly fern and autumn fern, China; southern wood fern, Texas.

Spacing: About 12 to 18 inches on center for Japanese painted fern; 2 to 3 feet on center for holly fern; 18 inches for southern wood fern; 2 to 3 feet on center for the autumn fern.

Cautions: Almost never eaten by deer.

Japanese painted ferns

Ferns are one of the easiest and most dependable plants for shade. Extremely deer-resistant. Rate a blue ribbon* because they are easy to grow. Here are some that have other outstanding qualities as well.

Japanese painted fern

Ferns are one of the best choices for shade in Texas. Their appearance evokes a pleasant woodland, and they are incredibly easy to care for if you provide them good drainage. Autumn fern is useful because it is one of the few ferns that are evergreen. Southern wood fern is the hardiest and most commonly grown fern in north central Texas. Holly fern is the coarsest, with foliage that resembles that of holly trees. Japanese painted fern is both the smallest and the prettiest because of its fascinating colorations. The Japanese painted fern 'Pictum' (shown in these photos) won the 2004 Perennial Plant of the Year award. The Fort Worth Botanic Garden has a fern garden that features many species that do well in north central Texas.

Regional Differences: These four ferns perform well in north central Texas. Of these, only autumn fern is completely evergreen throughout the area. Holly fern is semi-evergreen. Japanese painted fern dies back in winter north of zone eight. Southern wood fern dies back completely in winter.

Buying Tips: Ferns are easy to find at garden centers

Blue ribbon plants are defined on page 12. For blue ribbon performance, follow the planting and maintenance guidelines on pages 22 to 39.

Autumn Fern (*Dryopteris erythrosora*, left) merits attention because it is one of the few ferns that is evergreen in zone seven. It is also distinctive for its copper-colored, new growth in spring and its golden bronze color in fall.

GROWING CONDITIONS

Light: Shade, although southern wood fern and holly fern will take some sun, preferably morning sun.

Water: Medium after establishment. Likes water once or twice a week during the growing season, depending on its environment. See pages 28 to 33 for more information.

Soil: For the garden, plant in any fertile, well-drained soil that has been enriched with organic matter. Use only good-quality potting mix for containers. See pages 22 to 25 for specific instructions on soil preparation.

Southern Wood Fern (*Thelypteris kunthii*, right) is the hardiest and most commonly grown fern in north central Texas. Its light green foliage lights up when catching early morning or late afternoon sun. It spreads by rhizomes and demonstrates considerable drought tolerance. Native to Texas. Deciduous (dies back in winter).

Hardiness: Japanese painted fern, zones 4 to 9; holly and southern wood ferns, zones 7 to 10; autumn fern, zones 5 to 9.

Propagation: Division

Pest Problems: Rare

PLANTING & MAINTENANCE

When to Plant: Ferns from containers can be planted at any time. Fall is best because they establish more easily in cooler weather, but you are more likely to find them at your garden center in early spring.

Holly Fern (*Cyrtomium falcatum*, left) is an evergreen fern as far north as zone eight and semi-evergreen is zone seven. However, it only shows cold damage at about seven degrees, so it stays green in the winter in many parts of zone seven. Holly fern offers coarse texture that resembles a holly shrub. It also offers the darkest green color of any of these ferns.

Trimming: For evergreen ferns, each year in spring, remove older fronds that are lying on the ground. For deciduous ferns, cut back the dead foliage to the ground after it freezes in late fall or early winter.

Fertilization: Medium. Fertilize at planting time and annually with a timed-release product. Less fertilizer is needed with the application of more organics. See pages 36 to 39 for more instructions.

Japanese Painted Fern (*Athyrium niponicum*, right) is the most attractive and smallest of these ferns. Its silver and burgundy color pattern really stands out and brightens a dull spot. Japanese painted fern dies back during the winter north of zone eight.

Division: Every 3 to 5 years, divide clumps with a sharp spade in late fall or just before new growth starts in spring.

Only the southern wood fern is a Texas native.

PERENNIALS

CHARACTERISTICS

Plant Type: Varies by type

Average Size: 2 to 24 inches tall.

Growth Rate: Varies by type

Leaf: Long, grass-like leaves

Flower: Tall, upright spikes

Origin: Varies by type

Spacing: Mondo grass, 6 to 12 inches on center; *Carex* 'Toffee Twist,' 24 inches on center; Liriope, 12 to 18 inches on center; dwarf sweet flag, 8 to 12 inches on center (measure from the center of each plant). Closer in containers.

Cautions: None known

Colors: Flowers are lavender-blue for liriope. The rest have insignificant flowers.

Juncus grass forms the centerpiece of this container, surrounded by impatiens and creeping Jenny. This grass is good for summer containers but turns brown in winter. Cut back this warm-season grass to a few inches in fall or spring. Divide anytime from spring through mid summer. Sun or partial shade. Zones 4 to 10.

We use small grasses both in the landscape and in containers. Here are five of our favorites. All of them are incredibly easy to use and definitely rate a blue ribbon.*

'Toffee Twist' grass has worked quite well in our container gardens. It is shown here surrounded by coleus in a side-planted basket from www.kinsmangarden.com.

Carex 'Toffee Twist' is an award-winning grass we have used extensively as a centerpiece in containers. It grows 18 to 24 inches, smaller than the similar purple fountain grass shown on pages 130 and 131. We like the fact that the grass stays evergreen down to five degrees. Cut this grass back in very early spring (see "Trimming," far right). Divide this grass in early spring. It grows well in zones seven and eight but dies back in winter in zone seven. Use this grass in full sun to light shade.

Color Period: Most grasses bloom in summer and fall

Buying Tips: Garden centers are loaded with many different grasses in spring or summer. Most are labeled clearly with their names. Unfortunately, the labels don't include bad tendencies of the grasses, such as the aggressive growth that some have. Take this book with you, so you can check them out.

Blue ribbon plants are defined on page 12. For blue ribbon performance, follow the planting and maintenance guidelines on pages 22 to 39.

Dwarf White-Striped Sweet Flag (*Acorus gramineus*, left) We have used this grass in containers and loved it because of its small size - only six to fifteen inches tall. It is quite useful as a small filler in containers or massed as a groundcover in the garden.

It grows as a perennial in zones five to eleven and takes light shade to full sun. This is an evergreen, grass-like plant that can only be divided in spring and prefers normal to wet soils.

Mondo Grass (*Ophiopogon japonicus*, right) Small (two to six inches tall) grass used as a border and groundcover in dense to light shade. It takes morning sun, but protect it from afternoon sun. Its leaves are narrower than the similar liriope (shown below). Mondo grass requires almost no maintenance but grows so slowly that it can take quite a while to cover a large area. It looks attractive enough in winter but gets a bit raggedy if temperatures drop to under ten degrees. Cut back the bad leaves in late winter. Zones seven to ten.

Liriope (*Liriope muscari*, left) is a useful, 18- to 24- inch grass used for borders or massed as a groundcover. It blooms in July and August with a small white or purple flower.

Green liriope does well in full sun to medium shade, while the variegated forms may bleach out some in full sun. It needs no irrigation once it's established (in normal conditions), and it lives in zones six to ten.

GROWING CONDITIONS

Light: For full sun to light shade, use dwarf sweet flag, *Carex* 'Toffee Twist,' *Juncus* grass, or liriope. For medium to dense shade, use liriope or mondo grass. Mondo takes light shade as well.

Water: Liriope can live without irrigation after establishment. Water the rest once or twice a week.

Soil: For the garden, plant in any fertile, well-drained soil that has been enriched with organic matter. Use only good-quality potting mix for containers. See pages 22 to 25 for specific instructions on soil preparation.

Hardiness: Varies by type

Propagation: Division

Pest Problems: Rare

PLANTING & MAINTENANCE

When to Plant: Grasses from containers can be planted at any time. Fall is best because they establish easier in cooler weather. Spring is the best time to plant divisions.

Trimming: Cut it back to the ground just before new growth begins: February in zone 8 and March in zone 7. Your goal is to trim off the old growth from the previous year. Don't wait too long because, if you cut back new growth that appears in spring, the tips will be blunt and discolored.

Fertilization: Medium. Fertilize at planting time and annually with a timed-release product. Less fertilizer is needed with the application of more organics.

Division: We don't divide these small grasses often because they don't spread too quickly. However, if they spread too much or if you simply want more plants, dig the whole root ball out of the ground in spring, divide it into 4 pieces, and replant .

PERENNIALS

Liriope lives on rainwater alone in all but the most extreme situations. Both mondo grass and acorus grass need more water.

1ST

CHARACTERISTICS

Plant Type: Many grasses are deciduous (leaves die after a freeze). All of the grasses shown here are evergreen except purple fountain grass, which is an annual in north central Texas.

Average Size: From 24 to 36 inches tall.

Growth Rate: Varies by type

Leaf: Long, grass-like leaves

Flower: Tall, upright spikes

Origin: Varies by type

Spacing: Varies by type

Cautions: None known

Colors: Flowers are as follows: white for 'Hameln' fountain grass; rust for purple fountain grass; tan for inland sea oats; pink or purple for purple muhly grass.

Purple fountain grass is often used in the landscape with other annuals. Here, it is planted with pentas and celosia.

Grasses are the rage in Texas landscapes, and the photo below shows why. They are gorgeous! But choosing the right ones can be tricky. Some last only one season, and some last for years. Some require maintenance only once a year, and others will take over your garden in no time. Here are some of the best, blue ribbon* grasses for north central Texas.

'Hameln' (Pennisetum alopecuroides 'Hameln'), dwarf form of green fountain grass

'Hameln' has been growing at the Fort Worth Botanic Garden for many years. Its two and one half foot height makes it useful in many landscape situations. This showy grass produces tan-colored, foxtail plumes from midsummer to frost and holds its character well in winter, too. Since it only requires annual trimming, it easily wins a blue ribbon. 'Hameln' prefers well-drained, irrigated soils in full sun and is hardy to zone six.

Color Period: Fountain grasses bloom from midsummer until frost, but 'Hameln' remains attractive in winter as well. Pink muhly grass flowers from August until the first frost. Mexican feather grass turns straw-colored in summer, which is colorful in itself. Inland sea oats bloom for about two weeks in June or July. The seed pods that follow turn tan by fall and persist all winter.

Buying Tips: Garden centers are loaded with many different grasses in spring or summer. Most are labeled clearly with their names. Unfortunately, the labels don't include bad tendencies of the grasses, such as the aggressive growth that some have. Take this book with you, so you can check them out.

Blue ribbon plants are defined on page 12. For blue ribbon performance, follow the planting and maintenance guidelines on pages 22 to 39.

Mexican Feather Grass (*Nasella tenuissima*, right) is a native, drought-tolerant, grass that is the finest-textured of them all. Green during cool weather, it turns a straw color as it goes dormant in summer. Grows about two feet tall. Requires extremely well-drained soil. Excessive winter moisture will kill this grass. Zones seven to eleven.

Purple Fountain Grass (*Pennisetum setaceum* 'Rubrum', right) is an annual (living for only one season) in any zone colder than zone 9. However, it's worth using because its striking, purplish-red foliage and pinkish-tan foxtail plumes show up so well when surrounded by contrasting annual plantings. Three feet tall and prefers full sun. Only grass on this page that is not native to Texas.

Inland Sea Oats (*Chasmanthium latifolium*, left) is a clump-forming, upright grass native to Texas. It prefers shade and grows two to three feet tall. Leaves are bright green and resemble bamboo foliage. Produces flat, tan, chevron-shaped, drooping seed heads. Self-seeds and may become invasive but looks great in a large drift under shade trees.

Pink Muhly Grass (*Muhlenbergia capillaris*, left) grows two to three feet tall and wide. Produces spectacular clouds of airy, pink plumes in the fall. The plumes later turn tan and persist through the winter. The glossy, wiry, dark green leaves are attractive and differ from the flat-bladed leaves of most other grasses. Plant in full sun. Pink muhly grass does well in zones seven to nine.

GROWING CONDITIONS

Light: Varies by plant

Water: Fountain grasses can survive with little irrigation once they are established. Pink muhly grass and inland sea oats are fairly drought tolerant, but they appreciate occasional irrigation. Mexican feather grass does best without any irrigation.

Soil: For the garden, plant in any fertile, well-drained soil that has been enriched with organic matter. Use only good-quality potting mix for containers.

Hardiness: Varies by type

Propagation: Seeds or division, but many don't come true by seed.

Pest Problems: Rare

PLANTING & MAINTENANCE

When to Plant: Anytime from containers. Spring is best when planted from divisions.

Trimming: Cut back to the ground just before new growth begins: February in zone 8 and March in zone 7. Your goal is to trim off the old growth from the previous year. Don't wait too long because if you cut back new growth that appears in spring, the tips will be blunt and discolored.

Fertilization: Low. Fertilize at planting time with a timed-release product. Less fertilizer is needed with the application of more organics. In the years after planting, fertilization needs vary, based on the nutrients in your soil. See pages 36 to 39 for more instructions.

Division: We don't divide these small grasses often because they don't spread too quickly. However, if they spread too much or if you simply want more plants, dig the whole root ball out in early spring, divide it into 4 pieces, and replant.

CHARACTERISTICS

Plant Type: Semi-evergreen, perennial grasses.

Average Size: Lindheimer muhly's foliage is 3 to 4 feet tall and wide; its plumes reach 5 to 6 feet tall. 'Adagio' foliage is 3 feet tall and wide; its plumes are 3 to 4 feet tall. Lowland switch grass may reach 8 feet tall and 5 feet wide; its plumes reach the same height.

Growth Rate: Fast

Leaf: Long, narrow leaf blades; color varies according to type: Lindheimer's muhly has grayish blue-green foliage; 'Adagio' has green leaves with a silver stripe down the center of the blade; and, switch grass has blue-green foliage that turns a cinnamon color in the fall.

Flower: Soft-textured plumes. Lindheimer's are long and feathery; 'Adagio' has plumes that open up a little more; and switch grass has loose, open panicles.

Origin: Lindheimer's muhly and switch grass are native to Texas; 'Adagio' is native to East Asia.

Spacing: 4 feet on center for Lindheimer's muhly; 3 feet on center for 'Adagio;' and 6 feet on center for switch grass.

Cautions: Deer resistant

Colors: Flowers are tan to creamy-white, depending on variety.

Here are three taller grasses (three to six feet) that offer high, blue ribbon* performance. Two are native to Texas. All three are very easy to grow, requiring only one annual pruning.

Lindheimer's muhly grass

The form, foliage, and plumes of these three grasses make an outstanding addition to the landscape, especially late summer through winter. Large grasses make a bold yet graceful statement in the landscape. Lindheimer's muhly, switch grass, and 'Adagio' make softer-textured substitutes for stiff shrubs. They have a greater sense of movement than unbending shrubs, too, since even a light breeze can rustle their foliage and make their plumes dance in the air. These three grasses are very well adapted to the soils and climate of north central Texas. Other than watering, the only maintenance they need is a cutting back in late winter before new spring foliage emerges.

Color Period: Late summer to fall; plumes persist through winter

Buying Tips: Garden centers that specialize in native plants will certainly carry native and ornamental grasses, and more and more mainstream garden centers are carrying these grasses as well.

Blue ribbon plants are defined on page 12. For blue ribbon performance, follow the planting and maintenance guidelines on pages 22 to 39.

Lindheimer's Muhly Grass (*Muhlenbergia lindheimeri,* **left**) is one of the best grasses for gardens in north central Texas. It forms a three- to four-foot mound of narrow-bladed, arching, blue-green foliage that remains evergreen to semi-evergreen during the winter. Starting in August, the grass sends up silvery-tan, feathery plumes five to six feet tall that complement the graceful foliage, persist through the winter, and add interest to the winter landscape.

Lowland Switch Grass (*Panicum virgatum,* **right**) is a Texas native that may reach eight feet tall and has blue-green, luxuriant foliage that turns a cinnamon color in the winter. It is topped by large, delicate panicles that wave in the wind. Although a large grass, lowland switch grass contributes a light, airy look to the landscape.

Maiden Grass (*Miscanthus sinensis* 'Adagio,' **left**) is an outstanding, imported grass for smaller gardens. It forms a gracefully-arching mound of foliage three feet tall and wide. The green leaves have a silver stripe down the center. Its tan-colored plumes reach four feet tall and persist through the winter.

GROWING CONDITIONS

Light: Full sun to light shade

Water: All three grasses have low water needs, requiring water every week or two after establishment (see pages 28 to 33).

Soil: Lindheimer's muhly and switch grass enjoy moist, heavy clay soil. 'Adagio' likes well-drained but moist soil.

Hardiness: All three thrive in zones 7 to 10.

Propagation: Division, although Lindheimer's muhly will occasionally reproduce from seed.

Pest Problems: No serious insect or disease problems.

PLANTING & MAINTENANCE

When to Plant: Anytime from a container, although fall is the best season to plant. Plant from divisions in late February or early March.

Trimming: Cut down foliage in late February or early March before new foliage emerges.

Fertilization: Low. Fertilize at planting time with a timed-release product. Less fertilizer is needed with the application of more organics. In the years after planting, fertilization needs vary, based on the nutrients in your soil. See pages 36 to 39 for more instructions.

Division: Once the clump has gotten too big, divide in late February or early March after you have cut back the foliage Dig the entire clump out of the ground, and split it into four parts with a sharp shovel. Plant the new divisions promptly.

PERENNIALS

Switch grass and Lindheimer's muhly are Texas natives.

Hibiscus, Perennial or Hardy

CHARACTERISTICS

Plant Type: Deciduous perennial (dies back in winter).

Average Size: 2 to 6 feet tall by 2 to 4 feet wide, depending on variety.

Growth Rate: Slow in cool, spring weather; growth rate increases substantially after the soil warms to above 70 degrees.

Leaf: Broad, lobed, green leaves, sometimes showing red veins.

Flower: Huge, open flowers, to 12 inches across, with prominent stamens. Individual flowers last only one day.

Origin: Native to Louisiana and other parts of the south.

Spacing: 3 to 6 feet on center (measure from the center of each plant), depending on variety.

Cautions: None known, except it is often damaged by deer.

Colors: Flowers are pink, red, white, lavender, or many bicolors.

Three hibiscus that do very well in north central Texas:
1. Hibiscus 'Flare'
2. Hibiscus 'Lord Baltimore'
3. Hibiscus 'Moy Grande'

Big splashes of bold color from summer to frost. Hibiscus produces the largest, showiest flowers in the summer garden. Requires a bit more trimming and fertilizer than most other plants in this book, so they don't rate a ribbon, but they are well worth the effort for the huge, beautiful flowers.

Hibiscus 'Luna White'

Several types of native hibiscus have been grown in Texas gardens for generations, but new, patented varieties of hardy hibiscus have set new standards for performance. These varieties feature fuller plants and larger, showier flowers in bright colors. They also come in manageable sizes, such as two-foot-tall dwarfs suitable for containers and five-foot-tall bushes ideal for the rear of sunny garden beds. Hardy hibiscus die back to the roots in winter and need no winter protection. They regrow after the soil warms in the spring.

The Fort Worth Botanic Garden features the three Texas Superstar™ hibiscus as designated by the Texas A & M University AgriLife Extension Service. The first is 'Flare,' a hybrid in almost constant bloom from summer until frost. It grows four feet tall and wide and has fuchsia-colored flowers six inches in diameter. 'Lord Baltimore,' another hybrid with stunning red flowers, grows five feet tall and wide and has flowers seven inches in diameter. The last is 'Moy Grande,' named after research scientist Dr. Moy of the San Antonio Botanical Garden. 'Moy Grande' grows five feet tall and wide and produces rose-pink flowers twelve inches in diameter!

Color Period: Starts blooming in early June in zone eight and mid-June in zone seven. Continues blooming until late September.

Buying Tips: Pay attention to the size listed on the plant tag at the garden center. Since different varieties of hibiscus vary from two to six feet tall, you need to be sure the one you choose fits your space.

Companions: The height of tall cultivars makes them useful for the back of sunny beds, while mid-sized and dwarf cultivars fit better up close where they can serve as specimen plants. The crepe-paper texture of hibiscus blossoms beckons up-close viewing, so it is nice to locate plants where the blossoms can be touched. The coarse texture of big hibiscus flowers and leaves are best offset by heat-tolerant flowers with a finer texture, such as angelonia, lantana, or 'Profusion' zinnias.

Try the flowers shown below for some textural as well as color contrast. All three bloom during the hottest part of summer.

'Purple Emperor'
Butterfly Bush
Plant Profile: Page 194

'Flamenco Samba' Cuphea
Plant Profile: Page 56

Hibiscus 'Luna White' and some companion plants

'Purple Emperor' Butterfly Bush (above, left) is one of the newer, more compact butterfly bushes that grows to about four feet tall and blooms at the same time as the 'Luna' hibiscus. Plant it behind the shorter hibiscus (two to three feet tall).

'Flamenco Samba' Cuphea (above, right) is a heat-loving annual that grows about 18 inches tall. Its smaller flowers and finer-textured foliage contrast well with the larger flowers and foliage of hibiscus. Samba's flowers look great with the hibiscus's flowers. 'Flamenco Samba' blooms all summer and fall and should be planted in front of the hibiscus.

GROWING CONDITIONS

Light: Full sun to slight afternoon shade.

Water: Medium after establishment. Likes water once or twice a week during the growing season, depending on its environment. See pages 28 to 33 for more information.

Soil: For the garden, plant in any fertile, well-drained soil that has been enriched with organic matter. Use only good-quality potting mix for containers. See pages 22 to 25 for specific instructions on soil preparation.

Hardiness: Most varieties grow well in zones 5 to 10. Tropical hibiscus have similar flowers but won't take freezes.

Propagation: The 'Belle' series can be grown from seed, but most superior varieties are grown from rooted stem cuttings.

Pest Problems: Japanese beetles can be a serious problem.

PLANTING & MAINTENANCE

When to Plant: Hibiscus from containers can be planted anytime. Fall is best because they establish more easily in cooler weather.

Trimming: To help plants grow bushy, pinch back growing tips at least twice in late spring and early summer. Even when pinched, plants often need staking when stems become heavy with buds. After cold weather kills back the plants, lop off the tops, leaving a 6-inch stub, and then mulch.

Fertilization: High. Fertilize at planting time and annually with a top-quality, timed-release product that includes minor elements. See pages 36 to 39 for more specifics.

Division: Hibiscus don't require division and are easier to propagate from stem cuttings. However, they can be divided every 5 years in spring.

PERENNIALS

Ice Plant

CHARACTERISTICS

Plant Type: Deciduous perennial (dies back in winter).

Average Size: 3 to 6 inches tall, spreading 18 to 24 inches wide.

Growth Rate: Fast

Leaf: Plump, gray-green, succulent leaves, needle-shaped; 1/4 inch wide and 2 inches long.

Flower: Star-like, daisy-shaped flowers about 2 inches across.

Origin: South Africa

Spacing: About 16 to 24 inches on center (measure from the center of each plant).

Cautions: Often damaged by deer

Colors: Flowers are lavender-blue, pink, coral, or yellow.

An excellent, blooming groundcover for hot, dry places, such as atop retaining walls or along walkways. Needs little maintenance, so it rates a red ribbon.* Best attribute is its low water needs. Lives on just rainwater after it is established.

Virtually unknown in gardens only ten years ago, ice plant has steadily gained ground in Texas gardens thanks to its tremendous tolerance of hot sun and dry conditions. The plants hoard moisture in their succulent leaves and can go without water even in times of summer drought. Their spreading habit makes them especially valuable when planted so that they cascade over walls, or use them to dress the edges of hot, concrete walkways. This plant's only weakness is a low tolerance for soggy winter conditions, so be sure to locate it where rainwater is quick to drain away.

Ice plants don't bloom as heavily in north central Texas as they do in cooler areas but are still worthwhile to plant.

Color Period: June through October

Buying Tips: If you can't find any ice plants at your garden center, try online suppliers.

1. 'Sequins' ice plant
2. 'Red Mountain' ice plant

Red ribbon plants are defined on page 13. For red ribbon performance, follow the planting and maintenance guidelines on pages 22 to 39.

Companions: In beds, ice plant makes a great groundcover to grow between widely-spaced roses, or you can use it as a low-growing companion plant for other drought-tolerant sun lovers such as agastache, coreopsis, gomphrena, or tall ornamental grasses.

For drought-tolerant color, use 'New Gold' lantana and 'Autumn Joy' sedum with ice plant. Both ice plant and sedum are succulents and can live on rainwater only. Lantana, however, looks better when watered every week or so.

'New Gold' Lantana
Plant Profile: Page 68

'Autumn Joy' Sedum
Plant Profile: Page 160

'Sequins' ice plant with some companions for drought-tolerant, color layers

'New Gold' Lantana (above, left) is an annual that blooms for the entire spring, summer, and fall season. It grows to about 18 to 24 inches tall and looks good with purple ice plant. Since the yellow lantana spreads quite a bit, keep the center of the lantana a full three feet away from the ice plant. That way, they won't crush each other. Both prefer full sun.

'Autumn Joy' Sedum (above, right) blooms in fall and grows 18 to 24 inches tall, like the lantana. Alternate the sedum with the lantana and border them with the ice plant. Plant all three in full sun.

GROWING CONDITIONS

Light: Full sun. Tolerates some afternoon shade.

Water: Very low after establishment. Lives on rainwater alone without supplemental water in all but the most extreme conditions.

Soil: Any fertile, well-drained soil that has been enriched with organic matter. Requires good drainage. See pages 22 to 25 for instructions.

Hardiness: Zones 6 to 10

Propagation: Division and cuttings. Root 4-inch-long stem tip cuttings whenever the plants are not in bloom. All varieties occasionally self-sow in areas where they are happy.

Pest Problems: Rare. Very wet winter conditions can cause plants to rot.

PLANTING & MAINTENANCE

When to Plant: Ice plants from containers can be planted at any time. Fall is best because they establish more easily in cooler weather, but you are more likely to find them at your garden center in early spring, when they are blooming.

Trimming: Ice plants need only casual deadheading (removal of dead flowers) through early summer. If plants appear ragged in midsummer, shearing them back by 1/3 of their size will encourage the development of new bud-bearing stems.

Fertilization: Low. This plant is not a heavy feeder and usually does fine with a single application of a balanced, timed-release fertilizer at planting time, provided it has organics added annually. See pages 36 to 39 for more instructions.

Division: Divide every 3 to 5 years in early spring if you want more plants.

PERENNIALS

*Lives on rainwater alone in all but the most extreme situations

Iris

CHARACTERISTICS

Plant Type: Most irises are evergreen perennials; some are deciduous (lose their leaves in winter).

Average Size: Sizes range from tiny (4 inches tall) to tall (5 feet tall). Most are from 18 to 24 inches tall and range from 6 to 18 inches wide.

Growth Rate: Medium

Leaf: Green to greenish-blue, flat, sword-shaped leaves.

Flower: Exotic, open blossoms with some petals curving down and others curving upward.

Origin: Various species native to America, Europe, and Asia.

Spacing: Varies with type. Set rhizomes of bearded iris at least 8 inches apart. Closer spacing is better with other types of iris, which grow into dense clumps when set 3 to 8 inches apart.

Cautions: Poisonous; often damaged by deer.

Colors: Flowers are blue, white, yellow, pink, purple, or with many blends and bicolors.

Bearded irises have a fuzzy spot on their petals that looks like a pipe cleaner.

Glamorous plants that are easy to grow in Texas, if you choose the right one. Thousands of different choices. Great plants to collect. Rates a blue ribbon* because of its ease of care.

Dutch iris 'Oriental Beauty'

Irises are the one of the most glamorous plants for Texas gardens. Although they bloom for a short time, the visual impact of the blooms, coupled with their ease of care, make them definitely worthwhile. The hardest part is choosing the right one for your garden because there are thousands available. The five described on the opposite page do well in Texas as a whole. The Fort Worth Botanic Garden features a collection of different types of irises.

Color Period: Most bloom early to late spring (for about two weeks), depending on variety. A few re-bloom in the fall.

Buying Tips: Not only are there thousands of irises on the market, hundreds more appear each year. Local garden centers are often good sources of information about how their irises do. Local iris societies often have sales in late summer. Online suppliers are endless (try www.johnscheepers.com or www.parkseed.com). For more information, see www.irises.org.

Blue ribbon plants are defined on page 12. For blue ribbon performance, follow the planting and maintenance guidelines on pages 22 to 39.

Botanical Name: *Iris* spp.
Family: Iridaceae

Bearded Iris 'Sarah Taylor'

Bearded Iris (*Iris germanica*, left): Eight to 24 inches tall. Hugely popular; often bloom for years with little care beyond regular feeding. Do not overwater because this one likes to be on the dry side. More susceptible to iris borer than the other varieties. Divide in September.

Dutch Iris (*Iris hollandica*, right): Dutch irises perform well in north central Texas and make excellent cut flowers. They grow 18 to 22 inches tall and create a formal look in beds. They come in an array of beautiful colors.

Dutch Iris

Japanese Iris (*Iris ensata*, left): Largest flowers of all irises and the last to bloom. They require full sun, acidic soil, and ample water. Two to four feet tall. Plant rhizomes two inches deep in fall or spring.

Japanese Iris 'Goldbound'

Louisiana Iris *(Iris spathula hexagonae*, right): Five species of marshland plants that thrive when given ample moisture and acid soil. A top choice for growing near or even in water or in low places where few other flowers are happy. Evergreen in most of Texas. Three to five feet tall. Divide in late summer.

Louisiana Iris 'James Dickenson'

Siberian Iris (*Iris sibirica* left): Resembles Louisiana iris, but the plants and flowers are smaller. Prefers moist and acidic soil. Varies from one to three feet tall. Fewer pests than the other varieties. Bloom best when allowed to grow into thick clump. They can be divided right after bloom or while they are dormant from fall to early spring.

Siberian Iris 'Butter and Sugar'

GROWING CONDITIONS

Light: Light shade to full sun

Water: Medium for most, but Louisiana iris needs more moisture and can even be grown in shallow water. Avoid overwatering other irises, however, because rot can result.

Soil: Fertile, well-drained soil that has been enriched with organic matter suits most irises. Louisiana iris requires acid soil.

Hardiness: Varies. Many irises are hardy to zone 3. Some Louisiana irises grow as far south as zone 10.

Propagation: Although some grow from seed, all grow from division.

Pest Problems: Iris borer can seriously damage bearded iris rhizomes. Affected plants are weak, bloom poorly, and have holes in their roots. Treat with the least toxic pesticide available. Another problem is rot caused by overwatering, mulch, or burying the rhizomes too deep.

PLANTING & MAINTENANCE

When to Plant: Irises from containers can be planted at any time. Fall is best because they establish more easily in cooler weather. Plant rhizomes or bulbs in early spring or in late summer. Arrange the rhizome or bulb, so the new leaf end is pointing up.

Planting Depth: Plant bearded iris rhizomes 1 inch deep, leaving the rhizome partially exposed.

Trimming: If desired, use scissors to cut away leaves or flower stems that turn brown. Cut back near to the ground the iris foliage that dies back in the winter.

Fertilization: Fertilize in early spring, soon after new growth appears (pages 36 to 39). If plants are set out (or divided) in late summer, fertilize them again.

PERENNIALS

Lenten Rose

CHARACTERISTICS

Plant Type: Evergreen perennial.

Average Size: About 12 to 16 inches tall and equally as wide.

Growth Rate: Medium. Plants need 2 to 3 years to attain mature size. They need 5 years to flower from seed.

Leaf: Glossy, green leaflets to 4 inches long, usually with serrated edges.

Flower: 1 to 2 inch wide, rose-like bracts with centers comprised of pincushion clusters of stamens.

Origin: Macedonia and Turkey

Spacing: About 14 inches on center (measure from the center of each plant). Closer in containers.

Cautions: All plant parts are poisonous. Almost never damaged by deer.

Colors: Flowers are shades of pink, purple, burgundy, green, white, and yellow, slate, red, or bicolors.

Lenten rose 'Royal Heritage Strain'

One of the few, evergreen perennials that is almost never damaged by deer! Lenten roses perform so well they earn a blue ribbon.* Their delightful, nodding blossoms in late winter are framed by glossy foliage. Before winter ends, lenten roses bring the woodland garden to life with up to two months of lovely flowers.

Any garden that gets winter sun followed by summer shade is a good home for lenten roses, which have the unusual talent of blooming in late winter, with flowers that survive ice and snow. Lenten roses need little help to form long-lived colonies beneath the shelter of large oaks or other shade trees. Because the blossoms face downward, you will enjoy this plant most if you grow it in raised beds, along steps, or atop a retaining wall. Lenten rose blossoms make good cut flowers if you sear the stem ends to hold in the sap. The blossoms look particularly nice when floating in a bowl.

Color Period: Late winter to spring. Plants often bloom for two to three months.

Buying Tips: Since lenten roses take five years from the time a seed is planted until the plant grows large enough to flower, buy the largest plants you can find and afford!

Blue ribbon plants are defined on page 12. For blue ribbon performance, follow the planting and maintenance guidelines on pages 22 to 39.

Companions: Shade garden plants, such as azaleas, hostas, and heucheras, make good partners for lenten roses, or you can grow them with daffodils or other spring-flowering bulbs. Edge lenten rose beds with liriope, and set annual begonias among the plants in early summer, when lenten rose foliage becomes thin. Also, try planting lenten roses beneath Japanese maples or ornamental cherries.

Gardeners who often feel impatient for the arrival of spring love to grow lenten roses in big window boxes, situated so the blooms can be enjoyed from indoors while cold winds still blow. Plant such a box in late spring, and keep it in a shady spot outdoors until mid winter.

For easy color layers, try camellias and azaleas with lenten rose, as shown below.

Camellia
Plant Profile: Page 196

Azalea
Plant Profile: Page 188

Lenten roses and some companion plants for easy color layers

Camellias (above, left) bloom at the same time as lenten roses, if you plant the right ones. Ask at your local garden center for a cultivar that shares the same bloom time. Both plants appreciate light shade.

Azaleas (above, right) also bloom at the same time as lenten roses. Plant the camellia as the tallest layer, with the azaleas as the mid layer. Border the grouping with lenten roses.

GROWING CONDITIONS

Light: Partial shade, or winter sun and summer shade.

Water: Medium after establishment. Likes water once or twice a week during the growing season, depending on its environment. See pages 28 to 33 for more information.

Soil: Any fertile, well-drained soil, enriched with organic matter. Requires good drainage. See pages 22 to 25 for instructions.

Hardiness: Zones 4 to 9

Propagation: Seeds or division. Plants often reseed on their own; flowers from seedlings are not necessarily the same color as their parents' flowers.

Pest Problems: None severe

PLANTING & MAINTENANCE

When to Plant: Lenten roses from containers can be planted at any time. Fall is best because they establish more easily in cooler weather. Lenten roses reseed, and young plants can be dug and moved to new locations in late summer, after the bloom season ends.

Trimming: Allow lenten rose foliage to grow freely until it yellows and dies back, which varies from early to late summer, depending on site and climate. Cut back faded foliage at the soil line.

Fertilization: Medium. Fertilize at planting time and each spring with a timed-release product. Less fertilizer is needed with the application of more organics. See pages 36 to 39 for more instructions.

Division: Lenten rose clumps can be left alone for up to 20 years. They recover from division very slowly. Use prolific seedlings if you want more plants.

PERENNIALS

Lilies, Naked Ladies

CHARACTERISTICS

Plant Type: Perennial bulb; tall foliage dies back in late spring, like daffodils. This is the reverse of most plants. The plant flowers in summer with no leaves.

Average Size: About 18 to 24 inches tall in bloom; 14 inches wide during foliar growth phase.

Growth Rate: Fast

Leaf: Medium green, strap-shaped, fleshy leaves to 16 inches long and 1 to 2 inches wide. Foliage emerges in the fall and persists until spring.

Flower: Clusters of 4 or more, 3 inch long florets atop bare stems; blossoms are flared trumpets, more typical of lilies.

Origin: China and Japan

Spacing: About 8 inches on center (measure from the center of each plant) and 6 inches deep.

Cautions: Bulbs are mildly toxic if eaten. Somewhat resistant to deer.

Colors: Flowers are pink or mauve

Incredibly easy plant that gives spectacular impact with very little care. Blooms in late summer or early fall, when many other summer bloomers are done. Easily rates a blue ribbon.*

Naked ladies with black-eyed Susans

After baking in hot soil through the summer dry season, naked ladies send up bare stems overnight after a deep, drenching rain; these stems are topped by dramatic clusters of lavender-pink blossoms. The plants are called "naked ladies" because they bloom when they are bare of leaves. Foliage appears in fall and dies down by early summer. Although the bloom time is short - less than three weeks - these bulbs endear themselves by persisting for decades with no care and by providing lovely color when little else is in bloom.

Naked ladies multiply quickly.

Color Period: From late July through August. Blooms last about three weeks.

Buying Tips: If you can't find these plants at your local garden center, they are readily available online or from catalog companies.

*Blue ribbon plants are defined on page 12. For blue ribbon performance, follow the planting and maintenance guidelines on pages 22 to 39.

Companions: Naked ladies steal the show when they are in bloom, so they are definitely a focal point flower. They attract the most attention when planted in large drifts. Plant them near a water feature, birdbath, mailbox, or close to your deck or patio where they can't be missed. Light pink naked ladies look great before a background of evergreen shrubs or coming up through groundcovers. They also work well interspersed among clumps of daylilies, which hide the failing foliage from view in early summer. These bulbs need a period of summer dryness, so avoid combining them with plants that need abundant water. They are easy to naturalize beneath deciduous trees, alongside daffodils and other spring-blooming bulbs.

Naked ladies flower in summer when a number of our best perennials and shrubs are in flower as well. Try layering them with the high performers shown below for a dazzling summer show.

'Endless Summer' Hydrangea
Plant Profile: Page 220

Southern Wood Fern
Plant Profile: Page 126

Naked ladies with companion plants that form easy color layers

'Endless Summer' Hydrangea (above, left) grows three to four feet tall and blooms for most of the summer, coordinating with the naked ladies' flower time. The large hydrangea flowers contrast well with the smaller naked ladies' flowers. Use this hydrangea as the tallest layer of this grouping.

Southern Wood Fern (above, right) grows two to three feet tall and provides a light green, soft-textured foil for the lavender-pink blossoms of naked ladies. Use it as the mid layer and border the grouping with the smaller naked ladies.

GROWING CONDITIONS

Light: Partial shade to sun in winter; partial shade in summer.

Water: Plants need water only in spring, their active period of growth. A dry period in summer, followed by drenching rain, triggers flowering.

Soil: Any well-drained soil. Drainage is essential, so be sure to loosen clay under the bulb if you are planting in clay.

Hardiness: Zones 5 to 9

Propagation: Division

Pest Problems: Rare

PLANTING & MAINTENANCE

When to Plant: Set out bulbs at any time except spring. Regardless of planting time, they may not bloom their first year. Dig, divide, and replant bulbs in early summer, just as the foliage fades away.

Planting Depth: Twice as deep as the diameter of the bulb.

Trimming: When the leaves turn brown in early summer, trim them off with a sharp knife or pruning shears if you find them unsightly.

Fertilization: Medium. Fertilize at planting time and each fall with a timed-release product. Less fertilizer is needed with the application of more organics. See pages 36 to 39 for more instructions.

Division: Dig, divide, and replant in early summer to increase your supply but no more often than every 4 or 5 years.

PERENNIALS

Lily, Philippine

CHARACTERISTICS

Plant Type: Deciduous perennial (dies back in winter).

Average Size: 3 to 5 feet tall by 1 foot wide.

Growth Rate: Fast

Leaf: Dark green and narrow; 8 inches long.

Flower: Trumpet-shaped, 5 to 8 inches long.

Origin: Taiwan and the Philippines

Spacing: About 2 feet on center (measure from the center of each plant).

Cautions: None known

Colors: Flowers are white

Easy-to-grow bulb that produces clusters of fragrant white flowers in late summer. This plant is definitely a blue ribbon plant* because of its carefree culture and its beautiful white blossoms that appear when few other bulbs are blooming.

Philippine lily is one of the best hardy lilies for the entire state of Texas. It adorns the late summer garden with showy clusters of drooping, white, fragrant, trumpet-shaped flowers that resemble Easter lily blossoms. Even after the flowers disappear, the seed capsules add visual interest to the plant the rest of the summer.

Color Period: Blooms in July or August for about two weeks

Buying Tips: Since this bulb is relatively obscure in Texas, few garden centers carry it. It can be ordered from online plant and bulb sources, like www.southernbulbs.com.

Blue ribbon plants are defined on page 12. For blue ribbon performance, follow the planting and maintenance guidelines on pages 22 to 39.

Companions: Philippine lily combines very well with summer-blooming annuals, perennials, ornamental grasses, and roses. Black-eyed Susans, cannas, and summer phlox are good companions. Or, plant them with esperanza 'Gold Star' and cleome, as shown below.

Esperanza 'Gold Star'
Plant Profile: Page 62

'Senorita Rosalita'
Cleome
Plant Profile: Page 52

Philippine lily and some companions

Esperanza 'Gold Star' (above, top) gets about as tall as Philippine lily and should be interplanted among the lilies. Its cheery, golden yellow flowers and bright green foliage combine well with the white lily flowers to create a fresh, summery look to the garden. The smaller, yellow flowers of 'Gold Star' contrast well with the larger, trumpet-shaped flowers of the lily.

'Senorita Rosalita' Cleome (above, bottom) makes a light, airy annual companion for Philippine lily. Since both reach about the same height, cleome should be planted among the lilies. The airy clusters of bright lavender-pink cleome flowers create a delicate and pastel contrast to the white lily blossoms. The lighter green, palm-shaped leaves of cleome contrast nicely with the darker green, grass-like leaves of the Philippine lily to create a striking foliar contrast.

GROWING CONDITIONS

Light: Light shade to full sun

Water: Medium after establishment. Likes water once or twice a week during the growing season, depending on its environment. See pages 28 to 33 for more information.

Soil: For the garden, plant in any fertile, well-drained soil that has been enriched with organic matter. See page 22 to 25 for specific instructions on soil preparation.

Hardiness: Zones 6 through 9

Propagation: Seeds or division

Pest Problems: No insect or disease problems.

PLANTING & MAINTENANCE

When to Plant: Spring

Planting Depth: Cover with soil to twice the height of the bulb.

Trimming: Cut back the dead foliage (to the ground) after it freezes in late fall or early winter. Other than that, no trimming is required, but you might want to remove the dead flowers.

Fertilization: Low. Fertilize at planting time with a timed-release product. Less fertilizer is needed with the application of more organics. In the years after planting, fertilization needs vary, based on the nutrients in your soil. See pages 36 to 39 for more instructions.

Division: Dig and divide in fall, but we have never divided ours yet. This plant has produced only one tall cane from a single bulb so far for us, so there has been no reason to divide.

PERENNIALS

Lilies, Spider or Hurricane

1ST

CHARACTERISTICS

Plant Type: Perennial bulb; winter foliage dies back in summer, which is the reverse of most bulbs. The plant flowers with no leaves. The flowers disappear by the time new leaves form.

Average Size: About 18 inches tall in bloom; 8 to 10 inches wide during foliar growth phase.

Growth Rate: Fast

Leaf: Dark green with a silver stripe down the center. Leaves are narrow, like grass. Foliage emerges in the fall and persists until spring.

Flower: Clusters of 4 or more florets atop bare stems; spider lilies have long stamens, with florets resembling those of azalea.

Origin: China and Japan

Spacing: About 7 to 9 inches on center (measure from the center of each plant).

Cautions: Bulbs are mildly toxic if eaten. Somewhat resistant to deer.

Colors: Flowers are red

ALTERNATE SELECTIONS

If you have a partially shaded, white garden, seek out the white flowering spider lily (*Lycoris x albiflora*), the perfect companion for 'Monroe White' liriope. Yellow-flowered species (*Lycoris aurea*) are available, but they are often not as dependable as red spider lilies.

Sudden bursts of color in late summer or early fall that provide strong and dramatic accents. Short bloom period but incredibly easy to grow. Survives both droughts and floods. Easily rates a blue ribbon.*

Like their cousins, the naked lady lilies (pages 142-143), spider lilies spend most of the summer hibernating until late August or early September. At that time, their bare stems pop out of the ground with clusters of predominately red flowers. They are often called hurricane lilies because their blooms often follow on the heels of tropical storms. They develop thin, grass-like leaves in fall that persist until spring. Although the bloom time is short, lasting less than three weeks, these bulbs endear themselves by persisting for decades with no care and providing lovely color when little else is in bloom. The slope behind the floral clock at the Fort Worth Botanic Garden features a beautiful display of red spider lilies every fall. These bulbs multiply rapidly.

Color Period: Late August to early October, depending on rainfall. Blooms last about two weeks. Spider lilies frequently don't bloom until their second year in the ground.

Buying Tips: If you can't find these plants at your local garden center, they are readily available online or from catalog companies.

Blue ribbon plants are defined on page 12. For blue ribbon performance, follow the planting and maintenance guidelines on pages 22 to 39.

Companions: Spider lilies steal the show when they are in bloom, so they are definitely a focal point flower. They work well interspersed among clumps of daylilies, which hide the failing foliage from view in early summer. These bulbs need a period of summer dryness, so avoid combining them with plants that need abundant water.

For major color impact, combine spider lilies with flowers of contrasting colors, like blue and yellow. Try layering this lily with blue perennial salvia and golden shrimp plants for a high-impact accent area, as shown below.

'Black and Blue' Salvia
Plant Profile: Page 156

Golden Shrimp Plant
Plant Profile: Page 84

Spider lilies with companion plants that form easy layers of color

Black and Blue Salvia (above, left) grows to about four feet tall and dependably blooms at the same time as spider lilies. This salvia also grows well in light shade, an ideal light condition for spider lilies. Use this salvia as the tallest layer in this grouping.

Golden Shrimp Plant (above, right) is an annual that is always blooming in the late summer to early fall period, when the spider lily flowers. Use it as the mid layer in this grouping, with the spider lilies as the border.

GROWING CONDITIONS

Light: Sun in winter; partial shade in summer.

Water: Plants need water only in spring, their active period of growth. A dry period in summer, followed by drenching rain, triggers flowering. Keeping them moist during the flowering period keeps them in bloom longer.

Soil: Any fertile, well-drained soil that stays dry in the summer.

Hardiness: Zones 7 to 10; survives in zone 7 if planted in a protected location and mulched.

Propagation: Division

Pest Problems: Rare

PLANTING & MAINTENANCE

When to Plant: Fall. Bulbs may not bloom their first year.

Planting Depth: 4 to 6 inches

Trimming: When the leaves turn brown in early summer, trim them off with a sharp knife or pruning shears if you find them unsightly.

Fertilization: Medium. Fertilize at planting time and each spring with a timed-release product. Less fertilizer is needed with the application of more organics. See pages 36 to 39 for more instructions.

Division: Dig, divide, and replant in early summer to increase your supply, but no more often than every 4 or 5 years. Newly-planted bulbs often take 2 years to bloom.

PERENNIALS

Mexican Mint Marigold

1ST

CHARACTERISTICS

Plant Type: Deciduous perennial (dies back in winter).

Average Size: 30 to 36 inches tall and 18 inches wide.

Growth Rate: Fast

Leaf: Medium green, 2 inches long and 1/2 inch wide; when crushed, the leaves smell like licorice.

Flower: Daisy-like, single flowers; slightly under 1 inch in diameter.

Origin: Mexico and Guatemala

Spacing: About 3 feet on center (measure from the center of each plant).

Cautions: None known. Almost never damaged by deer.

Colors: Flowers are golden yellow

This is a perennial marigold that looks nothing like the common, annual marigold. Mexican mint marigold is not plagued by spider mites, a pest that takes a toll on annual marigolds in our area. The golden yellow flowers appear in the fall. This plant earns a blue ribbon* because of its ease of care.

Mexican mint marigold is an easy-to-grow perennial that puts on a marvelous show in the fall. Even if this perennial didn't flower, it would be worth having in the garden because of its licorice-scented leaves which are a popular substitute for tarragon. Place this charming plant in an area where you can easily pick a few of its leaves for use in cooking – perhaps in a kitchen or herb garden. The golden yellow flowers brighten up the fall garden and bloom at the same time as the fall aster, its best companion plant. Mexican mint marigold dies down after a freeze in the fall but returns the following spring.

Color Period: Blooms in October or November for about three weeks

Buying Tips: Readily available in many garden centers and nurseries

Blue ribbon plants are defined on page 12. For blue ribbon performance, follow the planting and maintenance guidelines on pages 22 to 39.

Resists Deer   Avg. Weeks of Color   ③

Companions: Mexican mint marigold forms a nice little green shrub during the growing season and, because of its height, can be placed in the middle of the mixed border with taller plants behind it and lower ones in front of it (as shown on the opposite page). Good taller plants include the blue-flowering 'Henry Duelberg' salvia, the purple-flowering Mexican bush sage, or any number of ornamental grasses, such as *Miscanthus* 'Adagio.'

Fall aster is one of the best partners for this marigold. See that combination on page 131.

Red autumn sage grows about the same height as Mexican mint marigold, increases its flower production in the fall, and creates a striking contrast with the flowers of Mexican mint marigold. Pair the two as a border for the taller Mexican bush sage, as shown below.

Mexican Bush Sage
Plant Profile: Page 156

Autumn Sage
Plant Profile: Page 156

Mexican mint marigold and some companions

Mexican Bush Sage (above, left) is another spectacular, fall-blooming perennial that looks fantastic with this marigold. The sage grows taller (about four feet), so it works well as a background plant for the marigold. For best flowering, plant them in light shade to full sun.

Autumn Sage (above, right) is a perennial that grows about the same height as the marigold. It blooms from April through October, so its bloom period corresponds as well. Alternate clumps of the two plants in front of the taller sage for a spectacular fall show.

GROWING CONDITIONS

Light: Full sun, at least 6 hours per day.

Water: Low after establishment. Likes water every week or two during the growing season, depending on its environment. See pages 28 to 33 for more information.

Soil: Any fertile, well-drained soil that has been enriched with organic matter. Requires good drainage. See pages 22 to 25 for instructions.

Hardiness: Zones 8 to 10

Propagation: Rooted cuttings or division.

Pest Problems: Not plagued by spider mites the way common marigolds are in north central Texas.

PLANTING & MAINTENANCE

When to Plant: Mexican mint marigolds from containers can be planted at any time. Fall is best because they establish more easily in cooler weather.

Trimming: Cut back the dead foliage (to the ground) after it freezes in late fall or early winter.

Fertilization: Low. Fertilize at planting time with a timed-release product. Less fertilizer is needed with the application of more organics. In the years after planting, fertilization needs vary, based on the nutrients in your soil. See pages 36 to 39 for more instructions.

Division: Divide clumps in spring if they get too full or when you need more plants. No harm done if you don't divide them; you'll just have a bigger clump.

PERENNIALS

Phlox, Garden

1ST

CHARACTERISTICS

Plant Type: Deciduous perennial (dies back in winter).

Average Size: 3 feet tall by 2 feet wide.

Growth Rate: Moderate

Leaf: Dark green, narrow, pointed leaves to 3 inches long and up to 1 inch wide.

Flower: 6 to 12 inch long, terminal clusters of fragrant, star-shaped flowers; 1/2 to 1 inch in diameter with 5 flat petals.

Origin: In general, eastern and southeastern U.S. This particular cultivar was discovered in San Antonio and named after late Texas nurseryman John Fanick.

Spacing: 18 to 24 inches on center (measure from the center of each plant). Keep the plants well-spaced because they do better with some air circulation.

Cautions: Occasionally damaged by deer.

Colors: Flowers are light pink with a darker pink eye.

'John Fanick' is perhaps the best garden phlox for Texas because of its compact growth habit, resistance to powdery mildew, and its tolerance towards heat and drought. The Texas A & M AgriLife Extension Service has designated it a Texas Superstar™ plant, and it definitely rates a blue ribbon* designation as well.

This easy-to-grow phlox rewards the gardener with outstanding performance in the summer garden. 'John Fanick' makes a full, compact plant with sturdy stems that need no staking. The dark green leaves are very attractive and free of the powdery mildew that is common on phlox in Texas. They are a perfect foil for the large, showy clusters of light pink flowers. These flowers are fragrant, stand out from a distance, and attract butterflies and hummingbirds.

Color Period: June to September, continuously

Buying Tips: Available in better nurseries and garden centers in four-inch pots and one gallon containers. Available through online nurseries as well.

Blue ribbon plants are defined on page 12. For blue ribbon performance, follow the planting and maintenance guidelines on pages 22 to 39.

Companions: Garden phlox is a staple of the perennial border. 'John Fanick' mixes well with other perennials and provides summer long blooms. Plant it among other summer flowering perennials, such as Philippine lilies, black-eyed Susans, or coneflowers. It also looks great with blooming shrubs, such as butterfly bush, and dwarf crapemyrtles. Or, try it in front of dark-leafed loropetalum because its light pink flowers really stand out against the dark purple leaves.

For a long-blooming, color accent area, plant 'Knock Out' roses and salvia with this phlox, as shown below.

'John Fanick' phlox with some companions

'Knock Out' Roses (above, left). The light pink flowers of 'John Fanick' really stand out against the cherry red flowers of this rose that blooms almost continuously from spring to fall. The dark pink centers of 'John Fanick' create a "color echo" of the darker 'Knock Out' flowers. Since 'Knock Out' grows four to six feet tall, plant it as a backdrop behind 'John Fanick.'

'Henry Duelberg' Salvia (above, right). This three foot tall and wide perennial contrasts beautifully with 'John Fanick' and makes the flowers of 'John Fanick' stand out that much more. The smaller, lighter green leaves of 'Henry Duelberg' differ from those of the phlox. The dark blue spikes of salvia flowers provide contrast in form as well as color. Since these two perennials are about the same height, plant them side by side in the flower bed for a stunning effect. Plant them in front of the taller roses.

GROWING CONDITIONS

Light: Full sun

Water: Medium after establishment. Likes water once or twice a week during the growing season, depending on its environment. See pages 28 to 33 for more information.

Soil: Any fertile, well-drained soil that has been enriched with organic matter. Requires good drainage. See pages 22 to 25 for instructions.

Hardiness: Zones 4 to 9

Propagation: Division or rooted stem cuttings.

Pest Problems: None. 'John Fanick' is resistant to powdery mildew, which plagues most cultivars of garden phlox.

PLANTING & MAINTENANCE

When to Plant: Phlox from containers can be planted at any time. Fall is best because they establish more easily in cooler weather, but you are more likely to find them at your garden center in summer, when they are blooming.

Trimming: Remove faded flowers to prolong the bloom period. Cut back the dead foliage (to the ground) after it freezes in late fall or early winter.

Fertilization: Medium. Fertilize at planting time and annually with a timed-release product. Less fertilizer is needed with the application of more organics. See pages 36 to 39 for more instructions.

Division: Every third year, divide clumps in fall or early spring if you think the clump is too big or when you need new starts to transplant. Not much harm in not dividing; you'll just have a larger clump.

PERENNIALS

Purple Heart

CHARACTERISTICS

Plant Type: Deciduous perennial (dies back in winter).

Average Size: 10 to 14 inches tall by 16 inches wide.

Growth Rate: Fast

Leaf: Deep purple, 3 inch leaves on brittle, angular stems.

Flower: Small, triangular (orchid-pink) flowers to 1/2 inch across.

Origin: Eastern Mexico

Spacing: About 10 inches on center (measure from the center of each plant). Closer in containers.

Cautions: Sap is an irritant. Seldom bothered by deer.

Colors: Leaves are deep purple in sun, slightly greenish in shade; orchid-pink flowers. The flowers don't last long. The best feature of this plant is the colorful leaves.

BUDGET GARDENING TIP

Covering a lot of ground with purchased plants gets expensive. However, just one purple heart plant can cover a lot of ground, even in its first season, because it is so easy to propagate. Throughout summer, stem cuttings will root readily in moist soil or in a jar of water.

Purple heart's flowers are rather insignificant. Its best feature is the purple leaf color.

One of the few, low-growing perennials that offers five to six months of color with almost no care! Bold purple foliage with coarse texture is a high contrast player in the summer garden. Easily rates a blue ribbon.*

Purple heart planted with pink vinca

Purple heart is a champion, summer groundcover that tolerates heat, drought, and even comes back when mowed. Long billed as an annual under the name of setcreasea, this sprawling spreader is surprisingly hardy, capable of surviving winter temperatures to zero degrees. It's a great plant to use in areas bordered by grass or for remote spots that are difficult to water. A potent source of both dark purple color and coarse texture, purple heart is ideal for framing plantings when your goal is to maximize contrast.

Color Period: Late summer to fall. Flowers open in the morning and close at night. The flowers are rather insignificant, however. The main feature of this plant is the purple leaf.

Buying Tips: Purple heart is available at quite a few garden centers in spring. If you just buy a few, you can easily root cuttings from them to make quite a few more plants.

Blue ribbon plants are defined on page 12. For blue ribbon performance, follow the planting and maintenance guidelines on pages 22 to 39.

Companions: Purple heart is quite versatile in the spring, summer, and fall gardens. It works well in a number of different color schemes. Lime green is a wonderful companion color in the form of coleus, sweet potato vines, hostas, or heucheras. Pale pink or lavender is a softer choice, from the flowers of vinca, petunias, or pentas. Or, try it with yellow melampodium and red dragon wing begonias for a traffic-stopping combination.

For very easy color, try purple heart with the great performers shown below. This combination gives you drought tolerance as well.

'Cherry Dazzle' Crapemyrtle
Plant Profile: Page 206

'New Gold' Lantana
Plant Profile: Page 68

Purple heart with some companion plants

'Cherry Dazzle' Crapemyrtle (above, left) blooms for up to 90 days if you remove the dead flowers. Its bloom period coincides with the purple heart's summer color period. Since dwarf crapemyrtles grow from three to five feet tall, use them behind the shorter purple heart and yellow lantana.

'New Gold' Lantana (above, right) is an annual that blooms for the entire spring, summer, and fall season. Since it grows to about two feet tall, place it behind the purple heart. Because the yellow lantana spreads quite a bit, keep the center of the lantana a full two feet away from the center of the purple heart. That way, the lantana won't take over the purple heart. Both prefer full sun.

GROWING CONDITIONS

Light: Light shade to full sun. Loses color in too much shade.

Water: Low. Once established, purple heart's semi-succulent leaves and stems help it tolerate drought. Ours have always been watered weekly, so we haven't tried it without any irrigation.

Soil: Any fertile, well-drained soil that has been enriched with organic matter. Requires good drainage. See pages 22 to 25 for instructions.

Hardiness: Zones 8 to 11. In very cold winter areas, cuttings can be rooted, potted up, and kept through winter as indoor houseplants, then planted outdoors in spring.

Propagation: Stem cutting or division.

Pest Problems: No serious insect or disease problems.

PLANTING & MAINTENANCE

When to Plant: Purple heart from containers can be planted at any time. Fall is best because they establish more easily in cooler weather, but you are more likely to find them at your garden center in spring or summer.

Trimming: Purple heart doesn't need trimming in most situations during the growing season. However, if it gets too wild-looking for you, cut it back to half its size. Cut back the dead foliage to the ground after it freezes in late fall or early winter.

Fertilization: Medium. Fertilize at planting time and each spring with a timed-release product. Less fertilizer is needed with the application of more organics. See pages 36 to 39 for more instructions.

Division: Seldom needs division. Root cuttings for more plants.

PERENNIALS

Red-Hot Poker

CHARACTERISTICS

Plant Type: Deciduous perennial (dies back in winter).

Average Size: About 3 to 4 feet tall by 2 to 3 feet wide. Flower spikes often reach 4 feet tall.

Growth Rate: Fast

Leaf: Long, narrow, grass-like leaves about 2 feet long by 1/2 inch wide.

Flower: Unique, spiky flower shaped like a poker.

Origin: South Africa

Spacing: About 2 to 3 feet on center (measure from the center of each plant). Closer in containers.

Cautions: Almost never damaged by deer.

Colors: Flowers are orange, yellow, or red. Red flowers are often lime or yellow on the bottom of the bloom as they age.

Red-hot poker with gaillardia

Terrific color impact from a plant that loves heat and drought. Great, hot colors. Very easy to grow if you give it good drainage. Rates a red ribbon.*

Red-hot poker plants have been thriving at the Fort Worth Botanic Garden for over fifteen years.

The best features of red-hot poker are the unique flower shape and hot colors. Their bloom period is not the longest, but the color impact makes them worth planting. Use a few clumps of these flowers in your summer gardens for lots of oohs and aahs!

Color Period: Blooms for four to six weeks from June to August

Buying Tips: We have tried only a few different kinds, and all have done well.

*Red ribbon plants are defined on page 13. For red ribbon performance, follow the planting and maintenance guidelines on pages 22 to 39.

Attracts Butterflies

Attracts Hummingbirds

Resists Deer

(5)
Avg. Weeks of Color

Botanical Name: *Kniphofia uvaria*
Family: Liliaceae

Companions: Use red-hot poker in clumps to accent summer flower beds. They look best with flowers of different colors and shapes, including agastache, black-eyed Susan, lantana, coneflowers, coreopsis, verbena, and yarrow.

Red-hot poker looks good alternated with clumps of daylilies and bordered by purple heart, as shown below.

Red-hot poker with some companions

'Stella de Oro' Daylily (top left) is one of the longest blooming perennial daylilies, blooming for up to three months each summer. Its 18 to 24 inch height fits well in front of the 36 inch poker. Plant both in full sun for most blooms.

Purple Heart (bottom left) is an excellent perennial that gives your garden strong color from spring to the first frost of fall or early winter. Plant it in front of your daylilies and poker plants, as a border.

GROWING CONDITIONS

Light: Full sun, at least 6 hours per day.

Water: Medium after establishment. Likes water once or twice a week during the growing season, depending on its environment. See pages 28 to 33 for more information.

Soil: Any fertile, well-drained soil that has been enriched with organic matter. Requires good drainage. See pages 22 to 25 for instructions.

Hardiness: Zones 7 to 9. If you protect them with mulch in winter, they grow in zones 5 and 6.

Propagation: Division

Pest Problems: We have never had a pest on this plant, but root rot is a major problem in wet soils.

PLANTING & MAINTENANCE

When to Plant: Red-hot poker plants from containers can be planted at any time. Fall is best because they establish more easily in cooler weather, but you are more likely to find them at your garden center in spring or summer.

Trimming: For best appearance, cut off the dead flower spikes as they begin dying, if they bother you. Cut back the dead foliage on the ground after it freezes in late fall or early winter.

Fertilization: Medium. Fertilize at planting time and annually with a timed-release product. Less fertilizer is needed with the application of more organics. See pages 36 to 39 for more instructions.

Division: Red-hot poker becomes rather crowded about every 5 years. Remove the clump from the ground in spring or fall. Separate the clumping root system, and replant promptly. New plants take 2 to 3 years to bloom.

PERENNIALS

Salvia

CHARACTERISTICS

Plant Type: Deciduous perennial (loses its leaves in winter).

Average Size: 2 1/2 to 4 feet tall, depending on cultivar.

Growth Rate: Fast

Leaf: Varies by species

Flower: Tubular; sizes vary

Origin: 'Henry Duelberg' and autumn sage are native to Texas. 'Black and Blue' is native to Brazil, Paraguay, and northern Argentina. Mexican bush sage is native to Mexico.

Spacing: 3 feet on center for 'Henry Duelberg' and 'Black and Blue' sage; 2 to 3 feet on center for autumn sage; 3 to 5 feet on center for Mexican bush sage; and 3 feet on center for the smaller cultivar, 'Santa Barbara.'

Cautions: Autumn sage and Mexican bush sage are almost never eaten by deer.

Colors: Flower colors vary by species.

BUDGET GARDENING TIP

Look for this plant in 1-gallon containers, which should cost about $8. Since both Mexican and 'Black and Blue' sage spread so wide, one plant can cover at least 16 square feet or 50 cents per foot. Many other perennials in that price range only cover 2 to 4 square feet or $2 to $4 per foot.

'Black and Blue' salvia

Salvias are some of the best perennials for gardens in north central Texas. All but one bloom from spring to frost. 'Henry Duelberg' and autumn sage rate blue ribbons* because of their low maintenance. Mexican bush and 'Black and Blue' sage earn red ribbons* because they look best with two trimmings each year.

Mexican bush sage with yellow lantana

These salvias offer tremendous color, attract butterflies and hummingbirds, and thrive in the heat of north central Texas summers. All but Mexican bush sage bloom all season long, but it makes up for the difference by putting on a marvelous show in the fall. These salvias are easy to grow, requiring only one to a few trimmings each year. They fit well into a mass planting or toward the back of a mixed border.

'Black and Blue' salvia has the brightest blue flowers but also has a tendency to sprawl.

Color Period: Continuous blooms from spring through fall for all but Mexican bush sage, which blooms in late summer and fall for about three months.

Buying Tips: Commonly sold at many garden centers. Many salvias are annuals, lasting only one season. Be sure to check the tag for one of the names on these two pages if you want perennial salvia.

*Blue and red ribbon plants are defined on page 12 and 13. For blue and red ribbon performances, follow the planting and maintenance guidelines on pages 22 to 39.

Attracts Butterflies | Attracts Hummingbirds | Resists Deer | Avg. Weeks of Color | Texas Native *

30

Botanical Name: *Salvia* spp.
Family: Lamiaceae

Autumn Sage (*Salvia greggii,* **left)** is one tough, nearly ever-green perennial that grows two to three feet tall and blooms from April to November in red, pink, coral, or white. Flowering is especially strong in the spring and fall with lighter, yet steady, blooming during the summer. Autumn sage is a drought-tolerant plant and looks great in both native as well as more traditional landscapes.

'Black and Blue' Sage (*Salvia guaranitica* **'Black and Blue,' right)** grows three to four feet tall and wide and blooms all spring, summer, and fall. This plant blooms much longer than most other perennials, but it has a tendency to fall over, looking weedy to some and like a wonderful wild flower to others.

'Henry Duelberg' Mealy Cup Sage (*Salvia farinacea* **'Henry Duelberg,' left)** reaches three to four feet tall and three feet wide. From May through November, it produces eight-inch-long spikes of blue flowers. A white-flowering form, 'Augusta Duelberg,' has the same characteristics as the blue form. The two selections look great with each other.

Mexican Bush Sage (*Salvia leu-cantha,* **right)** grows four to five feet tall and wide; the compact cultivar, 'Santa Barbara,' grows two feet tall and three to four feet wide. Both selections have velvety spikes of purple flowers for three months late summer through fall. Mexican bush sage combines well with other fall-blooming perennials, such as the lavender-flowering fall aster and the yellow-flowering Mexican mint marigold.

GROWING CONDITIONS

Light: Light shade to full sun; flower more with full sun.

Water: Low for autumn sage, 'Henry Duelberg,' and Mexican bush sage. Likes water every week or two during the growing season, depending on its environment. Medium for 'Black and Blue' sage. Likes water once or twice a week during the growing season, depending on its environment.

Soil: Any fertile, well-drained soil that has been enriched with organic matter. Requires good drainage.

Hardiness: Zones 7 to 10 for autumn and 'Henry Duelberg' sage; zones 8 to 10 for 'Black and Blue' and Mexican bush sage. Both survive winters in zone 7 with protection.

Propagation: Cuttings or division

Pest Problems: No serious insect or disease problems.

PLANTING & MAINTENANCE

When to Plant: Sage from containers can be planted at any time. Fall is best because they establish more easily in cooler weather, but you are more likely to find them at your garden center in early spring, when they are blooming.

Trimming: Cut back to a few inches after a killing frost in the fall or late winter. If the plants look ragged during the summer, give them a light trimming. Cut autumn sage back by one third in late August to induce greater fall bloom.

Fertilization: Low. Fertilize at planting time and annually with a timed-release product. Less fertilizer is needed with the application of more organics. See pages 36 to 39 for more instructions.

Division: If clumps get too big, divide in early spring or fall.

PERENNIALS

* *'Henry Duelberg' and autumn sage are Texas natives.*

Scabiosa, Pincushion Flower

CHARACTERISTICS

Plant Type: Deciduous perennial (loses its leaves in winter).

Average Size: About 12 to 18 inches tall (including the flowers) by 12 to 15 inches wide.

Growth Rate: Fast

Leaf: Grayish-green, fine-textured

Flower: About 2 inches wide; resembles pincushions.

Origin: Europe and Asia

Spacing: About 12 inches on center (measure from the center of each plant). Closer in containers.

Cautions: Occasionally damaged by deer.

Colors: Flowers are white, lavender-blue, or pink.

Scabiosa 'Harlequin Blue'

Scabiosa offers a long, bloom period without too much care. Needs deadheading (removal of dead flowers) but returns the favor by attracting lots of butterflies. Misses a ribbon because of this chore but is quite easy to grow.

Scabiosa 'Butterfly Blue' is one of the butterfly's favorite foods when it first comes into bloom in spring. The Fort Worth Botanic Garden has been growing this plant successfully for many years.

If you love butterflies, treat them to some scabiosa. When it first opens up in spring, they flock to the newest delicacy on the block. It blooms most at first, slowing down as the season progresses. But it delivers an acceptable percentage of color for four to five months if you deadhead (remove the dead flowers). This high performance earned *Scabiosa* 'Butterfly Blue' the Perennial Plant of the Year Award in 2000.

The flowers are borne on top of the foliage.

Color Period: If you deadhead (remove dead flowers), scabiosa blooms nonstop from May until September. Without deadheading, it blooms from May until July or early August. It blooms most at first, slowing down as the season progresses.

Buying Tips: Scabiosa is quite fine-textured and looks somewhat scrawny in the containers in your garden center. However, if fills out nicely once you have it in the ground.

Attracts Butterflies · Avg. Weeks of Color

Botanical Name: *Scabiosa columbaria*
Family: Dipsacaceae

Companions: Scabiosa's low stature (12 to 18 inches tall) makes it an ideal border plant for many taller perennials and flowering shrubs. Try it with 'Knock Out' roses and coneflowers, as shown below.

Scabiosa 'Butterfly Blue' and some companions

'Knock Out' Roses (above, left) are shrubs that bloom spring, summer, and fall, so they will keep the bed in color for the entire growing season. Since scabiosa blooms heaviest in May, the roses will be at their showiest at the same time. These roses grow to four to six feet tall, so plant them as the tallest plant in the bed. The 'Knock Out' roses come in bright pink (as shown above) or a paler pink that would also look wonderful with the scabiosa.

'Big Sky Sunrise' Coneflower (above, right) is an excellent perennial choice for a companion for the roses and scabiosa. This yellow coneflower blooms from about May until August, which coincides with the flowering period of the other two plants. The textures of the plants are quite different, and all prefer sun. This coneflower grows to about three feet tall, so plant it as the middle layer in between the roses and the scabiosa.

GROWING CONDITIONS

Light: Full sun, at least 6 hours per day.

Water: Medium after establishment. Likes water once or twice a week during the growing season, depending on its environment. See pages 28 to 33 for more information. Scabiosa doesn't tolerate wet soils.

Soil: Any fertile, well-drained soil that has been enriched with organic matter. Requires good drainage. See pages 22 to 25 for instructions. Scabiosa doesn't tolerate wet soils.

Hardiness: Zones 5 to 9

Propagation: Seeds or division

Pest Problems: Rare

PLANTING & MAINTENANCE

When to Plant: Scabiosa from containers can be planted at any time. Fall is best because they establish more easily in cooler weather, but you are more likely to find them at garden centers when they are blooming in summer.

Trimming: Deadhead (remove dead flowers) throughout the blooming season to increase flower production. Cut back the dead foliage to the ground after it freezes in late fall or early winter.

Fertilization: Medium. Fertilize at planting time and annually with a timed-release product. Less fertilizer is needed with the application of more organics. See pages 36 to 39 for more instructions.

Division: Divide in fall if you want more plants. The clumps do well for years without division.

PERENNIALS

Within image 3: 'Knock Out' Rose Plant Profile: Page 246 · 'Big Sky Sunrise' Coneflower Plant Profile: page 136

Sedum 'Autumn Joy'

CHARACTERISTICS

Plant Type: Deciduous perennial (loses its leaves in winter).

Average Size: About 18 to 24 inches tall and equally as wide.

Growth Rate: Fast

Leaf: Light to medium green, fleshy, rounded; 2 to 3 inches across.

Flower: Large, flat-topped clusters; about 6 inches wide.

Origin: China and Korea

Spacing: About 12 to 18 inches on center (measure from the center of each plant). Closer in containers.

Cautions: Seldom damaged by deer.

Colors: Flowers start out lime green (shown below) and progress to pink or red.

1. *'Autumn Joy' sedum flowers start out lime green in July.*
2. *Flowers turn bright rosy-pink by late fall.*

'Autumn Joy' sedum is one of our showiest fall bloomers, with flower clusters the size of a softball for up to three months. Sedum is a succulent, which needs less water than most other plants. No deadheading (removal of dead flowers) required, which makes sedum easier than most other perennials. Requires two trimmings each year, so it rates a red ribbon.*

With hundreds of sedums on the market, 'Autumn Joy' outsells them all. While most plants that grow well in Texas store water primarily in the roots, sedums are succulents that also store water in their leaves, making them more tolerant of drought. And while many succulents can't adapt to rainy periods, 'Autumn Joy' handles them well, provided it has good drainage.

This sedum is one of the easiest perennials in this book because it requires no deadheading (removal of dead flowers).

Color Period: From August or September until frost, continuously.

Buying Tips: Look for the label 'Autumn Joy' in your garden center to be sure you are buying this one. However, many new cultivars are coming out each spring which show a lot of promise.

Red ribbon plants are defined on page 13. For red ribbon performance, follow the planting and maintenance guidelines on pages 22 to 39.

Companions: Plant sedums with other fall bloomers, like Mexican bush sage, chrysanthemums, asters, and pansies.

Try the combination shown below for easy color layers that will, once again, stop traffic on your street.

Mexican Bush Sage
Plant Profile: Page 156

Fall Aster
Plant Profile: page 130

'Autumn Joy' sedum with some companions

Mexican Bush Sage (above, left) works wonderfully with sedum because they bloom at the same time and offer lots of color. The taller varieties grow to five feet tall, so plant the shorter sedum in front as a border. Mexican bush sage lives without winter protection as far north as zone eight.

Fall Aster (above, right) also peaks in fall and grows to about two and a half feet tall. Plant them in between the tall sage and the shorter sedum. All three plants like sun but will bloom with some shade.

GROWING CONDITIONS

Light: Light shade to full sun

Water: Very low after establishment. Lives on rainwater alone, without supplemental water, in all but the most extreme conditions. See pages 28 to 33 for more information.

Soil: Any fertile, well-drained soil that has been enriched with organic matter. Requires good drainage. See pages 22 to 25 for instructions.

Hardiness: Zones 3 to 9

Propagation: Division or cuttings

Pest Problems: Rare. Root rot can develop if plants are kept too wet.

PLANTING & MAINTENANCE

When to Plant: Sedum from containers can be planted at any time. Fall is best because they establish more easily in cooler weather.

Trimming: In spring or early summer, cut them back to about half when they are 8 inches tall. This cutback will make them fuller for their fall season. Deadheading (removal of dead flowers) is not needed. Cut back the dead foliage to the ground after it freezes in late fall or early winter.

Fertilization: Medium. Fertilize at planting time and annually with a timed-release product. Less fertilizer is needed with the application of more organics. See pages 36 to 39 for more instructions.

Division: Divide every 3 to 5 years in spring, when the middle of the plant goes into a decline.

PERENNIALS

Lives on rainwater alone in all but the most extreme situations.

Spanish Bluebells

CHARACTERISTICS

Plant Type: Deciduous perennial (loses its leaves in winter).

Average Size: About 12 to 15 inches tall and 12 inches wide.

Growth Rate: Fast

Leaf: Dark green, strap-shaped leaves to 12 inches long.

Flower: Bell-shaped blossoms on upright spikes.

Origin: Spain and Portugal

Spacing: Set bulbs 4 to 6 inches apart; they will fill in to form a clump.

Cautions: None known. Somewhat resistant to deer.

Colors: Flowers are blue, pink, or white.

This old-fashioned, spring-flowering bulb is ideal for Texas shade gardens. Extremely easy, requiring almost no care. Unique color complements many other spring-blooming plants. Definitely rates a blue ribbon.*

Spanish bluebells bloom just as the last daffodils are fading.

If your spring color scheme calls for soft pastels beneath the open shade of deciduous trees, Spanish bluebells should be a garden essential. In mid to late spring, from a cluster of strappy green leaves, upright spikes emerge that are loosely studded with dozens of delicate, bell-shaped blossoms. Blue is the strongest color, but there are also varieties that bloom pink ('Queen of Pinks') or white ('White City'). This is the perfect bulb to grow at the base of trees or near pink or white azaleas. Once planted, Spanish bluebells persist for years with little attention. The bulbs actually benefit from a dry period in summer and then begin growing roots when the soil cools in the fall. Some varieties are fragrant, and all make excellent cut flowers.

Color Period: Bloom for about two weeks in mid to late spring, just as the last daffodils are fading.

Buying Tips: Available from internet suppliers if you can't find them at your local garden center.

*Blue ribbon plants are defined on page 12. For blue ribbon performance, follow the planting and maintenance guidelines on pages 22 to 39.

Companions: Spanish bluebells mix well with all of the spring-blooming, shade garden plants - azaleas, Mexican plums, lenten roses, hostas, and liriope. You can plant them near the base of a Mexican plum or other tree, or place them near big hostas, which leaf out at the perfect time to hide fading bluebell foliage from view. After the weather warms and bluebells become dormant, you can set caladiums or begonias over the resting bulbs.

The blue color of the bluebells looks wonderful with pink Encore azaleas and yellow forsythia, as shown below.

Encore Azalea
Plant Profile: Page 188

Forsythia
Plant Profile: Page 210

Spanish bluebells and some companion plants

Encore Azaleas (above, top) bloom at the same time as Spanish bluebells and create a colorful backdrop for the 18 inch tall bluebells. Both plants are comfortable in winter sun and summer shade.

Forsythia (above, bottom) is a shrub that blooms at the same time as both the azalea and the bluebells and grows to about six feet tall. Forsythia takes light shade, but too much shade will prevent it from blooming. Use it next to the azaleas with the bluebells bordering both taller plants.

GROWING CONDITIONS

Light: Partial shade (winter sun, summer shade).

Water: Low. Plants normally require supplemental water only in years when spring is extremely dry.

Soil: Any fertile, well-drained soil

Hardiness: Zones 4 to 8

Propagation: Division. Bulbs vary in size, but those that are more than 2 inches in diameter are the strongest bloomers. Seedlings or small bulblets will grow to blooming size in about 3 years.

Pest Problems: Rare. Bulbs may rot in extremely wet soil.

PLANTING & MAINTENANCE

When to Plant: Set out dormant bulbs in the fall.

Planting Depth: Plant 5 inches deep, to the base of the bulb.

Trimming: Spanish bluebells often reseed if ripe flower spikes are left on the plants until they die back naturally. If you don't want the plants to spread, clip off the spikes as soon as the flowers fade.

Fertilization: Medium. Fertilize at planting time and each spring with a timed-release product. Less fertilizer is needed with the application of more organics. See pages 36 to 39 for more instructions.

Division: Every 5 to 6 years in the summer or fall, dig, divide, and replant crowded clumps.

PERENNIALS

Stokesia, Stokes' Aster

CHARACTERISTICS

Plant Type: Deciduous perennial (loses its leaves in winter).

Average Size: 12 to 24 inches tall by 12 inches wide.

Growth Rate: Fast

Leaf: Oblong to pointed, lance-shaped, green leaves; 2 to 4 inches long.

Flower: Open, daisy-shaped blossoms with fringed edges; 2 to 4 inches across.

Origin: Southeastern U.S.

Spacing: About 12 inches on center (measure from the center of each plant). Plants grow into colonies. Closer in containers.

Cautions: Often damaged by deer

Colors: Flowers are lavender-blue, white, pink, or yellow.

1. *'Peachy' stokesia*
2. *'Purple Pixie' stokesia*
3. *'Color Wheel' stokesia*

Perennial that is extremely dependable and easy to grow. Its best qualities are its blue color and fairly long bloom period. However, you have to trim it to keep it blooming, so it doesn't rate a ribbon. Great butterfly plant.

Blue flowers always have a cooling influence in the garden, which is exactly the special effect you can expect with Stokes' aster. This low-growing perennial makes good cut flowers that are always trouble free in the garden. Although Stokes' aster doesn't bloom as long as the similar scabiosa, it is extremely easy to grow. This plant requires deadheading (removal of dead flowers) to keep it looking tidy and to increase the bloom period.

Stokes' aster has been thriving at the Fort Worth Botanic Garden for years.

Color Period: Heaviest bloom period is in spring, followed by a summer's rest, then a rebloom in fall. Blooms continue for six weeks in the spring without deadheading (removal of dead flowers) and six more weeks with deadheading.

Buying Tips: Look for 'Blue Danube' and 'Klaus Jelitto,' which have done well for us.

Companions: In low-maintenance borders, stokesias are perfect for planting in front of tall daylilies. But because gentle stokesias go with almost everything, why not put them to work as camouflage plants? For example, use stokesia as a foreground plant for late-blooming chrysanthemums. By the time the mums need elbow room, the stokesia can be cut back for a midsummer break. Grow stokesias alongside daffodils. In late spring, the stokesia foliage will hide the withering daffodil leaves from view.

Stokesia shows well when layered with other plants that also have peak bloom periods in early summer.

'Sunny Knock Out' Rose
Plant Profile: Page 246

Yarrow
Plant Profile: Page 172

Stokes' aster with some companions for easy color layers

'Sunny Knock Out' Rose (above, top) has a more compact growth habit than the original 'Knock Out,' growing to about four feet tall. The flowers start out yellow and fade to cream. Both colors complement the Stokes' aster. This rose blooms on and off from spring until fall, so it should be in bloom with the aster. Use the rose as the tallest plant of this grouping.

Yarrow (above, bottom) also starts blooming in early summer and continues until late summer. Use it as the mid layer, in between the roses and the Stokes' aster. Plant them in full sun.

GROWING CONDITIONS

Light: Light shade to full sun, preferring full sun.

Water: Low to medium. Stokesias are quite drought-tolerant once established. However, we have always watered ours weekly during the growing season, so we don't know how it does with no irrigation. See pages 28 to 33 for more information.

Soil: Any fertile, well-drained soil that has been enriched with organic matter. Requires good drainage. See pages 22 to 25 for instructions.

Hardiness: Zones 5 to 9

Propagation: Seed, cuttings, division (preferred). Plants divided and replanted in fall bloom reliably the following summer.

Pest Problems: Very rare. Stokes' asters are remarkably resistant to insects and diseases.

PLANTING & MAINTENANCE

When to Plant: Stokes' asters from containers can be planted at any time. Fall is best because they establish more easily in cooler weather.

Trimming: Cut back flowers, and remove spent stems (after they fade) to keep the plants from producing seeds and to prolong bloom time. Cut back the dead foliage to the ground after it freezes in late fall or early winter.

Fertilization: Medium. Fertilize at planting time and annually with a timed-release product. Less fertilizer is needed with the application of more organics. See pages 36 to 39 for more instructions.

Division: Dig, divide, and replant established clumps every 3 years in early spring or late summer. If necessary, plants dug in fall can be held in containers until the following spring.

PERENNIALS

Summer Snowflake

CHARACTERISTICS

Plant Type: Deciduous perennial (loses its leaves in winter).

Average Size: 12 to 15 inches tall by 8 inches wide.

Growth Rate: Moderate

Leaf: Medium green, narrow, 14 to 16 inches long.

Flower: Small, 3/4 inch, bell-shaped.

Origin: Central and southern Europe.

Spacing: About 6 inches on center (measure from the center of each plant).

Cautions: Rodent proof

Colors: Flowers are white with a green dot on the outside tip of each petal.

Easy-to-grow, spring-flowering bulb that naturalizes and reminds us of a delicate blanket of snow. This bulb is definitely a blue ribbon plant* because of its low maintenance, tolerance of clay soil, and dainty white blooms.

Summer snowflake is one of the best bulbs for naturalizing in north central Texas. Contrary to what the name suggests, summer snowflake actually blooms in early to mid spring and looks especially good planted in drifts beneath deciduous trees or along stream banks, where its dainty, white flowers adorn the woodland setting. It thrives in full sun or in the shade of deciduous trees. Clumps may persist for many years before needing to be divided. Division should take place in early summer after the foliage has died.

Color Period: Blooms in March or April for about two weeks

Buying Tips: Easily purchased through online bulb companies in the fall. The cultivar 'Gravetye Giant' sports larger flowers than the regular snowflake.

Blue ribbon plants are defined on page 12. For blue ribbon performance, follow the planting and maintenance guidelines on pages 22 to 39.

Companions: Summer snowflake combines well with other spring-flowering bulbs, such as daffodils. It looks good with spring-flowering annuals, such as pansies and perennials (such as 'Texas Gold' columbine).

Daffodils
Plant Profile: Page 120

Pansies
Plant Profile: Page 72

'Texas Gold'
Columbine
Plant Profile: page 124

Summer snowflake and some companions

Daffodils (above, left) bloom about the same time as summer snowflake and have similar looking foliage but larger flowers in yellow. Summer snowflakes and daffodils are similar in height (16 inches or so) and could therefore be planted in drifts adjoining each other.

Pansies (above, center) are in peak bloom when summer snowflakes bloom and look good with summer snowflake coming up through them. Because pansies are shorter (six to eight inches tall), they perform well as a border in front of summer snowflake.

'Texas Gold' Columbine (above, right), with its abundance of golden yellow, graceful flowers riding above its blue-green foliage, offers contrast in flower color, form of plant, and in leaf color and shape.

GROWING CONDITIONS

Light: Summer snowflake is one of the few plants that tolerates both sun and shade. It grows well in medium to light shade or full sun.

Water: Very low after establishment. Lives on rainwater alone, without supplemental water, in all but the most extreme conditions. See pages 28 to 33 for more information.

Soil: Any good garden soil; tolerates clay soil very well.

Hardiness: Zones 4 to 9

Propagation: Division of clumps

Pest Problems: None; these bulbs are even rodent-proof.

PLANTING & MAINTENANCE

When to Plant: Fall, if you are planting bulbs; early summer from division.

Planting Depth: 4 to 6 inches

Trimming: None needed

Fertilization: Low. Fertilize at planting time with a timed-release product. Less fertilizer is needed with the application of more organics. In the years after planting, fertilization needs vary, based on the nutrients in your soil. See pages 36 to 39 for more instructions.

Division: Early summer, after the foliage has died.

PERENNIALS

Lives on rainwater alone in all but the most extreme situations.

Turk's Cap

CHARACTERISTICS

Plant Type: Deciduous perennial (loses its leaves in winter).

Average Size: 2 to 4 feet tall and 2 to 3 feet wide.

Growth Rate: Fast

Leaf: Medium green, 3 inches wide; shaped like a maple leaf. The cultivar 'Fiesta' has green and white-marbled, variegated leaves.

Flower: A whorl of tightly-held petals that resembles a fez, or Turk's cap. Stamens extend through the top of the whorl and look something like a finial atop the petals.

Origin: Native to Texas

Spacing: 2 to 3 feet apart on center.

Cautions: Resistant to deer

Colors: Flowers of the most common Turk's cap are red. There is also a less common, white-flowering selection, and 'Pam Puryear' is a pink-flowering cultivar (shown, right).

Turk's cap is one of the best, flowering perennials for shade in north central Texas. Its apple-green leaves create a lush, woodland effect, and its bright red flowers sparkle in the shade, attracting hummingbirds and butterflies all season long. Turk's cap is definitely a blue ribbon* plant!

Turk's cap is a low-maintenance, high-performing perennial for the shade garden. It grows in sand, loam, clay or limestone soils as long as they are well drained. Once established, Turk's cap is a drought-tolerant perennial that holds up very well to the Texas heat. Many stems arise from the crown of the plant, growing out and up to assume a slightly spreading yet upright growth habit. Bright red flowers adorn the plant May through November and brighten up a shady spot.

'Big Momma' is a red-blooming cultivar with flowers about a third larger than those of the species. After the flowers disappear on all varieties, marble-sized red fruits appear and appeal to the appetites of many different birds. Turk's cap looks especially nice and creates a woodland effect when planted in large drifts beneath deciduous trees.

Color Period: From May to November, blooming continuously.

Buying Tips: Garden centers that specialize in native plants will certainly offer Turk's cap. If mainstream garden centers don't carry it, it's available through online nurseries.

Blue ribbon plants are defined on page 12. For blue ribbon performance, follow the planting and maintenance guidelines on pages 22 to 39.

Attracts Butterflies

Attracts Hummingbirds

Lives on Rain Water *

28
Avg. Weeks of Color

Texas Native

Botanical Name:
Malvaviscus arboreus var. drummondii
Family: Malvaceae

PERENNIALS

Companions: Turk's cap mixes beautifully with other shade-tolerant, woodland perennials, such as ferns, hostas, and grasses. For a monochromatic look, interplant it with red spider lily, the flowers of which match the color of Turk's cap flowers yet provide contrast in form and texture.

For a shade garden that offers great textural contrast, try Turk's cap with ferns and caladiums, as shown below.

Southern Wood Fern
Plant Profile: Page 126

Caladium
Plant Profile: Page 50

Turk's cap and some companions

Southern Wood Fern (above, top) grows two to three feet tall and provides a light green, soft-textured foil for the red blossoms of Turk's Cap. Use it as the mid layer for this grouping.

Caladiums (above, bottom) are a natural companion for Turks's cap and ferns because they contrast so much with both of them. Use a caladium that coordinates with the colors in Turk's cap flowers. Look for caladiums that stay lower than two feet tall, and plant them as a border because they are smaller than the Turk's cap and ferns. Plant all three in light to medium shade.

*Lives on rainwater alone in all but the most extreme situations.

GROWING CONDITIONS

Light: Light to medium shade

Water: Very low after establishment. Lives on rainwater alone, without supplemental water, in all but the most extreme conditions. See pages 28 to 33 for more information.

Soil: Any fertile, well-drained soil that has been enriched with organic matter. Requires good drainage. See pages 22 to 25 for instructions.

Hardiness: Zones 7 to 10

Propagation: Seed, rooted cuttings, or division.

Pest Problems: Susceptible to a little caterpillar that chews small holes in the leaves. Only a cosmetic problem, though; Turk's cap thrives in spite of the few holes that may appear. If they bother you, ask your garden center for the least toxic control.

PLANTING & MAINTENANCE

When to Plant: Plants from containers can be planted at any time. Fall is best because they establish more easily in cooler weather.

Trimming: Cut stems back to the ground after a hard freeze in the fall. Be patient for leaves to emerge the following spring!

Fertilization: Low. Fertilize at planting time with a timed-release product. Less fertilizer is needed with the application of more organics. In the years after planting, fertilization needs vary, based on the nutrients in your soil. See pages 36 to 39 for more instructions.

Division: No need to divide these at all. We just cut them back hard after a killing freeze in the fall or in late February. By leaving them in place, the plants expand a little and grow into a fuller bush, which we like.

Verbena 'Homestead Purple'

1ST

CHARACTERISTICS

Plant Type: Deciduous perennial (loses its leaves in winter).

Average Size: About 8 to 12 inches tall by 30 to 36 inches wide.

Growth Rate: Fast

Leaf: Dark green leaves on rambling stems.

Flower: Clusters of small flowers; attractive to butterflies.

Origin: Eastern U.S., Virginia to Florida.

Spacing: About 3 feet on center (measure from the center of each plant). Closer in containers.

Cautions: Often damaged by deer

Colors: Flowers are purple

'Homestead Purple' verbena alternated with yellow celosia and pink wave petunias.

Verbena 'Blue Princess'

One of the best, blooming groundcovers for Texas. Lots of blooms in spring and fall but has some blooms almost all season long. No deadheading (removal of dead flowers) necessary. Easily earns a blue ribbon* for outstanding performance with very little care. Great for butterflies. Short lived (three to four years) in north central Texas.

'Homestead Purple' verbena has been a popular verbena at the Fort Worth Botanic Garden.

'Homestead Purple' verbena is one of the longest-blooming, low-growing plants we have tried. It flowers for about six months, taking short breaks, but almost always has some blooms. This verbena spreads well, too, so be sure to give it space. 'Blue Princess' is another cultivar that produces a mass of lavender-blue flower clusters from early spring through late fall. It grows one foot tall and three feet wide. The Texas A & M AgriLife Extension Service has designated this cultivar as a Texas Superstar™ plant. Even though they only live three to four years in north central Texas, they are an excellent value.

Color Period: It starts blooming with a bang in early spring and is covered with flowers, as shown above. Although the blooms taper off during summer, it is almost never without flowers. And, in fall, it undergoes another big bang, blooming until the first hard frost.

Buying Tips: Check the plant tag to be sure it says 'Homestead Purple' or 'Blue Princess' verbena, if you want the perennial form.

*Blue ribbon plants are defined on page 12. For blue ribbon performance, follow the planting and maintenance guidelines on pages 22 to 39.

Companions: This verbena is quite useful in the flower garden because it is one of the lowest-growing perennials. Its small stature makes it ideal for borders, and the deep purple color complements most other colors well. Use it with other long-blooming perennials, like agastache, lantana, and black-eyed Susans. It also looks great with daylilies and flowering shrubs, like butterfly bush and 'Knock Out' roses.

For easy color layers that bloom a long time, try the combination shown below.

Canna
Plant Profile: Page 134

Coreopsis
Plant Profile: page 132

'Homestead Purple' verbena and some companions

Cannas (above, left) are perennials in most of Texas (zones seven to nine) and bloom for most of the summer. Their height varies from three to six feet, so use them as the tallest plant in this grouping.

Coreopsis (above, right) is a wonderful companion for both because its light texture is not only different from the coarser-textured canna but also quite a bit smaller than the verbena. It blooms from June until September and grows about 18 inches tall, so place it in between the taller canna and shorter verbena. All do well in full sun.

GROWING CONDITIONS

Light: Light shade to full sun

Water: Medium after establishment. Likes water once or twice a week during the growing season, depending on its environment. See pages 28 to 33 for more information.

Soil: Any fertile, well-drained soil that has been enriched with organic matter. Requires good drainage, especially in winter. See pages 22 to 25 for instructions.

Hardiness: Zones 7 to 10

Propagation: Cuttings or division. Plants eagerly develop roots where stems touch the ground.

Pest Problems: Rare. Powdery mildew occasionally.

PLANTING & MAINTENANCE

When to Plant: Verbenas from containers can be planted at any time. Fall is best because they establish more easily in cooler weather, but you are more likely to see them at garden centers in spring or summer.

Trimming: Cut back the dead foliage (to the ground) after it freezes in late fall or early winter.

Fertilization: Medium. Fertilize at planting time and annually with a timed-release product. Less fertilizer is needed with the application of more organics.

BUDGET GARDENING TIP

One plant can cover a lot of ground, even in its first season. When you plant it, understand that a single plant spreads a full three feet across. Look underneath the spreading stems, and you'll see roots. Cut off small pieces with roots, and plant them elsewhere. Since one plant can cover 9 square feet, you could have a lot of purple by the end of the summer!

PERENNIALS

Yarrow, Achillea

CHARACTERISTICS

Plant Type: Deciduous perennial (loses its leaves in winter).

Average Size: 18 to 30 inches tall, spreads into patches from 18 to 24 inches wide.

Growth Rate: Fast

Leaf: Finely-cut, feathery, green leaves; slightly aromatic.

Flower: Flat-topped clusters of tiny flowers; clusters 2 to 4 inches wide.

Origin: Europe

Spacing: About 24 inches on center (measure from the center of each plant). Closer in containers.

Cautions: Yarrow was historically used as a medicinal herb to stop bleeding of wounds. Almost never eaten by deer.

Colors: Flowers are white, pink, red, yellow, orange, lilac.

ALTERNATE SELECTIONS

Cultivars of fern-leaf yarrow (*Achillea filipendulina*) grow taller and produce large clusters of yellow flowers over a period of two months, from late spring through early summer. This species often performs well in zone 6 and in very well-drained beds in zone 7 gardens.

Feathery foliage all year; flowers in early summer. A truly low-care perennial for sunny spots, yarrow provides soft texture even when it is not in bloom. However, it looks better with several trimmings, so it misses a ribbon.

Yarrow with shasta daisies and monarda

Yarrow's ferny foliage spreads quickly to form a thick mass, so this perennial doubles as a flowering groundcover for sunny spots. Available in a rainbow of shades, you can grow a single color or choose from mixtures that are keyed to certain color schemes. For example, 'Summer Pastels' includes soft shades of pink, yellow and lilac; 'Debutante' features hotter shades of orange and red. 'Debutante' also reblooms more willingly than older varieties.

Yarrow is a must-have if you enjoy fresh cut flowers. The blossoms keep their colors well when dried, too. To dry them, pick the flowers as they get their full color and hang upside down in a cool, dry, shady place with low humidity (such as in a basement or storage room).

Color Period: Late May through the end of July without deadheading (removal of dead flowers). Blooms a month or so longer with deadheading. Foliage often persists year round.

Buying Tips: 'Coronation Gold,' 'Moonshine,' 'Cerise Queen,' and 'Rosea Paprika' have all done well at the Fort Worth Botanic Garden.

Attracts Butterflies   Resists Deer

(12)

Avg. Weeks of Color

Botanical Name: *Achillea millefolium*
Family: Asteraceae

Companions: Yarrow works best with other plants that bloom at the same time, including most of our summer perennials. Try it with the companions shown below for both color and butterfly attraction.

'Purple Emperor'
Butterfly Bush
Plant Profile: Page 194

Scabiosa
Plant Profile: Page 158

Yarrow and some companions

'Purple Emperor' Butterfly Bush (above, left) is one of the newer, more compact butterfly bushes that grows to about four feet tall and blooms at the same time as the yarrow. Plant it behind the shorter yarrow (18 to 30 inches tall).

Scabiosa (above, right) is a low-growing perennial (12 to 18 inches tall) that blooms for most of the growing season, from May until October. Plant it as the front border for the butterfly bush and yarrow. Plant them in full sun.

All three of these plants attract butterflies.

GROWING CONDITIONS

Light: Full sun, at least 6 hours per day.

Water: Low to medium. Yarrow is quite drought tolerant once established. However, we have always watered ours weekly during the growing season, so we don't know how it does with no irrigation. See pages 28 to 33 for more information.

Soil: Any fertile, well-drained soil that has been enriched with organic matter. Requires good drainage. See pages 22 to 25 for instructions.

Hardiness: Zones 3 to 9

Propagation: Seed, division. The best times to dig and divide established plantings are spring and fall.

Pest Problems: Root rot, if the soil is too wet or not well drained.

PLANTING & MAINTENANCE

When to Plant: Yarrow from containers can be planted at any time. Fall is best because they establish more easily in cooler weather, but you are more likely to find them at your garden center in summer, when they are blooming.

Trimming: Deadhead (remove dead flowers) to help prolong bloom time. Also, trim off any foliage that turns brown to keep the patch looking neat, which can be done in late July. You can even trim it down to the ground at this time if it is dead-looking. Cut back the dead foliage to the ground after it freezes in late fall or early winter.

Fertilization: Medium. Fertilize at planting time and annually with a timed-release product. Less fertilizer is needed with the application of more organics.

Division: The best times to dig and divide established plantings are spring and fall every 3 to 5 years or whenever the center dies out.

PERENNIALS

Other Perennials that Deserve Mention

Agapanthus
Agapanthus spp.

Excellent blue color for zones 8 to 10. Blooms in spring or early summer for about 6 weeks. 18 to 30 inches tall. Light shade to full sun. Medium water. Grows from a rhizome.

Ajuga
Ajuga reptans

Groundcover with beautiful green or purple-bronze foliage with blue flowers on 6 inch spikes. Ajuga provides a mat of dark-colored foliage that spreads by runners. Must have great drainage to prevent crown rot, which occurs frequently in Texas. 3 to 6 inches tall. Medium shade to morning sun. Medium water.

Chrysanthemum
Chrysanthemum spp.

Garden mums are a long-time, Texan favorite. New names and selections are everywhere. 'Clara Curtis' is an excellent, old-fashioned garden mum with beautiful pink flowers blooming in fall for about 2 weeks. 2 to 3 feet tall. Full sun. Medium water. Zones 5 to 9.

Confederate Rose
Hibiscus mutablis

Tender perennial in zones 6 to 7, Confederate rose astounds gardeners with its changing flower colors (from white to pink to red) as the sun moves from east to west. Blooms for 2 to 6 weeks, in the fall. Single and double flower forms. 6 to 8 feet tall. Full sun. Medium water. Zones 7 to 9.

Creeping Jenny
Lysimachia nummularia

We have only used this plant in containers so don't know how it does long term as a landscape plant. Outstanding container plant. About 3 inches tall. Trails over the edge of containers. Medium shade to full sun. Zones 3 to 9. Medium water.

Crinum
Crinum spp.

Dramatic, tropical looking plant with large flowers. Poisonous. Many sizes available. Some varieties are very susceptible to pests. Grows from a bulb. Zones 8 to 11. Full sun.

Crocus
Crocus spp.

Easy, small, flowering bulb suitable for naturalizing in zones 6 to 7; struggles in zone 8. Early to bloom (often in areas with snow on the ground) for about two weeks. Rich colors of yellow, purple, white and shades in between. 3 to 6 inches tall. Full sun. Low water. Zones 3 to 8.

Daisy, Shasta
Leucanthemum x superbum

Excellent perennial, but requires frequent deadheading to keep it looking good - more than most perennials in this book. White, daisy-like flowers with golden eyes. Flowers open in May and last several weeks. 2 feet tall. Full sun to light shade. Medium water. Zones 4 to 9.

Dianthus, Cottage Pinks
Dianthus gratianopolitanus

Wonderful, small perennials that flower in spring for 2 to 3 weeks heavily and sporadically for the rest of summer. 'Bath's Pink' and 'Tiny Rubies' have been recognized as superior selections. 8 to 12 inches tall. Full sun to light shade. Low water. Zones 4 to 8.

Foxglove
Digitalis purpurea

A short-lived perennial for most of Texas, but the flower show in spring is worth the effort. Spikes to 4 feet tall, bearing numerous flowers in rich colors open in spring for 2 to 3 weeks. Poisonous. 2 to 3 feet tall (foliage). Full sun to light shade. Medium water. Zones 4 to 9.

Gaillardia, Blanket Flower
Gaillardia pulchella

Excellent, drought-tolerant, native perennial that attracts butterflies. Hot colors of red, yellow, and orange in single or double forms bloom most of the summer. Heat and humidity tolerant. 1 to 2 feet tall. Full sun. Low water. Zones 4 to 9.

Gaura
Gaura lindheimeri

Drought-tolerant perennial native to the southwest that does very well in Texas. 2 to 3 foot plants send up numerous airy spikes of flowers in white, pink, or red for much of the summer. May need to be deadheaded to keep neat appearance. Full sun. Low water. Blooms 12 to 16 weeks. Zones 5 to 9.

Ginger Lily
Hedychium coronarium

Tender perennial for zones 6 to 7, this wonderful plant knocks you over with its sweet fragrance from late summer to the first frost. White flowers open atop stems of strap-shaped leaves. 4 to 6 feet tall. Full sun to light shade. Medium water (can take wet feet). Zones 7 to 9.

Grass, Pampas
Cortaderia selloana

Widely-planted, ornamental grass for zones 7 to 9. Prized for the magnificent floral plumes opening in August. Coarse-textured foliage (will cut you if not careful) is semi-evergreen. Cut back in late winter to 6 to 12 inches tall. 6 to 8 feet tall. Full sun. Low water. Zones 7 to 9.

Hosta
Hosta species and hybrids

One of the most common shade plants in the U.S. Doesn't do well in north central Texas because of heat, slugs, and snails. 1 to 3 feet tall. Medium water. Zones 3 to 8. Light to medium shade.

Hyacinth, Grape
Muscari armeniacum

Blooms for 2 to 3 weeks in early spring. Foliage is grass-like, and flower spikes are small, often getting lost in the garden. Easy to grow; multiplies rapidly; must be seen up close to appreciate. 3 to 6 inches tall. Full sun to light shade. Low water. Zones 3 to 8.

Joe Pye Weed
Eupatorium purpureum

Nice perennial that does well in north central Texas. Blooms in August and September for 4 to 6 weeks. Attracts hummingbirds. 5 to 7 feet tall by 4 feet wide. Medium water. Light shade to full sun. Zones 5 to 9.

Lamb's Ear
Stachys byzantina

Prized for the coarse-textured, hairy, almost quilted foliage in silvery-gray, lamb's ear is a great foil in the mixed perennial border among hot-color combinations. The soft, hairy leaves beg to be touched, and children love them. Good drainage a must. 1 to 2 feet tall. Full sun to light shade. Low water. Zones 4 to 8.

Lily of the Field
Sternbergia lutea

Excellent bulb for north central Texas. Easy to grow. Tolerates heat well. Spectacular yellow flowers for about 2 weeks in September to October, when few other bulbs are blooming. Zones 6 to 9. Light shade to full sun. Low to medium water.

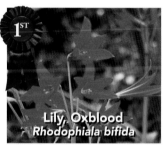

Lily, Oxblood
Rhodophiala bifida

One of the best bulbs for north central Texas. Takes heat well. Showy, red, attention-getting flowers for about 2 weeks in August or September. Zones 7 to 9. Low water, requiring no irrigation in summer. Light shade.

Monarda, Bee Balm
Monarda didyma

Old garden favorite that attracts butterflies and can be made into a tea. Rosy red flowers open in May and will flower all summer with deadheading. Heat tolerant but is prone to powdery mildew. 2 to 3 feet tall. Full sun. Medium water. Zones 4 to 8.

Phlox, Woodland
Phlox divaricata

One of the few blooming groundcovers that takes shade. Easy to grow. Blooms for 3 to 4 weeks in March and April. 12 to 15 inches tall. Zones 3 to 8. Low water. Light to medium shade.

Tulip
Tulipa species and hybrids

Most popular bulb sold in the U.S. Often gives Texans fits. Heat and rain spoil most tulip displays before their time, but we have found the peony-style selections, like 'Angelique,' will hold up to our weather conditions and bloom for about 2 to 3 weeks. Best to replant every year; they do not come back reliably. Full sun. Low water.

Zexmenia
Wedelia hispida

Outstanding, native perennial that blooms all summer, tolerates drought, and thrives in the heat of north central Texas summers. Flowers are sunny yellow and attract butterflies. 20 inches tall by 3 to 4 feet wide. Light shade to full sun, but prefers sun. Low water. Zones 7 to 10.

Chapter 4

Shrubs & Vines

The shrubs and vines in this chapter represent some of the best that Texas has to offer. And new cultivars make gardening with color easier than ever.

✿ Flowering shrubs are generally less work to maintain than perennials. Many shrubs in this chapter only require a chore or two per year and give you months of color in return.

✿ Since shrubs develop larger root systems than perennials, most need less water than perennials.

✿ Shrubs with short bloom periods, like hydrangeas and azaleas, are now available in reblooming forms. These new shrubs bloom about twice as much as the older ones.

✿ Many flowering shrubs - like butterfly bush, loropetalum, and althea - grow too large for most residences. Plant breeders have introduced many new, more compact forms that are much more useful in residential settings.

Above: The white-flowered hydrangeas are called 'Annabelle.' The blue ones are 'Penny Mac,' one of the new, reblooming hydrangeas.

Left: The dark-leaved shrub is loropetalum, with a bridalwreath spiraea blooming in the background. Loropetalums have grown huge in the past, but the new, dwarf varieties fit better in many residences.

Abelia

CHARACTERISTICS

Plant Type: Evergreen shrub.

Average Size: Both large and small abelias available, ranging from 3 to 5 feet tall to 6 to 10 feet tall.

Growth Rate: Fast

Leaf: Emerges bronze, changes to dark green in summer, and turns purplish in fall; 1 1/4 inches long.

Flower: Tubular-shaped, fragrant

Origin: China

Spacing: From 3 to 6 feet on center (measure from the center of each plant), depending on mature size of abelia you are planting.

Cautions: Seldom damaged by deer.

Colors: Flowers are white or pink.

Abelia chinensis

One of the easiest flowering plants in this book. Lives without irrigation in all but the most extreme situations. Butterfly and hummingbird attractor that is seldom damaged by deer. Blooms for most of the summer. New, smaller varieties give increased flexibility to this old, familiar plant. Easily rates a blue ribbon* for its ease of care.

Award-winning abelia 'Rose Creek'

Abelia has been used for generations in Texas. But, the original varieties (shown, left) grow quite tall, from six to ten feet, which limits their use in residential gardens. New, dwarf varieties (shown above) not only stay smaller but also bloom more. This smaller stature (three to five feet tall) has greatly increased the use of abelia, particularly as foundation planting for houses.

Color Period: Continuous from May until the first hard frost. Actually, the white flower falls off, but the sepals below are pink and persist even in winter.

Buying Tips: Be sure the abelia you are buying fits your space. 'Canyon Creek' and 'Rose Creek' abelia grow three to five feet tall and bloom more than older, larger varieties. 'Edward Goucher' and 'Sherwoodii' are popular cultivars in the Dallas-Fort Worth area. 'Edward Goucher' grows three to five feet tall and has lavender-pink flowers, while 'Sherwoodii' grows three to four feet tall and produces small, white flowers.

Blue ribbon plants are defined on page 12. For blue ribbon performance, follow the planting and maintenance guidelines on pages 22 to 39.

Companions: Abelia is frequently used with green shrubs like juniper and boxwood.

For easy color layers with green-leafed abelia, try the large abelia with the flowering plants below.

'Kaleidoscope' abelia (shown right) looks best with pink or peach flowers.

'Cherry Dazzle'
Dwarf Crapemyrtle
Plant Profile: Page 206

Phlox 'John Fanick'
Plant Profile: Page 150

Glossy abelia with some companions

'Cherry Dazzle' Dwarf Crapemyrtle (above, left) blooms from June through September. The bloom period coincides with the abelia's summer color period. Since dwarf crapemyrtles grow from three to five feet tall, use them in front of the taller glossy abelia.

Phlox 'John Fanick' (above, right) is a perennial that grows three feet tall and blooms June through September. Plant it as a border in front of the two other plants. All three do well in full sun.

*Lives on rainwater alone in all but the most extreme situations.

GROWING CONDITIONS

Light: Light shade to full sun

Water: Very low after establishment. Lives on rainwater alone, without supplemental water, in all but the most extreme conditions. See pages 28 to 33 for more information.

Soil: For the garden, plant in any fertile, well-drained soil that has been enriched with organic matter. Good drainage is essential for abelia. See pages 22 to 25 for instructions.

Hardiness: Zones 5 to 9

Propagation: Hardwood cuttings work well.

Pest Problems: Rare

PLANTING & MAINTENANCE

When to Plant: Abelia from containers can be planted at any time. Fall is best because they establish more easily in cooler weather.

Trimming: This shrub doesn't need much trimming as it has a nice, natural form. A frequent mistake is to cut the top out, which really hurts the form of the shrub for years. Shaping every 2 or 3 years is a better choice.

Large abelia: Every few years, cut 2 or 3 of the oldest, longest stems to the ground.

Small abelia: Trim off any wayward shoots that come out of the top. Cut them at the ground.

Fertilization: Low. Fertilize at planting time with a timed-release product. Less fertilizer is needed with the application of more organics. In the years after planting, fertilization needs vary, based on the nutrients in your soil. See pages 36 to 39 for more instructions.

SHRUBS & VINES

Agarita

CHARACTERISTICS

Plant Type: Evergreen shrub.

Average Size: 3 to 6 feet tall by 3 to 6 feet wide.

Growth Rate: Slow

Leaf: Gray-green to blue-gray, holly-like, 2 to 4 inches long.

Flower: Cup-shaped, 1/2 inch wide, 6 petals, fragrant.

Origin: Texas, New Mexico, Arizona.

Spacing: 3 to 6 feet on center (measure from the center of each plant).

Cautions: Animals (even deer) don't eat this shrub! Leaves have spines.

Color: Flowers are yellow

Attractive, evergreen, holly-like shrub that is tough as nails. Clusters of fragrant, yellow flowers appear in late winter/early spring and produce pea-size red berries from May through July. Agarita looks great in a native landscape. It definitely rates a blue ribbon* because of its beauty, low maintenance, and drought tolerance.

Extremely easy to grow, agarita contributes a regional, native Texas look to the landscape. The evergreen leaves provide year round beauty and attraction. The small, bright yellow flowers offer late winter interest, and the brick-red berries that follow in May through July provide summer interest and supply meals to songbirds and other wildlife. Many people enjoy making a delicious jelly from the fruits. Because of the needle-sharp tips on the leaves, agarita makes an excellent security hedge.

Although this shrub is native to central and west Texas, it does well in north central Texas, provided it is grown in well-drained soil.

Color Period: Agarita has color from its leaves all year. In addition to leaf color, it flowers for two to three weeks in February and March. Brick-red berries follow for about 12 weeks from May through July.

Buying Tips: Available in nurseries and garden centers that sell native plants.

Blue ribbon plants are defined on page 12. For blue ribbon performance, follow the planting and maintenance guidelines on pages 22 to 39.

Companions: Agarita combines very well with other native Texas plants, such as red yucca, white-flowering yucca, zexmenia, and grasses (such as Lindheimer's muhly). Combine it with native autumn sage and Mexican feather grass, as shown below, for a grouping that contrasts both in color and texture.

Autumn Sage
Plant Profile: Page 156

Mexican Feather Grass
Plant Profile: Page 130

Agarita and some companions

Autumn Sage (above, top) is a perennial that grows two and one half feet tall and wide. Since the agarita is taller, plant this sage in front of the agarita. Its green leaves contrast with the shape and color of the agarita leaves. Autumn sage blooms from April to November and attracts hummingbirds. Autumn sage and agarita share the same affinity for full sun and well-drained soil, and both are low water-use plants.

Mexican Feather Grass (above, bottom) provides the ultimate contrast with agarita in form and texture. This grass grows 24 to 30 inches tall and assumes an almost weeping form with foliage as fine as human hair. It, like agarita, prefers full sun to light shade and requires extremely well-drained soil. Plant a band or swath of Mexican feather grass in front of a grouping of agarita shrubs for a striking effect.

GROWING CONDITIONS

Light: Light shade to full sun

Water: Very low after establishment. Lives on rainwater alone, without supplemental water, in all but the most extreme conditions. See pages 28 to 33 for more information.

Soil: Any, as long as it is well-drained. See pages 22 to 25 for instructions.

Hardiness: Zones 7 to 9

Propagation: Seeds

Pest Problems: No serious insect or disease problems.

PLANTING & MAINTENANCE

When to Plant: Agarita from containers can be planted at any time. Fall is best because they establish more easily in cooler weather.

Trimming: None required. Let this shrub assume its natural form.

Fertilization: Low. Fertilize at planting time with a timed-release product. Less fertilizer is needed with the application of more organics. In the years after planting, fertilization needs vary, based on the nutrients in your soil. See pages 36 to 39 for more instructions.

SHRUBS & VINES

*Lives on rainwater alone in all but the most extreme situations

Agave, Century Plant

CHARACTERISTICS

Plant Type: Evergreen shrub.

Average Size: Varies according to species, although many are in the 2 to 5 feet range.

Growth Rate: Slow

Leaf: Stiff, sword-like, and succulent; many have a single spine at the tip and/or spines along the leaf margin.

Flower: Clusters of flowers at the ends of branches that extend from a single, tall, flowering stalk.

Lifespan: The central, mother plant dies after flowering (after years of growth, depending on species). Offshoots, or "pups," then emerge from the mother plant and continue the life cycle.

Origin: Texas, New Mexico, Arizona.

Spacing: Generally 3 to 5 feet on center, but it depends on the species.

Cautions: Most agave leaves end in a sharp point or have spines along the leaf margin; therefore, do not plant where pedestrians or playing children could be injured by them.

Color: Flowers are yellow

Blue agaves look striking in cobalt blue containers.

Agaves contribute a tremendous sculptural element to the landscape. Their striking form makes them useful as accent plants. The blue-colored agaves are especially eye-catching. Agaves survive on very little water and look great in a native or low water-use landscape. Agaves definitely rate a blue ribbon* because of their low maintenance requirements. Most agaves have dangerous spines, however.

Extremely easy to grow, agaves contribute a native Texas look to the landscape and add dramatic interest to the garden through their size, unique form, and color. Use a single plant as an accent next to an entrance or in front of a wall, or scatter several different species throughout the landscape to create a southwestern look. Because of their need for excellent drainage, it may be necessary to construct a raised bed or mound from well-drained soil and/or rock. Although the tip and leaf spines are part of the plant's beauty, they may pose a hazard to people who brush against them.

Color Period: Agaves give color from their leaves all year. They flower once when the mother plant matures, which varies by species from once in 10 to once in 40 years.

Buying Tips: Usually plentiful at garden centers. Look for species that do well in north central Texas, including the more cold-tolerant *Agave americana var. protoamericana*, *A. ferox* 'Green Goblet,' *A. flexispina*, *A. gentryi* 'Jaws,' *A. havardiana*, *A. neomexicana*, and *A. parryi* var. *truncata*.

Blue ribbon plants are defined on page 12. For blue ribbon performance, follow the planting and maintenance guidelines on pages 22 to 39.

Attracts Butterflies

Attracts Hummingbirds

Attracts Birds

Lives on Rain Water *

52
Avg. Weeks of Color

Texas Native

Botanical Name: *Agave* spp.
Family: Agavaceae

Companions: Agaves combine very well with other native Texas plants, such as red yucca, white-flowering yuccas, zexmenia, autumn sage, and grasses (such as Mexican feather grass).

Zexmenia
Plant Profile: Page 175

Mexican Feather Grass
Plant Profile: Page 130

Agave and some companions

Zexmenia (above, left) is a sprawling perennial that gets 20 inches tall and three to four feet wide. Its attractive foliage has a neat, clean appearance all summer long, and its golden-yellow, daisy-like, small flowers cover the plant for seven months and attract butterflies. The form, foliage, and flowers of this Texas native contrast well with and soften the strong structural form of agaves. Both zexmenia and agaves like full sun and well-drained soil.

Mexican Feather Grass (above, right) provides the ultimate contrast with agaves in form and texture. This grass grows 24 to 30 inches tall and assumes an almost weeping form with foliage as fine as human hair. It, like agaves, prefers full sun and requires extremely well-drained soil. Nestle a grouping of Mexican feather grass in front of or around a single agave or multiple agaves for a striking effect.

Lives on rainwater alone in all but the most extreme situations

GROWING CONDITIONS

Light: Full sun, at least 6 hours per day.

Water: Very low after establishment. Lives on rainwater alone, without supplemental water, in all but the most extreme conditions. See pages 28 to 33 for more information.

Soil: Well-drained, even rocky, soil. See pages 22 to 25 for instructions.

Hardiness: Zones 7 to 10

Propagation: Division of offshoots ("pups").

Pest Problems: No serious insect or disease problems.

PLANTING & MAINTENANCE

When to Plant: Agave from containers can be planted at any time. Fall is best because they establish more easily in cooler weather.

Trimming: Remove flowering stalk and dying mother plant after flowering. Also, remove dead leaves. Avoid any contact with the thorns and spines because they can render a painful injury.

Fertilization: Low. Fertilize at planting time with a timed-release product. Less fertilizer is needed with the application of more organics. In the years after planting, fertilization needs vary, based on the nutrients in your soil. See pages 36 to 39 for more instructions.

BUDGET GARDENING TIP

The mother plant of agaves produces multiple offshoots, or "pups." These can be easily severed and planted. Find a friend who has an agave, and ask him or her for a start! Pups make great pass-along plants.

SHRUBS & VINES

Althea, Rose of Sharon

1ST

CHARACTERISTICS

Plant Type: Deciduous shrub (loses its leaves in winter).

Average Size: Most altheas grow quite tall, 10 to 12 feet by 6 to 8 feet wide. New dwarfs grow only about 3 feet tall.

Growth Rate: Fast

Leaf: Green, 3-lobed leaves, about 3 inches long.

Flower: About 4 inches across with prominent stamens.

Origin: China and India

Spacing: About 6 feet on center (measure from the center of each plant). Closer for the dwarfs.

Cautions: Seedlings from the older varieties are a nuisance. Occasionally damaged by deer.

Colors: Flowers are white, purple, violet, pink, blue, including many bicolors.

1. 'Blue Chiffon' althea
2. 'Little Kim' althea
3. 'Rose Satin' althea

Exotic, tropical-looking flowers from early summer to fall. Heat tolerant and easy to grow. Old ones seed enough to be a nuisance, but new ones don't. Easily rates a blue ribbon* because of high performance with very little care.

'White Chiffon' althea

Thomas Jefferson planted seeds of this shrub at Monticello in 1794, and it went on to become a popular garden plant. Old varieties tend to release too many seeds and become weedy, and their flowers are often small and not very showy. Newer altheas have much more to offer, including larger flowers and a longer period of bloom, and several varieties produce very few seeds. If you are looking for low maintenance, be sure you choose a sterile one!

Color Period: Older varieties bloom in midsummer, with some flowering continuing until fall. Newer varieties begin blooming in June and continue to set buds through October.

Buying Tips: We have done well with the Goddess series, as well as with 'Chiffon' and 'Satin.' 'Little Kim' is a tiny dwarf we have tried for only one season with great success.

Blue ribbon plants are defined on page 12. For blue ribbon performance, follow the planting and maintenance guidelines on pages 22 to 39.

Companions: Altheas go well with many summer-blooming perennials and shrubs that like sun, including agastache and black-eyed Susans.

For a long-blooming shrub garden, combine althea with 'Knock Out' roses and shrub crapemyrtle, as shown below.

'Sunny Knock Out' Rose
Plant Profile: Page 246

'Cherry Dazzle' Crapemyrtle
Plant Profile: Page 206

Althea and some companions

'Sunny Knock Out' Rose (above, top) has a more compact growth habit than the original 'Knock Out,' growing to about four feet tall. The flowers start out yellow and fade to cream. Both colors complement the althea. This rose blooms on and off from spring until fall, so it should bloom with the althea. Use the althea as the tallest plant of this grouping, with the rose in front of it.

'Cherry Dazzle' Crapemyrtle (above, bottom) blooms from June through September. Their bloom period coincides with althea's summer color period. Since dwarf crapemyrtles grow from three to five feet tall, plant them beside the roses. All three of these plants prefer sun.

GROWING CONDITIONS

Light: Full sun, at least 6 hours per day.

Water: Low after establishment. Likes water every week or two during the growing season, depending on its environment. See pages 28 to 33 for more information.

Soil: For the garden, plant in any fertile, well-drained soil that has been enriched with organic matter. Use only good-quality potting mix for containers. See pages 22 to 25 for specific instructions on soil preparation.

Hardiness: Zones 4 to 9

Propagation: Seeds or cuttings

Pest Problems: Rare. White flies, aphids, and Japanese beetles occasionally.

PLANTING & MAINTENANCE

When to Plant: Althea from containers can be planted at any time. Fall is best because they establish more easily in cooler weather.

Trimming: Don't need annual pruning unless you are trying to maintain it at a smaller-than-mature size. Any pruning should be done in early spring, before new growth starts.

Fertilization: Low. Fertilize at planting time with a timed-release product. Less fertilizer is needed with the application of more organics. In the years after planting, fertilization needs vary, based on the nutrients in your soil. See pages 36 to 39 for more instructions.

ALTERNATE SELECTIONS

See hibiscus on page 134 if you want the showy flowers of althea on a smaller plant that dies back to the ground in winter.

SHRUBS & VINES

Aucuba

CHARACTERISTICS

Plant Type: Evergreen shrub.

Average Size: Easily maintained at sizes between 4 to 8 feet tall by 3 to 4 feet wide.

Growth Rate: Slow to medium

Leaf: 3 to 4 inches wide by 6 to 8 inches long. Oval, with a pointed tip.

Flower: Insignificant

Origin: Japan

Spacing: 4 to 5 feet on center (measure from the center of each plant). Closer in containers.

Cautions: Frequently damaged by deer.

Colors: Leaves are solid green or variegated (yellow and green).

Great plant for shade, brightening up an otherwise dark spot. Adds interest in an area that doesn't have enough light for most flowering plants. Keep it out of any sun. Very easy to grow - one of the easiest plants in this book, easily rating a blue ribbon.*

Aucuba japonica 'Golden King'

While many evergreens stretch and grow lanky in shade, aucuba loves it! Take care with its placement, however, because it doesn't like any sun at all, even winter sun. (If you need tips on judging the year-round shade potential of a spot, see pages 20 to 21).

Aucuba does well when planted under large trees. It also does quite well in containers.

Color Period: Flowers are insignificant. However, green forms of aucuba have bright red berries in fall. They hang under the foliage, so they are not easy to see. Female plants don't produce fruit unless a male plant is in the neighborhood. Variegated leaves provide continuous color interest.

Buying Tips: All the aucubas we have tried have done equally well.

Aucuba japonica 'Crotonifolia'

Blue ribbon plants are defined on page 12. For blue ribbon performance, follow the planting and maintenance guidelines on pages 22 to 39.

Companions: Plant aucuba with other, shade-loving plants, like ferns, hostas, mondo grass, and heucheras.

For a woodland look, layer aucuba with the two plants shown below.

Aucuba japonica 'Picturata' and some companions

Autumn Fern (above, left) is an evergreen fern that grows two feet tall, so plant it in front of the taller aucuba. The coarse-textured aucuba contrasts well with the light-textured fern. Both do well in shade.

Mondo Grass (above, right) is an evergreen grass-like ground cover that grows three to six inches tall depending upon variety. It is an ideal groundcover under trees because it is very easy to rake through it when the tree leaves drop in the fall. Since mondo grass is the smallest of the three, use it as a border.

GROWING CONDITIONS

Light: Medium to dense shade. Burns in any sun at all, even in winter.

Water: Medium after establishment. Likes water once or twice a week during the growing season, depending on its environment. We have seen it hold up pretty well with no irrigation in deep shade. See pages 28 to 33 for more information.

Soil: For the garden, plant in any fertile, well-drained soil that has been enriched with organic matter. Good drainage is essential. See pages 22 to 25 for specific instructions on soil preparation.

Hardiness: Zones 6 to 10, but expect a little die-back in zone 6.

Propagation: Cuttings

Pest Problems: Root rot with poor drainage.

PLANTING & MAINTENANCE

When to Plant: Aucuba from containers can be planted at any time. Fall is best because they establish more easily in cooler weather.

Trimming: Aucuba grows fairly slowly, so it requires little trimming - just a touch up every 2 to 3 years in fall or early spring. Be sure to remove any dead branches when you trim it.

Fertilization: Medium. Fertilize at planting time and each spring with a timed-release product. Less fertilizer is needed with the application of more organics. See pages 36 to 39 for more instructions.

SHRUBS & VINES

Azalea, Encore Series

CHARACTERISTICS

Plant Type: Evergreen shrub.

Average Size: 2 to 12 feet tall and wide, depending on variety.

Growth Rate: Medium

Leaf: Small, green to bronze, slightly hairy leaves with pointed tips.

Flower: Petunia-like blossoms to 3 inches across with prominent stamens.

Lifespan: At least 30 years

Origin: Japan and Taiwan

Spacing: About 2 to 8 feet on center (measure from the center of each plant), depending on variety.

Cautions: Toxic to some people, so don't eat this plant. Frequently damaged by deer.

Colors: Flowers are white, pink, lavender, red, salmon, or orange.

1. *'Autumn Cheer'*
2. *'Autumn Chiffon'*
3. *'Autumn Royalty'*
4. *'Autumn Twist'*

Evergreen azaleas, long-lived and dependable, are one of the most popular flowering plants for partial shade. Gorgeous flowers in spring, fall, or both. Qualifies for a blue ribbon,* but likes more water than most plants in this book.

Encore azaleas and ferns

There are 10,000 to 15,000 different kinds of azaleas. They range in size from small dwarfs to large shrubs. Many bloom only in spring, with flowers so dense they cover the shrub entirely, as shown, right. Others, like the popular, reblooming Encore azaleas shown above, bloom strong in the spring, lightly during the summer, and fairly strong in the fall. The Fort Worth Botanic Garden and the Dallas Arboretum have an entire collection of Encore series azaleas.

Color Period: Most older varieties bloom only in spring, with different cultivars starting at different times from March through May. Each plant blooms for about three weeks. Encore azaleas are repeat bloomers.

Buying Tips: Most azaleas sold in garden centers do well but check the zone hardiness on the label to be sure they work well in your area.

*Blue ribbon plants are defined on page 12. For blue ribbon performance, follow the planting and maintenance guidelines on pages 22 to 39.

Companions: Plant azaleas with other plants that bloom in spring, including trees, like Mexican plum. Shrubs, such as some camellias and forsythia, also make good companions for azaleas.

For an easy, spring color accent, try azalea with ferns and kerria, as shown below.

Southern Wood Fern
Plant Profile: Page 126

Kerria
Plant Profile: Page 226

Encore azaleas and some companions

Southern Wood Fern (above, left) grows two to three feet tall and provides a light green, soft-textured contrast against the coarser leaves of the azaleas. Plant southern wood fern in front of Encore azaleas for a refreshing woodland effect. Both do well in light shade.

Kerria (above, right) usually blooms at the same time as the azaleas. Let it grow to its full height of six feet, and plant it alongside or behind the azaleas, with the southern wood fern as a border. These three plants do well in light shade.

GROWING CONDITIONS

Light: Light shade with no afternoon sun. Takes morning sun well.

Water: High the first season after planting, when azaleas should not be allowed to dry out. Medium after establishment. Likes water once or twice a week during the growing season, depending on its environment.

Soil: For the garden, plant in any fertile, well-drained soil that has been enriched with organic matter. Azaleas are picky about pH (5.5 to 6 is ideal), so take some soil to your county extension agent for testing prior to planting.

Hardiness: Zones 4 to 9

Propagation: Rooted stem cuttings taken in late spring.

Pest Problems: Root rot is the leading cause of death. Good drainage is essential. Aphids or lacebugs can usually be controlled with insecticidal soap.

PLANTING & MAINTENANCE

When to Plant: Azaleas from containers can be planted at any time. Fall is best because they establish more easily in cooler weather.

Trimming: Azaleas need very little trimming and should be pruned only if they become extremely overgrown or have damaged branches that need to be removed. Trim only in early summer because azaleas bloom on old wood. Thinning is much better than trimming them into little meatballs.

Fertilization: Medium. Fertilize at planting time and after flowering each spring with a timed-release product. Less fertilizer is needed with the application of more organics. Encore azaleas need more fertilizer than the others.

SHRUBS & VINES

Beautyberry, American

CHARACTERISTICS

Plant Type: Deciduous shrub (loses its leaves in winter).

Average Size: 4 to 6 feet tall on the average. Occasionally grows as tall as 9 feet.

Growth Rate: Fast

Leaf: Green, up to 6 inches long and half as wide, egg-shaped.

Flower: Small, in dense clusters at the bases of the leaves; inconspicuous.

Origin: Southeastern U.S., including Texas.

Spacing: 4 to 6 feet on center (measure from the center of each plant).

Cautions: Deer love the leaves!

Color: Flowers are inconspicuous. Berries are purple or white.

Large native shrub with branches that gracefully arch downwards. The best feature of this shrub is the spectacular, iridescent-purple berries that line the stems late summer through fall. The clusters of berries really stand out after the leaves drop in the fall, and they persist through winter unless devoured by birds. Rates a blue ribbon* because of its size, form, shade tolerance, low maintenance, and brilliant purple berries.

American beautyberry functions well in part shade, especially beneath the canopy of large trees. It is easy to grow and looks good in a landscape with other native plants. Its gorgeous display of purple berries adds eye-catching interest to the garden during late summer and fall. In late winter, it can be cut back to 12 inches to encourage more compact growth. It attracts birds and butterflies, making it an excellent plant for a garden that invites wildlife.

Color Period: Berries provide color from late summer into fall and may persist into winter. They are very visible after leaves fall.

Buying Tips: Available in nurseries and garden centers that sell native plants. A white-berried selection may also be found.

Blue ribbon plants are defined on page 12. For blue ribbon performance, follow the planting and maintenance guidelines on pages 22 to 39.

Companions: American beautyberry makes a good companion for other shade-tolerant, native plants, such as southern wood fern, inland sea oats, and Turk's cap. It also combines well with such adapted plants as purple-flowering Encore azaleas, oakleaf hydrangeas, and yew.

Beautyberry and some companions

Southern Wood Fern (above, left) grows two to three feet tall in light to medium shade and provides a light green, soft-textured contrast against the large-leafed foliage of American beautyberry. Plant the ferns in front of American beautyberry for a striking woodland effect.

Encore Azaleas (above, right) bloom again in the fall, just when the brilliant, purple berries of beautyberry are showing off. Interplant beautyberry with azalea varieties of similar height with purple or pink flowers, such as 'Autumn Royalty' or 'Autumn Twist' (purple and white streaked flowers, pictured above) for a dazzling display in fall.

*Lives on rainwater alone in all but the most extreme situations but defoliates in droughts.

GROWING CONDITIONS

Light: Light shade

Water: Very low after establishment. Lives on rainwater alone, without supplemental water, in all but the most extreme conditions. However, plants defoliate in drought conditions. See pages 28 to 33 for more information.

Soil: Plant in any fertile, well-drained soil that has been enriched with organic matter. See pages 22 to 25 for instructions.

Hardiness: Zones 7 to 10

Propagation: Seeds or cuttings

Pest Problems: No serious insect or disease problems. Deer love the foliage.

PLANTING & MAINTENANCE

When to Plant: Anytime from a container, although fall is best because plants establish more easily in cooler weather.

Trimming: Avoid shearing or shaping into a hedge. If it gets too tall and lanky, cut back to 12 inches to encourage more compact growth.

Fertilization: Low. Fertilize at planting time with a timed-release product. Less fertilizer is needed with the application of more organics. In the years after planting, fertilization needs vary, based on the nutrients in your soil. See pages 36 to 39 for more instructions.

SHRUBS & VINES

Boxwood

1ST

CHARACTERISTICS

Plant Type: Evergreen shrub.

Average Size: Easily maintained between 1 to 6 feet tall by 1 to 3 feet wide.

Growth Rate: Slow

Leaf: Tiny, green leaves

Flower: Inconspicuous

Origin: Europe, Mediterranean region, Asia, Central America, and the Caribbean.

Spacing: About 1 to 4 feet on center (measure from the center of each plant).

Cautions: Juice or sap can cause skin problems. Seldom damaged by deer.

Colors: Leaves are green; flowers are insignificant.

1. *'Wintergreen' Korean boxwood*
2. *Buxus sempervirens*

One of the most popular shrubs for hedges. Historically thought of as a plant of the aristocracy. Looks the same all year. Gives structure to the garden. Rates a blue ribbon* because of its ease of care.

There are 70 different species of boxwoods, which vary primarily in their cold tolerance and growth rate. Although all make good hedges and foundation plants, choose the one that fits your climate as well as the ultimate size desired for your space.

Boxwoods are considered the premier hedge material.

Several different varieties do well in north central Texas. Japanese boxwood is the most susceptible to winter damage; Korean boxwood is the hardiest of all selections.

Color Period: Insignificant

Buying Tips: Be sure to purchase boxwoods that take your climate well. The descriptions on the opposite page give you that information.

Blue ribbon plants are defined on page 12. For blue ribbon performance, follow the planting and maintenance guidelines on pages 22 to 39.

Japanese Boxwood (*Buxus microphylla* var. *japonica*, right) grows faster than the rest, to about four feet tall and wide. Does better in the heat of zones eight and nine than the English or Williamsburg boxwood.

Little Leaf Boxwood (*Buxus microphylla*, right). Dwarf boxwoods (like 'Kingswood Dwarf,' 'Morris Midget,' or 'Justin Bauer') grow only one foot tall by one foot wide. They are not widely available. They do well in zones eight and nine.

English or Common Boxwood (*Buxus sempervirens*, left) is used primarily for rounded foundation plantings of four to six feet tall and wide. Does well in zones six and seven. Struggles with the heat in zones eight and nine.

Korean Boxwood (*Buxus microphylla* var. *koreana*, left) is quite cold tolerant, growing from zone seven north to Canada, but not in zones eight and nine. Grows as tall as four feet tall and wide. 'Winter Gem' and 'Winter Green' hold their color better in winter.

English Boxwood (*Buxus sempervirens* 'Suffruticosa,' left) grows only 18 to 36 inches tall, so it is used only for small hedges and edging. Does well in zones six and seven but is not happy in zones eight or nine. Grows only about two inches per year, so it seldom needs trimming.

GROWING CONDITIONS

Light: Light shade to full sun

Water: Medium after establishment. Likes water once or twice a week during the growing season, depending on its environment. See pages 28 to 33 for more information.

Soil: Any fertile, well-drained soil that has been enriched with organic matter. Requires good drainage. See pages 22 to 25 for more information.

Hardiness: Zones 4 to 9, depending on type.

Propagation: Cuttings

Pest Problems: Rare. Root rot can develop if plants are kept too wet.

PLANTING & MAINTENANCE

When to Plant: Boxwood from containers can be planted at any time. Fall is best because they establish more easily in cooler weather.

Trimming: Tolerant of pruning and shearing. Shape as desired.

Fertilization: Medium. Fertilize at planting time and each spring with a timed-release product. Less fertilizer is needed with the application of more organics. See pages 36 to 39 for more instructions.

SHRUBS & VINES

Butterfly Bush

CHARACTERISTICS

Plant Type: Semi-evergreen shrub (loses some of its leaves in winter).

Average Size: 4 to 8 feet tall and wide, depending on variety.

Growth Rate: Fast

Leaf: Gray-green to blue-green, narrow leaves to 4 inches long, with lighter undersides.

Flower: 6 to 12 inch panicles studded with hundreds of tiny florets. Fragrant.

Origin: China

Spacing: Set plants 8 feet apart, or grow them as a single specimen.

Cautions: Almost never damaged by deer.

Colors: Flowers are lilac, purple, pink, magenta-red, blue, or white.

This 'Davidii' mix shows many of the different colors of butterfly bushes.

Through the hottest part of summer, butterflies flock to the flowers that may grow 12 inches long. This is a very easy shrub to grow and invaluable for its ability to bloom through the hottest part of summer. Deer leave it alone, too. Needs dead-heading (removal of dead flowers) to look good, so it misses a ribbon.

'Peacock' butterfly bush is one of the newer, more compact varieties

Butterfly bushes are one of the best plants for attracting butterflies. The older varieties are quite tall and have a tendency to look straggly. Some newer varieties are quite a bit more compact and are a great improvement over previous species. They grow relatively compactly, reaching about four feet tall by four feet wide, and look great all season. All butterfly bushes look quite a bit better with dead-heading (removal of dead flowers).

Color Period: Continuous from mid May to fall, provided old flower spikes are removed every few weeks.

Buying Tips: For compactness, look for the 'English Butterfly' series, which includes 'Adonis,' 'Peacock,' and 'Purple Emperor.' If you can't find them at your local garden center, try online suppliers. 'Black Knight' is a great, large species (eight foot) because the dark purple color really shows up well.

Attracts Butterflies   Attracts Hummingbirds   Resists Deer   Avg. Weeks of Color

(27)

Botanical Name: *Buddleia davidii*
Family: Loganiaceae

Companions: Use buddleia to anchor an island bed filled with other butterfly magnets such as lantana, pentas, verbena, and zinnias. Because the plants need regular trimming during their flowering season, be sure to allow easy access space.

Combine butterfly bush with coneflower and coreopsis for easy color layers, as shown below.

'Big Sky Twilight' Coneflower
Plant Profile: Page 116

Threadleaf Coreopsis
Plant Profile: Page 118

'Purple Emperor' butterfly bush and some companions

'Big Sky Twilight' Coneflower (above, left) is an excellent choice as a companion for butterfly bush. The textures of the flowers are quite different, they both like sun, and they share the same bloom period. This coneflower grows to about 30 inches tall. Place it in front of the taller butterfly bush.

Threadleaf Coreopsis (above, right) also blooms at the same time as both the butterfly bush and the coneflower. The fine texture of the coreopsis contrasts well with the coarser-textured flowers. Use the shorter coreopsis (about 18 inches tall) as a border for the butterfly bush and the coneflower. All three plants do well in full sun.

GROWING CONDITIONS

Light: Full sun, at least 6 hours per day.

Water: Medium after establishment. Likes water once or twice a week during the growing season, depending on its environment. Plants are drought-tolerant after establishment, but they don't bloom as much without water.

Soil: For the garden, plant in any fertile, well-drained soil that has been enriched with organic matter. Use only good-quality potting mix for containers. See pages 22 to 25 for specific instructions on soil preparation.

Hardiness: Most varieties are adapted in Zones 5 to 9; plants usually shed their leaves in winter in Zones 5 and 6.

Propagation: Cuttings

Pest Problems: Rare; aphids and spider mites occasionally.

PLANTING & MAINTENANCE

When to Plant: Butterfly bushes from containers can be planted at any time. Fall is best because they establish more easily in cooler weather.

Trimming: In late winter, cut plants back to at least 24 inches. If desired, they may be pruned back to the ground. In early summer, shape plants if needed. This pruning delays flowering but improves the overall bushiness of the plants. Throughout summer, clip off old flowers as they turn brown. As new growth emerges, every stem tip will bear blooms.

Fertilization: Low. Fertilize at planting time with a timed-release product. Less fertilizer is needed with the application of more organics. In the years after planting, fertilization needs vary, based on the nutrients in your soil. See pages 36 to 39 for more instructions.

SHRUBS & VINES

Camellia

CHARACTERISTICS

Plant Type: Evergreen shrub.

Average Size: 4 to 15 feet tall, depending on cultivar, by 4 to 8 feet wide.

Growth Rate: Slow. Once established, camellias grow slowly for decades.

Leaf: Glossy green, oval leaves; with pointed tips 2 to 4 inches long.

Flower: Single or double blossoms to 5 inches across, often with prominent stamens; numerous novel flower forms.

Origin: China and Japan

Spacing: Usually grown as specimen shrubs in foundation or boundary planting but can be planted 6 feet apart to form an evergreen hedge.

Cautions: Occasionally damaged by deer. Some varieties bear the leaves used to make green tea.

Colors: Flowers are pink, white, red, a few yellows, or bicolors.

Evergreen shrubs with gorgeous flowers in winter and spring. Wonderful as cut flowers to bring inside and float in a bowl of water.

For decades, beautiful camellias were grown only in the warmest parts of Texas, but in recent years, cold-hardy hybrids have extended this shrub's range northward into zone six. Many revered, old, winter-blooming varieties are still best grown in zones eight and nine, but hardy fall or spring blooming varieties can be grown throughout the region. *Camellia sasanqua* is better suited for north central Texas than *Camellia japonica* because it blooms in the fall before flower-damaging cold weather arrives in January and February. The best performers at the Fort Worth Botanic Garden are *Camelia sasanqua* 'Shishigashira' and 'Chansonette.' The Fort Worth Botanic Garden also has a collection of *Camellia japonica* varieties, which bloom beautifully if January and February are mild. Camellias are not as dependable as azaleas.

Regional Differences: All camellias will grow in zones eight and nine, and most will grow in zone seven.

Color Period: October to December for fall bloomers, November to January for winter bloomers, and March to April for spring bloomers. Each type blooms for about two to three weeks.

Buying Tips: Buy plants locally or from nurseries nearby, and ask them if their camellias are cold tolerant for your area.

Blue ribbon plants are defined on page 12. For blue ribbon performance, follow the planting and maintenance guidelines on pages 22 to 39.

Companions: Camellias are ideal evergreen shrubs to work into foundation plantings on the east side of your house where they will get morning sun and afternoon shade. Camellias are also an excellent choice for a blooming, evergreen hedge that rarely needs pruning.

Combine camellias with azaleas and Spanish bluebells, as shown below, for easy color layers.

White Azalea
Plant Profile: Page 188

Spanish Bluebells
Plant Profile: Page 162

White Azaleas (above, left) bloom in early spring, usually in April. Since camellias' bloom periods vary by species, check to see when yours blooms before pairing it with the azalea if you want both to bloom at the same time. Plant the shorter azalea in front of the camellia.

Spanish Bluebells (above, right) look wonderful planted in front of native azaleas. They bloom at the same time and like the same light shade. Spanish bluebells grow 18 inches tall, which is an ideal size for bordering camellias and azaleas.

GROWING CONDITIONS

Light: Light shade. Morning sun and afternoon shade is ideal.

Water: Low after establishment. Likes water every week or two during the growing season, depending on its environment. See pages 28 to 33 for more information.

Soil: For the garden, plant in any fertile, well-drained soil that has been enriched with organic matter. Camellias, like azaleas, like acidic soil. See pages 22 to 25 for specific instructions on soil preparation.

Hardiness: Zones 6 to 9

Propagation: Seeds or grafts. Named cultivars are usually grafted onto seedling rootstock.

Pest Problems: Scale insects occasionally. Squirrels often harvest buds for breakfast. Sudden cold snaps can ruin otherwise perfect camellia blossoms. To avoid this occurrence, cover blossom-bearing bushes with blankets when temperatures fall into the 20's.

PLANTING & MAINTENANCE

When to Plant: Camellias from containers can be planted at any time. Fall is best because they establish more easily in cooler weather.

Trimming: These slow-growing, woody shrubs need very little pruning. Cut back branches that grow awkwardly long, but generally allow the plants to find their own natural shape.

Fertilization: Low. Fertilize at planting time with a timed-release product. Less fertilizer is needed with the application of more organics. In the years after planting, fertilization needs vary, based on the nutrients in your soil. See pages 36 to 39 for more instructions.

SHRUBS & VINES

Carolina Jessamine

CHARACTERISTICS

Plant Type: Evergreen vine

Average Size: 10 to 20 feet tall with support; will climb most anything.

Growth Rate: Fast

Leaf: Bright green, lance-shaped leaves; 2 inches long by 1/2 inch wide.

Flower: Bright yellow, funnel-shaped flowers, 1 inch long by 1 inch wide.

Origin: Virginia to Florida, west to Texas.

Spacing: Plant one at each post of a pergola or arbor or about 6 feet on center (measure from the center of each plant). One vine will cover a mailbox.

Cautions: All parts are poisonous, and sap or juice can cause skin irritation. Seldom damaged by deer.

Colors: Flowers are yellow

Native to the woodlands of east Texas, this vine blooms profusely in early spring. Fast-growing, evergreen. Excellent selection for covering arbors, pergolas, and fences. Earns a blue ribbon* because of its ease of care.

This vigorous evergreen vine is easy to grow, provided you begin with young plants and do not spoil them with too much water or fertilizer. Carolina jessamine is happiest growing as the wild thing that it is and will reward you with thousands of fragrant, yellow flowers each spring. Although found naturally growing in sandy loam, it grows well in the black clay soils of north central Texas.

Color Period: Blooms for about three weeks in early spring in zone eight and mid April in zone seven. May rebloom sporadically throughout summer.

Buying Tips: Several cultivars are available, but 'Staright' is an excellent choice. 'Pride of Augusta,' a double-flowering form, received the 2008 Georgia Gold Medal for vines.

'Margarita' Carolina jessamine

Blue ribbon plants are defined on page 12. For blue ribbon performance, follow the planting and maintenance guidelines on pages 22 to 39.

Attracts Butterflies

Attracts Hummingbirds

Avg. Weeks of Color

Texas Native

Botanical Name: *Gelsemium sempervirens*
Family: Loganiaceae

Companions: Space companion plantings at least four to six feet away from this vine, so they don't get tangled up.

Plant Carolina jessamine with other plants that bloom at the same time or with foliage plants that provide contrast. Below is an idea for plants that look good in front of Carolina jessamine that is supported by a wall or fence.

Mexican Plum
Plant Profile: Page 300

Loropetalum
Plant Profile: Page 288

Carolina jessamine and some companions

Mexican Plum (above, left) is a small tree that blooms about the same time as Carolina jessamine. It grows 15 to 35 feet tall and up to 20 feet wide in full sun or light shade. It covers itself with fragrant, white blossoms in early spring. Plant this tree close to a wall or arbor covered with Carolina jessamine for springtime impact.

Loropetalum (above, right, 'Ever Red Sunset') is a shrub with purplish-burgundy foliage year round. Most varieties grow six to eight feet tall and wide, but there are some compact varieties, such as 'Purple Pixie,' which grows only one to two feet tall by four to five feet wide. The dark burgundy foliage of loropetalum contrasts nicely with the bright yellow flowers of Carolina jessamine. Loropetalum blooms in spring but is most useful for its year round leaf color. Plant it in front of the jessamine in full sun to light shade.

GROWING CONDITIONS

Light: Full sun to light shade

Water: Low after establishment. Likes water every week or two during the growing season, depending on its environment. Takes wet soils as well. See pages 28 to 33 for more information.

Soil: Any fertile, well-drained soil that has been enriched with organic matter. Requires good drainage. See pages 22 to 25 for instructions.

Hardiness: Zones 7 to 10

Propagation: Improved varieties are propagated by rooting stem tip cuttings taken in late spring. You also can dig out basal sprouts and transplant them to where you want them to grow.

Pest Problems: None serious. Most frequent problem with this vine is lack of flowers due to over-fertilization.

PLANTING & MAINTENANCE

When to Plant: Carolina jessamine from containers can be planted at any time. Fall is best because they establish more easily in cooler weather, but you are more likely to find them at your garden center in early spring when they are blooming.

Trimming: Trim it shortly after flowering. This vine doesn't require much trimming, only to train it or to control its growth. Remove any dead branches. Don't prune it in winter or early spring, or it might not bloom that season.

Fertilization: Low. Fertilize at planting time with a timed-release product. Less fertilizer is needed with the application of more organics. In the years after planting, fertilization needs vary, based on the nutrients in your soil. See pages 36 to 39 for more instructions.

SHRUBS & VINES

Clematis, Evergreen

CHARACTERISTICS

Plant Type: Evergreen vine

Average Size: Up to 20 feet tall by 10 feet wide.

Growth Rate: Medium

Leaf: Dark, glossy green; composed of 3 narrow leaflets 5 to 7 inches long by 1 to 2 inches wide; leathery in texture; very attractive.

Flower: 2 inches wide; 5 petals with prominent stamens and vanilla fragrance.

Origin: China

Spacing: 10 to 12 feet on center (measure from the center of each plant).

Cautions: None known

Colors: Flowers are white

An evergreen vine with the darkest green, most attractive foliage you'll ever see on a vine. Evergreen clematis effortlessly climbs on arbors, trellises, fences, and walls. Where other kinds of clematis are grown primarily for their beautiful flowers, this clematis should be used where its handsome, evergreen foliage will make a statement throughout the year. Its flowers are simply an added bonus! For these reasons, it definitely rates a blue ribbon.*

Not fussy like its more delicate clematis cousins, evergreen clematis is tough and easy to grow. Its handsome foliage is its most salient and attractive feature. In late winter/early spring, the dark foliage serves as the perfect foil for the fragrant, white flowers that are borne in clusters at the ends of the branches. These delicate flowers emit a wonderful vanilla fragrance. Established plants tolerate dry conditions.

Color Period: Two weeks in late winter/early spring

Buying Tips: Available in better nurseries and garden centers. 'Apple Blossom' has flowers that resemble large apple blossoms, opening pink and fading to white. 'Snowdrift' has white, very fragrant flowers.

*Blue ribbon plants are defined on page 12. For blue ribbon performance, follow the planting and maintenance guidelines on pages 22 to 39.

Companions: Because of its dark green, leathery foliage, evergreen clematis makes a nice backdrop for such spring-flowering shrubs as forsythia, Encore azaleas, bridalwreath spiraea, and loropetalum (fringe flower). It also serves as nice foil for daffodils and columbine.

Forsythia
Plant Profile: Page 210

Encore Azalea
Plant Profile: Page 188

Evergreen clematis and some companions

Forsythia (above, left) is an early spring-flowering shrub that bursts into an explosion of bright yellow flowers. It grows up to six feet tall in full sun to partial shade. Plant forsythia in front of a fence or trellis with evergreen clematis growing on it. Forsythia's bright yellow flowers and, later, its lime green leaves really stand out against the dark green foliage of evergreen clematis.

Encore Azalea (above, right) also blooms at the same time as evergreen clematis and offers an additional bloom in fall. Plant the clematis against a fence or wall with the forsythia (six feet tall) in front. Border with the azaleas (four feet tall). Plant all three in light shade.

GROWING CONDITIONS

Light: Like other clematis, evergreen clematis prefers "its head in the sun and its feet in the shade." Morning sun and afternoon shade are ideal, as is dappled shade throughout the day. Shade the roots by planting low shrubs, perennials, or ground covers at the base of the vines. Cool the roots even more by mulching 2 to 3 inches thick.

Water: Medium after establishment. Likes water once or twice a week during the growing season, depending on its environment. See pages 28 to 33 for more information.

Soil: Any fertile, well-drained soil that has been enriched with organic matter. Requires good drainage. See pages 22 to 25 for instructions.

Hardiness: Zones 7b to 10

Propagation: Cuttings

Pest Problems: No serious insect or disease problems.

PLANTING & MAINTENANCE

When to Plant: Evergreen clematis from containers can be planted at any time. Fall is best because they establish more easily in cooler weather.

Trimming: To prevent dead, underlying layers of leaves, prune every year immediately after flowering. Pruning any later will reduce next spring's flowering.

Fertilization: Low. Fertilize at planting time with a timed-release product. Less fertilizer is needed with the application of more organics. In the years after planting, fertilization needs vary, based on the nutrients in your soil. See pages 36 to 39 for more instructions.

SHRUBS & VINES

Clematis, Sweet Autumn

CHARACTERISTICS

Plant Type: Semi-ever-green vine (sometimes loses its leaves in winter).

Average Size: Up to 30 feet tall and wide.

Growth Rate: Fast

Leaf: Each leaf consists of 3 to 5 leaflets; each leaflet 2 to 3 inches long by 1 1/4 inches wide; leathery-textured; shiny green.

Flower: Star-shaped, 1 inch in diameter, sweetly fragrant; flowers cover the foliage when in bloom so that the leaves look as if they're covered with snow.

Origin: Japan

Spacing: 15 feet on center (measure from the center of each plant).

Cautions: Can invasively self-seed in the landscape, and has escaped cultivation and naturalized in many parts of the U.S.

Colors: Flowers are creamy white

Vigorous vine that can cover a fence, trellis, or arbor within a growing season. Attractive leaves and creamy-white flowers cover the vine in late summer/early fall and emit a sweet fragrance. After flowering, you will find silvery-gray, featherlike seed heads adorn the vine. Rates a blue ribbon* because of its fast growth, late summer bloom, and low maintenance requirements.

Sweet autumn clematis signals the end of summer by providing billowy masses of creamy-white flowers that absolutely cover the vine and release a sweet fragrance into the air. This is the easiest of all clematis varieties to grow. It thrives on neglect and can even become a nuisance by engulfing nearby shrubs and trees and self-seeding all over the place. This is a great vine for covering a fence, trellis, arbor, or unsightly building.

Color Period: Late August through September

Buying Tips: Available in better nurseries and garden centers

*Blue ribbon plants are defined on page 12. For blue ribbon performance, follow the planting and maintenance guidelines on pages 22 to 39.

Attracts Butterflies

Attracts Hummingbirds

Lives on Rain Water *

3
Avg. Weeks of Color

Botanical Name: *Clematis terniflora*

Family: Ranunculaceae

Companions: Sweet autumn clematis combines very well with butterfly bush, the deep purple, foliage of loropetalum, and the purple fruit-laden American beautyberry. It's also a beautiful backdrop for late summer-blooming ornamental grasses and the bright red flowers of Turk's cap.

Loropetalum
Plant Profile: Page 288

Lindheimer's Muhly Grass
Plant Profile: Page 132

Sweet autumn clematis and some companions

Loropetalum (above, top, 'Little Rose Dawn') is a large evergreen to semi-evergreen shrub six to 15 feet tall by four to eight feet wide. It has purplish-burgundy foliage that really stands out against the glossy green leaves and profusion of creamy-white flowers of sweet autumn clematis. Plant loropetalum in front of a fence that has sweet autumn clematis growing on it for a stunning effect in late summer/early fall.

Lindheimer's Muhly Grass (above, bottom) forms a three to four foot mound of narrow-bladed, gracefully-arching, blue-green foliage that remains evergreen to semi-evergreen during the winter. Starting in August, the grass sends up silvery-tan, feathery plumes five to six feet tall. Plant clumps of this grass in front of a wall of sweet autumn clematis for a beautiful fall composition.

*Lives on rainwater alone in all but the most extreme situations.

GROWING CONDITIONS

Light: This clematis likes its roots in the shade and its foliage in the sun. Morning sun and afternoon shade are ideal, as is dappled shade throughout the day. Shade the roots by planting low shrubs, perennials, or ground covers at the base of the vines. Cool the roots even more by mulching 2 to 3 inches thick.

Water: Very low after establishment. Lives on rainwater alone, without supplemental water, in all but the most extreme conditions. See pages 28 to 33 for more information.

Soil: Any fertile, well-drained soil that has been enriched with organic matter. Requires good drainage. See pages 22 to 25 for instructions.

Hardiness: Zones 5 to 10

Propagation: Seeds or cuttings

Pest Problems: No serious insect or disease problems.

PLANTING & MAINTENANCE

When to Plant: Clematis from containers can be planted at any time. Fall is best because they establish more easily in cooler weather.

Trimming: Whenever needed to keep in bounds; sweet autumn clematis blooms on new growth, so pruning anytime doesn't interfere with blooming.

Fertilization: Low. Fertilize at planting time with a timed-release product. Less fertilizer is needed with the application of more organics. In the years after planting, fertilization needs vary, based on the nutrients in your soil.

BUDGET GARDENING TIP

Sweet autumn clematis is a great "pass-along plant." You can easily dig up seedlings and share with a neighbor or gardening friend.

SHRUBS & VINES

Cleyera

CHARACTERISTICS

Plant Type: Evergreen shrub

Average Size: 'Big Foot' grows 10 to 12 feet tall by 6 feet wide. 'Bronze Beauty' and 'Leann' grow 8 to 10 feet tall by 8 feet wide.

Growth Rate: Slow

Leaf: 3 to 4 inches long by 1 inch wide; elliptical; new growth is copper-colored.

Flower: Flowers are insignificant, but fruit that follows is good bird food.

Origin: Japan

Spacing: About 4 to 6 feet on center (measure from the center of each plant). Closer in containers.

Cautions: None known

Colors: Flowers are white, but insignificant.

Cleyera 'Big Foot' planted as a hedge.

Nice, glossy, green shrub where soils are acidic. Great substitute for red-tip photinia, which is plagued with fungal leaf spot. Excellent, low-maintenance hedge material. Doesn't rate a ribbon because of its susceptibility to chlorosis (yellowing of the leaves) in alkaline soils.

Cleyera 'Leann'

Cleyera is a good evergreen shrub for foundation plantings or a hedge. It keeps its full shape nicely without requiring a lot of trimming. It grows upright but full and rounded. Before planting, have your soil tested through the county extension service, and amend as necessary.

Color Period: Late spring, but flowers are insignificant

Buying Tips: 'Bronze Beauty,' 'Leann,' and 'Big Foot' are three new cultivars that show promise.

Blue ribbon plants are defined on page 12. For blue ribbon performance, follow the planting and maintenance guidelines on pages 22 to 39.

Companions: Cleyera comes in many shades of green, including the solid, dark green 'Big Foot,' shown right. For contrast, mix it with bright-colored flowers like crapemyrtle. Or, combine any of the different green cleyeras with plants that have contrasting textures, like the yew and southern wood fern, shown below.

GROWING CONDITIONS

Light: Light to medium shade. Stretches a bit in shade.

Water: Medium after establishment. Likes water once or twice a week during the growing season, depending on its environment. See pages 28 to 33 for more information.

Soil: Any fertile, well-drained, acidic soil that has been enriched with organic matter. Requires good drainage. See pages 22 to 25 for instructions.

Hardiness: Zones 7 to 10. Shows damage at 0 degrees.

Propagation: Seeds or cuttings

Pest Problems: Rare

PLANTING & MAINTENANCE

When to Plant: Cleyera from containers can be planted at any time. Fall is best because they establish more easily in cooler weather.

Trimming: Cleyera doesn't need much trimming, at most once a year. Late winter or early spring is the best time.

Fertilization: Low. Fertilize at planting time with a timed-release product designed for azaleas and camellias. Less fertilizer is needed with the application of more organics. In the years after planting, fertilization needs vary, based on the nutrients in your soil. See pages 36 to 39 for more instructions.

Yew
Plant Profile: Page 260

Southern Wood Fern
Plant Profile: Page 126

Cleyera 'Bronze Beauty' and some companions

Yew (above, left) makes a good companion for cleyera because of the strong textural difference. Since the yew grows three to four feet tall, plant it in front of the taller-growing cleyera.

Southern Wood Fern (above, right) grows two to three feet tall in light to medium shade and provides a light green, soft-textured contrast to the dark green, stiff needles of the yew shrub. The lime green color of southern wood fern is the same color as the new growth on yew, so the two complement each other very well.

SHRUBS & VINES

Crapemyrtle, Dwarf

1ST

CHARACTERISTICS

Plant Type: Deciduous shrub (loses its leaves in winter).

Average Size: Easily maintained at sizes between 3 to 5 feet tall by 3 to 4 feet wide.

Growth Rate: Fast

Leaf: Deep green with shades of red, 2" long by 1" wide. Nice fall color, turning yellow to bright red, depending on cultivar.

Flower: Frilly, like crepe paper-like

Origin: China

Spacing: About 2 to 3 feet on center (measure from the center of each plant). Closer in containers.

Cautions: Almost never damaged by deer.

Colors: Flowers are red, pink, white, or lavender.

1. 'Dazzle Me Pink'
2. 'Raspberry Dazzle'
3. 'Snow Dazzle'
4. Fall color on leaves of 'Raspberry Dazzle.'

One of the top flowering shrubs for Texas. Blooms for 90 to 120 days during the heat of summer. Great color impact with very little care. Lives without irrigation. Easily earns a blue ribbon.*

'Victor' crapemyrtle hedge

Most Texans are familiar with crapemyrtle tree, which is one of the best flowering trees for Texas. New, dwarf crapemyrtles grow into shrubs instead of trees. They are incredibly easy to grow and offer a long bloom period. Crapemyrtles are also quite dependable - blooming through both wet and dry years.

Color Period: Varies some from year to year. They start blooming in June, when they have the highest intensity of color. In August, they continue blooming, but the seed pods are forming, so they don't have quite as much color. If you trim the seed pods, they should continue blooming through September.

Buying Tips: Go online to www.crapemyrtletrails.org, click on "Varieties," and make your selection. Purchase crapemyrtles at the nursery while they're in bloom, so you know you're getting the color you want. Choose varieties that are resistant to powdery mildew.

Blue ribbon plants are defined on page 12. For blue ribbon performance, follow the planting and maintenance guidelines on pages 22 to 39.

Attracts Butterflies

Resists Deer

Lives on Rain Water *

23
Avg. Weeks of Color

Botanical Name: *Lagerstroemia indica*
Family: Lythraceae

Companions: The long blooming period for crapemyrtles (June through September) overlaps that of many other shrubs and perennials. Altheas are a particularly nice background plant for crapemyrtle.

For easy color layers, plant reblooming daylilies and scabiosa in front of dwarf crapemyrtle, as shown below.

'Cherry Dazzle' crapemyrtle and some companions

'Stella de Oro' Daylily (top left) is one of the longest-blooming perennial daylilies, blooming for up to three months each summer. Its 18 to 24 inch height fits well in front of the taller crapemyrtles. Plant both in full sun for optimal blooming.

Scabiosa (above, right) is another one of the longest-blooming perennials for Texas, flowering from May until September, if you dead-head (remove dead flowers). It grows 12 to 18 inches tall, so use it as a front border for the taller crapemyrtle and daylilies.

Lives on rainwater alone in all but the most extreme situations.

GROWING CONDITIONS

Light: Full sun, at least 6 hours per day. The number one reason crapemyrtles don't flower is too much shade.

Water: Very low after establishment. Likes water every week or two during the growing season, depending on its environment, but lives without irrigation after it is established.

Soil: Any fertile, well-drained soil that has been enriched with organic matter. Requires good drainage. See pages 22 to 25 for instructions.

Hardiness: Zones 6 to 10, but occasionally damaged in zone 6 if the temperatures fall below -10 degrees.

Propagation: Seeds or cuttings

Pest Problems: Powdery mildew, a fungus, is the most common disease on crapemyrtles. Avoid this problem altogether by planting mildew-resistant varieties in full sun where there's plenty of air circulation. The crapemyrtle aphid, an insect, secretes honeydew on the leaves, and sooty mold follows.

PLANTING & MAINTENANCE

When to Plant: Crapemyrtle from containers can be planted at any time. Fall is best because they establish more easily in cooler weather, but you are more likely to find them at your garden center in summer when they are blooming.

Trimming: Cut the whole shrub back to the ground every year in late fall, or cut it back every few years if you want it to grow taller.

Fertilization: Low. Fertilize at planting time with a timed-release product. Less fertilizer is needed with the application of more organics. In the years after planting, fertilization needs vary, based on the nutrients in your soil.

SHRUBS & VINES

Crossvine

CHARACTERISTICS

Plant Type: Evergreen vine

Average Size: Up to 50 feet tall.

Growth Rate: Fast

Leaf: Glossy, waxy, and dark green; 4 to 6 inches long by 2 inches wide.

Flower: Trumpet-shaped flowers; 2 inches long by 1 1/2 inches wide, borne in clusters of 2 to 5.

Origin: Southeastern U.S., including east Texas.

Spacing: 6 to 8 feet on center (measure from the center of each plant).

Cautions: Highly deer resistant

Colors: Flowers are yellow, orange, or red.

Crossvine provides a spectacular display of showy flowers in the spring and attracts hummingbirds on their spring migration. The vine blooms so profusely that the foliage is covered by the flowers. Attractive, evergreen leaves year round. Crossvine earns a blue ribbon* for its spring flower production, adaptability to a range of soil and light conditions, and drought tolerance once established.

This easy-to-grow vine thrills the gardener each spring with a profusion of yellow, orange, or red, trumpet-shaped flowers that absolutely cover the vine. Crossvine tolerates shade but produces the most flowers in full sun. After the flowers disappear, the handsome foliage makes an attractive vine the rest of the season. Claws at the end of its tendrils enable crossvine to cling to brick, stone, or fences, so it is not necessary to string up support wires for it.

Color Period: Blooms heavily in March/April and then again lightly in the fall. Green foliage year round.

Buying Tips: The native species has yellow flowers with rust-colored throats. 'Tangerine Beauty' produces orange flowers with yellow throats. *Bignonia capreolata var. atrosanguinea* produces red to reddish-burgundy flowers.

Blue ribbon plants are defined on page 12. For blue ribbon performance, follow the planting and maintenance guidelines on pages 22 to 39.

Companions: Crossvine combines well with other, spring-flowering plants, such as daffodils, forsythia, columbine, and Mexican plum tree. It also looks great against the burgundy foliage of loropetalum.

Daffodils
Plant Profile: Page 120

Mexican Plum
Plant Profile: Page 300

Crossvine and some companions

Daffodils (above, left) bloom in March through early April - the same time crossvine blooms. Daffodils reach a height of 16 inches or so and produce one to several flowers atop each stem, depending on the variety. Like crossvine, daffodils bloom best in full sun. Plant a large drift of daffodils in front of crossvine for a stunning springtime display.

Mexican Plum (above, right) also blooms at the same time as crossvine. This native tree usually grows about 15 feet tall and wide and produces an abundance of honey-scented, white blossoms. A few Mexican plum trees blooming behind a fence of flowering crossvines will create a breathtaking spring scene.

GROWING CONDITIONS

Light: Full sun to part shade

Water: Low to very low. Crossvine will live without irrigation but looks better with water every week or two during the growing season, depending on its environment. See pages 28 to 33 for more information.

Soil: Any fertile, well-drained soil that has been enriched with organic matter. Requires good drainage. See pages 22 to 25 for instructions.

Hardiness: Zones 6 to 9

Propagation: Seed

Pest Problems: No serious insect or pest problems.

PLANTING & MAINTENANCE

When to Plant: Crossvine from containers can be planted at any time. Fall is best because they establish more easily in cooler weather.

Trimming: Very little, if any, trimming needed.

Fertilization: Low. Fertilize at planting time with a timed-release product. Less fertilizer is needed with the application of more organics. In the years after planting, fertilization needs vary, based on the nutrients in your soil. See pages 36 to 39 for more instructions.

SHRUBS & VINES

Forsythia

CHARACTERISTICS

Plant Type: Deciduous flowering shrub (loses its leaves in winter).

Average Size: To 6 feet tall and wide.

Growth Rate: Fast

Leaf: Narrow green leaves turn yellow or bronze in late fall. 3 to 5 inches long.

Flower: Abundant, four-petaled flowers cover the bare stems in early spring.

Origin: Hybrid of *F. suspensa* and *F. viridissima*, which are native to China.

Spacing: About 6 to 8 feet on center (measure from the center of each plant).

Cautions: Occasionally damaged by deer.

Colors: Flowers are golden yellow. Leaves are green in summer, turning yellow or bronze in late fall.

Forsythia and pansies are great companions.

Sudden explosion of golden yellow announces the arrival of spring. Blooms in March, before the last freeze. Continues blooming for about a month. Spectacular color with very little care. Easily earns a blue ribbon.*

In addition to opening the color season with a bang, forsythias are among the easiest shrubs to grow. They adapt to sun or partial shade, good soil or bad, and they are at their most beautiful when left unpruned. The natural fountain shape of a mature forsythia is breathtaking, but patience is required. Young plants often appear a bit stiff, but after three years or so, the branches lengthen into a graceful arch.

In late winter's bare landscape, forsythias are easily seen from afar, so they are ideal for the distant corners of your yard. They are also good for accenting fences or other boundaries, and they mix easily with other flowering and evergreen shrubs.

Color Period: Late winter or very early spring, usually in mid March. It keeps blooming for two to four weeks.

Buying Tips: There are quite a few different varieties for sale. We have not found too much difference among them.

Blue ribbon plants are defined on page 12. For blue ribbon performance, follow the planting and maintenance guidelines on pages 22 to 39.

Companions: Forsythia looks great planted near Mexican plum trees, which bloom at the same time. Pansies and violas make a great border for forsythia.

Or, try forsythia with irises and loropetalum, as shown below.

Forsythia and some companions

Iris (above, left) blooms in mid spring, like the forsythia. They grow in clumps that reach about two feet tall. Plant them in clumps in front of the forsythia. They both do well in sun.

Loropetalum (above, right, 'Little Rose Dawn') is a large shrub 6 to 15 feet tall. It has purplish-burgundy foliage that makes a striking foil for the golden yellow flowers of forsythia. Furthermore, loropetalum produces fringe-like, fuchsia-colored flowers in late winter/early spring that will stand out against the yellow flowers of forsythia as well. Use a large variety of loropetalums behind forsythia.

GROWING CONDITIONS

Light: Full sun to partial shade. Blooming is not as heavy in the shade.

Water: Low after establishment. Likes water every week or two during the growing season, depending on its environment. See pages 28 to 33 for more information.

Soil: For the garden, plant in any fertile, well-drained soil that has been enriched with organic matter. See pages 22 to 25 for specific instructions on soil preparation.

Hardiness: Zones 5 to 8

Propagation: Rooted cuttings. Or, follow this procedure for layering: In late spring, bend a long branch down, and pin it to the ground with a stone or brick (after removing the leaves from the section of stem that will be in contact with the ground). By the following spring, the layered stem will be rooted and ready to transplant.

Pest Problems: None serious

PLANTING & MAINTENANCE

When to Plant: Forsythia from containers can be planted at any time. Fall is best because they establish more easily in cooler weather.

Trimming: Every three to four years, just after the flowers fade, cut the oldest branches close to the ground, removing no more than 1/4 of the total branches. Do not attempt to shear this one into a mushroom, or it will look ridiculous.

Fertilization: Low. Fertilize at planting time with a timed-release product. Less fertilizer is needed with the application of more organics. In the years after planting, fertilization needs vary, based on the nutrients in your soil.

SHRUBS & VINES

Groundcovers, Small Vining

CHARACTERISTICS

Plant Type: Evergreen groundcover.

Average Size: Varies by type.

Growth Rate: Medium

Leaf: Varies by type

Flower: Both ivy and pachysandra have inconspicuous flowers. Vinca has small flowers that resemble periwinkles.

Origin: Vinca and ivy are native to Europe. Japanese pachysandra is from Japan. Allegheny spurge is native from Virginia to Florida, west to Texas.

Spacing: Varies by type

Cautions: None known

Colors: Ivy and pachysandra have insignificant flowers. Vinca vine has blue or white flowers.

Variegated ivy is alternated with coleus and red wax begonias in the sides and along the edges of this 36-inch, side-planted window box from www.kinsmangarden.com. The trellis is hung separately and is available from the same source. We like ivy better in containers than in the ground because it is easier to control.

Three vining groundcovers for shady areas. Grow in areas that are too shady for grass. They use less water and require less care than grass. Rate a blue ribbon* because of their ease of care.

Small, vining groundcovers can be used to cover fences or walls, as shown above. Take great care with ivy because it can go wild in natural areas, killing whole forests that stand in its way.

These three, shade, groundcovers thrive in areas that are too shady for grass. Take care with ivy, however, because it is considered invasive, damaging our native forests by smothering the trees and other vegetation.

Color Period: Vinca vine is the only one that has significant flowers. It blooms for about three weeks, starting sometime in April.

Buying Tips: These groundcovers are available at many garden centers. Or, check out online suppliers.

Blue ribbon plants are defined on page 12. For blue ribbon performance, follow the planting and maintenance guidelines on pages 22 to 39.

English Ivy (*Hedira helix*, left) covers the ground quickly in areas that are so dark that not too many other plants grow. However, it grows up as well as out, covering everything in its way. Ivy has covered whole forests and can kill the trees that get in its way. It climbs up houses, damaging the wood behind it. So, be very careful with this one. Space ivy plantings one to two feet on center, depending on the size of the plants. It takes morning sun to dense shade.

Pachysandra (Japanese Pachysandra *P. terminalis* and Allegheny spurge, *P. procumbens*, right) are two related groundcovers that are better suited for zones five to seven than farther south. They take light to dense shade in zone seven and medium to dense shade in zone eight. Japanese pachysandra grows faster than Allegheny spurge, but neither is as fast as ivy. Japanese pachysandra is bright green, while Allegheny spurge is bluish-green with some variegation.

Vinca Vine (*Vinca minor*, left) is an attractive groundcover with dark green leaves and blue flowers that bloom in spring for about three weeks (usually in mid April). It covers the ground fairly quickly. Avoid its relative, *Vinca major*, because it is quite difficult to control. Vinca with solid green leaves do better as landscape plants than those with variegated leaves. Requires light to medium shade. Stick to medium to light shade in zones eight or nine. Vinca vine grows about six inches tall. Space new plants one to two feet on center.

GROWING CONDITIONS

Light: All of these groundcovers prefer varying degrees of shade. See individual descriptions for more specifics.

Water: Ivy has very low water needs and lives without supplemental irrigation after establishment. Both pachysandra and vinca have medium water needs after establishment. They like water once or twice a week during the growing season, depending on their environment. See pages 28 to 33 for more information.

Soil: Any fertile, well-drained soil that has been enriched with organic matter. Requires good drainage. See pages 22 to 25 for instructions.

Hardiness: Vinca vine is hardy from zones 4 to 8. Ivy's cold tolerance depends on the cultivar. Pachysandra grows in zones 5 to 9.

Propagation: Division or cuttings

Pest Problems: Rare

PLANTING & MAINTENANCE

When to Plant: Groundcovers from containers can be planted at any time. Fall is best because they establish more easily in cooler weather.

Trimming: Vinca vine and pachysandra need only occasional trimming to keep them within bounds. Ivy needs hard trimming every few years. Set the blade of a mower on high and mow it, or cut it with a weed eater.

Fertilization: Medium. Fertilize at planting time and each spring with a timed-release product. Less fertilizer is needed with the application of more organics. See pages 36 to 39 for more instructions.

Ivy lives on rainwater alone in all but the most extreme situations. Vinca and pachysandra need more water.

SHRUBS & VINES

Hollies, Smaller

CHARACTERISTICS

Plant Type: Evergreen shrub.

Average Size: Easily maintained at sizes between 2 to 10 feet tall and 2 to 6 feet wide.

Growth Rate: Most are fast, but dwarf forms are slower.

Leaf: Rounded, glossy green or bronze leaves, 1 to 2 inches long and wide.

Flower: Hundreds of small, open-centered blossoms.

Origin: Several species are native to the southeastern U.S.; the rest are from the Far East.

Spacing: About 4 feet on center (measure from the center of each plant). Closer in containers.

Cautions: Some of the leaves have spines. Berries of some hollies are poisonous. Seldom to occasional damage by deer. Lots of bees when blooming.

Colors: Holly flowers are insignificant, but some have attractive berries in both red and dark blue to black.

1. *Ilex helleri*
2. *Ilex cornuta*

One of the most popular evergreen shrubs in Texas. Most landscapes include at least one holly. Very easy to grow, rating a blue ribbon.*

Dwarf yaupon holly makes an excellent hedge.

Hollies are quite well adapted to the climate in north central Texas. There are many different kinds that vary mostly in leaf shape and the size of the plant. Some hollies have smooth leaf edges, and others have spines, like the ones associated with Christmas. The two photos, left, show how different the leaves can be.

Color Period: Blooms are insignificant. Berries appear on some species in fall and winter.

Buying Tips: The most important consideration is size and light. All of these smaller hollies do well in light shade to full sun. In medium shade, choose another shrub, like aucuba. Also, know the mature size you need. A frequent mistake is to plant hollies that outgrow their spaces.

Blue ribbon plants are defined on page 12. For blue ribbon performance, follow the planting and maintenance guidelines on pages 22 to 39.

Attracts Birds   Lives on Rain Water *

Chinese Holly (*Ilex cornuta*, left) is the standard for foundation planting and features red fruit and spines on the leaves. There are many different cultivars, ranging from three to 15 feet tall, so be sure you get the right one! Zones seven to nine.

Japanese Holly (*Ilex crenata*, right) is also known as the "poor man's boxwood." Resembles boxwood from a distance, but not quite as refined, although it has the smallest leaves of any of the hollies. Often trimmed like little green meatballs, and looks better thinned than sheared. Averages three to four feet tall by three feet wide, so space them two to three feet apart. Zones seven to nine.

Dwarf Yaupon holly, (*Ilex vomitoria* left, and on opposite page), is one of the twenty most popular landscape plants. Good substitute for boxwood and suitable for shearing. Easy to maintain at two to three feet tall by equally as wide, so space them at two to three feet apart. Grows five feet without trimming. 'Shillings' is the best cultivar for hedges. Very drought tolerant, surviving without irrigation in interstate plantings. Zones six to ten.

GROWING CONDITIONS

Light: Light shade to full sun

Water: Varies by type. Yaupon holly has very low water needs after establishment. Lives on rainwater alone, without supplemental water, in all but the most extreme conditions. Chinese holly and Japanese holly have low water needs after establishment. They like water every week or two during the growing season, depending on the environment. See pages 28 to 33 for more information.

Soil: Any fertile, well-drained soil that has been enriched with organic matter. Requires good drainage. See pages 22 to 25 for instructions.

Hardiness: Varies by species from zones 6 to 10.

Propagation: Cuttings; seeds are difficult.

Pest Problems: Rare. Root rot can develop if plants are kept too wet.

PLANTING & MAINTENANCE

When to Plant: Holly from containers can be planted at any time. Fall is best because they establish more easily in cooler weather.

Trimming: Most hollies look good with one annual pruning in late winter to early spring. Some require a few more shapings throughout the growing season.

Fertilization: Medium. Fertilize at planting time and each spring with a timed-release product. Less fertilizer is needed with the application of more organics. See pages 36 to 39 for more instructions.

SHRUBS & VINES

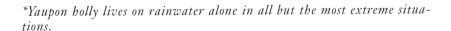

*Yaupon holly lives on rainwater alone in all but the most extreme situations.

Hollies, Larger

1ST

CHARACTERISTICS

Plant Type: Evergreen or deciduous shrub, depending on species (see opposite page).

Average Size: Easily maintained at sizes between 8 to 20 feet tall by 6 to 12 feet wide.

Growth Rate: Depends on type

Leaf: Rounded, glossy, green leaves, 1 to 2 inches long and wide.

Flower: Insignificant

Origin: See individual descriptions on opposite page.

Spacing: About 6 to 12 feet on center (measure from the center of each plant), depending on cultivar.

Cautions: Some of the leaves have spines; berries of some hollies are poisonous; hollies attract lots of bees when blooming but seldom attract any deer.

Colors: Holly flowers are insignificant, but some have attractive berries in both red and dark blue to black.

One of the most popular shrubs or small trees in Texas. Most landscapes include at least one holly. Very easy to grow, rating a blue ribbon.*

Some holly species are quite tall, like this 'Nellie R. Stevens' (the tallest plant in the photo), while others are small, like these small, round, Japanese hollies in front.

Hollies are quite well adapted to the Texas climate. There are many different kinds that vary mostly in leaf shape and the size of the plant. Some hollies have smooth leaf edges, and others have spines, like the ones associated with Christmas. Hollies vary quite a bit in size, as shown in the photo above. Plant any of these large hollies at least eight feet away from your house. A common landscape mistake is to plant them too close to the house.

Color Period: April, but flowers are insignificant. Fruits appear on some species in fall and winter.

Buying Tips: The most important consideration is size and light. All of these hollies do well in light shade to full sun. In medium shade, choose another shrub, like aucuba. Also, know the mature size you need. A frequent mistake is to plant hollies that outgrow their spaces.

1. 'Nellie R. Stevens' holly
2. 'Mary Nell' holly
3. Possumhaw holly

Blue ribbon plants are defined on page 12. For blue ribbon performance, follow the planting and maintenance guidelines on pages 22 to 39.

'Mary Nell' Holly (*Ilex* x 'Mary Nell,' left) is a pyramidal-shaped, large shrub with dark green, glossy, serrated leaves with a point on each of the many tips along the leaf margin. 'Mary Nell' gets 10 to 15 feet tall by six to eight feet wide. This holly has a very formal look and produces clusters of bright red berries. Excellent as a background shrub, screen, or accent plant. 'Mary Nell' is a hybrid of hollies from China and Japan. Evergreen. Zones seven through nine.

'Nellie R. Stevens' Holly (*Ilex* 'Nellie R. Stevens', right) is another pyramidal-shaped, large shrub with dark, evergreen leaves to four inches long with two to three spines on each side of the leaf. This holly grows 15 to 20 feet tall by eight to 12 feet wide and produces abundant clusters of large, bright red berries. 'Nellie R. Stevens' makes an excellent screen or background shrub. It is a hybrid of hollies native to England and China. Zones six through nine.

Possumhaw Holly (*Ilex decidua*, left) is a native Texas holly. Unlike the others, this one is deciduous (loses its leaves in winter). Up to 20 feet tall, with a spread of 12 feet. Glossy, medium-green leaves and gray bark. Only the female trees produce the red berries, so be sure to buy a plant with berries on it if you want a female. 'Warren's Red' is a female cultivar that has particularly large and very red berries. Fruit production is heaviest in full sun, although the plant will tolerate light shade. Fairly drought tolerant once established. Zones five through nine.

GROWING CONDITIONS

Light: Light shade to full sun

Water: 'Nellie R. Stevens' and possumhaw hollies have low water needs after establishment. They like water every week or two during the growing season, depending on the environment. 'Mary Nell' has medium water needs, doing best with water every week or two after it is established. See pages 28 to 33 for more information.

Soil: Any fertile, well-drained soil that has been enriched with organic matter. Requires good drainage. See pages 22 to 25 for instructions.

Hardiness: Varies by species from 5 to 9.

Propagation: Cuttings; seeds are difficult.

Pest Problems: Rare

PLANTING & MAINTENANCE

When to Plant: Holly from containers can be planted at any time. Fall is best because they establish more easily in cooler weather.

Trimming: Most hollies look good with one annual pruning in late winter to early spring. Some require a few more shapings throughout the growing season.

Fertilization: Medium. Fertilize at planting time and each spring with a timed-release product. Less fertilizer is needed with the application of more organics. See pages 36 to 39 for more instructions.

SHRUBS & VINES

Only possumhaw holly is a Texas native

Honeysuckle, Coral

CHARACTERISTICS

Plant Type: Semi-ever-green vine (loses some of its leaves in winter).

Average Size: 10 to 20 feet tall; needs support.

Growth Rate: Fast

Leaf: Small, rounded leaves emerging in early spring with tinges of red or purple changing to a blue-green in summer.

Flower: Abundant tubular flowers, 4 inches long.

Origin: New England to Florida, west to Texas.

Spacing: Plant one at each post of a pergola or arbor or 6 feet on center (measure from the center of each plant).

Cautions: Occasionally damaged by deer. Poisonous to some, so don't eat this plant.

Colors: Red, orange, yellow, or pink.

1. 'Mardi Gras' honeysuckle
2. 'Harlequin' honeysuckle
3. 'John Clayton' honeysuckle

Spectacular coral red to yellow spring flowers on a fast-growing, twining vine. Native to Texas and easy to grow. Rates a blue ribbon* because of ease of care.

Coral honeysuckle is an outstanding native vine for showy spring flowers. It is a great hummingbird attractor, with butterflies enjoying it as well. This large vine grows to 20 feet with support or stays in a large clump if allowed to grow on its own. This is a good selection for Texas gardens - not as aggressive as the Japanese honeysuckle, which is an invasive species.

Color Period: Early to mid spring for about two months. May re-bloom sporadically throughout summer.

Buying Tips: Cultivars are available based on color of flowers. 'Magnifica' and 'Alabama Crimson' both have red flowers. 'John Clayton' is pure yellow, and 'Cedar Lane' is a selection from Madison, Georgia, that blooms over a longer period of time.

*Blue ribbon plants are defined on page 12. For blue ribbon performance, follow the planting and maintenance guidelines on pages 22 to 39.

Companions: Space companion plantings at least four to six feet away from this vine, so they don't get tangled up with each other.

Plant this vine with other plants that bloom at the same time. Plants that look good in front of honeysuckle that is supported by a wall or fence are listed below.

'Sunny Knock Out' Rose
Plant Profile: Page 246

Autumn Sage
Plant Profile: Page 156

Honeysuckle and some companions

'Sunny Knock Out' Rose (above, left) has a more compact growth habit than the original 'Knock Out,' growing to about four feet tall. The flowers start out yellow and fade to cream. Both colors complement the honeysuckle. This rose blooms on and off from spring until fall, so it should bloom with the honeysuckle. Use the honeysuckle as the tallest plant of this grouping, with the rose in front of it.

Autumn Sage (above, right) is a perennial that grows about 30 inches tall and wide. It starts blooming at the same time coral honeysuckle does in April and, like coral honeysuckle, attracts hummingbirds. Continuing to bloom to November, this sage shares the same affinity for full sun to light shade with coral honeysuckle. Place autumn sage in front of the 'Sunny Knock Out' roses as a border for the two taller plants.

GROWING CONDITIONS

Light: Light shade to full sun

Water: Very low after establishment. Lives on rainwater alone, without supplemental water, in all but the most extreme conditions. See pages 28 to 33 for more information.

Soil: Any fertile, well-drained soil that has been enriched with organic matter. Requires good drainage. See pages 22 to 25 for instructions.

Hardiness: Zones 4 to 9

Propagation: Seeds or cuttings

Pest Problems: None serious. Powdery mildew can be a problem on the leaves that are in shade and have poor air circulation.

PLANTING & MAINTENANCE

When to Plant: Honeysuckle from containers can be planted at any time. Fall is best because they establish more easily in cooler weather, but you are more likely to find them at your garden center in early spring when they are blooming.

Trimming: Trim it shortly after flowering. This vine doesn't require much trimming, only to train it or remove some of the older branches. Remove any dead branches.

Fertilization: Medium. Fertilize at planting time and each spring with a timed-release product. Less fertilizer is needed with the application of more organics. See pages 36 to 39 for more instructions.

SHRUBS & VINES

Lives on rainwater alone in all but the most extreme situations

Hydrangea, Mophead and Lacecap

1ST

CHARACTERISTICS

Plant Type: Deciduous shrub. (loses its leaves in the winter).

Average Size: Varies by type from 3 to 8 feet tall and wide.

Growth Rate: Fast

Leaf: Rounded, medium-green leaves, 4 to 6 inches tall and wide.

Flower: Large, pom-pom or delicate, lacecap blooms.

Origin: Japan

Spacing: About 4 to 6 feet on center (measure from the center of each plant), depending on the mature size of the hydrangea.

Cautions: Poisonous to some people, so don't eat this plant. Juice or sap is a skin irritant. Occasionally damaged by deer.

Colors: Flowers are pink or blue. Color depends on pH of the soil and availability of aluminum. See http://www.hydrangeashydrangeas.com/colorchange.html for instructions.

1. 'Endless Summer'
2. 'Endless Summer Blushing Bride'
3. 'Endless Summer Pink'
4. 'Midnight Dutchess' lacecap

Two of the most common hydrangeas planted in the eastern half of Texas. New, reblooming types are more dependable than older varieties, particularly in areas that might have a severe spring freeze. The most cold-sensitive hydrangeas. Qualifies for a blue ribbons,* but like more water than most plants in this book.

'Mini Penny' blue reblooming hydrangea

"Why doesn't my mophead hydrangea bloom?" Nine times out of ten, it's because of a late spring freeze, which is a frequent occurrence in zone seven. Older mopheads and lacecap hydrangeas will have no flowers for an entire year after a late freeze. However, the new, reblooming mopheads will bloom later on if it freezes in spring. In years without late freezes, the rebloomers flower twice, once in spring and again in fall. This doubles the normal bloom time of this type of hydrangea.

Regional Differences: Mophead and lacecap hydrangeas often show cold damage in zone seven. This cold damage can keep them from blooming that season.

Color Period: Without a late freeze, they bloom for about a month in May or June. Rebloomers bloom again later in the summer or in early fall.

Buying Tips: It makes sense to buy reblooming hydrangeas. They are now available in both mophead and lacecap forms. We have had good luck with 'Endless Summer,' 'Blushing Bride,' 'Penny Mac,' and 'Let's Dance.' Reblooming hydrangeas are commonly available in most garden centers in spring.

*Blue ribbon plants are defined on page 12. For blue ribbon performance, follow the planting and maintenance guidelines on pages 22 to 39.

Companions: Mophead and lacecap hydrangeas look good planted with Encore azaleas, evergreen hollies, rusty blackhaw viburnum, and southern wood fern.

Using an annual border around your hydrangeas will keep the bed in color for the entire growing season, as shown below.

Hydrangea with some companions

White Begonias (above, left) are one of the best annuals to use for borders of reblooming hydrangeas. They like the same light shade and keep blooming for the entire season.

Trailing Torenia (above, right) makes a great border for hydrangeas. It is frequently sold in hanging baskets but also thrives when planted in the ground. The blue color is a perfect contrast to the pink hydrangea. Plant this combination in light shade.

GROWING CONDITIONS

Light: Light shade, or morning sun and afternoon shade.

Water: Medium after establishment. Likes water once or twice a week during the growing season, depending on its environment. Quite intolerant of drought. See pages 28 to 33 for more information.

Soil: Any fertile, well-drained soil that has been enriched with organic matter. Requires good drainage and likes the same acid soil as azaleas. See pages 22 to 25 for instructions.

Hardiness: Zones 6 to 9. Often shows cold damage in zones six and seven. This cold damage can keep them from blooming that season.

Propagation: Cuttings or layering

Pest Problems: Root rot is the worst. Leaf spots sometimes from overhead irrigation.

PLANTING & MAINTENANCE

When to Plant: Hydrangea from containers can be planted at any time. Fall is best because they establish more easily in cooler weather, but you are more likely to find them at your garden center in spring when they are blooming.

Trimming: Prune immediately after flowering. Do not cut them any later, or they won't bloom the next season. Remove 1/3 of older canes by cutting them to the ground. Tip prune the other stems to control growth.

Fertilization: Medium. Fertilize at planting time and each spring with a timed-release product. Less fertilizer is needed with the application of more organics. See pages 36 to 39 for more instructions.

SHRUBS & VINES

1ST

CHARACTERISTICS

Plant Type: Deciduous shrub (loses its leaves in winter).

Average Size: 6 to 12 feet tall and wide, depending on variety.

Growth Rate: Medium

Leaf: Oak-like, deeply-lobed, green leaves to 8 inches long; turns red in the fall.

Flower: Elongated clusters 6 to 18 inches long, 6 inches in diameter.

Origin: Southeastern U.S.

Spacing: Set plants 5 to 8 feet apart. Allow plenty of room for lateral growth when planting this shrub near walls or buildings.

Cautions: Poisonous to some people, so don't eat this plant. Juice or sap is a skin irritant. Occasionally damaged by deer.

Colors: All oakleaf hydrangea flowers start out white and then change color, as shown on the opposite page. But, there is a lot of variability in the species. Most age to pink, cream, or red.

A four-season performer with different looks from the same plant. Clusters of white flowers open in early summer and persist until fall, changing colors along the way. Very easy to grow. Qualifies for a blue ribbon* but likes more water than most plants in this book.

Oakleaf hydrangea has something for every season. In winter, the exfoliating, coppery-tan bark is interesting. In spring, the large leaves emerge, giving a coarse, tropical texture to the garden, more so than any of the other hydrangeas. In summer, huge, white clusters of flowers appear and change colors as they age, as shown opposite. In fall, the leaves turn orange, red, and purple. Oakleaf hydrangeas perform well in north central Texas provided the soil is slightly acidic and plenty of water is supplied.

Color Period: Early May to June, with flowers remaining white for about a month. As the flowers dry, they often turn pale or blush pink and persist as light brown clusters until fall.

Buying Tips: Be sure to choose a variety that fits the space you have for it. The best-selling cultivar is 'Snowflake,' which grows eight feet tall and has huge, 18 inch long flower clusters. 'Alice' and 'Alison' will eventually grow to 12 feet wide, while 'Pee Wee' is much smaller at 6 to 8 feet wide.

Blue ribbon plants are defined on page 12. For blue ribbon performance, follow the planting and maintenance guidelines on pages 22 to 39.

All oakleaf hydrangea flowers start out white and then change color, as shown above. But, there is a lot of variability in the species. Most age to pink, cream, or red.

GROWING CONDITIONS

Light: Light shade, or morning sun and afternoon shade.

Water: Medium after establishment. Likes water once or twice a week during the growing season, depending on its environment. Quite intolerant of drought. See pages 28 to 33 for more information.

Soil: Any fertile, well-drained soil that has been enriched with organic matter. Requires good drainage and likes the same acid soil as azaleas. See pages 22 to 25 for instructions.

Hardiness: Zones 5 to 9

Propagation: Cuttings or layering

Pest Problems: Root rot is the worst. Leaf spot sometimes from overhead irrigation.

PLANTING & MAINTENANCE

When to Plant: Hydrangea from containers can be planted at any time. Fall is best because they establish more easily in cooler weather, but you are more likely to find them at your garden center in spring or early summer when they are blooming.

Trimming: After they finish with the white flowers, cut one or two of the tallest old canes to the ground. This plant does not branch too well, so this thinning encourages more branching. Also, remove any branches that are killed by accidents or winter weather. If you find the withered flower clusters unsightly in winter, simply snip them off.

Fertilization: Medium. Fertilize at planting time and each spring with a timed-release product. Less fertilizer is needed with the application of more organics. See pages 36 to 39 for more instructions.

SHRUBS & VINES

Juniper Shrubs

CHARACTERISTICS

Plant Type: Evergreen shrub.

Average Size: Varies according to cultivar. See opposite page.

Growth Rate: Slow to medium

Leaf: Parson's juniper has scale-like, grey-green needles on a long spray of branches. 'Nick's Compact' and 'Blue Rug' leaves are more like needles than scales, and they are darker green.

Flower: Insignificant

Origin: Parson's juniper is from Asia, Siberia, and Japan. 'Nick's Compact' is from China. 'Blue Rug' is from North America.

Spacing: About 4 feet on center (measure from the center of each plant), if you want them to grow together quickly. 5 or 6 feet on center otherwise.

Cautions: None known. Seldom damaged by deer.

Colors: Flower is insignificant. Berries are blue-black.

Parson's juniper with berries

Juniper is a popular shrub in Texas. It is also one of the easiest to grow. Deer leave it alone, and it lives without irrigation in all but the most severe situations. Just give it good drainage, and you may never need to touch it again! Easily rates a blue ribbon* because of its ease of care.

Parson's juniper

Junipers are durable, sun-loving, narrow-leafed evergreens for hot, dry locations. They are commonly planted in difficult environments, like along interstate highways. Juniper is also quite useful for stabilizing slopes. The nice, green foliage is attractive and contrasts well with other shrubs.

There are many different sizes and shapes of junipers - from low, creeping groundcovers to large, conical trees.

The two most common mistakes made with junipers are planting them too close together or in wet soil. They need good air circulation to prevent diseases.

Color Period: Flowers are insignificant. Blue berries appear in September and October on some varieties.

Buying Tips: Easy to find at most garden centers.

*Blue ribbon plants are defined on page 12. For blue ribbon performance, follow the planting and maintenance guidelines on pages 22 to 39.

Botanical Name: *Juniperus* spp.
Family: Cupressaceae

Blue Rug Juniper (*Juniperus horizontalis* 'Wiltonii,' *left*) is the most popular of the so-called "carpet" junipers, which resemble rugs. It is only about six or eight inches tall and spreads six to eight feet wide. This juniper is especially common on hillsides because it helps to stabilize the slope. Its foliage is blue-green during the warm months, but develops a purplish cast in winter. Cascades well over the sides of planters. Zones four to nine.

'Nick's Compact' Juniper (*Juniperus chinensis* 'Nick's Compact,' *right*) is a medium-sized, flat-topped juniper growing two and a half feet tall by six feet wide. Zones four to nine. Does well as a border (as shown) or as a groundcover over large areas.

Parson's Juniper (*Juniperus davurica* 'Parsonii,' *left*) grows to about two feet tall by six feet wide. Well-suited for slopes, but the branches are too stiff to cascade over the sides of planters. Showy, blue fruit. Zones six to nine.

GROWING CONDITIONS

Light: Full sun for all junipers. Plants receiving less that 4 hours of sun thin out.

Water: Very low after establishment. Lives on rainwater alone, without supplemental water, in all but the most extreme conditions. See pages 28 to 33 for more information.

Soil: Any fertile, well-drained soil that has been enriched with organic matter. Requires good drainage. See pages 22 to 25 for instructions.

Hardiness: Zones 6 to 9 for parson's juniper; 4 to 9 for 'Blue Rug' juniper and 'Nick's Compact.'

Propagation: Cuttings

Pest Problems: Root rot can develop if plants are kept too wet. Watch out for blackening of stems. Spider mites and bagworms occasionally.

PLANTING & MAINTENANCE

When to Plant: Junipers from containers can be planted at any time. Fall is best because they establish more easily in cooler weather.

Trimming: Trim junipers if they outgrow their space or to remove dead branches. Other than that, they don't need trimming.

Fertilization: Medium. Fertilize at planting time and annually with a timed-release product. Less fertilizer is needed with the application of more organics. See pages 36 to 39 for more instructions.

BUDGET GARDENING TIP

Junipers in 1-gallon containers will save you about 70 percent over the same plant in a 3-gallon container. Since they grow fairly quickly, they will make up the difference in no time!

SHRUBS & VINES

Lives on rainwater alone in all but the most extreme situations

Kerria, Japanese

CHARACTERISTICS

Plant Type: Deciduous shrub (loses its leaves in winter).

Average Size: 5 to 10 feet tall and wide.

Growth Rate: Medium to fast

Leaf: Long, pointed, serrated, with prominent veins, 2 inches long. Bright green color.

Flower: Bright orange-yellow, about 1 1/2 inches wide. The double-flowered form is the most common.

Origin: China and Japan

Spacing: About 4 feet on center (measure from the center of each plant). This plant tends to sucker, so it forms a large mass over time.

Cautions: Seldom damaged by deer.

Colors: Yellow flowers in spring. Yellow leaves in fall. Light green stems in winter.

Graceful, spring-flowering shrub that grows in shade. Old-fashioned, carefree, and tough. Attractive flowering shrub for woodland garden or shrub borders. Easily rates a blue ribbon* because of its ease of care.

This is a great choice for spring color in shade. Nice, open, arching, growth habit with bright green leaves and stems; the pretty flowers brighten up a shady spot.

Japanese kerria offers interest in each season. One of the first shrubs to leaf out in spring, its best feature is its yellow flowers that quickly follow. The leaves turn a nice yellow color in fall. The light green stems show up well in winter.

Color Period: Blooms for three to four weeks in April and May. Sometimes, it has intermittent blooms in summer. The leaves turn a nice shade of yellow in fall.

Buying Tips: 'Pleniflora' has double flowers and is the cultivar most commonly sold in nurseries.

Double flower of 'Pleniflora' kerria

Blue ribbon plants are defined on page 12. For blue ribbon performance, follow the planting and maintenance guidelines on pages 22 to 39.

Botanical Name: *Kerria japonica*
Family: Rosaceae

Companions: Use kerria with other plants that share the same bloom period. Azaleas and bridal wreath spiraea look good with kerria.

Or, try these yellow flowers with lenten rose and phlox, as shown below.

Double flowers of 'Pleniflora' kerria

GROWING CONDITIONS

Light: Light to medium shade. Morning sun is fine, but protect it from afternoon sun.

Water: Low after establishment. Likes water every week or two during the growing season, depending on its environment. See pages 28 to 33 for more information.

Soil: Kerria will grow in clay, but it prefers better soil. See pages 22 to 25 for instructions.

Hardiness: Zones 4 to 9

Propagation: Division or cuttings

Pest Problems: Rare. Root rot can develop if plants are kept too wet.

PLANTING & MAINTENANCE

When to Plant: Kerria from containers can be planted at any time. Fall is best because they establish more easily in cooler weather, but you are more likely to find them at your garden center in early spring, when they are blooming.

Trimming: Prune in May or June, after it flowers. Thin out the older branches when their stems turn light brown.

Fertilization: Low. Fertilize at planting time with a timed-release product. Less fertilizer is needed with the application of more organics. In the years after planting, fertilization needs vary, based on the nutrients in your soil. See pages 36 to 39 for more instructions.

Lenten Rose
Plant Profile: Page 140

Woodland Phlox
Plant Profile: Page 150

Kerria with some companions

SHRUBS & VINES

Lenten Rose (above, left) blooms in early spring in shade, as does kerria.

Woodland Phlox (above, right) is another shade plant that blooms in early spring. Since the phlox and the lenten rose both stay low (about 12 to 16 inches tall), alternate clumps of them in front of the taller kerria.

Loropetalum, Fringe Flower

CHARACTERISTICS

Plant Type: Evergreen to semi-evergreen shrub.

Average Size: Easily maintained at sizes between 2 to 12 feet tall by 4 to 8 feet wide. There are compact varieties that have been on the market for less than 2 years which we have not tested thoroughly. 'Purple Pixie' grows only 2 feet tall by 4 1/2 feet wide. 'Purple Diamond' grows to 5 feet tall by 5 feet wide.

Growth Rate: Fast

Leaf: Burgundy or light green, 2 inches long by 1 inch wide, oval shaped.

Flower: Fringe-like, 1 inch long by 1/4 inch wide, four petals.

Origin: China and Japan

Spacing: About 4 to 5 feet on center (measure from the center of each plant).

Cautions: This plant grows quickly and gets much larger than most people expect. Since many different sizes are available, be sure the size you buy fits your space. Deer seldom damage this plant.

Colors: Flowers are pink, red, white, lavender, or fuchsia.

1. 'Forever Red' loropetalum
2. 'Little Rose Dawn' loropetalum

One of the few shrubs that give year round color - even in winter - with very little care. Burgundy evergreen leaves form a wonderful contrast in the landscape. Easily rates a blue ribbon.*

Loropetalum with daylilies, red cannas, purple heart, and periwinkles

With the advent of the new burgundy leaf forms of this shrub, garden centers can't keep this plant in stock. It is a wonderful evergreen shrub that retains color year round and is easy to grow. As an added bonus it blooms, most in the spring and sporadically throughout the summer into fall. However, the blooms are not always dependable, so buy this plant for its leaf color. Since there are many sizes available, be sure you buy one that fits your space. Large loropetalums make great screens or hedges and can also be grown as small trees, with a maximum height of 12 feet when mature.

Color Period: Blooms most for about three weeks in late winter or early spring. Flowers sporadically through summer but has much more color impact from leaves than flowers.

Buying Tips: Garden centers have a variety of the burgundy-leafed shrub. So far, all the ones we have tried have done well except for the 'Bill Wallace' variety, which did not tolerate the cold in zone seven. Ask for a compact or dwarf variety if your space for planting is limited.

Blue ribbon plants are defined on page 12. For blue ribbon performance, follow the planting and maintenance guidelines on pages 22 to 39.

Companions: Loropetalum is one of the most useful shrubs in Texas because it gives year round color in sun to partial shade. Its leaf color lasts all year, so use it primarily for that feature. The dark leaves show up quite well against lime green.

Or, combine loropetalum with plants that have a long bloom period, like the 'Knock Out' roses or scabiosa shown below.

Loropetalum is spectacular when it blooms, but the color from the flowers doesn't last as long as the leaf color.

GROWING CONDITIONS

Light: Full sun to partial shade. Blooms best and has most attractive leaf color in full sun. Very heat tolerant.

Water: Low after establishment. Likes water every week or two during the growing season, depending on its environment. See pages 28 to 33 for more information.

Soil: For the garden, plant in any fertile, well-drained soil that has been enriched with organic matter. Use only good-quality potting mix for containers. See pages 22 to 25 for specific instructions on soil preparation.

Hardiness: Zones 7 to 10

Propagation: Seeds or rooted cuttings taken in early summer.

Pest Problems: Rare. Aphids may occasionally feed on tender, new growth but seldom require control.

PLANTING & MAINTENANCE

When to Plant: Loropetalum from containers can be planted at any time. Fall is best because they establish more easily in cooler weather.

Trimming: Trim back very long branches in early summer, after the biggest show of blooms has ended. When planted in a site it likes, loropetalum can grow very large and may need to be cut back rather aggressively in late winter. Do not be timid about trimming this shrub, but do maintain its natural shape, and never attempt to prune it into a ball.

Fertilization: Medium. Fertilize at planting time and each spring with a timed-release product. Less fertilizer is needed with the application of more organics. See pages 36 to 39 for more instructions.

'Knock Out' Rose
Plant Profile: Page 246

Scabiosa
Plant Profile: Page 158

Loropetalum with some companions

'Knock Out' Roses (above, left) bloom spring, summer, and fall, so they keep the bed in color for the entire growing season. Since 'Knock Out' grows to about five feet tall, place it in front of taller loropetalums and behind shorter loropetalums. The 'Knock Out' roses come in bright pink (as shown above) or a paler pink that would also look wonderful with the burgundy loropetalum.

Scabiosa (above, right) is another one of the longest-blooming perennials for Texas, flowering from May until September if you deadhead (remove dead flowers). It grows 12 to 18 inches tall, so use it as a front border for the taller roses and loropetalum.

SHRUBS & VINES

Mahonia, Leatherleaf

CHARACTERISTICS

Plant Type: Evergreen shrub.

Average Size: 4 to 6 feet tall by 3 to 4 feet wide.

Growth Rate: Slow

Leaf: Grayish- or bluish-green above, lighter green underneath. Each leaflet is 2 to 4 inches long and features sharp, marginal spines that give the foliage a holly-like appearance.

Flower: Terminal spikes of fragrant flowers in late winter. The flowers attract bees.

Origin: China

Spacing: 3 feet on center (measure from the center of each plant).

Cautions: Spiny leaves hurt if you back into them.

Colors: Flowers are bright lemon yellow.

Well-suited for shade gardens, leatherleaf mahonia is a tough, beautiful, evergreen shrub that produces holly-like leaves in horizontal layers. Flowers appear in late winter, followed by attractive clusters of purplish-blue berries that persist throughout the summer unless devoured by birds. Exhibits considerable drought tolerance once established. Definitely rates a blue ribbon* for its beauty and low maintenance.

Leatherleaf mahonia has a sculptural quality about it and adds beauty to a shade or woodland garden. Although the plant is tough and the leaves are stiff, the horizontal branching habit of this shrub gives it a graceful look. Its yellow flowers bring cheer to the winter garden, and its clusters of blue fruits set against the holly-like foliage offer beauty during the growing season. Leatherleaf mahonia is easy to grow. Use it as an accent plant on the north or east side of the house, or place several beneath the canopy of deciduous trees for a woodland look.

Color Period: Blooms in January and February for two to three weeks, with additional color provided by the clusters of blue fruits throughout the summer for about 12 weeks.

Buying Tips: Commonly available in nurseries and garden centers

Blue ribbon plants are defined on page 12. For blue ribbon performance, follow the planting and maintenance guidelines on pages 22 to 39.

Companions: Because of its coarse texture, leatherleaf mahonia contrasts well with such fine-textured, shade-tolerant plants as yew, southern wood fern, inland sea oats, and columbine. The coarse-textured Turk's cap also combines well with mahonia in the shade.

Southern Wood Fern
Plant Profile: Page 126

'Texas Gold' Columbine
Plant Profile: Page 104

Mahonia with some companions

Southern Wood Fern (above, left) grows two to three feet tall in light to medium shade and provides a soft-textured contrast to the stiff leaves of mahonia. Plant a drift of the lower-growing fern in front of a grouping of mahonia for a striking effect.

'Texas Gold' Columbine (above, right) is an 18 inch tall perennial that produces bright yellow flowers in April. 'Texas Gold' enjoys the same amount of shade that mahonia does, and for that reason, the two can be used together. Plant a swath of columbine in front of the taller fern.

GROWING CONDITIONS

Light: Light to medium shade

Water: Low after establishment. Likes water every week or two during the growing season, depending on its environment. See pages 28 to 33 for more information.

Soil: Any fertile, well-drained soil that has been enriched with organic matter. Requires good drainage. See pages 22 to 25 for instructions.

Hardiness: Zones 6 to 9

Propagation: Seeds or cuttings

Pest Problems: No serious insect or disease problems.

PLANTING & MAINTENANCE

When to Plant: Mahonia from containers can be planted at any time. Fall is best because they establish easier in cooler weather.

Trimming: If the plant gets too tall or thin, cut off the tallest canes at the ground. The shrub will then fill out with more canes arising from the ground level.

Fertilization: Low. Fertilize at planting time with a timed-release product. Less fertilizer is needed with the application of more organics. In the years after planting, fertilization needs vary, based on the nutrients in your soil. See pages 36 to 39 for more instructions.

SHRUBS & VINES

Nandina

CHARACTERISTICS

Plant Type: Evergreen shrub.

Average Size: Standard size is 5 to 7 feet tall by 3 to 5 feet wide. Many smaller cultivars exist (see "Buying Tips").

Growth Rate: Medium to fast

Leaf: Compound leaf with many small leaflets 1 to 2 inches long by 1/2 to 1 inch wide. Deep green to blue-green in shade or lighter green in sun.

Flower: Terminal clusters of small white flowers in spring; quite showy.

Origin: China

Spacing: 3 to 4 feet on center for the standard size; closer for the smaller cultivars.

Cautions: Can become invasive through animal-dispersed seeds.

Colors: Flowers are white

Nandina 'Firepower'

Tough, durable, and versatile evergreen shrub for the landscape. Demonstrates considerable drought tolerance. Definitely rates a blue ribbon* for its year round beauty, usefulness in the landscape, freedom from problems, and low maintenance.

Nandina 'Gulf Stream'

Nandina is an old-fashioned plant that is extremely easy to grow. It grows in sun or shade; in fact, the foliage of the standard form actually looks better in the shade, where it takes on a metallic blue-green color. New, dwarf cultivars, like 'Firepower' (shown, left), have incredible leaf color in fall.

Original *Nandina domestica* is an invasive plant in Texas. Birds are dropping its fruit in natural areas, and it takes over our native plants' space. 'Gulf Stream' (as shown on these two pages) does not produce fruit.

Color Period: Nandina offers leaf color year round. It flowers for two to three weeks in April. Clusters of red berries appear for about 28 weeks in fall and winter on the old, invasive variety.

Buying Tips: Commonly available at nurseries and garden centers. Many cultivars exist. Many new, compact, and dwarf varieties exist, such as 'Compacta' (four to five feet), 'Gulf Stream' (three to four feet), 'Firepower' (18 to 24 inches), and 'Harbour Dwarf' (18 to 24 inches). Be sure to look at the tag to see which cultivar you're getting and how big it gets.

Blue ribbon plants are defined on page 12. For blue ribbon performance, follow the planting and maintenance guidelines on pages 22 to 39.

Botanical Name: *Nandina domestica*
Family: Berberidaceae

Companions: Nandina combines very well with other shrubs and perennials that offer contrast in size, form, color, and texture. Examples include abelia, beautyberry, hollies, and ornamental grasses.

Autumn Fern
Plant Profile: Page 126

Mondo Grass
Plant Profile: Page 128

Nandina 'Gulf Stream' and some companions

Autumn Fern (above, left) combines very well with 'Gulf Stream' nandina because both have copper-colored new growth, and the fern's fine-textured foliage contrasts with the larger leaves of the nandina. Both enjoy light shade. Plant the lower-growing autumn fern in front of the nandina.

Mondo Grass (above, right) is an evergreen groundcover that gets about six inches tall and forms a carpet of green foliage that contrasts starkly against the lighter green of the autumn fern. Plant the mondo grass in front of the fern as a border in this grouping.

GROWING CONDITIONS

Light: Sun to shade, although some cultivars prefer more shade than others.

Water: Low after establishment. Likes water every week or two during the growing season, depending on its environment. Although it survives on just rainwater, it could get leaf scorch from so little water. See pages 28 to 33 for more information.

Soil: Any fertile, well-drained soil that has been enriched with organic matter. Requires good drainage. See pages 22 to 25 for instructions.

Hardiness: Zones 6 to 9

Propagation: Cuttings or division

Pest Problems: No serious insect or disease problems. Leaves may develop chlorosis (yellowing) in alkaline soils.

PLANTING & MAINTENANCE

When to Plant: Nandina from containers can be planted at any time. Fall is best because they establish easier in cooler weather.

Trimming: If the plant gets too tall or thin, cut off the tallest canes at the ground. The shrub will then fill out with more canes arising from the ground level.

Fertilization: Low. Fertilize at planting time with a timed-release product. Less fertilizer is needed with the application of more organics. In the years after planting, fertilization needs vary, based on the nutrients in your soil. See pages 36 to 39 for more instructions.

SHRUBS & VINES

Pomegranate

CHARACTERISTICS

Plant Type: Deciduous shrub or small tree (loses its leaves in winter).

Average Size: 3 to 20 feet tall by 4 to 15 feet wide, depending on cultivar.

Growth Rate: Moderate

Leaf: Bright, medium green; 1 to 3 inches long by 1/4 to 1/2 inch wide. Yellow fall color.

Flower: Trumpet-shaped, double, somewhat like a carnation; 1 1/2 to 2 inches across; grows either as a single or in clusters at the ends of branches; very showy.

Origin: Southeastern Europe to India.

Spacing: 2 to 8 feet on center (measure from the center of each plant), depending on cultivar.

Cautions: None known. Almost never eaten by deer.

Colors: Red, red-orange, or white, depending on cultivar.

Flowers and fruit of the dwarf pomegranate.

Attractive shrub or multi-trunked small tree with glossy green leaves, showy flowers, and attractive fruit. Tolerates a wide range of soils. Blooms for five months each summer. Rates a blue ribbon* for its spectacular flowers, heat tolerance, and low maintenance.

Dwarf pomegranate

Easy to grow, pomegranate rewards the gardener with showy, double, red-orange flowers from summer to fall and attractive fruits that mature in September or October. Few other shrubs offer such an intense color of orange flowers. The cultivar 'Wonderful' forms a small tree, sports red-orange flowers, and produces large fruits. 'Nana' grows three to six feet tall with scarlet flowers and two inch fruits.

Color Period: Pomegranate offers color for five to seven months from both flowers and fruit. It flowers from early June through October. In October, colorful fruits form and remain until December.

Buying Tips: May be hard to find, but better nurseries will either carry it or be able to order it.

*Blue ribbon plants are defined on page 12. For blue ribbon performance, follow the planting and maintenance guidelines on pages 22 to 39.

Companions: The orange flowers of pomegranate combine well with dwarf white crapemyrtles, the purple flowers of butterfly bush, and even the burgundy foliage of loropetalum. Both the tree and dwarf shrub forms look good in a low water-use garden that features rosemary, agaves, red yucca, and ornamental grasses. The bright yellow flowers of lantana and esperanza 'Gold Star' also look great against the bright orange flowers of pomegranate.

Try a simple planting of crapemyrtle, pomegranate, and purple heart for a great color accent.

Dwarf White Crapemyrtle
Plant Profile: Page 206

Purple Heart
Plant Profile: Page 152

Pomegranate with some companions

Dwarf White Crapemyrtle (above, top) grows three to five feet tall and blooms for the same time period as pomegranate. The crinkly, white flowers of dwarf crapemyrtle differ in form and color with those of pomegranate and make the orange flowers of pomegranate stand out that much more.

Purple Heart (above, bottom) is a low-growing groundcover that looks good all season long. Plant it as a border for the taller crapemyrtle and pomegranate.

GROWING CONDITIONS

Light: Full sun, at least 6 hours per day.

Water: Low after establishment. Likes water every week or two during the growing season, depending on its environment. See pages 28 to 33 for more information.

Soil: Any fertile, well-drained soil that has been enriched with organic matter. Requires good drainage. See pages 22 to 25 for instructions.

Hardiness: Zones 7 to 11

Propagation: Cuttings; seedlings are extremely variable.

Pest Problems: No serious insect or disease problems.

PLANTING & MAINTENANCE

When to Plant: Pomegranates from containers can be planted at any time. Fall is best because they establish easier in cooler weather.

Trimming: Prune in late winter as needed to shape or control growth. Lower branches can be removed to create a tree form. Remove unwanted stems that come up from the ground as they develop.

Fertilization: Low. Fertilize at planting time with a timed-release product. Less fertilizer is needed with the application of more organics. In the years after planting, fertilization needs vary, based on the nutrients in your soil. See pages 36 to 39 for more instructions.

SHRUBS & VINES

Rosemary

CHARACTERISTICS

Plant Type: Evergreen shrub.

Average Size: From 2 to 6 feet tall by 3 to 6 feet wide, depending on variety.

Growth Rate: Medium

Leaf: Needle-like, 1/2 to 1 1/2 inches long by 1/8 inch wide, leathery. Dark sage green above, white and wooly underneath. Very aromatic when crushed. Some cultivars are more silver than green.

Flower: Small, about 1/2 inch in diameter.

Origin: Mediterranean region

Spacing: 2 to 4 feet on center (measure from center of each plant), depending on cultivar.

Cautions: Almost never eaten by deer.

Colors: Flowers are light blue

A tough, evergreen shrub that takes full sun and tolerates drought. Grows well in most any soil, provided it is well-drained. Creates a Mediterranean look in the landscape. Excellent in combination with native and other low water-use plants. Definitely a blue ribbon* plant because of its ease of care.

Rosemary offers many attractive features as a shrub in north central Texas. It is easy to grow as long as it is in full sun and well-drained soil. As an evergreen, it makes a nice backdrop for lower perennials and annuals. Rosemary has an attractive form – upright, spreading, or prostrate – and interesting texture. The aromatic leaves are the best feature of rosemary. If for no other reason, include rosemary in the garden for a delightful olfactory experience! The leaves, of course, can also be used in cooking and seasoning.

Rosemary doesn't live as long as many Texas shrubs. However, expect several years from it.

Color Period: Rosemary offers year round color from its leaves. It flowers in late winter through April and May for about six to eight weeks.

Buying Tips: Readily available in garden centers and nurseries, usually in the herb section.

Rosemary in flower

*Blue ribbon plants are defined on page 12. For blue ribbon performance, follow the planting and maintenance guidelines on pages 22 to 39.

Companions: Rosemary does quite well in container gardens, as shown, right. It does well alone or paired with other plants in containers. Rosemary is one of the few great centerpieces for containers that look good in winter.

It also fits well in the ground as part of a mixed border. Good companions include such perennials as autumn sage, *Artemisia* 'Powis Castle,' and Mexican feather grass. The silver-leafed rosemary looks great with red and purple, as shown below.

'Cherry Dazzle' Crapemyrtle
Plant Profile: Page 206

'Homestead Purple' Verbena
Plant Profile: Page 170

Rosemary with some companions

'Cherry Dazzle' Crapemyrtle (above, left) blooms for up to 90 days if you remove the dead flowers. Since this dwarf crapemyrtle grows from three to five feet tall, use it behind the shorter rosemary and verbena.

'Homestead Purple' Verbena (above, right) is one of the longest-blooming perennial groundcovers for Texas. It starts blooming with a burst in spring and slows down somewhat in summer. This verbena grows to about one foot tall. It makes the ideal border for crapemyrtle and rosemary.

GROWING CONDITIONS

Light: Full sun, at least 6 hours per day.

Water: Low after establishment. Likes water every week or two during the growing season, depending on its environment. See pages 28 to 33 for more information.

Soil: Plant in any fertile, well-drained soil that has been enriched with organic matter. Rosemary must have good drainage to survive. See pages 22 to 25 for instructions.

Hardiness: Zones 7 to 11; some cultivars are more cold hardy than others.

Propagation: Stem cuttings

Pest Problems: No serious insect or disease problems.

PLANTING & MAINTENANCE

When to Plant: Rosemary from containers can be planted at any time. Fall is best because they establish easier in cooler weather.

Trimming: Prune in late February to early March to shape, if needed.

Fertilization: Low. Fertilize at planting time with a timed-release product. Less fertilizer is needed with the application of more organics. In the years after planting, fertilization needs vary, based on the nutrients in your soil. See pages 36 to 39 for more instructions.

SHRUBS & VINES

Roses, Climbers

CHARACTERISTICS

Plant Type: Deciduous shrub (loses its leaves in winter).

Average Size: Varies with variety. See opposite page.

Growth Rate: Medium. Roses need a year to become established; reach mature size after 3 to 4 seasons.

Leaf: Glossy, green, oval leaves with serrated edges, often turning reddish in cold weather.

Flower: Huge range in flower size and form. Most disease-resistant shrub roses bear double flowers to 3 inches across, with prominent stamens in the centers.

Origin: Man-made hybrids, most involving parent species from China.

Spacing: To allow ample space for air to circulate through the foliage, add 2 feet to the mature width of plants when using roses in groups or as hedge plants. Plants that grow to 3 feet wide should be set 5 feet on center (measure from center of each plant).

Cautions: Beware of thorns, and do not plant roses with thorns in high traffic areas. 'Lady Banks' roses are thornless. Rose berries, or hips, make a nutritious tea, provided the plants are grown without using systemic pesticides. Roses are frequently damaged by deer.

Colors: Pink, white, red, yellow, and many bicolors and blends.

Satin-petaled blossoms in flushes from late spring to autumn. Advances in disease resistance are bringing sentimental, softly-scented roses back into our gardens. Rates a blue ribbon* because of its ease of care.

'Lady Banks' rose will cover an arbor with soft yellow blossoms in spring. It is an aggressive grower, so use a strong support.

Roses bring a romantic presence to the garden, so they are on every gardener's wish list. Some new, modern hybrids called shrub or landscape roses are capable of season-long bloom and perform well without constant spraying. These varieties produce smaller but more plentiful blooms with only a little fragrance, but they are pretty! Another group of roses, called EarthKind™ roses, demonstrate outstanding landscape performance as well as disease and insect resistance. They also tolerate a wide range of soils, heat, and drought. Visit http://earthkindroses.tamu.edu to learn more about these outstanding roses.

Color Period: Blooms most in late spring and early summer. Reblooming varieties continue to bloom sporadically through summer and often bloom heavily in the fall as well.

Buying Tips: Garden centers carry many varieties that are clearly tagged. They are also available online. Three great online suppliers are www.chambleeroses.com, www.antiqueroseemporium.com, and www.JacksonandPerkins.com. Look for roses grown on their own roots and not grafted.

*Blue ribbon plants are defined on page 12. For blue ribbon performance, follow the planting and maintenance guidelines on pages 22 to 39.

'Lady Banks' (right), one of the great classic roses, grows to twenty feet and is thornless. This rose is generally too large for the small garden.

Clusters of yellow flowers cover the plant for three to four weeks in early spring. Although it does not bloom again until the next year, it is spectacular in bloom and one of the showiest climbers.

This rose is evergreen in zone eight and deciduous farther north. Hardy in zones seven to nine.

'Climbing Pinkie' (left) is a mannerly climber to 12 feet tall with a spread of seven feet. It produces fragrant, semi-double, pink blossoms primarily in spring. 'Climbing Pinkie' blooms sporadically in summer and again rather heavily in fall.

Since 'Climbing Pinkie' is almost thornless, it is easy to work with the canes when training it onto an arbor or fence.

'Climbing Pinkie' grows well in zones six through nine.

'Seafoam' (left) is a shrub-type rose that produces creamy-white, double blossoms in spring, summer, and fall. It grows eight feet tall by four feet wide in the hot, Texas climate. It is very well suited for growing on pillars and trellises. Since it is a small climber, it is a good choice for smaller spaces.

This rose grows as a groundcover if it is not trained to grow up a support.

'Seafoam' rose grows in zones four to nine and is deciduous (loses its eaves in winter).

GROWING CONDITIONS

Light: Full sun, at least 8 hours per day.

Water: Low after establishment, provided it is well mulched. Likes water every week or two during the growing season, depending on its environment. See pages 28 to 33 for more information.

Soil: For the garden, plant in any fertile, well-drained soil that has been enriched with organic matter. Use only good-quality potting mix for containers. See pages 22 to 25 for specific instructions on soil preparation.

Hardiness: Zones 6 to 9; varies with variety.

Propagation: Rooted cuttings or grafts.

Pest Problems: Black spot and powdery mildew are two fungal diseases that produce symptoms on leaves. EarthKind™ roses will grow and bloom in spite of these diseases and without being sprayed. Thrips, extremely small insects barely visible to the naked eye, attack buds and flowers, causing them not to open or to be disfigured if they do open. They are a minor problem, however, and we don't spray for them.

PLANTING & MAINTENANCE

When to Plant: Roses from containers can be planted at any time. Fall is best because they establish more easily in cooler weather.

Trimming: Once a year on February 14th, reduce the plant size by 1/3 to 1/2, if desired or needed.

Fertilization: Medium. Fertilize at planting time and each spring with a timed-release product. Less fertilizer is needed with the application of more organics. See pages 36 to 39 for more instructions.

SHRUBS & VINES

Roses, EarthKind™ Small Shrubs

1ST

CHARACTERISTICS

Plant Type: Deciduous shrub (loses its leaves in winter).

Average Size: Varies with variety. Most shrub roses grow 3 to 5 feet tall by 3 feet wide.

Growth Rate: Medium. Roses need a year to become established; reach mature size after 3 to 4 seasons.

Leaf: Glossy, green, oval leaves with serrated edges, often turning reddish in cold weather.

Flower: Huge range in flower size and form. Most disease-resistant shrub roses bear double flowers to 3 inches across, with prominent stamens in the centers.

Origin: Man-made hybrids, most involving parent species from China.

Spacing: To allow ample space for air to circulate through the foliage, add 2 feet to the mature width of plants when using roses in groups or as hedge plants. Plants that grow to 3 feet wide should be set 5 feet on center (measure from center of each plant).

Cautions: Beware of thorns, and do not plant roses with thorns in high traffic areas. Rose berries, or hips, make a nutritious tea, provided the plants are grown without using systemic pesticides. Roses are frequently damaged by deer.

Colors: Pink, white, red, yellow, and many bicolors and blends.

Reaching a mature size of only three to four feet tall and wide, the small EarthKind™ rose is ideal for smaller yards and large containers. Perform well with no spraying. Blooms from spring to fall. Rates a blue ribbon* for its designation as EarthKind™ roses and because if require so little maintenance.

'Caldwell Pink' roses

EarthKind™ roses are those that have undergone extensive testing and research by scientists at the Texas A & M University AgriLife Extension Service. Over 117 rose varieties were grown during a five year study across the state in unamended clay soil with no pesticides, fertilizer, deadheading (removal of spent blossoms), pruning, or supplemental watering after the second year. Fifteen varieties emerged as "winners" of this testing and were designated as EarthKind™ roses. These are roses any homeowner can grow with ease and good results. They don't require all the care that typical hybrid tea roses do. Visit http://earthkindroses.tamu.edu to learn more about these outstanding roses.

Color Period: Blooms heavily in spring, sporadically through summer, and heavily again in fall.

Buying Tips: Garden centers carry many varieties that are clearly tagged. They are also available online. Three great online suppliers are www.chambleeroses.com, www.antiqueroseemporium.com, and www.JacksonandPerkins.com. Look for roses grown on their own roots and not grafted.

*Blue ribbon plants are defined on page 12. For blue ribbon performance, follow the planting and maintenance guidelines on pages 22 to 39.

'Caldwell Pink' (left) has lilac-pink, fully double, almost carnation-like blossoms. The flowers are not fragrant and grow in clusters. Blooms from mid spring, throughout the summer, and into fall. Four feet tall and wide. Zones six to nine.

'The Fairy' (right) features an abundance of small, double, light pink blossoms. Flowers are the pinkest in spring and fall but fade to almost white during the summer. Blooms spring, summer, and fall. The plant has small, glossy, very attractive leaves and lots of thorns! Three feet tall by four feet wide. Zones four to nine.

'Marie Daly' (left) has very fragrant, semi-double pink flowers. Blooms spring, summer, and fall. Few thorns. Three feet tall and wide. Must have excellent air circulation around its foliage; does well in large containers because the plant is higher and exposed to more air. Zones five to nine.

'Perle d'Or' (right) produces perfect, orange buds that open to fragrant, peach flowers. Blooms spring, summer, and fall. Healthy, strong grower well suited to highly alkaline, clay soils. Four feet tall and wide. Named 2007 EarthKind™ Rose of the Year by the Texas A&M AgriLife Extension Service. Zones six to nine.

'Georgetown Tea' (left) has long-budded, fragrant, double blossoms of dark pink in the center and lilac pink on the outer edge. Petals are pointed at the tips, giving the open flower a star-like appearance. Blooms spring, summer, and fall. Four feet tall and wide. Hardiness zones seven to nine.

GROWING CONDITIONS

Light: Full sun, at least 8 hours per day.

Water: Low after establishment, provided it is well mulched. Likes water every week or two during the growing season, depending on its environment. See pages 28 to 33 for more information.

Soil: For the garden, plant in any fertile, well-drained soil that has been enriched with organic matter. Use only good-quality potting mix for containers. See pages 22 to 25 for specific instructions on soil preparation.

Hardiness: Zones 4 to 9; varies with variety, so see individual descriptions.

Propagation: Rooted cuttings or grafts.

Pest Problems: Black spot and powdery mildew are two fungal diseases that produce symptoms on leaves. EarthKind™ roses will grow and bloom in spite of these diseases and without being sprayed. Thrips, extremely small insects barely visible to the naked eye, attack buds and flowers, causing them not to open or to be disfigured if they do open. They are a minor problem, however, and we don't spray for them.

PLANTING & MAINTENANCE

When to Plant: Roses from containers can be planted at any time. Fall is best because they establish more easily in cooler weather.

Trimming: Once a year on February 14th, reduce the plant size by 1/3 to 1/2, if desired or needed.

Fertilization: Medium. Fertilize at planting time and each spring with a timed-release product. Less fertilizer is needed with the application of more organics. See pages 36 to 39 for more instructions.

SHRUBS & VINES

CHARACTERISTICS

Plant Type: Deciduous shrub (loses its leaves in winter).

Average Size: Varies with variety. Most shrub roses grow 3 to 5 feet tall by 3 feet wide.

Growth Rate: Medium. Roses need a year to become established; reach mature size after 3 to 4 seasons.

Leaf: Glossy, green, oval leaves with serrated edges, often turning reddish in cold weather.

Flower: Huge range in flower size and form. Most disease-resistant shrub roses bear double flowers to 3 inches across, with prominent stamens in the centers.

Origin: Man-made hybrids, most involving parent species from China.

Spacing: To allow ample space for air to circulate through the foliage, add 2 feet to the mature width of plants when using roses in groups or as hedge plants. Plants that grow to 3 feet wide should be set 5 feet on center (measure from center of each plant).

Cautions: Beware of thorns, and do not plant roses with thorns in high traffic areas. Rose berries, or hips, make a nutritious tea, provided the plants are grown without using systemic pesticides. Roses are frequently damaged by deer.

Colors: Pink, white, red, yellow, and many bicolors and blends.

Medium EarthKind™ roses reach a mature size of five or six feet tall by four to five feet wide. These easy-to-grow shrub roses offer gorgeous blooms from spring to fall. They easily rate a blue ribbon* for their EarthKind™ status alone but also for their long bloom period and high performance without the need for spraying.

EarthKind™ roses function as blooming shrubs and offer old-fashioned charm as well as lots of color in the landscape. They must be grown in full sun (at least eight hours each day), where they have plenty of air circulation around them. Avoid planting them in enclosed areas, such as courtyards or small backyards surrounded by tall fences that block the movement of air. Mulch them with three to four inches of organic mulch. Water them from drip irrigation, soaker hoses, or bubblers rather than by overhead sprinklers, which keep the leaves wet and invite disease. Use the largest EarthKind™ roses at the back of a flower bed that features other shrubs, perennials, and annuals, as a screen to hide ugly views, or to define a property line. The medium EarthKind™ roses can be used in beds close to the house.

Color Period: Blooms heavily in spring, sporadically through summer, and heavily again in fall.

Buying Tips: Garden centers carry many varieties that are clearly tagged. They are also available online. Three great online suppliers are www.chambleeroses.com, www.antiqueroseemporium.com, and www.JacksonandPerkins.com. Look for roses grown on their own roots and not grafted.

Blue ribbon plants are defined on page 12. For blue ribbon performance, follow the planting and maintenance guidelines on pages 22 to 39.

'Belinda's Dream' (left) has the classic look of a high-centered, hybrid tea rose, but is a shrub rose! This gorgeous rose has large, moderately fragrant, very double, pink flowers that are four inches across. This rose has over 100 petals per blossom. Blooms spring, summer, and fall. Five feet tall and wide. Zones five to nine.

'Carefree Beauty' (right) is also known as 'Katy Road Pink.' It produces large, moderately fragrant, semi-double, pink blossoms. Blooms spring, summer, and fall. This rose also produces large orange hips. Named the 2006 EarthKind™ Rose of the Year by the Texas A&M AgriLife Extension Service. Five feet tall and wide. Zones four to nine.

'Ducher' (left) is an old rose that was introduced in 1869. The round buds open to form fragrant, very double, ivory blossoms. Blooms spring, summer, and fall. New growth is bronze, and mature foliage is a light green. Six feet tall and wide. Zones six to nine.

'Duchesse de Brabant' (right) is a tea rose introduced in 1857. It produces large, very fragrant, double, rose-pink blossoms. This was President Teddy Roosevelt's favorite rose, which he often wore as a boutonnière. Blooms spring, summer, and fall. Foliage is apple green. Six feet tall and four feet wide. Zones seven to nine.

GROWING CONDITIONS

Light: Full sun, at least 8 hours per day.

Water: Low after establishment, provided it is well mulched. Likes water every week or two during the growing season, depending on its environment. See pages 28 to 33 for more information.

Soil: Any fertile, well-drained soil that has been enriched with organic matter. Requires good drainage. See pages 22 to 25 for instructions.

Hardiness: Zones 4 to 9

Propagation: Rooted cuttings or grafts.

Pest Problems: Black spot and powdery mildew are two fungal diseases that produce symptoms on leaves. EarthKind™ roses will grow and bloom in spite of these diseases and without being sprayed. Thrips, extremely small insects barely visible to the naked eye, attack buds and flowers, causing them not to open or to be disfigured if they do open. They are a minor problem, however, and we don't spray for them.

PLANTING & MAINTENANCE

When to Plant: Roses from containers can be planted at any time. Fall is best because they establish more easily in cooler weather.

Trimming: Once a year on February 14th, reduce the plant size by 1/3 to 1/2, if desired or needed.

Medium: Fertilize at planting time and annually with a timed-release product. Less fertilizer is needed with the application of more organics. See pages 36 to 39 for more instructions.

SHRUBS & VINES

1ST

CHARACTERISTICS

Plant Type: Deciduous shrub (loses its leaves in winter).

Average Size: Varies with variety. Most shrub roses grow 3 to 5 feet tall by 3 feet wide.

Growth Rate: Medium. Roses need a year to become established; reach mature size after 3 to 4 seasons.

Leaf: Glossy, green, oval leaves with serrated edges, often turning reddish in cold weather.

Flower: Huge range in flower size and form. Most disease-resistant shrub roses bear double flowers to 3 inches across, with prominent stamens in the centers.

Origin: Man-made hybrids, most involving parent species from China.

Spacing: To allow ample space for air to circulate through the foliage, add 2 feet to the mature width of plants when using roses in groups or as hedge plants. Plants that grow to 3 feet wide should be set 5 feet on center (measure from center of each plant).

Cautions: Beware of thorns, and do not plant roses with thorns in high traffic areas. Rose berries, or hips, make a nutritious tea, provided the plants are grown without using systemic pesticides. Roses are frequently damaged by deer.

Colors: Pink, white, red, yellow, and many bicolors and blends.

Here are more of the high-performing EarthKind™ roses in sizes ranging from five to six feet. See the previous two pages for alternate selections in this same size range. Rates a blue ribbon* because of its ease of care.

Complement the charm and beauty of EarthKind™ roses by planting other shrubs, perennials, or annuals with them in the same flower bed. These "companion plants" can form backdrops for the roses, fill in gaps in the bed, and supply color when the roses aren't blooming. They also offer contrast in form, texture, and color. Simply put, companion plants add variety to the rose bed.

Combine your roses with such shrubs as abelia, spiraea, and compact forms of Texas sage. Ornamental grasses look beautiful with roses, as do perennials, like salvia or phlox. Annual companion plants include old-fashioned petunias and melampodium.

Color Period: Blooms heavily in spring, sporadically through summer, and heavily again in fall.

Buying Tips: Garden centers carry many varieties that are clearly tagged. They are also available online. Three great online suppliers are www.chambleeroses.com, www.antiqueroseemporium.com, and www.JacksonandPerkins.com. Look for roses grown on their own roots and not grafted.

Blue ribbon plants are defined on page 12. For blue ribbon performance, follow the planting and maintenance guidelines on pages 22 to 39.

Attracts Butterflies   Avg. Weeks of Color   25

'Else Poulsen' (left) has medium-large, semi-double blossoms that have light pink petals and a slightly darker color on the underside of the petals. The flowers are not fragrant. Blooms spring, summer, and fall. Needs excellent air circulation to reduce disease problems on the foliage. Five feet tall and wide. Zones five to nine.

This rose has been around for quite a while. It was introduced by Danish breeder S. Poulsen in 1924.

'Mutabilis' (right) was introduced prior to 1894. It forms a large, sprawling shrub six feet tall and wide. New growth is bronze, mature foliage is medium green, and the stems are red. Produces single blossoms with silk-like petals that start out yellow, change to pink, and then to crimson. The flowers are not fragrant. Blooms spring, summer, and fall. Named 2005 EarthKind™ Rose of the Year by the Texas A&M AgriLife Extension Service. Zones six to nine. Very easy to grow. Give it plenty of room.

'Spice' (left) is a China-type rose found growing on the island of Bermuda. Produces blush-pink, almost white, double blossoms with a peppery fragrance. Blooms spring, summer, and fall. Mature size is five feet tall and four feet wide. Hardiness zones seven to nine. Very healthy and easy to grow.

Light: Full sun, at least 8 hours per day.

Water: Low after establishment, provided it is well mulched. Likes water every week or two during the growing season, depending on its environment. See pages 28 to 33 for more information.

Soil: For the garden, plant in any fertile, well-drained soil that has been enriched with organic matter. Use only good-quality potting mix for containers. See pages 22 to 25 for specific instructions on soil preparation.

Hardiness: Zones 4 to 9; varies with variety.

Propagation: Rooted cuttings or grafts.

Pest Problems: Black spot and powdery mildew are two fungal diseases that produce symptoms on leaves. EarthKind™ roses will grow and bloom in spite of these diseases and without being sprayed. Thrips, extremely small insects barely visible to the naked eye, attack buds and flowers, causing them not to open or to be disfigured if they do open. They are a minor problem, however, and we don't spray for them.

PLANTING & MAINTENANCE

When to Plant: Roses from containers can be planted at any time. Fall is best because they establish more easily in cooler weather.

Trimming: Once a year on February 14th, reduce the plant size by 1/3 to 1/2, if desired or needed.

Fertilization: Medium. Fertilize at planting time and each spring with a timed-release product. Less fertilizer is needed with the application of more organics. See pages 36 to 39 for more instructions.

SHRUBS & VINES

Rose, 'Knock Out' (EarthKind™ Rose)

1ST

CHARACTERISTICS

Plant Type: Deciduous (loses its leaves in winter) or semi-evergreen shrub.

Average Size: Easily maintained at 4 to 6 feet tall by 4 to 6 feet wide.

Growth Rate: Fast

Leaf: New growth is maroon; mature leaves are green. Oval-shaped with serrated edges.

Flower: Singles have 5 to 7 overlapping petals. Doubles have 20 to 30 petals. All have yellow stamens. Flower is 3 to 3 1/2 inches wide.

Origin: Roses are originally native to China. This one was hybridized in the U.S.

Spacing: About 6 to 8 feet on center (measure from the center of each plant).

Cautions: Frequently damaged by deer. Be careful of thorns.

Colors: See opposite page

'Double Knock Out' rose

This shrub blooms the longest with the least amount of care of any shrub in this book. Good color from spring until hard frost. Probably the best choice of roses for beginning gardeners. Produces the most color of any of the EarthKind™ roses. Rates a blue ribbon* because of its ease of care.

If you have ever been surprised by a plant - this is it! While many in the past considered roses too much work, the 'Knock Out' roses have changed all the rules. They are low maintenance, carefree shrubs that require no deadheading and little spraying, fertilizing, or trimming. And, they bloom continuously from spring until the first heavy frost. They are planted on the ramp in the rose garden of the Fort Worth Botanic Garden, where they command center stage and offer spectacular color all season long. The only limitation is that they do not produce a long-stemmed rose suitable for cutting.

Color Period: Blooms heavily in spring, sporadically through summer, and heavily again in fall. This shrub blooms heavier and longer than any other shrub in this book.

Buying Tips: Garden centers are carry many varieties that are clearly tagged. They are also available online. Three great online suppliers are www.chambleeroses.com, www.antiqueroseemporium.com, and www.JacksonandPerkins.com. Look for roses grown on their own roots and not grafted.

*Blue ribbon plants are defined on page 12. For blue ribbon performance, follow the planting and maintenance guidelines on pages 22 to 39.

Botanical Name: *Rosa* spp.
Family: Rosaceae

1. *'Knock Out' rose*
2. *'Double Knock Out' rose*
3. *'Pink Knock Out' rose*
4. *'Pink Double Knock Out' rose*
5. *'Rainbow Knock Out' rose*
6. *'Blushing Knock Out' rose*
7. *'Sunny Knock Out' rose*

At the Fort Worth Botanic Garden, the single red variety (simply called 'Knock Out' rose) is the most vigorous bloomer, with 'Rainbow' the least prolific.

GROWING CONDITIONS

Light: Full sun, at least 8 hours per day.

Water: Low after establishment, provided it is well mulched. Likes water every week or two during the growing season, depending on its environment. See pages 28 to 33 for more information.

Soil: For the garden, plant in any fertile, well-drained soil that has been enriched with organic matter. Use only good-quality potting mix for containers. See pages 22 to 25 for specific instructions on soil preparation.

Hardiness: Zones 5 to 9

Propagation: Prohibited; plants are currently patented.

Pest Problems: Black spot and powdery mildew are two fungal diseases that produce symptoms on leaves. EarthKind™ roses will grow and bloom in spite of these diseases and without being sprayed. Thrips, extremely small insects barely visible to the naked eye, attack buds and flowers, causing them not to open or to be disfigured if they do open. They are a minor problem, however, and we don't spray for them.

PLANTING & MAINTENANCE

When to Plant: Roses from containers can be planted at any time. Fall is best because they establish more easily in cooler weather, but you are more likely to find them at your garden center in early spring and summer.

Trimming: Once a year on February 14th, reduce the plant size by one third to one half if desired or needed.

Fertilization: Medium. Fertilize at planting time and each spring with a timed-release product. Less fertilizer is needed with the application of more organics.

SHRUBS & VINES

Spiraea, Bridal Wreath

1ST

CHARACTERISTICS

Plant Type: Deciduous shrub (loses its leaves in winter).

Average Size: With annual pruning after it blooms, easily maintained at 6 to 8 feet tall by 5 to 6 feet wide

Growth Rate: Fast

Leaf: Bright green, 1 to 1 1/2 inches long by 1/2 inch wide, finely toothed.

Flower: Clusters of double, rose-like flowers up and down the stem, about 1/2 inch wide.

Origin: China

Spacing: 4 to 6 feet on center (measure from the center of each plant).

Cautions: Seldom damaged by deer.

Color: Flowers are white

Loropetalum with spiraea

The pure white blossoms tell us spring has arrived. Great beauty and impact in exchange for an annual pruning that takes less than ten minutes! Easily rates a blue ribbon.*

This shrub is a favorite because of its graceful, arching form that is covered with tiny, rose-like blossoms in early spring. The blooms, which occur on old wood, appear before the leaves emerge, so the effect is spectacular. Tough as nails, bridal wreath spiraea is easily maintained with annual pruning. But be aware that, without this regular pruning, the shrub becomes unwieldy.

To lengthen spring bloom time of spiraeas, you might want to consider adding Vanhoutte spiraea (*Spiraea x vanhouttei*) to your landscape. While this shrub is similar to the bridal wreath, the bloom time is two to three weeks later, giving you over a month of early spring blossoms. Although this shrub flowers after the leaves appear, the flower is twice the size of bridal wreath and clearly visible. The dark green leaves make a beautiful contrasting background to the pure white blossoms.

Color Period: Blooms in early spring (March or early April) for two to three weeks.

Buying Tips: If you can't find this one at your local garden center, it is available from online suppliers.

Blue ribbon plants are defined on page 12. For blue ribbon performance, follow the planting and maintenance guidelines on pages 22 to 39.

Companions: Plant bridal wreath spiraea with other plants that bloom in early spring, as shown below.

Azalea
Plant Profile: Page 188

Woodland Phlox
Plant Profile: Page 150

Bridal wreath spiraea and some companions

Azalea (above, left) blooms in early spring, usually at the same time as the spiraea. Since the azalea is smaller (four to five feet tall), plant it in front of the spiraea. Both will grow in partial shade.

Woodland Phlox (above, right) is another plant that blooms in early spring. Since the phlox stays low (about 12 to 16 inches tall), use it as a border for the spiraea and azalea.

GROWING CONDITIONS

Light: Full sun to light shade

Water: Low after establishment. Likes water every week or two during the growing season, depending on its environment. See pages 28 to 33 for more information.

Soil: For the garden, plant in any fertile, well-drained soil that has been enriched with organic matter. Use only good-quality potting mix for containers. See pages 22 to 25 for specific instructions on soil preparation.

Hardiness: Zones 5 to 8

Propagation: Cuttings

Pest Problems: No serious insect or disease problems.

PLANTING & MAINTENANCE

When to Plant: Spiraea from containers can be planted at any time. Fall is best because they establish more easily in cooler weather, but you are more likely to find them at your garden center in early spring, when they are blooming.

Trimming: Prune 1/3 of the old canes right down to the ground after blooming, which means only (on the average) 4 to 5 pruning cuts. This quick pruning will give you a beautiful, well-groomed, flowering shrub year after year.

Fertilization: Medium. Fertilize at planting time and each spring with a timed-release product. Less fertilizer is needed with the application of more organics. See pages 36 to 39 for more instructions.

SHRUBS & VINES

Texas Sage, Cenizo

CHARACTERISTICS

Plant Type: Evergreen shrub.

Average Size: 3 to 5 feet tall, occasionally to 8 feet tall; 4 to 6 feet wide.

Growth Rate: Moderate

Leaf: Silvery-gray to greenish, lightly fuzzy to the touch; 1 inch long.

Flower: Bell-shaped, 1 inch in diameter; blooms periodically over several months, often after summer showers, which is why another common name is the barometer bush.

Origin: Texas

Spacing: 4 to 6 feet on center, depending on cultivar.

Cautions: Highly resistant to deer

Colors: The most common color is lavender to violet, although there are some that bloom white and pink.

1. *Texas sage not flowering*
2. *Texas sage 'Compactum'*

Great silver leaves on a medium sized shrub. Texas native that rates a blue ribbon* because of its ease of care. Lives on rainwater.

Texas sage makes a good screen or hedge and adds a southwestern/native Texas look to the landscape. It rewards the gardener with a gorgeous display of flowers at different times during the summer and early fall. Native to west Texas, this is a shrub that prefers low humidity and takes full sun and the Texas heat. It is easy to grow as long as it has excellent drainage. It is susceptible to cotton root rot, a soil fungus common in alkaline soils and for which there is no chemical control.

Regional Differences: Performs well in zone eight of north central Texas.

Color Period: Texas sage offers leaf color all year, which is the primary reason for using it. It also blooms on and off from summer to early fall for a total of about eight weeks. You never know exactly when this intermittent bloomer will produce its beautiful purple flowers, although it often blooms after a summer or fall rain.

Buying Tips: Several cultivars exist that differ slightly in size, leaf color, and flower color. 'Compactum' (three to feet tall and wide), 'Green Cloud' (four to six feet tall with green leaves), and 'Lynn's Everblooming' (four to five feet tall and wide with green foliage and lavender-blue flowers). If you are really particular about the flower color, purchase Texas sage while it is in bloom to make sure of the color.

Blue ribbon plants are defined on page 12. For blue ribbon performance, follow the planting and maintenance guidelines on pages 22 to 39.

Attracts Butterflies

Resists Deer

Lives on Rain Water *

52
Avg. Weeks of Color

Texas Native

Botanical Name:
Leucophyllum frutescens
Family: Scrophulariaceae

Companions: The silvery-gray foliage of Texas sage makes this shrub a beautiful background or companion shrub for plants with blue, purple, red, or pink flowers. Great companions include 'Henry Duelberg' salvia, fall aster, 'Raspberry' autumn sage, summer phlox, purple heart, and 'Knock Out' roses.

GROWING CONDITIONS

Light: Full sun to light shade

Water: Very low after establishment. Lives on rainwater alone, without supplemental water, in all but the most extreme conditions. See pages 28 to 33 for more information.

Soil: Any fertile, well-drained soil that has been enriched with organic matter. Requires good drainage. See pages 22 to 25 for instructions.

Hardiness: Zones 8 to 9

Propagation: Seeds or cuttings

Pest Problems: Susceptible to cotton root rot.

PLANTING & MAINTENANCE

When to Plant: Anytime from a container, although fall is best because plants establish more easily in cooler weather.

Trimming: As necessary to keep compact.

Fertilization: Low. Fertilize at planting time with a timed-release product. Less fertilizer is needed with the application of more organics. In the years after planting, fertilization needs vary, based on the nutrients in your soil. See pages 36 to 39 for more instructions.

'Raspberry' Autumn Sage
Plant Profile: Page 156

Fall Aster
Plant Profile: Page 110

Texas sage with some companions

'Raspberry' Autumn Sage (above, left) is a nearly evergreen perennial that grows two and a half feet to three feet tall and blooms from April to November. 'Raspberry' has vibrant, fuchsia-colored flowers that really stand out against the silvery-gray foliage of Texas sage. Also a west Texas native, autumn sage is a drought-tolerant plant and looks great in both native as well as more traditional landscapes. Use autumn sage in front of the taller-growing Texas sage.

Fall Aster (above, right) is a perennial that grows about two and one half feet tall by three feet wide. It is a green mound all summer long, but come mid October, it absolutely covers itself with lavender, daisy-like flowers that are beautiful against the foliage of Texas sage. Use fall aster as a border in front of Texas sage.

Lives on rainwater alone in all but the most extreme situations

SHRUBS & VINES

Viburnum, Chinese Snowball

CHARACTERISTICS

Plant Type: Deciduous shrub (loses its leaves in winter).

Average Size: Easily maintained at sizes between 8 to 12 feet tall by 6 to 8 feet wide.

Growth Rate: Fast

Leaf: Deep green, whitish on underside, oval shaped; 4 inches long by 2 inches wide.

Flower: A round ball, 6 to 8 inches across, composed of florets less than 1 inch across.

Origin: China

Spacing: About 8 feet on center (measure from the center of each plant).

Cautions: Blossoms do not hold up when dried for arrangements. Occasionally damaged by deer.

Colors: As the flower unfolds, it is a Granny Smith apple color, eventually turning white.

This plant puts on a breathtaking show when it comes into bloom in early spring. A tough shrub and easily maintained, rating a blue ribbon.*

Chinese snowball viburnum and purple pansies in spring

The giant snowballs that cover this shrub cause a "jaw dropping" experience for all those who see it in early spring. At the Fort Worth Botanic Garden, there is one inside the entry courtyard of the Japanese garden. When it blooms, it stops traffic! This plant needs a lot of space, so be sure to keep that in mind when placing it in your landscape.

Color Period: Blooms for two to three weeks from late March to mid-April.

Buying Tips: There is more than one plant called a snowball bush. For the very large, softball-sized blossoms shown here, be sure you have *Viburnum macrocephalum* (which means big head). Other, smaller blooming shrubs that are available include the Japanese snowballs whose blooms are half the size: 'Kern's Pink' viburnum (pictured, opposite), whose blossoms are shades of pink; and 'Popcorn,' which also has a white blossom.

'Kern's Pink' viburnum has blossoms tinged with pink. Its blooms are smaller than those of the Chinese snowball.

Blue ribbon plants are defined on page 12. For blue ribbon performance, follow the planting and maintenance guidelines on pages 22 to 39.

Companions: You will love the effect of early-blooming flowers planted in front of it. And when it finishes blooming, it is a great backdrop for tall perennials and annuals.

Try this viburnum with azaleas and forsythia, as shown below.

Chinese snowball viburnum with some companions

Azalea (above, left) blooms in early spring, usually at the same time as the viburnum. Since the azalea is smaller (four to five feet tall), plant it in front of the viburnum. Both will grow in light shade.

Forsythia (above, right) is an early spring-flowering, deciduous shrub that can grow as tall and wide as six feet in full sun to partial shade. Its gracefully arching branches produce a profusion of bright, golden yellow flowers before the leaves emerge. Plant forsythia in front of the taller Chinese snowball for a spectacular display of spring flowers.

Be sure to place the viburnum where it gets at least half a day's sun. Ideal light for this group of plants would be on the east side of your house or in an area that gets morning sun and afternoon shade. The viburnum and forsythia can take full sun, but the azalea will burn up with that much light.

GROWING CONDITIONS

Light: Full sun to partial shade. Blooms best and has most attractive leaf color in full sun. Very heat tolerant.

Water: Low after establishment. Likes water every week or two during the growing season, depending on its environment. See pages 28 to 33 for more information.

Soil: For the garden, plant in any fertile, well-drained soil that has been enriched with organic matter. Use only good-quality potting mix for containers. See pages 22 to 25 for specific instructions on soil preparation.

Hardiness: Zones 6 to 9

Propagation: Cuttings

Pest Problems: Rare

PLANTING & MAINTENANCE

When to Plant: Viburnum from containers can be planted at any time. Fall is best because they establish more easily in cooler weather, but you are more likely to find them at your garden center in early spring, when they are blooming.

Trimming: Annual pruning right after bloom time in late April to early May.

Fertilization: Medium. Fertilize at planting time and each spring with a timed-release product. Less fertilizer is needed with the application of more organics. See pages 36 to 39 for more instructions.

BUDGET GARDENING TIP

Since this plant grows quickly, you can buy small, inexpensive ones that will fill out in no time! And since this plant stops traffic, it is a high-impact plant for a low price.

SHRUBS & VINES

Viburnum, Doublefile

CHARACTERISTICS

Plant Type: Deciduous shrub (loses its leaves in winter).

Average Size: With annual pruning, easily maintained at 8 to 12 feet tall by 12 to 15 feet wide.

Growth Rate: Fast

Leaf: Deep green leaf, 4 to 5 inches long by 2 to 3 inches wide. Leaves grow opposite of one another with prominent veins. Leaves are rough to the touch.

Flower: White lace caps that are 2 inches across; flower clusters appear in two rows, or files, along the branches.

Origin: China and Japan

Spacing: About 12 feet on center (measure from the center of each plant).

Cautions: May get a little leaf scorch on hot, summer days. Occasional damage from deer.

Colors: Flowers are white

A native viburnum, the rusty blackhaw viburnum (V. rufidulum), forms a large shrub or small tree 10 to 20 feet tall and wide that grows slowly with little care. It blooms in April and has berries in fall that attract birds. The leaves turn red and yellow in fall. Plant this viburnum in light shade to full sun.

A beautiful, floral display in late spring, after the dogwoods have stopped blooming. Blue ribbon plant* that requires very little care.

This shrub gives a magnificent floral display in late spring. Its horizontal branching is quite distinctive. The lace cap blossoms come in pairs, opposite each other along the stem, and are presented for viewing against beautiful, dark green foliage. Butterflies love the flowers, and in summer, for a short period, this plant produces red berries that are a treat for the birds.

Color Period: Late spring, for about two weeks

Buying Tips: Available at your local garden center and also from online suppliers. Other cultivars to look for that were introduced by the National Arboretum's breeding project are 'Shasta' (its flowers are three to four inches across and will completely cover the bush) and 'Shoshoni' (a more compact shrub that grows to six feet tall by six feet wide). You also may want to try 'Mariesii,' which is a vigorous floral performer.

*Blue ribbon plants are defined on page 12. For blue ribbon performance, follow the planting and maintenance guidelines on pages 22 to 39.

Companions: This shrub has a shallow root system that is best left undisturbed, so it is wise to provide long-lived companion plants stationed nearby but not right atop its root zone.

Plant it near hydrangeas and woodland phlox, as shown below.

Doublefile viburnum with some companions

'Mini Penny' Hydrangea (above, left) is a reblooming shrub that blooms for the first time in late spring, usually at the same time as the viburnum in zones seven to nine (provided there is no late freeze). Since the hydrangea is smaller (three to four feet tall), plant it in front of the viburnum. Both will grow in light shade.

Woodland Phlox (above, right) is another plant that blooms in spring. Since the phlox stays low (about 12 to 16 inches tall), use it as a border for the hydrangea and the viburnum. This group of plants does best in light shade.

GROWING CONDITIONS

Light: Light shade to full sun. Takes more shade than the snowball viburnum.

Water: Low after establishment. Likes water every week or two during the growing season, depending on its environment. See pages 28 to 33 for more information.

Soil: For the garden, plant in any fertile, well-drained soil that has been enriched with organic matter. Use only good-quality potting mix for containers. See pages 22 to 25 for specific instructions on soil preparation.

Hardiness: Zones 5 to 8 for doublefiles; 5 to 9 for rusty blackhaw.

Propagation: Cuttings

Pest Problems: None serious

PLANTING & MAINTENANCE

When to Plant: Viburnum from containers can be planted at any time. Fall is best because they establish more easily in cooler weather, but you are more likely to find them at your garden center in late spring, when they are blooming.

Trimming: Prune doublefile as needed after flowering. Prune rusty blackhaw as needed to shape.

Fertilization: Medium for doublefile. Fertilize at planting time and each spring with a timed-release product. Less fertilizer is needed with the application of more organics. Low for rusty blackhaw. See pages 36 to 39 for more instructions.

SHRUBS & VINES

Virginia Creeper

CHARACTERISTICS

Plant Type: Deciduous vine (loses its leaves in the winter).

Average Size: May reach 40 to 50 feet.

Growth Rate: Fast

Leaf: Each leaflet is 3 to 6 inches long by 1 to 2 inches wide. Dark green above, pale green below. Leaves provide early fall color, turning brilliant red and orange.

Flower: Small, white clusters; inconspicuous. Flowers give way to dark blue to black berries, which are attractive to birds.

Origin: Eastern and southeastern U. S., including Texas.

Spacing: 8 feet on center (measure from the center of each plant).

Cautions: Berries are highly toxic to humans if eaten. Also, once attached to the side of a building or home, it becomes difficult to remove and will damage painted surfaces and leave residues.

Color: Leaves turn red and orange in fall.

Virginia creeper is an excellent native vine. Its most outstanding feature is its fall color. Since it turns color earlier than most other deciduous plants, its flaming red-orange leaves really stand out in the landscape. It rates a blue ribbon* because of its ease of care.

Virginia creeper provides beauty as well as energy conservation to a sunny wall on a house. Its lush green leaves shade the wall during the summer and, as a bare vine during the winter, allows the sun to warm the wall. In addition, the small, black berries provide food for birds during the winter. Very easy to grow, this vine attaches to brick, stone, or wooden walls via adhesive discs at the ends of its tendrils. These discs leave their mark on walls when you remove the vines. This is a very large vine, however, so don't attempt to use it in small spaces.

Color Period: Green leaves in spring and summer, brilliant red and orange fall color, and black berries late fall and winter.

Buying Tips: The cultivar 'Engelmanii' has smaller leaves than the species. Very similar if not identical to a variety discovered in Mexico called 'Hacienda Creeper.'

*Blue ribbon plants are defined on page 12. For blue ribbon performance, follow the planting and maintenance guidelines on pages 22 to 39.

Texas Native

Attracts Birds

4
Avg. Weeks of Color

Lives on Rain Water *

Botanical Name: *Parthenocissus quinquefolia*
Family: Vitaceae

Companions: Virginia creeper forms a dramatic backdrop against a wall or fence for any other plant in the landscape. In other words, it combines well with anything! For outstanding fall impact, you might combine it with other plants that produce brilliant fall color, as shown below.

Rusty Blackhaw Viburnum
Plant Profile: Page 254

Chinese Pistache
Plant Profile: Page 298

Virginia creeper with some companions

Rusty Blackhaw Viburnum (above, left) forms a large shrub or small tree, 10 to 20 feet tall and wide. The leaves are dark green and glossy in the summer but turn reddish-purple, orange and yellow in the fall, which puts on quite a show when combined with the colored leaves of the Virginia creeper. Plant rusty blackhaw viburnum in full sun or part shade.

Chinese Pistache (above, right) is a medium-sized tree that reaches 30 to 40 feet tall. Its compound leaves consist of attractive, lance-shaped leaflets that set the landscape on fire each fall when they turn brilliant red, orange, and yellow.

GROWING CONDITIONS

Light: Full sun to medium shade

Water: Very low after establishment. Lives on rainwater alone, without supplemental water, in all but the most extreme conditions. See pages 28 to 33 for more information.

Soil: Any fertile, well-drained soil that has been enriched with organic matter. Requires good drainage. See pages 22 to 25 for instructions.

Hardiness: Zones 3 to 9

Propagation: Seeds

Pest Problems: No serious insect or pest problems.

PLANTING & MAINTENANCE

When to Plant: Virginia creeper from containers can be planted at any time. Fall is best because they establish easier in cooler weather.

Trimming: Only to control growth.

Fertilization: Low. Fertilize at planting time with a timed-release product. Less fertilizer is needed with the application of more organics. In the years after planting, fertilization needs vary, based on the nutrients in your soil. See pages 36 to 39 for more instructions.

SHRUBS & VINES

Lives on rainwater alone in all but the most extreme situations.

Wax Myrtle

CHARACTERISTICS

Plant Type: Evergreen shrub.

Average Size: The largest type grows 10 to 15 feet tall as far north as zone 7, and 20 feet tall or more further south. If you need a smaller one, try dwarf wax myrtle *Myrica pumilia,* which grows to 6 feet tall and 4 to 6 feet wide.

Growth Rate: Fast

Leaf: Willow shaped, long and elliptical; 3 inches long by 1/2 inch wide; yellow-green and aromatic when crushed.

Flower: Very tiny (inconspicuous) flowers that cluster at the base of the leaves. Male and female flowers on separate plants.

Origin: Southeastern U.S., including east Texas.

Spacing: About 12 to 15 feet on center (measure from the center of each plant).

Cautions: Almost never damaged by deer.

Colors: Flowers are yellow but not showy.

A fantastic, native evergreen that is particularly useful for shady areas, although it takes full sun as well. A large shrub or small tree, often multi-trunked, it makes an attractive tall screen or specimen tree. Extremely easy to grow, attracts birds, and rates a blue ribbon.*

Since many evergreens are coarse textured, like many hollies, wax myrtle adds another texture to the mix. The leaves are light-textured, like a willow. The shrub has beautiful, blue fruit in fall that attracts birds.

Wax myrtles are native to many different types of environments, from zone seven to zone ten. Plants that can live in so many different temperature zones and adapt to wet and dry regions tend to be quite easy to grow.

Color Period: Flowers are insignificant in late winter to mid spring. Blue fruit that follows is attractive.

Buying Tips: Only female wax myrtles produce the blue fruit. If you want a female, purchase your wax myrtle while it has fruit on it. The best fruit set will occur if there is a male nearby.

Blue ribbon plants are defined on page 12. For blue ribbon performance, follow the planting and maintenance guidelines on pages 22 to 39.

Texas Native

Attracts Birds

Resists Deer

Companions: For an evergreen grouping featuring different textures, try wax myrtle with yew and dwarf yaupon holly, as shown below.

Wax myrtle with some companions

Yew (above, left) has dark green foliage and adds a different texture to the group. Plant the yew, which grows three to four feet tall, in front of the wax myrtle.

Dwarf Yaupon Holly (above, right) is a small evergreen holly that assumes a round shape three to four feet tall at maturity. Its small, light green leaves contrast well with those of yew and wax myrtle.

GROWING CONDITIONS

Light: Medium shade to full sun. Grows looser in shade.

Water: Low after establishment. Likes water every week or two during the growing season, depending on its environment. See pages 28 to 33 for more information.

Soil: Wax myrtles prefer good soil but will make it in clay. For best results, plant them in any fertile, well-drained soil that has been enriched with organic matter. Requires good drainage. See pages 22 to 25 for instructions.

Hardiness: Zones 7 to 10

Propagation: Seeds or cuttings

Pest Problems: Rare. Root rot can develop if plants are kept too wet.

PLANTING & MAINTENANCE

When to Plant: Wax myrtles from containers can be planted at any time. Fall is best because they establish more easily in cooler weather.

Trimming: Trim once a year or as needed. Thinning is better than shearing, but the dwarfs take shearing well enough. Wax myrtles are more attractive with a natural growth habit than sheared into a meatball.

Fertilization: Medium. Fertilize at planting time and annually with a timed-release product. Less fertilizer is needed with the application of more organics. See pages 36 to 39 for more instructions.

SHRUBS & VINES

Yew

CHARACTERISTICS

Plant Type: Evergreen shrub.

Average Size: 3 to 4 feet tall by 4 to 6 feet wide.

Growth Rate: Slow to medium

Leaf: Needle-like, 1 to 1 1/2 inches long by 1/4 inch wide; arranged spirally around the stem.

Flower: Insignificant

Origin: Japan and England

Spacing: About 3 feet on center (measure from the center of each plant).

Cautions: All parts of the plant are poisonous if eaten. Almost never damaged by deer.

Colors: Leaves are dark green. Flowers are insignificant.

Yew is a fine-textured, evergreen shrub that makes an excellent small hedge or foundation planting for part shade or shade. Because of its slow growth rate, it seldom needs pruning. Rates a blue ribbon* for its low maintenance.

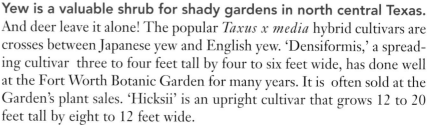

Yew is a valuable shrub for shady gardens in north central Texas. And deer leave it alone! The popular *Taxus x media* hybrid cultivars are crosses between Japanese yew and English yew. 'Densiformis,' a spreading cultivar three to four feet tall by four to six feet wide, has done well at the Fort Worth Botanic Garden for many years. It is often sold at the Garden's plant sales. 'Hicksii' is an upright cultivar that grows 12 to 20 feet tall by eight to 12 feet wide.

Yew is easy to grow if you give it good drainage. It has no serious insect or disease problems.

Color Period: Insignificant

Buying Tips: Available at nurseries and garden centers

Blue ribbon plants are defined on page 12. For blue ribbon performance, follow the planting and maintenance guidelines on pages 22 to 39.

Resists Deer

Companions: The dark green, fine-textured foliage of yew provides the perfect backdrop for lighter-colored plants with different textures. Layer it with 'Bronze Beauty' cleyera and southern wood fern to accentuate the interesting textures of all three plants, as shown below.

'Bronze Beauty' Cleyera
Plant Profile: Page 204

Southern Wood Fern
Plant Profile: Page 126

Yew and some companions

'Bronze Beauty' Cleyera (above, left) is a shrub that grows up to eight feet tall, making a nice backdrop for the shorter yew. The textures of both plants are quite different, which makes each plant show up better.

Southern Wood Fern (above, right) grows two to three feet tall in light to medium shade and provides a light green, soft-textured contrast to the dark green, needle-like foliage of yew. The reason southern wood fern looks so good with yew is that its lime green color is the same color as the new growth on the yew. Since southern wood fern is shorter than yew, use it as the lowest plant in this grouping.

GROWING CONDITIONS

Light: Light to medium shade in north central Texas. Takes more sun in colder climates.

Water: Low after establishment. Likes water every week or two during the growing season, depending on its environment. See pages 28 to 33 for more information.

Soil: Any fertile, well-drained soil that has been enriched with organic matter. Requires good drainage. See pages 22 to 25 for instructions.

Hardiness: Zones 4 to 7

Propagation: Seeds can take up to 2 years to germinate and are extremely variable.

Pest Problems: Rare

PLANTING & MAINTENANCE

When to Plant: Yew from containers can be planted at any time. Fall is best because they establish more easily in cooler weather.

Trimming: Very little trimming needed. Prune out dead branches whenever you notice them.

Fertilization: Medium. Fertilize at planting time and annually with a timed-release product. Less fertilizer is needed with the application of more organics. See pages 36 to 39 for more instructions.

SHRUBS & VINES

Yucca

CHARACTERISTICS

Plant Type: Evergreen shrub.

Average Size: Easily maintained at sizes between 2 to 3 feet tall by equally as wide.

Growth Rate: Slow to medium

Leaf: Sword-like, elongated leaves; 2 to 2 1/2 feet long by 1 inch wide, with a sharp point. Blue green, bright green, or variegated.

Flower: Clusters of bell-shaped flowers on tall spikes (5 to 8 feet tall).

Origin: Southeast and southwest U.S.

Spacing: About 3 to 4 feet on center (measure from the center of each plant).

Cautions: Pointed tips, particularly on Spanish bayonet (*Yucca aloifolia*). Almost never damaged by deer.

Colors: Flowers are white

Hardy, dependable, and tough as nails. Provides dramatic accent in the garden. Easy to grow, but some have sharp tips that can puncture your hands. Easily wins a blue ribbon,* but be sure to wear heavy gloves while handling any sharp yuccas!

The only way you can kill this plant is to overwater it. Give it any other extreme, and it does quite well. Yuccas thrive in hot, sunny parking lots and in front of walls that reflect a lot of heat.

Color Period: Blooms once in June. One spike per clump. Variegated leaf cultivars provide additional color interest year round.

Buying Tips: All of the yuccas we have planted have done well. 'Bright Edge' has yellow along the edge of the leaves, while 'Color Guard' (pictured above) has yellow in the center of the leaf.

'Color Guard' yucca. When you first buy yuccas, they are usually about the size of this one. They form clumps as they grow, thickening like the one at the top of this page.

'Ivory Tower' yucca

*Blue ribbon plants are defined on page 12. For blue ribbon performance, follow the planting and maintenance guidelines on pages 22 to 39.

Texas Native

Lives on Rain Water *

Resists Deer

52
Avg. Weeks of Color

Botanical Name: *Yucca filamentosa*
Family: Agavaceae

Companions: Use yucca as an accent in the garden to break up groups of plants with different colors or textures.

For color contrast, use this yucca with the darkest leaves you can find, like the loropetalum and purple heart, shown below.

Loropetalum
Plant Profile: Page 228

Purple Heart
Plant Profile: Page 152

Yucca with some companions

Loropetalum (above, left) is an evergreen shrub that has dark burgundy leaves that contrast well with the yellow-green leaves of the yucca. Plant the taller loropetalum behind the shorter yucca.

Purple Heart (above, right) is a low-growing, perennial groundcover that also contrasts well with the yellow-green yucca. Plant it in front of the taller yucca. All do well in light shade to full sun.

*Lives on rainwater alone in all but the most extreme situations

GROWING CONDITIONS

Light: Light shade to full sun

Water: Very low after establishment. Lives on rainwater alone, without supplemental water, in all but the most extreme conditions. See pages 28 to 33 for more information.

Soil: Yucca tolerates clay but prefers a better soil. Best to plant it in fertile, well-drained soil that has been enriched with organic matter. Requires good drainage. See pages 22 to 25 for instructions.

Hardiness: Zones 4 to 9

Propagation: Seeds, cuttings, or division. Yuccas form clumps that can be divided every few years by digging them out of the ground, cutting the plants apart, and replanting.

Pest Problems: Rare. A little aphid gets on the flowers occasionally. Leaf spots in wet weather.

PLANTING & MAINTENANCE

When to Plant: Yucca from containers can be planted at any time. Fall is best because they establish more easily in cooler weather.

Trimming: Remove flower stalk after it fades. Be very careful of the spiky tips on this plant.

Fertilization: Low. Fertilize at planting time with a timed-release product. Less fertilizer is needed with the application of more organics. In the years after planting, fertilization needs vary, based on the nutrients in your soil. See pages 36 to 39 for more instructions.

SHRUBS & VINES

Yucca, Red

CHARACTERISTICS

Plant Type: Evergreen shrub.

Average Size: 3 feet tall and wide.

Growth Rate: Medium

Leaf: 2 to 4 feet long; stiff and succulent, narrow, and adorned with white fibrous threads on the margins.

Flower: 1 inch long, bell-shaped flowers that appear in clusters up and down the stalks that rise 4 to 6 feet above the ground. Flowers are full of nectar and attract hummingbirds all season long.

Origin: Native to west Texas

Spacing: 3 to 4 feet on center (measure from the center of each plant).

Cautions: Almost never eaten by deer.

Color: Flowers are coral on the outside, pale yellow on the inside. There is also a solid yellow flowering selection.

A yellow flower selection

Dramatic flowers that last a full 30 weeks per year with only minutes of maintenance! Rates a blue ribbon* because it thrives under the hot Texas sun with very little care. Lives on rainwater, resists deer, and attracts hummingbirds.

Red yucca rewards the gardener with striking form, foliage, and flowers. It lends a native Texas/southwestern look to the landscape and holds up beautifully during the blazing summers of north central Texas. Red yucca is an excellent choice for use around swimming pools and patios because of its clean, litter-free nature. Extremely easy to grow, it survives beautifully on annual rainfall. The only maintenance required is the removal of the spent flowering stalks at the end of the season.

Color Period: Blooms from April through October for an average of 30 weeks.

Buying Tips: Available at nurseries and garden centers. Both red- and yellow flowering forms are available, although the red flowering selection is more common.

Blue ribbon plants are defined on page 12. For blue ribbon performance, follow the planting and maintenance guidelines on pages 22 to 39.

Attracts Hummingbirds

Resists Deer

Lives on Rain Water *

30
Avg. Weeks of Color

Texas Native

Botanical Name: *Hesperaloe parviflora*

Family: Agavaceae

Companions: Use companion plants that play off the colors on the stems and in the flowers. The yellow flowers of Dahlberg daisy or 'New Gold' lantana correspond to the yellow centers of the flowers. Use coral autumn sage to reinforce the color of red yucca's flowers and stems. Use purple trailing lantana or 'Blue Princess' verbena to reinforce the purplish hue on the stems.

Coral Autumn Sage
Plant Profile: Page 156

Purple Trailing Lantana
Plant Profile: Page 68

Red yucca with some companions

Coral Autumn Sage (above, left) is the best color of *Salvia greggii* to use with red yucca. It blooms April through October and, therefore, corresponds perfectly to the blooming period of red yucca. It gets about two and one half feet tall and wide and contrasts nicely in shape and leaf form with red yucca.

Purple Trailing Lantana (above, right) grows one foot tall by four feet wide. Its spreading habit contrasts strikingly with the clumping, arching leaves of red yucca and softens the whole appearance of red yucca. Its purple flowers correspond to the purplish hues on the flowering stalks of red yucca and contrast with the vivid coral flowers of red yucca. Plant it as a border for the taller yucca and sage.

*Lives on rainwater alone in all but the most extreme situations

GROWING CONDITIONS

Light: Full sun, at least 6 hours per day.

Water: Very low after establishment. Lives on rainwater alone, without supplemental water, in all but the most extreme conditions. See pages 28 to 33 for more information.

Soil: Tolerates any soil as long as it is well-drained. Does not do well with poor drainage.

Hardiness: Zones 7 to 10

Propagation: Seeds or division

Pest Problems: None

PLANTING & MAINTENANCE

When to Plant: Red yucca from containers can be planted at any time. Fall is best because they establish easier in cooler weather.

Trimming: Remove the spent flowering stalks at the end of the season.

Fertilization: Low. Fertilize at planting time with a timed-release product. Less fertilizer is needed with the application of more organics. In the years after planting, fertilization needs vary, based on the nutrients in your soil. See pages 36 to 39 for more instructions.

SHRUBS & VINES

Other Shrubs & Vines that Deserve Mention

Barberry, Japanese
Berberis thunbergii

Deciduous shrub noted for its thorny stems and red leaves. 'Crimson Pygmy' is the best-selling cultivar that provides beautiful foliage color. Larger barberries are tough and vigorous but are proving to be invasive in some parts of the country. Full sun to light shade. Low water. Zones 4 to 8.

Burning Bush
Euonymus alatus

Burning bush lights up the landscape in fall. The name is appropriate because the foliage turns an intense, bright red like few other plants. Dwarf form is best selection for home gardeners. Becoming invasive in more northern locales. Full sun to light shade. Low water. Zones 4 to 9.

Fraser, Red-Tip Photinia
Photinia x fraseri

Glossy green foliage with brilliant red new growth on a fast growing shrub. Unfortunately, very prone to a leaf spot that will defoliate plants in our hot weather. Does not grow well here. Cleyera is a much better plant, although it doesn't have the brilliant, red, new growth. Full sun. Medium water. Zones 7 to 9.

Gardenia
Gardenia japonica

Great plant for fragrance in acid soil, not the alkaline soils of north central Texas. Does not grow well here. Evergreen. 6 to 8 feet tall. Blooms for several months of the summer. Zones 8 to 10. Often needs protection in zone 7. Insects and nutritional deficiencies are frequent problems. Light shade to morning sun. Medium water.

Duranta, Brazilian Sky Flower
Duranta erecta

Butterfly and hummingbird magnet. Lavender-blue flower panicles bloom almost all summer long. Dies to the ground in zone 8. Not hardy in zones 6 or 7. Range from 4 to 12 feet tall, depending on growing season. Full sun. Medium water. Zones 8 to 11.

Indian Hawthorn
Raphiolepis indica

Very popular shrub in zones 7B to 10 that doesn't do well in north central Texas because of a leaf spot that will defoliate plants in our hot weather. Light shade to full sun. Low water. Blooms for about 2 weeks in spring. 3 to 6 feet tall.

Jasmine, Asiatic
Trachelospermum asiaticum

Most common groundcover in Dallas-Fort Worth. Dark green, glossy leaves. Easy to grow. May suffer freeze damage in severe winters but comes back vigorously. In late winter, cut back old or damaged growth by mowing over with lawn mower at highest setting. Sun to shade. 12 inches tall, but can be maintained at 6 inches. Medium water.

Jasmine, Confederate
Trachelospermum jasminoides

Evergreen vine used extensively in zones 8 to 10 for green foliage and fragrant, white flowers. The flowers open in late April and flower heavily for 4 weeks and then sporadically throughout the summer. Vines grow 12 feet to 20 feet tall with support. Full sun to medium shade. Medium water.

Laurel 'Otto Luyken'
Prunus laurocerasus 'Otto Luyken'

Evergreen shrub that is excellent in masses or low hedges. Dark green foliage susceptible to shot hole disease. 3 to 4 feet tall by 4 to 5 feet wide with small, white flowers in May. Must have good drainage to survive. Full sun to medium shade. Medium water. Zones 6 to 8.

Ligustrum
Ligustrum japonicum

Evergreen, large shrub or small tree. Glossy foliage on plants 6 to 12 feet tall. White flowers open in May and are quite fragrant, but some might say they stink. While not as invasive as the Chinese privet, some caution should be taken in planting profusely. Full sun to light shade. Medium water. Zones 7 to 10.

Oleander
Nerium oleander

Commonly used in zones 8 to 11 for its durability and long bloom period. Grows about 6 feet tall in areas that freeze. Blooms for most of the warm season. Very toxic (can kill people), and attracts caterpillars that can completely defoliate it. Low water. Full sun.

Pittosporum
Pittosporum tobira

Widely planted, evergreen shrub in zones 8 to 10. Variegated or solid green leaves. 2 to 8 feet tall with equal spread. Tolerant of poor soils, but needs good drainage. Not reliably cold hardy below 10 degrees. Full sun to medium shade. Low water.

Podocarpus
Podocarpus macrophyllus

Often called the yew of warm areas, podocarpus has deep green foliage. Frequently used as a large, evergreen hedge. Cannot tolerate wet soils. Winter damage below 10 degrees. Full sun to light shade. Medium water. Zones 8 to 10.

Pyracantha
Pyracantha coccinea

Brilliant, orange berry displays that ripen in September and persist for several months before being eaten by birds. Evergreen shrub growing 6 to 10 feet tall with small glossy foliage and thorny stems. Fireblight can be a problem. Full sun. Low water. Zones 5 to 9.

Silverthorn
Elaeagnus pungens

Large, evergreen shrub (8 to 12 feet tall) known for its fast growth and unruly character. Shearing makes it grow faster, so let it grow naturally. There is concern over invasive potential of several of the *Elaeagnus* species, so consider an alternative like wax myrtle for an evergreen screen. Full sun. Low water. Zones 7 to 10.

Tea Olive
Osmanthus fragrans

Flowers are incredibly fragrant. Blooms heavily in spring and fall; sporadically in summer. Makes an excellent, large, evergreen, growing 10 to 15 feet tall. Plants may be damaged if temperatures fall below 10 degrees. Full sun to light shade. Medium water. Zones 7 to 10.

Trumpet Creeper
Campsis radicans

Older cultivars of this plant are beautiful but quite aggressive. Considered invasive. Improved cultivars ('Madame Galen') are less aggressive and bloom for about 4 months each summer. Very showy. 25 to 40 feet tall. Full sun. Low water. Zones 5 to 9.

Viburnum 'Awabuki'
Viburnum awabuki

Evergreen shrub with white flowers in May. Nice, green foliage on fast-growing plants. Bright red berries can be seen if good pollination occurs. 'Chindo' is a superior cultivar. Must have good drainage. Full sun to light shade. Medium water. Zones 8 to 9.

Viburnum, Burkwood
Viburnum x burkwoodii

Excellent deciduous to semi-evergreen shrub with beautiful, fragrant, spring flowers. 8 to 10 feet tall. Flowers appear pink to red in bud, opening to a pure white, emanating a heady fragrance in the garden. Blooms for 2 to 3 weeks in April. Full sun to light shade. Medium water. Zones 5 to 8.

Viburnum, Leatherleaf
Viburnum x rhytidophyllum

Coarse-textured, evergreen shrub that grows 8 to 10 feet tall. Foliage is quilted, dark green in color, 8 inches long by 4 inches wide. Creamy white flowers open in April and are showy for 2 to 3 weeks followed by clusters of red berries in fall. Full sun to light shade. Medium water. Zones 5 to 8.

Wintercreeper
Euonymus fortunei

Widely planted groundcover to small shrub, depending upon cultivar selection. Very susceptible to Euonymus scale. Often grows out of control and has to be removed. Interesting foliage colors include plum-red and white and gold variegated forms. Full sun to medium shade. Medium water. Zones 5 to 9.

Wisteria, American
Wisteria frutescens

Beautiful blooms in late spring. Flowers are 4 to 6 inches long and last 2 to 3 weeks. Vines are more restrained than the very aggressive Japanese or Chinese wisterias (that are more commonly sold). Full sun to light shade. Low water. Zones 5 to 9.

Wisteria, Evergreen
Millettia reticulata

Beautiful vine that does very well in north central Texas if you give it cold protection in zone 7. Blooms in late summer through fall. Flowers visible better from close up than from a distance. Medium water. Produces branches that require sturdy support. Full sun. 15 feet tall by 10 feet wide. Zones 8 to 10.

Wisteria, Japanese & Chinese
Wisteria floribunda, Wisteria sinensis

This plant is commonly used in Texas and is one of the most destructive to our natural environment. Kills trees and whatever other plants get in its way. Do not plant it! 2 other wisterias on this page that give you the same look without the risk.

Chapter 5

Trees

✿ Trees are one of the easiest plants in your garden. Many require no maintenance at all other than a fall cleanup of the fallen leaves.

✿ Trees provide shade for your house. Houses with 50 percent of their roof shaded save up to 50 percent on their air conditioning bills.

✿ Trees also provide shade to the plants underneath, which saves over 50 percent of the water the plants need to grow.

✿ One of the most common gardening mistakes is choosing trees that outgrow their space. Check out tree size carefully before planting.

Above: Shantung maple in fall
Left: 'Fire Dragon' shantung maple with ginkgo in fall

Chaste Tree, Vitex

CHARACTERISTICS

Plant Type: Deciduous shrub or multi-trunked tree (loses its leaves in the winter).

Average Size: 10 to 15 feet tall and wide.

Growth Rate: Fast

Wind Tolerance: Unknown

Leaf: 2 to 4 inches long. Dull, gray-green on top with whitish gray on the bottom. Leaves have a spicy fragrance when crushed. Fall color is yellow.

Flower: Terminal spikes of tiny, fragrant, bluish-lavender; spikes are up to 12 inches long and attractive to butterflies.

Origin: Southern Europe

Spacing: About 10 to 15 feet on center (measure from the center of each plant).

Cautions: Juice or sap is an irritant, which can cause painful blisters. Bees all over flowers in summer. Almost never damaged by deer.

Colors: Flowers are various shades of light blue, white, or pink. Leaves are green.

Chaste tree trimmed like a shrub

An outstanding small tree that blooms for up to five months with very little care. Great for butterflies. Easily wins a blue ribbon* for its high performance with very little care.

Vitex, or chaste tree, is an outstanding, small, multi-trunked tree for your butterfly garden. Beautiful panicles of blue flowers attract hundreds of native butterflies throughout the five-month bloom period. Provide full sun and good drainage, and watch it take off, blooming profusely from a very young age. The leaves are attractive, resembling Japanese maple leaves without the red coloration. Vitex tolerates heat, drought, and pests. It is a Texas Superstar™ plant.

Color Period: Mid May to early October. Deadheading keeps plants full of flowers, if you can reach them!

Buying Tips: Several selections based on flower color are available in garden centers. 'Mississippi Blues' is an excellent deep blue selection; 'Abbeville Blue' and 'Shoal Creek' are good blue selections; 'Alba' and 'Silver Spire' have white flowers; and 'Rosea' has pink flowers.

*Blue ribbon plants are defined on page 12. For blue ribbon performance, follow the planting and maintenance guidelines on pages 22 to 39.

Companions: Chaste tree is excellent for attracting butterflies, so pair with other butterfly-attracting plants like butterfly bush, abelia 'Rose Creek,' black-eyed Susans, and cone flowers. Both lantana and pentas are also butterfly favorites, so try planting them with vitex, as shown below.

'New Gold' Lantana
Plant Profile: Page 68

Pentas
Plant Profile: Page 74

Chaste tree and some companions

'New Gold' Lantana (above, left) is an annual that is one of the best butterfly attractors. It grows about two feet tall and blooms all spring, summer, and all fall.

Pentas (above, right) are annuals that are also among the best butterfly flowers. They bloom on and off from May until the first frost. Alternate clumps of lantana with pentas under the chaste tree in an area where they both get sun.

GROWING CONDITIONS

Light: Full sun, at least 6 hours per day.

Water: Low after establishment. Likes water every week or two during the growing season, depending on its environment. See pages 28 to 33 for more information.

Soil: Grows in unimproved soil, including clay, provided the soil has not been compacted. Compaction occurs most commonly from heavy equipment working around a house under construction. See page 27 for instructions on tree planting.

Hardiness: Zones 6 to 9

Propagation: Seeds or cuttings

Pest Problems: None serious

PLANTING & MAINTENANCE

When to Plant: Chaste trees from containers can be planted at any time. Fall is best because they establish more easily in cooler weather, but you are more likely to find them at your garden center in spring, when they are blooming.

Trimming: Late winter to early spring. Thin out older canes to encourage new growth from the base. Blooms on new wood, so prune before foliage emerges in the spring. Occasional deadheading will keep flowers coming over a longer period of time.

Fertilization: Medium. Fertilize at planting time and each spring with a timed-release product. Less fertilizer is needed with the application of more organics. See pages 36 to 39 for more instructions.

TREES

Crapemyrtle

CHARACTERISTICS

Plant Type: Deciduous tree or shrub (loses its leaves in winter).

Average Size: Ranges from 3 to 25 feet tall; width varies from broad bushes to upright, vase-shaped trees. Check plant tags for a cultivar's mature size. For information on shrub crapemyrtles, see pages 206 and 207.

Growth Rate: Medium

Wind Tolerance: High

Leaf: Dark green, oval leaves to 4 inches long. Turns yellow, orange, or red in the fall.

Flower: Terminal clusters of crinkled flowers; some with conspicuous, yellow stamens. Clusters measure up to 10 inches long by 5 inches wide.

Origin: China, Japan, and Korea

Spacing: Varies with plant size. At maturity, plants should have ample space to stretch their limbs into unobstructed sun.

Cautions: Almost never damaged by deer. Flowers that drop on pavement can make it slippery.

Colors: Flowers are white and many shades of pink, red, or lavender. Leaves are green in spring and summer, turning yellow, orange, or red in the fall.

One of the easiest and longest-blooming trees in Texas. Blooms over 90 days and follows with gorgeous fall color. Requires very little care; even lives without irrigation. Almost never damaged by deer, but birds love it. Easily wins a blue ribbon.*

Crapemyrtles are one of the most common trees grown in the southern half of the country. Whether grown as a shrub or a small, multi-trunked tree, crapemyrtle thrives in hot sun, and humid heat actually intensifies its bloom. Crapemyrtles come in many more sizes (three to 30 feet tall) than most other plants, so know the size you need before you buy. One of the most common mistakes is planting crapemyrtles that outgrow their space. Crapemyrtles naturally have a beautiful form and don't take well to severe pruning. If you need a 10 foot tree, don't buy a 30 foot crapemyrtle. Most modern cultivars resist powdery mildew, once a persistent problem, and some bloom much longer than others. For information about shrub crapemyrtles, see pages 206 and 207.

Color Period: Most varieties begin blooming in late May or early June. If early blooms are pruned off, many crapemyrtles continue to bloom until September. If blooms are not trimmed off, blooms continue until August. Leaves usually turn yellow, orange, or red for about two weeks in fall, but this color change depends on temperatures and rainfall.

Buying Tips: Varieties that bloom for three months or more include red 'Centennial Spirit' (10 to 20 feet tall), light lavender 'Muskogee' (20 to 25 feet tall) and white, best-selling 'Natchez' (20 to 25 feet tall).

Blue ribbon plants are defined on page 12. For blue ribbon performance, follow the planting and maintenance guidelines on pages 22 to 39.

Resists Deer

Lives on Rain Water *

Attracts Birds

16
Avg. Weeks of Color

Botanical Name: *Lagerstroemia indica* hybrids

Family: Lythraceae

Companions: Crapemyrtles look great lining a street or drive. Or, play up contrast by growing yellow daylilies or black-eyed Susans near red or lavender crapemyrtles.

For a low water use garden, plant crapemyrtle with loropetalum and abelia, as shown below.

GROWING CONDITIONS

Light: Full sun, at least 6 hours per day. The number one reason crapemyrtles don't flower is too much shade.

Water: Very low after establishment. Lives on rainwater alone, without supplemental water, in all but the most extreme conditions.

Soil: Any well-drained soil that is not extremely compacted.

Hardiness: Zones 6 to 10

Propagation: Seeds, rooted cuttings taken in late spring.

Pest Problems: Aphids often are controlled by natural predators, or you can spray infested plants with insecticidal soap. Japanese beetles often eat leaves, but feeding stops as the plants begin to bloom. Older varieties are sometimes weakened by powdery mildew.

PLANTING & MAINTENANCE

When to Plant: If you plant in summer when the plants are blooming, you will be sure of the color. If you plant in fall, however, it will be easier to establish the trees.

Trimming: Many crapemyrtles are radically over-pruned. In late summer, a single deadheading will encourage reblooming, and you can lop off old flower clusters in early winter. Do not cut back plants to their trunks, regardless of what you see happening in your neighbor's yard. Mature crapemyrtles look best when pruning is limited to removing twiggy suckers that spring up around the base of the plant.

Fertilization: Low. Fertilize at planting time with a timed-release product. Less fertilizer is needed with the application of more organics. In the years after planting, fertilization needs vary, based on the nutrients in your soil.

'Ever Red Sunset'
Loropetalum
Plant Profile: Page 228

'Rose Creek' Abelia
Plant Profile: Page 178

Crapemyrtle with some low water-use companions

'Ever Red Sunset' Loropetalum (above, left) is one of the few plants that offers year round color (from its leaves) with very little water. It grows six feet tall, so place it on either side of a taller crapemyrtle. Both plants thrive in sun.

'Rose Creek' Abelia (above, right) is a wonderful shrub that blooms for about six months during spring, summer, and early fall. It grows three to four feet tall, so put it in front of the crapemyrtle and the loropetalum.

*Lives on rainwater alone in all but the most extreme situations

TREES

Cypress, Bald

CHARACTERISTICS

Plant Type: Deciduous tree (loses its leaves in winter).

Average Size: 60 to 80 feet tall by 20 to 40 feet wide.

Growth Rate: Fast

Wind Tolerance: High. (Pond cypress has a low to medium wind tolerance.)

Leaf: Bright green, needle-like leaves, 1/2 to 3/4 inch long, feather-like.

Flower: Inconspicuous

Origin: Native to the southeastern U. S., including Texas.

Spacing: About 40 feet on center (measure from the center of each plant).

Cautions: Almost never damaged by deer.

Colors: Flowers are inconspicuous. Leaves are green in summer and a beautiful shade of coppery orange in fall.

1. *Fall color*
2. *Seeds*

One of the best trees for creating a strong statement in the landscape. Fast-growing with a pyramidal growth habit. Wonderful tree for the home landscape that has plenty of room. Takes wet or dry situations well. Easily wins a blue ribbon* because of high performance with very little care.

Bald cypress in summer and fall

While most people assume that it needs a wet site to grow, bald cypress is tolerant of a wide variety of soil conditions. Once established, this tree can withstand long periods of drought. The strong, vertical growth habit helps to soften large brick homes, and the needle-like leaves have such a soft look and feel in the landscape. Fall color is outstanding, with rich shades of copper standing out in the autumn sun. Since the leaves are so small, leaf litter is not a problem for the homeowner, and fallen leaves can be chopped up by the lawn mower or used as mulch in planting beds. In winter, this tree presents a wonderful silhouette with a flared trunk, reddish-brown fibrous bark, and pyramidal shape. New growth in spring is a wonderful yellow-green that radiates from the brown stems. All in all, bald cypress is an outstanding native tree that produces shade in a hurry.

Color Period: Inconspicuous flowers in March and April. Leaves usually turn coppery orange for about three weeks in fall, but this color change depends on temperatures and rainfall.

Buying Tips: The original, native species, *Taxodium distichum,* is an excellent choice. 'Shawnee Brave' is a cultivar that is narrower (20 feet wide). Pond cypress, *Taxodium ascendens,* is upright, narrow, and has string-like leaves.

Blue ribbon plants are defined on page 12. For blue ribbon performance, follow the planting and maintenance guidelines on pages 22 to 39.

Resists Deer

Lives on Rain Water *

Attracts Birds

Texas Native

③
Avg. Weeks of Color

Botanical Name: *Taxodium distichum*

Family: Taxodiaceae

Companions: Since bald cypress is native and attracts birds, combine it with other natives that also attract wildlife. Bald cypress looks good with plants that have different textures, so look for natives that are coarser. Both wax myrtle and yaupon holly are native, attract birds, and have a coarser texture than the fern-like cypress. All three of these plants need almost no maintenance at all! Combine them as shown below.

Bald cypress and some companions for a low water, low-maintenance garden that attracts birds.

Yaupon Holly (above, left) grows 15 to 20 feet tall, so plant a few on either side of the much taller (60 to 80 feet) bald cypress.

Wax Myrtle (above, right) grows 10 to 15 feet tall in zones six through eight. Plant a group of three in front of the bald cypress. Plant them in full sun so that all three do well.

Lives on rainwater alone in all but the most extreme situations

GROWING CONDITIONS

Light: Full sun

Water: Adapts to wet or dry situations. Can take very low water situations after establishment. Lives on rainwater alone, without supplemental water, in all but the most extreme conditions. See pages 28 to 33 for more information.

Soil: Tolerant of a wide range of soils. Great choice for sites with poor drainage.

Hardiness: Zones 4 to 10

Propagation: Seeds or cuttings

Pest Problems: Rare

PLANTING & MAINTENANCE

When to Plant: Bald cypress from containers can be planted at any time. Fall is best because they establish more easily in cooler weather. Likewise, winter is the best time for balled-and-burlapped cypresses.

Trimming: Trim only to shape trees when young or to raise the canopy. Raising the canopy means removing branches from the trunk that are closest to the ground. The green tree shown on the left (opposite page) has had its canopy raised, while the orange tree on the right has not.

Fertilization: Low. Fertilize at planting time with a timed-release product. Less fertilizer is needed with the application of more organics. In the years after planting, fertilization needs vary, based on the nutrients in your soil. See pages 36 to 39 for more instructions.

Desert Willow

1ST

CHARACTERISTICS

Plant Type: Deciduous tree (loses its leaves in the winter).

Average Size: 15 to 25 feet tall by 15 to 20 feet wide.

Growth Rate: Fast

Leaf: Medium green, willow-like leaves, 3 1/2 inches long by 3/16 inch wide.

Flower: Trumpet-shaped, appearing in showy clusters at the ends of branches; 1 to 1 1/2 inches long, spreading at the opening into five, ruffled, petal-like lobes. Flowers attract hummingbirds.

Origin: West Texas

Spacing: About 10 to 15 feet on center (measure from the center of each plant).

Cautions: Moderately deer resistant.

Colors: White, pink, or burgundy

Slender-twigged, small tree with showy clusters of gorgeous, trumpet-shaped flowers that bloom all season long. Definitely rates a blue ribbon* because of its delicate beauty, long flowering period, drought tolerance, and low maintenance.

Desert willow is an outstanding, native tree that rewards the gardener with an airy, willow-like appearance and attractive flowers all season long. Despite its name, this tree is not a willow at all. Rather, it is related to trumpet vine, crossvine, and catalpa. Because it reaches a mature height of only 25 feet, it easily fits into smaller, suburban landscapes. It casts only light shade, allowing grass to grow beneath it. At the end of the blooming season, pencil-thin seed pods, four to six inches long, appear and persist through the winter. Depending on your viewpoint, these pods either adorn the tree during winter or make it look tacky. For those who don't want to look at the seed pods all winter, there's a seedless variety called 'Art's Seedless.'

Color Period: Blooms continuously May through September for about 20 weeks. Leaves turn yellow in the fall and then drop from the tree.

Buying Tips: Available at better nurseries and garden centers, especially those that sell native plants. You might want to purchase the tree while it is in bloom to make sure of the color.

Blue ribbon plants are defined on page 12. For blue ribbon performance, follow the planting and maintenance guidelines on pages 22 to 39.

Companions: Desert willow combines well with other native, Texas plants such as agarita, dwarf yaupon holly, or yucca.

Mexican feather grass and autumn sage are two more natives that look particularly good with desert willow, as shown below. You can create a strong, regional look with these plants that are so indicative of Texas.

Autumn Sage
Plant Profile: Page 156

Mexican Feather Grass
Plant Profile: Page 130

Desert willow and some companions

Autumn Sage (above, top) is a native perennial that grows two and one half feet tall and wide and blooms April through October, coinciding with the desert willow. Plant autumn sage underneath the open canopy of the desert willow for season-long color and interest.

Mexican Feather Grass (above, bottom) grows 24 to 30 inches tall and assumes an almost weeping form, with foliage as fine as human hair. This light texture really complements the desert willow. Plant a drift of Mexican feather grass under or in front of a desert willow for a striking effect. Plant all three in light shade to full sun.

*Lives on rainwater alone in all but the most extreme situations

GROWING CONDITIONS

Light: Full sun, at least 6 hours per day.

Water: Very low after establishment. Lives on rainwater alone, without supplemental water, in all but the most extreme conditions. See pages 28 to 33 for more information.

Soil: Grows in unimproved soil, including clay, provided the soil has not been compacted. Compaction occurs most commonly from heavy equipment working around a house under construction. See page 27 for instructions on tree planting.

Hardiness: Zones 7 to 9

Propagation: Seeds or cuttings

Pest Problems: None. Resistant to cotton root rot.

PLANTING & MAINTENANCE

When to Plant: Desert willows from containers can be planted at any time. Fall is best because even container specimens establish more easily in cooler weather. Balled-and-burlapped trees are best planted in fall.

Trimming: Trim only to shape trees when young or to raise the canopy. Raising the canopy means removing branches from the trunk that are closest to the ground. Since it blooms on new wood, the more it is trimmed, the more it blooms.

Fertilization: Low. Fertilize at planting time with a timed-release product. Less fertilizer is needed with the application of more organics. In the years after planting, fertilization needs vary, based on the nutrients in your soil. See pages 36 to 39 for more instructions.

TREES

Eastern Red Cedar

Plant Type: Evergreen tree

Average Size: The original native tree is 40 feet tall by 20 feet wide. Cultivars vary from 3 to 25 feet tall by 4 to 12 feet wide. Sizes of some specific cultivars are listed under Buying Tips on this page.

Growth Rate: Medium to fast

Wind Tolerance: Unknown

Leaf: Narrow, scale-like needles; short, about 1 inch long, aromatic when crushed.

Flower: Yellow flower is inconspicuous.

Origin: This tree has the largest native range of any plant in this book. It is native to the entire U.S., with the exception of south Florida.

Spacing: About 20 feet on center (measure from the center of each plant), depending on cultivar.

Cautions: Slightly poisonous. Do not eat this plant. Sap or juice is a skin irritant to some. Pollen from flowers aggravates allergies in some. Almost never damaged by deer.

Colors: Flowers are insignificant. Leaves are different shades of green, including blue-green, light green, and very dark green. Fruit is blue.

One of the most durable trees in Texas, seen in abandoned fields and homesteads. Tolerates extremes of drought, heat, and cold. No ribbon because it gets a few pests.

Eastern red cedar is one of the most common, native trees in Texas. Indigenous to 37 states, its adaptability to a large climate range shows that it is tough enough to take adverse conditions, except for insects and floods. Unfortunately, this tree is susceptible to both bagworms and spider mites; it is an alternate host for cedar apple rust (see "Pest Problems" in the right sidebar), and it will not tolerate wet soils. Its foliage is quite aromatic, however, and varies in color from medium to dark green during the growing season; all foliage may become a bronze-brown in winter. There are separate male and female trees; only the female trees produce the fruits that attract many birds.

Color Period: Foliage is green year round; blue fruits appear only on female trees mid summer until early winter.

Buying Tips: Both the original, native species and the cultivars do equally as well. Most of the cultivars are smaller or are a different shade of green. 'Canaertii,' which features the darkest green foliage, grows 20 feet tall by eight to 15 feet wide in a pyramidal shape. 'Emerald Sentinel,' a lighter shade of green, grows 15 to 20 feet tall by six to eight feet wide. 'Burkii,' with steel blue foliage, grows 10 to 15 feet tall by eight to 10 feet wide.

Attracts Birds

Lives on Rain Water *

Texas Native

Resists Deer

Botanical Name: *Juniperus virginiana*
Family: Cupressaceae

Companions: Eastern red cedars are often planted together to screen an area. Be sure to use the smaller cultivars described in "Buying Tips" on the previous page if you want a screen less than 20 feet wide.

Since eastern red cedars grow to the ground, it is difficult to plant shrubs underneath. Other trees are the best companions. Eastern red cedar is evergreen, so it works well with trees that lose their leaves in winter. When mixing eastern red cedars with other trees, choose different textures, as shown below.

Pistache Tree
Plant Profile: Page 298

'Natchez' Crapemyrtle
Plant Profile: Page 272

Eastern red cedar and some companions

Pistache Tree (above, left) exhibits a completely different texture than the cedar tree, and its brilliant fall color stands out against the dark green of the cedar.

'Natchez' Crapemyrtle (above, right) is one of the tallest crapemyrtles, growing 20 feet tall or more. During the summer, its large clusters of white flowers stand out in stark contrast against the dark green foliage of eastern red cedar. In the fall, the leaves of 'Natchez' turn red and orange and provide even more contrast against the foliage of the cedar.

Lives on rainwater alone in all but the most extreme situations

GROWING CONDITIONS

Light: Full sun

Water: Very low after establishment. Lives on rainwater alone, without supplemental water, in all but the most extreme conditions. Requires good drainage, and dies without it.

Soil: Grows in unimproved soil, including clay, provided the soil has not been compacted. Compaction occurs most commonly from heavy equipment working around a house under construction. See page 27 for instructions on tree planting.

Hardiness: Zones 2 to 9

Propagation: Seeds or cuttings

Pest Problems: Susceptible to bagworms, which can be severe. Spray in May with the least toxic product from your garden center. Also, a host of cedar apple rust, which is only a problem if you grow this tree near apples, crabapples, pyracanthas, or hawthorns.

PLANTING & MAINTENANCE

When to Plant: Eastern red cedar from containers can be planted at any time. Fall is best because they establish more easily in cooler weather. Likewise, late fall or winter are the best times for balled-and-burlapped cedars.

Trimming: Since eastern red cedar grows into a nice, pyramidal form with no shaping, this tree seldom needs any trimming at all. Remove dead branches as needed.

Fertilization: Low. Fertilize at planting time with a timed-release product. Less fertilizer is needed with the application of more organics. In the years after planting, fertilization needs vary, based on the nutrients in your soil. See pages 36 to 39 for more instructions.

Elm, Lacebark and Cedar

CHARACTERISTICS

Plant Type: Deciduous tree (loses its leaves in the winter).

Average Size: Lacebark elm grows 40 to 50 feet tall by 30 to 40 feet wide.

Growth Rate: Fast for lacebark elm; slow to moderate for cedar elm.

Wind Tolerance: 'Drake' elm (a cultivar of lacebark elm, but far from the best one) has a low wind tolerance.

Leaf: Small, dark green, oval leaves with serrated margins measuring 1 to 1 1/2 inches long by 1/2 to 1 inch wide.

Flower: Inconspicuous but occurring in late summer.

Origin: Lacebark elm is from China, Japan, and Korea. Cedar elm is a Texas native.

Spacing: About 50 feet on center (measure from the center of each plant).

Cautions: Juice or sap of the lacebark elm can be a skin irritant. Seldom damaged by deer. Cedar elm can cause allergic reactions.

Colors: Flowers are insignificant. Leaves are green in spring and summer, turning yellow with red-orange hues in fall.

Bark of the lacebark elm

Lacebark elm is an award-winning tree noted for its tough constitution. Performs well as a street tree that handles adverse urban environments. This translates well for the homeowner who, by exercising just a little care, can have a wonderful shade tree in a short period of time. Easily wins a blue ribbon.*

Lacebark elm

Lacebark elm is an excellent, fast-growing shade tree for the home landscape. Dark green foliage with good fall color are fine attributes, but the exfoliating bark is the outstanding characteristic (shown, left). The small leaves make fall cleanup a snap, and fast growth makes it an excellent selection for a new home void of trees. The choice of cultivars with rounded canopies or the striking vase shape of our beloved American elm provides great selections for homeowners.

This elm is known as lacebark elm for good reason - as trees mature, the smooth bark begins peeling away, exposing colors of varying hues of copper and orange.

Color Period: Flowers in late summer, but blooms are inconspicuous. Profuse clusters of small, round seeds appear among the leaves in September or October, maroon in color, somewhat showy. Leaves turn a pale yellow for three to four weeks in the fall and then drop. The orange- and gray-colored, lacy-textured bark stands out year round, but especially in winter after the leaves have dropped.

Buying Tips: Several excellent cultivars are available in local garden centers or online.

Blue ribbon plants are defined on page 12. For blue ribbon performance, follow the planting and maintenance guidelines on pages 22 to 39.

Cedar elm is a large, round-crowned tree with slightly weeping branches at maturity. Native to north central Texas and tough as nails. Rates a blue ribbon* because of its attractive form, tolerance of drought and poor soils, and low maintenance.

Cedar elm

Cedar elm forms a large, attractive tree and, because it is native to north central Texas, thrives in the climate of this region. Each tree has a unique, often irregular form. The small leaves give the tree a neat, clean appearance and don't even need to be raked in the fall because they compost in place so nicely. One of the best characteristics of this tree is its tolerance of heavy clay soils, which may be wet for extended periods of time during spring or fall rains. On the negative side, this tree is susceptible to Dutch elm disease, although that hasn't been a problem in north central Texas. Cedar elm also develops an extensive network of roots in the top 12 inches of the soil, and these roots can easily infiltrate nearby flowerbeds. Lastly, the pollen of the late summer-blooming flowers can bother some people's allergies.

Color Period: Green leaves April through November; yellow leaves late November through December. Green flowers July through August. Green seeds September through October.

Buying Tips: Available in better nurseries, especially those that sell native plants.

GROWING CONDITIONS

Light: Light shade to full sun

Water: Very low after establishment. Lives on rainwater alone, without supplemental water, in all but the most extreme conditions. See pages 28 to 33 for more information.

Soil: Grows in unimproved soil, including clay, provided the soil has not been compacted. Compaction occurs most commonly from heavy equipment working around a house under construction. See page 27 for instructions on tree planting.

Hardiness: Zones 6 to 9

Propagation: Seeds or cuttings

Pest Problems: Lacebark elm is resistant to Dutch elm disease, not affected by elm leaf beetles or Japanese beetles. Cedar elm is susceptible to Dutch elm disease.

PLANTING & MAINTENANCE

When to Plant: Elms from containers can be planted at any time. Fall to spring is best because they establish easier in cooler weather. Stick to the cooler months if you are planting a balled-and-burlapped tree.

Trimming: Trim only to shape trees when young or to raise the canopy. Raising the canopy means removing branches from the trunk that are closest to the ground.

Fertilization: Low. Fertilize at planting time with a timed-release product. Less fertilizer is needed with the application of more organics. In the years after planting, fertilization needs vary, based on the nutrients in your soil. See pages 36 to 39 for more instructions.

Both trees live on rainwater alone in all but the most extreme situations. Only cedar elm is a Texas native and attracts butterflies.

Eve's Necklace

CHARACTERISTICS

Plant Type: Deciduous tree (loses its leaves in the winter).

Average Size: 15 to 25 feet tall by 10 to 20 feet wide.

Growth Rate: Medium

Wind Tolerance: Medium

Leaf: Consists of 6 to 9 pairs of leaflets, each to 1 1/2 inches long and 1/2 to 3/4 inch wide.

Flower: 4- to 6-inch-long clusters of pea-like flowers; each flower is 1/2 inch long. Flowers turn into 4- to 6-inch-long chains of 1/2 inch seeds that look like beads in a necklace.

Origin: Arkansas and Texas

Spacing: About 15 feet on center (measure from the center of each plant).

Cautions: The fruits contain a poisonous substance.

Colors: Leaves are green during summer and yellow in the fall. Flowers are light pink. Fruit is black.

Seeds look like beads in a necklace

After its leaves emerge in the spring, Eve's necklace produces chains of pink, wisteria-like flowers. Eve's necklace rates a blue ribbon* because of its drought tolerance, low maintenance, and decorative flowers and seeds.

Eve's necklace makes a very attractive, small, ornamental tree that works well in smaller yards or as a patio or courtyard tree. It rewards the gardener with chains of pink blossoms in the spring, glossy green leaves all summer, yellow fall color, and decorative seed pods during the fall and winter. As a native tree, it is very easy to grow in a wide range of soils, as long as they are well drained.

Color Period: Leaves turn yellow in fall for two to three weeks. It flowers for a week or so in late spring, and black seed pods remain on the tree in fall and winter.

Buying Tips: Available in better nurseries and garden centers, especially those that sell native plants.

Blue ribbon plants are defined on page 12. For blue ribbon performance, follow the planting and maintenance guidelines on pages 22 to 39.

Companions: Eve's necklace can grow at the edge of or slightly under large shade trees, like shumard oak or cedar elm. It creates a light canopy under which small shrubs, ferns, other perennials, and annuals can grow.

Two other native plants, southern wood fern and Turk's cap, do quite well under the canopy of Eve's necklace, as shown below.

Southern Wood Fern
Plant Profile: Page 126

Turk's Cap
Plant Profile: Page 168

Eve's necklace and some companions

Southern Wood Fern (above, top) grows about two feet tall in light to medium shade. It has lime-green, soft-textured foliage that contrasts with the darker green leaves of Eve's necklace. Create a woodland effect by planting a bed of these ferns under an Eve's necklace.

Turk's Cap (above, bottom) is a native perennial that grows two to three feet tall in full sun or dappled shade. It grows well under the canopy of Eve's necklace. Alternate clumps of the ferns and Turk's cap under the canopy of the Eve's necklace.

*Lives on rainwater alone in all but the most extreme situations

GROWING CONDITIONS

Light: Light shade to full sun

Water: Very low after establishment. Lives on rainwater alone, without supplemental water, in all but the most extreme conditions. See pages 28 to 33 for more information.

Soil: Grows in unimproved soil, including clay, provided that the soil has not been compacted. Compaction occurs most commonly from heavy equipment working around a house under construction. See page 27 for instructions on tree planting.

Hardiness: Zones 7 to 9

Propagation: Seed

Pest Problems: No serious insect or disease problems.

PLANTING & MAINTENANCE

When to Plant: Eve's necklace from containers can be planted at any time. Fall is best because even containerized specimens establish more easily in cooler weather. Balled-and-burlapped trees are best planted in late fall and winter.

Trimming: Trim only to shape trees when young or to raise the canopy. Raising the canopy means removing branches from the trunk that are closest to the ground.

Fertilization: Low. Fertilize at planting time with a timed-release product. Less fertilizer is needed with the application of more organics. In the years after planting, fertilization needs vary, based on the nutrients in your soil. See pages 36 to 39 for more instructions.

TREES

Ginkgo

CHARACTERISTICS

Plant Type: Deciduous tree (loses its leaves in the winter).

Average Size: 50 to 80 feet tall by 30 to 40 feet wide.

Growth Rate: Slow

Wind Tolerance: Medium

Leaf: Very unusual, fan-shaped leaves measuring 2 to 3 inches long by 2 to 3 inches wide. They occur in clusters of 3 to 5 and are a rich, emerald-green color, changing to vibrant, golden yellow in fall.

Flower: Male and female flowers are on separate trees. Both are small and inconspicuous. Select a male plant since the fruit on the female tree has a foul odor.

Origin: China

Spacing: About 40 to 50 feet on center (measure from the center of each plant).

Cautions: Poisonous. Do not eat this plant. Also, sap or juice can be a skin irritant. Odor from female fruits is objectionable (see "Buying Tips," right). Almost never damaged by deer.

Colors: Flowers are insignificant. Leaves are green in summer, turning golden yellow in fall.

A fall day in the presence of a golden ginkgo is truly evidence of nature's handiwork. To see a blanket of gold resting upon a fresh green carpet of grass looks more like a painting than something that nature provides. Rates a blue ribbon* because of its ease of care.

When choosing a ginkgo, make sure you buy a named cultivar so you are positive you have a male tree. The smell from the seeds of a female is memorable and not in a good way. Growth habit and fall color are the basis for cultivar selection, and several make excellent choices. Ginkgos are slow growers but become large trees, so give them room to grow. If space is a factor, try 'Princeton Sentry,' a narrow, columnar tree that does not have a large spread. Ginkgos are not particular about soil and have proven to be excellent urban trees, if given space to grow.

Color Period: Inconspicuous flowers in March or April for two weeks. Leaves turn golden yellow for about two weeks in fall.

Buying Tips: Look for named cultivars when purchasing a ginkgo tree. All named cultivars are male and fruitless. Excellent choices include 'Princeton Sentry' (a very narrow form), 'Autumn Gold' and 'Golden Globe.' All have wonderful, golden yellow, fall color.

*Blue ribbon plants are defined on page 12. For blue ribbon performance, follow the planting and maintenance guidelines on pages 22 to 39.

Companions: Ginkgo looks magnificent as a single specimen with a lawn growing beneath. The blanket of gold created by the fallen leaves is a natural masterpiece.

GROWING CONDITIONS

Light: Full sun, at least 6 hours per day.

Water: Low after establishment. Likes water every week or two during the growing season, depending on its environment. See pages 28 to 33 for more information.

Soil: Grows in unimproved soil, including clay, provided the soil has not been compacted. Compaction occurs most commonly from heavy equipment working around a house under construction. See page 27 for instructions on tree planting.

Hardiness: Zones 4 to 8

Propagation: Seeds or grafts

Pest Problems: Rare

PLANTING & MAINTENANCE

When to Plant: Ginkgo trees from containers can be planted at any time. Fall is best because they establish more easily in cooler weather. Late fall and winter are the best times for balled-and-burlapped ginkgos.

Trimming: Trim only to shape trees when young or to raise the canopy. Raising the canopy means removing branches from the trunk that are closest to the ground.

Fertilization: Low. Fertilize at planting time with a timed-release product. Less fertilizer is needed with the application of more organics. In the years after planting, fertilization needs vary, based on the nutrients in your soil. See pages 36 to 39 for more instructions.

TREES

Holly, Yaupon

CHARACTERISTICS

Plant Type: Evergreen tree

Average Size: 15 to 20 feet tall by 8 to 12 feet wide.

Growth Rate: Medium

Wind Tolerance: High

Leaf: 1 1/2 inches long by 1/2 inch wide. Oval with slightly-serrated margins. No spines.

Flower: Inconspicuous, greenish-white flowers in spring.

Origin: Southeastern U.S.

Spacing: About 10 to 15 feet on center (measure from the center of each plant).

Cautions: Poisonous. Do not eat this plant. Hollies attract quite a few bees when they bloom. Seldom damaged by deer.

Colors: Flowers are greenish-white, but inconspicuous. Leaves are glossy and medium green. Berries are bright red.

Dwarf yaupon holly is used as a shrub.

Outstanding, small, award-winning tree. Native evergreen that provides berries for birds. Needs no irrigation after establishment. Takes sun or shade. Extremely easy, so it rates a blue ribbon.*

Yaupon holly is the ideal, small tree, having all the characteristics that most homeowners want. It grows quickly, is evergreen, attracts birds, needs little water, grows in sun or shade, adapts to a variety of soils, and seldom needs fertilizer or trimming. Not too many plants exhibit that many positive characteristics. However, yaupon holly looks different from the more common hollies we use for holiday decorations. Instead of the coarse leaves with spines, its leaves are smaller, with only slightly serrated margins. It looks best grown as a multi-trunked tree, like a crapemyrtle, rather than with a single trunk. Its branches will grow to the ground, or you can trim off the bottom branches to expose the trunk. Let it grow into a natural form instead of trimming it into a lollipop shape.

Color Period: Blooms in April with inconspicuous flowers. The berries give the most color. They appear in late October or early November and persist through the winter. Only female trees produce berries.

Buying Tips: 'Folsom's Weeping' is the most popular weeping form. Favorite upright forms that have the most fruit include 'Shadow's Female,' 'Kathy Ann,' and 'Pride of Houston.'

Blue ribbon plants are defined on page 12. For blue ribbon performance, follow the planting and maintenance guidelines on pages 22 to 39.

Companions: Yaupon hollies are often planted in groups for screening. They also fit well with other native trees, like bald cypress and eastern red cedar.

For a low water-use garden, combine yaupon holly with lantana and 'Hameln' grass, as shown below.

'New Gold' Lantana
Plant Profile: Page 68

'Hameln' Dwarf
Fountain Grass
Plant Profile: Page 130

Yaupon holly and some companions

'New Gold' Lantana (above, left) is an annual that is one of the best butterfly attractors. It grows about two feet tall and blooms all spring, summer, and all fall. Plant it under the holly but in an area where it gets full sun.

'Hameln' Dwarf Fountain Grass (above, right) is a perennial grass that blooms from July until October with the lantana. It also lives on very little extra water. Since it reaches about two feet tall, plant it along-side of the lantana.

GROWING CONDITIONS

Light: Light shade to full sun

Water: Very low after establishment. Lives on rainwater alone, without supplemental water, in all but the most extreme conditions. See pages 28 to 33 for more information.

Soil: Grows in unimproved soil, including clay, provided the soil has not been compacted. Compaction occurs most commonly from heavy equipment working around a house under construction. See page 27 for instructions on tree planting.

Hardiness: Zones 7 to 10

Propagation: Seeds or cuttings

Pest Problems: Rare

PLANTING & MAINTENANCE

When to Plant: Hollies from containers can be planted at any time. Fall is best because they establish more easily in cooler weather. Late fall and winter are the best times for balled-and-burlapped hollies.

Trimming: Yaupon holly seldom needs trimming. Let it grow into a natural form instead of trimming it into a lollipop shape. It looks best grown as a multi-trunked tree, like a crapemyrtle, rather than with a single trunk. Its branches will grow to the ground, or you can trim off the bottom branches to expose the trunk. Remove the suckers (small branches) that emerge from the bottom, if you like.

Fertilization: Low. Fertilize at planting time with a timed-release product. Less fertilizer is needed with the application of more organics. In the years after planting, fertilization needs vary, based on the nutrients in your soil. See pages 36 to 39 for more instructions.

TREES

Lives on rainwater alone in all but the most extreme situations

Magnolia, Southern & 'Little Gem'

CHARACTERISTICS

Plant Type: Evergreen tree

Average Size: 'Little Gem' is 15 to 20 feet tall by 10 feet wide. Southern is 60 to 80 feet tall by 30 to 45 feet wide.

Growth Rate: Slow to medium

Wind Tolerance: High

Leaf: Leaves are dark, glossy green on top and rusty brown underneath. 'Little Gem' leaves measure 3 to 4 inches long by 1 to 2 inches wide. Southern magnolia's leaves reach 6 to 10 inches long by 3 to 5 inches wide

Flower: Large, white, fragrant flowers measure 3 to 4 inches wide on 'Little Gem' and 8 to 12 inches wide on the southern. Red seeds, quite attractive to birds, appear in fall.

Origin: Southeastern U.S., west to Texas.

Spacing: About 20 feet on center for 'Little Gem' and 25 to 30 feet on center for southern magnolias planted as a screen (measure from the center of each plant).

Cautions: Seldom damaged by deer. Bees love flowers.

Colors: White flowers. Leaves are green on top and rust on the bottom.

Summer in Texas means the sweet smell of magnolia blossoms in the air. Large, southern magnolias dominate the landscape where planted. Give this tree room to grow, and you will be amply rewarded with beautiful flowers, intoxicating fragrance, bright red fruits, and glossy green foliage. Rates a blue ribbon* because of its ease of care.

Southern magnolia

Southern magnolia has become one of the most widely planted trees throughout the southern states. The thick, coarse texture of the magnolia is a testament to its strength and longevity. Southern magnolias still dot antebellum plantations and provide breathtaking beauty and fragrance when in bloom. Magnolias look best when the lower branches grow to the ground.

Color Period: Heavy flower production in May and June; blooms sporadically through the rest of summer.

Buying Tips: Numerous cultivars are available, selected for uniform growth habit, size, and leaf color, especially the presence of the rusty brown texture on the underside of the leaves. If planting more than one southern magnolia, it is best to plant a cultivar, so your trees will grow uniformly. Excellent choices include 'D.D. Blanchard,' 'Claudia Wannamaker,' 'Bracken's Brown Beauty,' and 'Cinnamon Twist.'

Blue ribbon plants are defined on page 12. For blue ribbon performance, follow the planting and maintenance guidelines on pages 22 to 39.

Botanical Name: *Magnolia grandiflora,*
Magnolia grandiflora 'Little Gem'
Family: Magnoliaceae

Smaller in stature than its older brother, 'Little Gem' is definitely not short on performance. Flowers, fragrance, and foliage are all beautiful in a dense, compact package.

'Little Gem' magnolia

For the home landscape, 'Little Gem' magnolia is most often the best choice due to its smaller size and stature. The beautiful, dark green foliage with rusty brown undersides creates a thick screen or hedge, and the flower production on this magnolia is fantastic. This is a perfect magnolia for creating an espalier on a large, brick wall or fence. Again, understand the full size before placing in the landscape, and you will be rewarded with years of beauty.

Color Period: Heavy flower production in May and June and then sporadically throughout the rest of summer. Green foliage year round. Tan cone splits to expose bright red seeds.

Buying Tips: The 'Little Gem' is the southern magnolia sold as a "dwarf." While much smaller in stature than southern magnolia, it still can reach heights of 20 feet. Other dense, compact selections include 'Teddy Bear,' 'Alta,' and 'Greenback."

GROWING CONDITIONS

Light: Light shade to full sun

Water: Low after establishment. Likes water every week or two during the growing season, depending on its environment. See pages 28 to 33 for more information.

Soil: Grows in unimproved soil, including clay, provided the soil has not been compacted. Compaction occurs most commonly from heavy equipment working around a house under construction. See page 27 for instructions on tree planting.

Hardiness: Zones 6 to 9. Trees in zone 6 may experience winter burn.

Propagation: Cuttings

Pest Problems: Rare. Root rot can develop if plants are kept too wet.

PLANTING & MAINTENANCE

When to Plant: Magnolias from containers can be planted at any time. Fall is best because they establish more easily in cooler weather. Late fall or winter are the best times for balled-and-burlapped magnolias.

Trimming: Since magnolias grow into a nice, pyramidal form with no shaping, this seldom needs any trimming at all. Remove dead branches as needed.

Fertilization: Low. Fertilize at planting time with a timed-release product. Less fertilizer is needed with the application of more organics. In the years after planting, fertilization needs vary, based on the nutrients in your soil. See pages 36 to 39 for more instructions.

TREES

Maple, Japanese and Shantung

CHARACTERISTICS

Plant Type: Deciduous tree (loses its leaves in the winter).

Average Size: Japanese maples grow 15 to 20 feet tall by 10 to 20 feet wide. Shantung maples grow 25 feet tall by 20 feet wide.

Growth Rate: For Japanese maples, slow growth rate, if grafted; medium for seedlings. Shantung maple has a medium rate of growth.

Wind Tolerance: Medium for Japanese maples; high for shantung maples.

Leaf: For Japanese maples, delicate leaves 2 to 5 inches long by same width. Rich colors of green to deep burgundy available - all with excellent fall color. For shantung maples, medium green leaves up to 5 inches across with 5 lobes.

Flower: Insignificant

Origin: Japan and Korea for Japanese maple; China for shantung maple.

Spacing: For Japanese maples, about 15 to 20 feet on center (measure from the center of each plant). For shantung maples, 20 feet on center.

Cautions: Japanese maples occasionally damaged by deer. Shantung maples can cause toxicity problems in some animals.

Colors: Japanese maple leaves are available in rich colors of green to deep burgundy, all with excellent fall color. Shantung has medium green leaves in summer. Fall color is golden yellow with some orange and red mixed in. 'Fire Dragon' has consistent red fall color.

Japanese maple is a true aristocrat of the garden. Delicate, lacy, and formal in appearance, Japanese maples exude an aura of importance and dignity as they take their place of prominence in the landscape. They are pickier than most trees, however, requiring well-drained, organically-enriched soil, more than average water, and protection from late afternoon sun and scorching winds. They miss a ribbon for these reasons.

Aristocratic, regal, and statuesque are all apt descriptions of how a Japanese maple fills a space. Decide whether you want an upright-growing selection that makes a small tree or a weeping selection that fills a space from the top down. The next choice is color, as Japanese maples come in a wide variety of greens, rusts, and reds. Japanese maples require more water than most of the trees in this book. And, it sometimes leafs out before the last frost, which can weaken the tree. Visit the Fort Worth Botanic Garden's Japanese Garden around Thanksgiving for a spectacular show of fall color from the Japanese maples.

Color Period: Insignificant flowers appear in April for about two weeks. Japanese maples with rust or burgundy leaves have color all season. All Japanese and shantung maples have fall color for about two to three weeks.

Buying Tips: Excellent, red-leafed cultivars for north central Texas include 'Bloodgood,' 'Emperor I,' 'Crimson Queen,' and 'Fire Glow.' Green-leafed selections include 'Viridis' and 'Osakazuki.'

A Texas Superstar™ plant, shantung maple definitely rates a blue ribbon* for its tolerance of a wide range of soils, heat, and drought. Nurseryman Keith Johansson of Metro Maples Nursery calls shantung maple "the tree of the millennium" and thinks it is the best shade tree the Dallas-Fort Worth metroplex has ever had!

Shantung maple in fall

Shantung maple is an ideal-sized tree for smaller, suburban lots in north central Texas. One of its best features is brilliant, fall color. And because the leaves are thick and waxy, they do not lose a lot of water during our hot summers. With age, the bark becomes deeply fissured and very attractive; the wood is strong and resistant to ice and wind storms. Shantung maple tolerates a wide range of soils, both acidic and alkaline, as long as the soil is not water-logged. This tree holds up to full sun and the Texas heat.

Color Period: Small, insignificant flowers in April. Green leaves all summer long. Spectacular fall color for two to three weeks.

Buying Tips: Metro Maples in Mansfield, Texas, has the best selection of shantung maples in the Dallas-Fort Worth metroplex. Visit this nursery online at www.metromaples.com. Choose the cultivar 'Fire Dragon' if you want consistent, red, fall color year after year.

GROWING CONDITIONS

Light: Morning sun to light shade for Japanese maple; full sun for shantung maple.

Water: Medium after establishment for Japanese maple. Likes water once or twice a week during the growing season, depending on its environment. For shantung maple, low after establishment, meaning water every week or two. See pages 28 to 33 for more information.

Soil: Plant in any fertile, well-drained soil that has been enriched with organic matter. This tree cannot tolerate poor drainage. See page 24 for specific instructions on soil preparation.

Hardiness: Zones 5 to 8

Propagation: Seeds or grafts

Pest Problems: Rare

PLANTING & MAINTENANCE

When to Plant: Japanese and shantung maples from containers can be planted at any time. Fall is best because they establish more easily in cooler weather. Late fall and winter are the best times for balled-and-burlapped maples. Take care not to plant these trees too deeply.

Trimming: Trim only to shape trees when young or to raise the canopy. Raising the canopy means removing branches from the trunk that are closest to the ground.

Fertilization: Medium. Fertilize at planting time and each spring with a timed-release product. Less fertilizer is needed with the application of more organics. See pages 36 to 39 for more instructions.

TREES

Blue ribbon plants are defined on page 12. For blue ribbon performance, follow the planting and maintenance guidelines on pages 22 to 39.

Oaks, Bur and Lacey

CHARACTERISTICS

Plant Type: Deciduous tree (loses its leaves in the winter).

Average Size: Bur oak grows 60 to 80 feet tall and 60 to 80 feet wide. Lacey oak grows up to 35 feet tall by 30 feet wide.

Growth Rate: Slow to moderate for bur oak; moderate for lacey oak.

Wind Tolerance: Medium

Leaf: Bur oak has leaves 6 to 10 inches long, 4 to 5 inches wide; 5 to 9 lobes separated by deep cuts; dark green above, pale green underneath. Lacey oak has leathery, oblong-shaped leaves with a few shallow lobes.

Flower: On the bur oak, inconspicuous male and female flowers appear on the same tree in the spring. The lacey oak has yellow, drooping flower spikes in the spring that are rather inconspicuous.

Origin: Bur oak is native from the eastern U.S. to Texas. Lacey oak is native to central Texas.

Spacing: For the bur oak, 60 to 80 feet on center (measure from the center of each plant). For lacey oak, 20 to 30 feet on center.

Cautions: Bur oak acorns and leaves have low toxicity if eaten, and the tree is sensitive to root zone disturbance caused by construction. Deer will eat lacey oak foliage.

Colors: Bur oak has dark green leaves during summer, dull yellow-brown leaves in fall. Lacey oak leaves are peach in the spring, blue-green in summer, and peach in the fall.

Bur oak forms a huge, majestic tree that likes plenty of room. Tough and durable. Tolerant of poor soils and low rainfall. Bur oak definitely rates a blue ribbon* because of its low maintenance.

Above, mature bur oak; below, large acorns that grow as large as golf balls

Bur oak is a native tree, adapts to a wide range of soils, and tolerates drought. It is definitely not for small yards. This slow growing, long-lived oak rewards the gardener with large, attractive leaves and plenty of shade when it reaches its mature size. Bur oak produces very large acorns, almost golf ball size. The acorn sits in a deep cup that has coarse scales and a fringed margin. It is resistant to oak wilt.

Color Period: Yellow-brown fall color for two to three weeks.

Buying Tips: Available in nurseries and garden centers.

Blue ribbon plants are defined on page 12. For blue ribbon performance, follow the planting and maintenance guidelines on pages 22 to 39.

Lacey oak's most appealing feature is its foliage. The leaves emerge a peach color in spring, turn a beautiful blue-green in summer, and turn peach again in the fall. Lacey oak deserves a blue ribbon* because it tolerates alkaline soil, high heat, and drought.

Above, mature lacey oak; below, leaves of the lacey oak

Lacey oak is an attractive small to medium-sized tree that is ideal for small yards. Branches are erect and spreading, and the tree can have single or multiple trunks. The more trunks the tree has, the smaller it is. This is a good tree for a wildscape because it provides food and cover for small mammals and birds. It is native to limestone or rocky soils, but it will tolerate a wide range of soils as long as they are well drained.

Color Period: Leaves assume a different color in spring, summer, and fall.

Buying Tips: Available in nurseries and garden centers, especially those that sell native plants.

GROWING CONDITIONS

Light: Full sun for bur oak; light shade to full sun for lacey oak.

Water: Very low after establishment. Lives on rainwater alone, without supplemental water, in all but the most extreme conditions. See pages 28 to 33 for more information.

Soil: Grows in unimproved soil, including clay, provided the soil has not been compacted. Compaction occurs most commonly from heavy equipment working around a house under construction. See page 27 for instructions on tree planting.

Hardiness: Zones 3 to 9 for bur oak; zones 8 to 9 for lacey oak.

Propagation: Fresh acorns

Pest Problems: No serious insect or disease problems.

PLANTING & MAINTENANCE

When to Plant: Bur and lacey oaks from containers can be planted at any time. Fall is best because they establish more easily in cooler weather. Likewise, fall is the best time for balled-and-burlapped oaks.

Trimming: Trim only to shape trees when young or to raise the canopy. Raising the canopy means removing branches from the trunk that are closest to the ground.

Fertilization: Low. Fertilize at planting time with a timed-release product. Less fertilizer is needed with the application of more organics. In the years after planting, fertilization needs vary, based on the nutrients in your soil. See pages 36 to 39 for more instructions.

Both oaks live on just rainwater in all but the most extreme conditions. Only the bur oak attracts butterflies.

TREES

Oaks, Live and Shumard

1ST

CHARACTERISTICS

Plant Type: Live oak is evergreen; shumard oak is deciduous (loses its leaves in the winter).

Average Size: Live oak grows 40 to 80 feet tall by 60 to 100 feet wide. Shumard oak grows 80 to 100 feet tall by 50 to 60 feet wide.

Growth Rate: Live oak is a slow to moderate grower, whereas shumard oak is a moderate to rapid grower.

Wind Tolerance: High for live oak; unknown for shumard oak.

Leaf: Live oak has leathery, elliptical leaves 1 1/2 to 4 inches long by 1/2 to 2 inches wide; dark green above and a lighter, gray-green underneath. Shumard oak has leaves 4 to 8 inches long by 3 to 6 inches wide, oval in outline, but with 7 to 9 lobes; glossy and dark green above with paler green underneath.

Flower: Live oak has male and female flowers on the same tree; female flowers are inconspicuous, but long yellow male catkins (drooping flower spikes) form in early spring. Shumard oak has male and female flowers on the same tree; not showy.

Origin: Both are native to the southeastern U.S., including Texas.

Spacing: 60 to 100 feet on center (measure from the center of each plant) for live oak; 50 to 60 feet on center for shumard.

Cautions: Avoid pruning both trees February 1 to June 1 to prevent the spread of oak wilt.

Colors: Live oak is green throughout the year. Shumard oak is dark green during the summer and orange to red in the fall.

Live oak is a spectacular and long-lived tree that needs plenty of room to do it justice. Its only liability is its susceptibility to oak wilt, a fungal disease that interferes with the tree's ability to conduct water to its extremities. This is still a blue ribbon* plant because of its tolerance of a wide range of soils and drought.

Live oak is the majestic, Spanish moss-laden tree of southern plantations. Its horizontal and arching branches form a round crown that can spread twice its height. Live oak is a tough tree that tolerates poor soils, a range of soil pH, and drought. It is a good choice for urban areas because of its tolerance of soil compaction and disturbance of soil around its root system.

Color Period: Green leaves year round. Flowers are insignificant.

Buying Tips: Readily available in nurseries and garden centers.

*Blue ribbon plants are defined on page 12. For blue ribbon performance, follow the planting and maintenance guidelines on pages 22 to 39.

Wonderful, native oak with brilliant, red, fall color. Excellent tree for a wide variety of soil types, even drier limestone soils and those with high pH levels. Fast growth and easy care are great attributes of this long-lived, blue ribbon* shade tree.

Shumard oak

Far superior to pin oak in the landscape, shumard oak does not suffer from the unsightly chlorosis (leaf yellowing) that often plagues pin oak. This is an excellent tree for street tree plantings in urban environments and for use as a large shade tree on the lawn. Foliage develops brilliant red to orange colors in the fall. Shumard oak is an outstanding shade tree for the long haul - it will give you many years of superb service, providing cooling shade in summer, outstanding fall color, and a distinctive, statuesque form in the winter landscape. Shumard oaks attract much attention during the fall at the Fort Worth Botanic Garden.

Color Period: Insignificant flowers for about two weeks in April. Leaves usually turn red to orange for two to three weeks in fall, but this color change depends on temperatures and rainfall.

Buying Tips: The original, native species is the only one available, and you can't go wrong with it. No cultivars have been developed yet.

*Lives on rainwater alone in all but the most extreme situations

GROWING CONDITIONS

Light: Full sun

Water: Very low after establishment. Lives on rainwater alone, without supplemental water, in all but the most extreme conditions.

Soil: Grows in unimproved soil, including clay, provided the soil has not been compacted. Compaction occurs most commonly from heavy equipment working around a house under construction. See page 27 for instructions on tree planting.

Hardiness: Zones 7 to 10 for live oak; zones 4 to 9 for shumard oak.

Propagation: Acorns

Pest Problems: Both are susceptible to oak wilt. To protect these trees, avoid pruning February 1 to June 1, the period when fungal mats and nitidulid beetles are most active.

PLANTING & MAINTENANCE

When to Plant: Live oak and shumard oak from containers can be planted at any time. Fall is best because they establish more easily in cooler weather. Late fall and winter are the best times for balled-and-burlapped live and shumard oaks.

Trimming: Trim only to shape trees when young or to raise the canopy. Raising the canopy means removing branches from the trunk that are closest to the ground. The best time to prune is December 1 to February 1. Protect cuts and wounds greater than 1/2 inch in diameter by painting them with latex paint within a few minutes of pruning.

Fertilization: Low. Fertilize at planting time with a timed-release product. Less fertilizer is needed with the application of more organics. In the years after planting, fertilization needs vary, based on the nutrients in your soil.

TREES

Palms

CHARACTERISTICS

Plant Type: Evergreen tree, although the needle palm is so short it is also considered a shrub.

Average Size: Varies by type

Wind Tolerance: Varies according to variety.

Growth Rate: All four of these palms grow slowly, particularly at the northern limits of their temperature range.

Leaf: European fan palm's leaves are about 2 feet in diameter. California fan palm has leaves 3 to 6 feet across. Windmill palm leaves are 2 to 3 feet wide. Needle palm leaves are 3 feet wide.

Flower: Insignificant

Origin: Needle palms are native to the southeastern U.S. European fan palms are native to the Mediterranean region. Windmill palms come from China. California fan palms are native to southern California.

Spacing: About 5 to 10 feet on center (measure from the center of each plant).

Cautions: Sap is a skin irritant to some. European fan palms have sharp spines along the fronds. Windmill and needle palms are slightly spiny.

Colors: Flowers are insignificant. Leaves are different shades of green.

These are exceptionally easy palms for north central Texas. They require little water and easily win a blue ribbon.*

Needle palm, Rhapidophyllum hystrix

The needle palm (shown, above) is one of the most cold-hardy palms, performing well in the southern half of zone seven through zone 10. It provides a wonderful, large, evergreen mass of coarse textured-foliage and requires no maintenance at all. The name comes from the six-inch-long, black needles that protrude from the leaf stalk that protect the plant's seeds. These needles make the plant deer-proof, so this is an excellent choice for gardeners who are struggling to confound deer. It is a slow-growing, rather shrubby palm that reaches only six to eight feet tall by four to eight feet wide.

Cold tolerance is more important for palms than for most other types of plants. If the new bud (growth emerging from the center) of the palm is killed, the entire plant dies. (Not so for most other plants. If the new growth dies on them, the roots still live.) If temperatures should drop too low, wrap the crown to protect the new bud.

Palms are ideal candidates for containers, particularly European fan palms and windmill palms. They stay for many years in the same pot without the need for transplanting to a larger container.

Regional Differences: Dependable as far north as zone eight, although needle palms will grow in zone seven.

Color Period: Green foliage year round

Buying Tips: These palms are becoming more available every year in garden centers. All of them grow slowly, so buy the largest one you can find or afford. For more information about hardy palms for north central Texas, visit www.dallaspalms.com.

Blue ribbon plants are defined on page 12. For blue ribbon performance, follow the planting and maintenance guidelines on pages 22 to 39.

European Fan Palm (*Chamaerops humilis,* left). A slow-growing palm that looks shrub-like until it is old enough to develop a trunk. Single and multiple trunk specimens available.

Grows 10 feet tall eventually, but very slowly. Very low water requirements after establishment. Light shade to full sun. Zones eight to ten.

California Fan Palm (*Washingtonia filifera,* right). A slow to moderate grower, this tree grows 30 to 40 feet with a crown 12 to 18 feet wide. Tolerates heat and dry conditions. Performs well in a wide range of soils, including extreme alkaline soils that have a pH as high as 9.2. This palm is very disease and pest resistant and withstands temperatures of 15 to 20 degrees with only minor foliage damage. Prefers full sun but will also grow well in part sun. Zones eight to 11.

Windmill Palm (*Trachycarpus fortunei,* left). One of the best cold-hardy palms.

Slowly grows to 25 feet tall. Needs regular watering to thrive. Light shade is best. Southern parts of zone seven to zone 10.

GROWING CONDITIONS

Light: Light shade to full sun

Water: Low after establishment for European and California fan palms. They like water every week or two during the growing season depending on the environment. Windmill palm may need water once or twice a week during the growing season to thrive and look good. They grow faster with water 2 or 3 times a week. (All palms need supplemental water for the two years after they have been transplanted.)

Soil: European fan and California fan palms adjust to poor soil as long as it is well drained. Fertile, well-drained soil high in organic matter is best for needle and windmill palms.

Hardiness: Zones 8 to 11 for the European fan and California fan palms; 7B to 10 for windmill and needle palms.

Propagation: Seeds

Pest Problems: European fan palm is susceptible to scale, ganoderma, and potassium deficiency. Windmill palm is moderately susceptible to lethal yellowing.

PLANTING & MAINTENANCE

When to Plant: Anytime

Trimming: Trim off the old fronds if they persist on the trunk after they turn brown. Don't pull them off the trunk, or you could damage it.

Fertilization: European fan palms have a low need for fertilizer. Windmill, California fan and needle palms have a medium fertilization need. Fertilize at planting time with a timed-release product. Less fertilizer is needed with the application of more organics.

TREES

Pistache or Chinese Pistache

1ST

CHARACTERISTICS

Plant Type: Deciduous tree (loses its leaves in the winter).

Average Size: 30 to 40 feet tall by 20 to 30 feet wide.

Growth Rate: Medium

Leaf: Compound green leaves measuring 8 to 10 inches long with even rows of 10 to 12 lance-shaped leaflets, 4 inches long by 1 inch wide. Foliage is aromatic when crushed.

Flower: Dioecious (meaning male and female flowers on separate trees). Flowers are small, greenish in color, but not very showy. Blue fruit clusters on female trees are enjoyed by birds.

Origin: China, Philippines

Spacing: About 30 to 40 feet on center (measure from the center of each plant).

Cautions: Seldom damaged by deer.

Colors: Flowers are small, greenish, and inconspicuous. Leaves are bright red to orange to yellow in fall. Fruit clusters are blue.

A medium-sized tree, it is a perfect solution for lot sizes that cannot take the larger sizes found in oaks and maples. A fast grower that requires little care, it rates a blue ribbon.* Brilliant fall color stops traffic.

Pistache literally sets the landscape on fire during the fall of the year. Its bright red canopy cannot be ignored by those passing by this magnificent tree.

When faced with a site with poor soils, pistache fits the bill. Excellent plantings can be found along interstate interchanges and harsh, urban environments. Once established, pistache can withstand prolonged droughts and is not bothered by insects or diseases. A little gangly when young, the canopy matures to a nice, rounded crown with age.

Color Period: Flowers appear in April, but they are greenish and inconspicuous. Fruit clusters are blue and borne in fall. Leaves usually turn red, orange, or yellow for two to three weeks in fall, but this color change depends on temperatures and rainfall.

Buying Tips: This tree is available in many garden centers.

Blue ribbon plants are defined on page 12. For blue ribbon performance, follow the planting and maintenance guidelines on pages 22 to 39.

Companions: Chinese pistache looks great planted alone in a lawn, which grows well underneath it. Groundcovers and small perennials or evergreen shrubs can be planted under the canopy as well. Mondo grass and ferns are good choices for under this tree, as shown below.

Autumn Fern
Plant Profile: Page 126

Mondo Grass
Plant Profile: Page 128

Chinese pistache and some companions

Autumn Fern (above, left) is one of the few evergreen ferns. Since Chinese pistache loses its leaves in winter, it is nice to have something evergreen beneath the tree. The autumn fern grows two to two and a half feet tall and likes shade.

Mondo Grass (above, right) is an evergreen grass-like groundcover that grows three to six inches tall, depending upon variety. Mondo grass is an ideal groundcover under trees because it is very easy to rake through when the tree leaves drop in the fall.

GROWING CONDITIONS

Light: Full sun

Water: Low after establishment. Likes water every week or two during the growing season, depending on its environment. See pages 28 to 33 for more information.

Soil: Grows in unimproved soil, including clay, provided the soil has not been compacted. Compaction occurs most commonly from heavy equipment working around a house under construction. See page 27 for instructions on tree planting.

Hardiness: Zones 6 to 9

Propagation: Seeds

Pest Problems: Rare

PLANTING & MAINTENANCE

When to Plant: Chinese pistaches from containers can be planted at any time. Fall is best because they establish more easily in cooler weather. Stick to the colder months (fall to winter) if you are planting a balled-and-burlapped tree.

Trimming: Trim only to shape trees when young or to raise the canopy. Raising the canopy means removing branches from the trunk that are closest to the ground.

Fertilization: Low. Fertilize at planting time with a timed-release product. Less fertilizer is needed with the application of more organics. In the years after planting, fertilization needs vary, based on the nutrients in your soil. See pages 36 to 39 for more instructions.

TREES

Plum, Mexican

CHARACTERISTICS

Plant Type: Deciduous tree (loses its leaves in the winter).

Average Size: 15 to 35 feet tall by up to 20 feet wide.

Growth Rate: Medium

Leaf: Up to 5 inches long by 2 inches wide with finely-serrated margins; medium green during summer and yellow, orange and red in the fall.

Flower: White, 1-inch-wide, honey-scented flowers in early spring. Small, oval-shaped plums appear in late summer and change color from yellow to mauve to purple as they ripen from July through September. These fruits are appealing to the eye as well as to birds and small mammals

Origin: Southeastern U.S. and Great Plains states, including Texas.

Spacing: About 20 feet on center (measure from the center of each plant).

Cautions: Susceptible to deer. Don't plant next to a driveway, sidewalk, or patio because the fruits will drop and create a mess on the pavement.

Colors: White flowers in early spring, bright green foliage during summer, and shades of yellow, orange, and red in fall.

The profusion of white blossoms on this small tree in early spring creates the appearance of clouds in the landscape. The flowers have a wonderful fragrance like that of honey and attract butterflies. This is an excellent, native tree with year round interest. Rates a blue ribbon* for its springtime beauty, adaptability to a wide range of soils, and drought tolerance.

Mexican plum announces the arrival of spring with its abundance of fragrant, white blossoms. After the flowers disappear, bright green foliage covers the tree during the summer. From mid summer through fall, beautifully-colored fruits adorn the tree and beckon birds and wildlife. Shades of yellow, orange, and red embellish the tree in the fall. An easy tree to grow, Mexican plum makes an outstanding tree for small lots or an understory tree beneath the canopy of larger trees.

Color Period: White blossoms for seven to 10 days in March; green leaves in summer; colorful foliage two to three weeks in the fall. Dark, attractive trunk stands out in winter.

Buying Tips: Available in garden centers and nurseries, especially those that sell native plants.

Blue ribbon plants are defined on page 12. For blue ribbon performance, follow the planting and maintenance guidelines on pages 22 to 39.

Attracts Butterflies

Attracts Birds

Lives on Rain Water

5
Avg. Weeks of Color

Texas Native

Botanical Name: *Prunus mexicana*
Family: Rosaceae

Companions: Mexican plum combines well with other, early, spring-flowering shrubs and trees, like agarita and forsythia. Redbuds and daffodils also bloom in spring and create traffic-stopping color when combined with this plum, as shown below.

Daffodil
Plant Profile: Page 120

Redbud
Plant Profile: Page 302

Mexican plum and some companions

Daffodils (above, left) bloom at the same time as Mexican plum. Most reach a height of 16 inches and produce one to several bright yellow flowers per stem, depending on variety. Plant a large drift of daffodils under and around Mexican plum for a stunning springtime display.

Redbud (above, right) is a small tree that corresponds to Mexican plum in both size and bloom time. The magenta-colored flowers that line the bare branches of redbud really stand out against the white blossoms of Mexican plum. Plant the trees together along your property line or as understory trees in wooded areas for a spectacular profusion of color in spring.

*Lives on rainwater alone in all but the most extreme situations

GROWING CONDITIONS

Light: Light shade to full sun

Water: Very low after establishment. Lives on rainwater alone, without supplemental water, in all but the most extreme conditions. See pages 28 to 33 for more information.

Soil: Grows in unimproved soil, including clay, provided the soil has not been compacted. Compaction occurs most commonly from heavy equipment working around a house under construction. See page 27 for instructions on tree planting.

Hardiness: Zones 4 to 8

Propagation: Seeds or cuttings

Pest Problems: No serious insect or pest problems.

PLANTING & MAINTENANCE

When to Plant: Mexican plums from containers can be planted at any time. Fall is best because they establish more easily in cooler weather. Late fall and winter are the best times for balled-and-burlapped trees.

Trimming: Trim only to shape trees when young or to raise the canopy. Raising the canopy means removing branches from the trunk that are closest to the ground.

Fertilization: Low. Fertilize at planting time with a timed-release product. Less fertilizer is needed with the application of more organics. In the years after planting, fertilization needs vary, based on the nutrients in your soil. See pages 36 to 39 for more instructions.

Redbud, Texas and Mexican

1ST

CHARACTERISTICS

Plant Type: Deciduous tree (loses its leaves in the winter).

Average Size: 15 to 20 feet tall and wide for Texas redbud; 10 to 15 feet tall and wide for Mexican redbud.

Growth Rate: Medium

Wind Tolerance: Medium

Leaf: Both trees have thick, heart-shaped green leaves. The leaves of Mexican redbud are simply smaller and glossier than its Texas counterpart.

Flower: Both have magenta, 1/2-inch-long, pea-like flowers.

Origin: Texas redbud is native to central and north central Texas. Mexican redbud is native to central and west Texas.

Spacing: 15 to 20 feet on center (measure from the center of each plant) for Texas redbud; 10 to 15 feet on center for Mexican redbud.

Cautions: Moderately resistant to deer.

Colors: Magenta flowers in spring, and yellow leaf color in fall.

Eastern redbud

There is nothing showier in spring than the pink flowers lining the bare branches of redbuds. Texas redbud is a small tree with great color impact in the early spring landscape. It rates a blue ribbon* for its showy flowers, adaptability to a range of soils, and its heat tolerance.

Texas redbud

Texas redbud puts on quite a show in early spring with its magnificent display of pink flowers that appear before the leaves emerge. Texas actually has three native redbuds: eastern redbud (*C. canadensis var. canadensis*), that grows in the eastern part of the state; Texas redbud, that grows in the central and north central parts of the state; and Mexican redbud, that grows in central and west Texas. The farther west you go, the smaller and more drought-tolerant the redbuds become. Texas redbud is an easy-to-grow, ideal, blooming tree for small yards. It is commonly multi-trunked and will grow in clay or rocky soils as long as they are well drained.

Color Period: Two to three weeks of spring bloom in March or early April, glossy green leaves all summer, and yellow leaf color for two to three weeks in the fall.

Buying Tips: Available in nurseries and garden centers, especially those that sell native plants. The cultivar, 'Oklahoma,' has darker flowers (rosy magenta to wine red), and its leaves are a richer green, with more gloss and wax. 'Texas White' is a white-blooming cultivar.

*Blue ribbon plants are defined on page 12. For blue ribbon performance, follow the planting and maintenance guidelines on pages 22 to 39.

Mexican redbud is shorter, has smaller leaves, and is more drought tolerant than Texas redbud. It is no less stunning than Texas redbud when in bloom, though. Mexican redbud rates a blue ribbon* for its showy flowers, ability to grow in rocky limestone soils and tolerate drought.

One of three redbuds naturally occurring in Texas, Mexican redbud is the shortest, the most compact, and the most drought tolerant. It grows as a multi-trunked tree on the limestone soils of west Texas and must be planted in well-drained soil. The leaves are thicker, darker, glossier, and more ruffled along the margins than those of the Texas redbud. Easy to grow, Mexican redbud rewards the gardener with spectacular flowers in the spring and low maintenance requirements.

Color Period: Two to three weeks of flowers in March, glossy green leaves in summer, and yellow leaf color for two to three weeks in fall.

Buying Tips: If you want the more drought-tolerant Mexican redbud, be sure it is properly labeled as such at the nursery. If you select the tree after the leaves have emerged, their ruffled margin is a good indication that the tree is a Mexican redbud.

Lives on rainwater alone in all but the most extreme situations

GROWING CONDITIONS

Light: Both Texas and Mexican redbuds take light shade to full sun.

Water: Very low after establishment. Lives on rainwater alone, without supplemental water, in all but the most extreme conditions. See pages 28 to 33 for more information.

Soil: Grows in unimproved soil, including clay, provided the soil has not been compacted. Compaction occurs most commonly from heavy equipment working around a house under construction. See page 27 for instructions on tree planting.

Hardiness: Zones 6 to 8 for Texas redbud; zones 7 to 8 for Mexican redbud.

Propagation: Seeds

Pest Problems: No serious insect or pest problems.

PLANTING & MAINTENANCE

When to Plant: Redbuds from containers can be planted at any time. Fall is best because they establish more easily in cooler weather. Late fall and winter are the best times for planting balled-and-burlapped redbuds.

Trimming: Trim only to shape trees when young or to raise the canopy. Raising the canopy means removing branches from the trunk that are closest to the ground.

Fertilization: Low. Fertilize at planting time with a timed-release product. Less fertilizer is needed with the application of more organics. In the years after planting, fertilization needs vary, based on the nutrients in your soil. See pages 36 to 39 for more instructions.

TREES

Soapberry, Western

CHARACTERISTICS

Plant Type: Deciduous tree (loses its leaves in the winter).

Average Size: 20 to 30 feet tall with a spread of 10 to 20 feet.

Growth Rate: Medium

Wind Tolerance: High

Leaf: Compound leaves, 5 to 12 inches long with 8 to 18 leaflets. Each leaflet is 1 1/2 to 3 1/2 inches long, 1/2 to 1 inch wide, and slightly curved or sickle-shaped.

Flower: 5- to 10-inch terminal panicles of creamy white flowers in May. Attractive clusters of 1/2 inch, translucent, amber colored fruits on female trees. The seed inside the fruit is black.

Origin: Southwestern U.S., including Texas.

Spacing: 10 to 20 feet on center (measure from the center of each plant).

Cautions: The fruits contain a substance called saponin, which, if ingested, is poisonous to people but not to birds.

Colors: Flowers are white

Soapberry fruit

Western soapberry is a tough yet attractive, medium-sized tree that performs well in urban and suburban landscapes. Its best features include its upright form, colorful bark, showy flowers, interesting fruit, and brilliant fall color. Western soapberry rates a blue ribbon* for its adaptability to a wide range of soils, its ease of transplanting, and its tolerance of drought and heat.

Western soapberry enhances the landscape several times each year. It produces showy flowers in spring, splendid fall color, fruit that appeals to the eye as well as to birds, and bark that adds winter interest. Western soapberry is easy to grow because it transplants easily, establishes well, and requires little maintenance. It is well suited to the smaller yards and disturbed soils found in many, newer, housing divisions. Be aware that suckers and seedlings can be an issue. You may wish to mulch surrounding beds heavily, so seedlings don't have a chance to come up.

Color Period: Produces showy, creamy-white flowers in May for two or three weeks, golden yellow fall color for two to three weeks in November, and amber colored fruit fall through winter.

Buying Tips: Most available in nurseries that sell native plants. Try to buy a male plant that produces no fruit at all, so that you won't have a problem with unwanted seedlings.

Blue ribbon plants are defined on page 12. For blue ribbon performance, follow the planting and maintenance guidelines on pages 22 to 39.

Attracts Butterflies

Attracts Birds

Resists Deer

Lives on Rain Water *

27
Avg. Weeks of Color

Texas Native

Botanical Name:
Sapindus drummondii
Family: Sapindaceae

Western soapberry combines well with a number of plants but looks the best with other low water-use, native Texas plants. Its yellow- to pumpkin-colored, fall foliage stands out against a backdrop of eastern red cedar or live oak. Agarita or dwarf yaupon holly shrubs would look good near it, as would native grasses, such as Mexican feather grass. Your best bet would be to plant perennials that get two to three feet high beneath the tree, as shown below.

Autumn Sage
Plant Profile: Page 156

Turk's Cap
Plant Profile: Page 168

Western soapberry and some companions

Autumn Sage (above, left) grows two and one half feet tall and wide and blooms April through October. It prefers full sun or light shade. Since the soapberry has an open canopy that permits light to reach what is growing under it, autumn sage will do well beneath the soapberry tree. If you remove the lower branches of the soapberry tree, you will make room for even more sunlight to reach what is growing beneath the canopy.

Turk's Cap (above, right) is a perennial that grows two to three feet tall in sun or shade. Turk's cap is a good choice once your soapberry casts more shade because its leaves are held horizontally and look perkier in the shade. Flowers adorn this plant May through October, attract hummingbirds, and contrast well with the golden yellow, fall foliage of western soapberry.

GROWING CONDITIONS

Light: Full sun

Water: Very low after establishment. Lives on rainwater alone, without supplemental water, in all but the most extreme conditions. See pages 28 to 33 for more information.

Soil: Grows in unimproved soil, including clay, provided the soil has not been compacted. Compaction occurs most commonly from heavy equipment working around a house under construction. See page 27 for instructions on tree planting.

Hardiness: Zones 5 to 9

Propagation: Seed or softwood cuttings.

Pest Problems: No serious insect or disease problems.

PLANTING & MAINTENANCE

When to Plant: Western soapberry from containers can be planted at any time. Fall is best because they establish more easily in cooler weather. Late fall and winter are the best times for planting balled-and-burlapped western soapberry trees.

Trimming: Trim only to shape trees when young or to raise the canopy. Raising the canopy means removing branches from the trunk that are closest to the ground. Keep removing suckers at the base of the tree until they stop appearing.

Fertilization: Low. Fertilize at planting time with a timed-release product. Less fertilizer is needed with the application of more organics. In the years after planting, fertilization needs vary, based on the nutrients in your soil. See pages 36 to 39 for more instructions.

Lives on rainwater alone in all but the most extreme situations

TREES

Other Trees That Deserve Attention

Ash, Green
Fraxinus pennsylvanica

Native deciduous tree known for its vigorous growth. 50 to 60 feet tall with a rounded crown. Large, compound leaves that can be messy in the home landscape. 'Urbanite' and 'Emerald' are two of the best cultivars. Full sun to light shade. Low water. Zones 3 to 9.

Buckeye, Bottlebrush
Aesculus parvifolia

Excellent native tree that grows like a large, multi-stemmed shrub. White flower panicles resembling an old-fashioned bottlebrush open in June for 2 to 3 weeks. 10 to 12 feet tall by an equal spread. Fall color is a golden yellow. Light shade to morning sun. Low water. Zones 4 to 9.

Buckeye, Flame
Aesculus pavia

Small, native tree. 15 to 20 feet tall. Brilliant, red flower panicles open in mid spring and provide much needed nectar for migrating hummingbirds. Flowers visible for two weeks. Large, fruit capsules ripen in October. Fall color is yellow. Full sun to medium shade. Low water. Zones 5 to 9.

Cedar, Deodar
Cedrus deodara

Handsome, needle-like evergreen. Pyramidal with almost weeping stem tips present a soft, lacy picture. Deep green to blue-green, depending on selection. 40 to 60 feet tall. Damaged by temperatures below 5 degrees ('Shalimar' & 'Kashmir' most cold hardy). Full sun. Low water.

Cherry, Kwanzan
Prunus serrulata 'Kwanzan'

Spring blooming cherry tree flowering after Yoshino cherry. Large, double, deep pink flowers open after foliage has emerged. 25 to 30 feet tall. Needs supplemental water during drought. Borers and root rot diseases are significant problems. Full sun. Medium water. Zones 5 to 9.

Cherry, Okame
Prunus x incamp 'Okame'

First of the flowering cherries to bloom in spring, with pink flowers lasting for 2 weeks. Trees will reach 20 to 30 feet tall with an upright to oval growth habit. Fall color is yellow to orange-red. U.S. National Arboretum introduction - most cold hardy of the flowering cherries. Medium water. Zones 6 to 9.

Cherry, Yoshino
Prunus x yedoensis

The most widely planted cherry tree in the south. Exquisite, white to pale pink flowers cover the tree in mid spring for 10 to 14 days. 15 to 20 feet tall. Not known for long life span (numerous insects and disease problems-not drought tolerant). Full sun. Medium water. Zones 5 to 8.

Fringe Tree
Chionanthus virginicus

Spectacular, small, native tree with pure white flowers in mid spring. Delicate petals resembling fringe are showy for 10 to 14 days. Clusters of deep blue fruits ripen in late summer and are a gourmet meal for songbirds. Yellow fall color. 15 to 20 feet tall. Light shade to morning sun. Low water. Zones 4 to 9.

Goldenrain Tree
Koelreuteria paniculata

Known for its spectacular, floral display of bright yellow flowers in late May to early June. After flowering, dull brown fruit capsules cover the tree, detracting from the bright green foliage. 30 to 35 feet tall by equal spread. Full sun. Low water. Zones 5 to 9.

Jerusalem Thorn
Parkensonia aculeata

Evergreen in tropical areas. Deciduous in temperate zones. Fine-textured, yellow flowers in spring for a few months. Easy to grow in areas that are warm enough; but have dangerous thorns. 15 to 30 feet tall. Very low water. Light shade to full sun. Zones 8 to 11.

Loquat
Eriobotrya japonica

Small, evergreen tree growing 15 to 20 feet tall. Thick, leathery, dark green leaves. Creamy white flowers followed by orange fruits. Flowers may open anytime from November to March, depending on weather. Low water. Not cold hardy in zones 6 and 7. Full sun. Zones 8 to 11.

Magnolia, Tulip
Magnolia x soulangiana

Lovely, spring flowering trees that disappoint many because they don't bloom if there is a late frost. Tulip-shaped, pink blossoms. Look for late-spring blooming selections (Little Girl series, 'Alexandrinia') to minimize threat. 15 to 30 feet tall. Full sun. Low water. Zones 4 to 10.

Palm, Pindo
Butia capitata

A small palm that grows as wide as it is tall. 12 to 15 feet tall. Bluish-grey leaves. Orange fruit that is used to make jelly. Easy to grow. High wind tolerance. Low water. Light shade to full sun. Zones 8 to 9.

Palm, Saw Palmetto
Serenoa repens

Native palm that looks more like a shrub in temperate areas. Great plant to attract wildlife. Bees are attracted to the flowers, and birds follow for the seeds. Zones 8 to 10. Light shade to full sun. Very low water. Very high wind tolerance.

Pecan
Carya illinoensis

State tree of Texas. Moderate rate of growth. Does best in deep soil but adapts to a range of soil types. Develops zinc deficiency in alkaline soils. Drops nuts, twigs, leaves and branches; susceptible to unsightly web worms. Full sun. 90 feet tall and 75 feet wide. Low water.

Poplar, Yellow
Liriodendron tulipifera

First cousin to the southern magnolia (creamy yellow flowers in spring that resemble tulips), yellow poplar needs plenty of room - 70 to 90 feet tall. Can be messy in the home landscape. Drought tolerant but leaves shed early as a result. Full sun. Medium water. Zones 4 to 9.

Redwood, Dawn
Metasequoia glyptostroboides

Large, deciduous, tree with a flared trunk. Medium to bright green leaves are fine-textured; pinkish-tan to reddish-bronze fall color. Best grown on moist, well-drained, slightly acidic soils. Easy to grow. Full sun. 75 to 100 feet tall. Medium water.

Sweet Gum
Liquidambar styraciflua

Doesn't do well in alkaline and limestone soils. Native to east Texas. Reaching 50 to 60 feet tall with attractive, green leaves changing to hues of red, orange and purple in fall. Fruit capsules are a mess - especially in a small yard. Full sun to medium shade. Medium water. Zones 5 to 9.

Sycamore
Platanus occidentalis

Very large, native tree with branches and stems of pure white in the upper canopy - incredible winter silhouette. 60 to 80 feet tall by equal spread. Leaves are large, fruit capsules are abundant, and both are messy to clean up. Very tolerant of urban pollution. Full sun. Medium to high water (but will drop leaves). Zones 4 to 9.

Walnut, Black
Juglans nigra

Large, native tree known for its beautiful wood, tasty nuts and the fact that few things can grow near it! Black walnut exudes a chemical that limits competition. Site it away from other plants and watch out for falling, green baseballs that hide the tasty nuts. 60 to 80 feet tall. Full sun. Low water. Zones 4 to 9.

Willow, Weeping
Salix babylonica

Dramatic growth habit of pendulous branches. Fast growing. 30 feet tall. Quick fix for open site but not known for longevity. Be careful around septic systems - extensive root system can clog field lines. Great accent for lake or pond setting. Full sun. Low to medium water. Zones 6 to 8.

Index

Index